THE ROOTS, VERB-FORMS AND PRIMARY DERIVATIVES OF THE SANSKRIT LANGUAGE

The Roots, Verb-forms and Primary Derivatives of the Sanskrit Language

(A Supplement to His Sanskrit Grammar)

WILLIAM DWIGHT WHITNEY

MOTILAL BANARSIDASS PUBLISHERS
PRIVATE LIMITED • DELHI

Reprint : Delhi, 1963, 1976, 1979, 1983, 1988
1991, 1994, 1997, 2000, 2003, **2006**

ISBN: 81-208-0484-8 (Cloth)
ISBN: 81-208-0485-6 (Paper)

Also available at:
MOTILAL BANARSIDASS
41 U.A. Bungalow Road, Jawahar Nagar, Delhi 110 007
8 Mahalaxmi Chamber, 22 Bhulabhai Desai Road, Mumbai 400 026
203 Royapettah High Road, Mylapore, Chennai 600 004
236, 9th Main III Block, Jayanagar, Bangalore 560 011
Sanas Plaza, 1302 Baji Rao Road, Pune 411 002
8 Camac Street, Kolkata 700 017
Ashok Rajpath, Patna 800 004
Chowk, Varanasi 221 001

PRINTED IN INDIA
BY JAINENDRA PRAKASH JAIN AT SHRI JAINENDRA PRESS,
A-45 NARAINA, PHASE-I, NEW DELHI 110 028
AND PUBLISHED BY NARENDRA PRAKASH JAIN FOR
MOTILAL BANARSIDASS PUBLISHERS PRIVATE LIMITED,
BUNGALOW ROAD, DELHI 110 007

PREFACE.

This work is intended especially as a Supplement to my Sanskrit Grammar (Leipzig, 1879), giving, with a fulness of detail that was not then practicable, nor admissible as part of the grammar itself, all the quotable roots of the language, with the tense and conjugation-systems made from them, and with the noun and adjective (infinitival and participial) formations that attach themselves most closely to the verb; and further, with the other derivative noun and adjective-stems usually classed as primary: since these also are needed, if one would have a comprehensive view of the value of a given root in the language. And everything given is dated, with such accuracy as the information thus far in hand allows — whether found in the language throughout its whole history, or limited to a certain period.

My leading authority has necessarily been that magnificent thesaurus of authentic information respecting the Sanskrit language of every period, the great St. Petersburg Lexicon of Böhtlingk and Roth.[1] This I have gone carefully over, excerpting all the material needed for my purpose. So far, indeed, as concerns the epic and classical literature, the Lexicon has been almost my sole source, since my own collections, for verification or of additional material, though not wholly wanting, have yet been altogether insignificant as compared with it. But in the older language, of Veda and Brāhmaṇa and Upanishad and Sūtra, I have done much more independent work. I have, namely,

[1] With its abbreviation and supplement, the minor lexicon of Böhtlingk, so far as this has yet appeared: namely, in the body of the work, to **rajaka**; in the Additions and Corrections, to the end of **l**.

gone over all the texts of the earlier period accessible to me, including (by the kindness of Professor Weber) the as yet unpublished Kāuṣītaki-Brāhmaṇa and Kāṭhaka, and (by the kindness of the late Dr. Burnell) the immense Jāiminīya or Talavakāra-Brāhmaṇa, which has as yet hardly been accessible to any one else;[1] and from them I have excerpted all the noteworthy verbal forms and (less completely) the primary derivatives; thus verifying and occasionally correcting the material of the Lexicon, supplying chance omissions, and especially filling in not a few details which it had not lain in the design of that work to present in their entirety.

As a matter of course, no such work as the present can pretend to completeness, especially at its first appearance. The only important texts of which we have exhaustive verbal indexes are the Rig-Veda and the Atharva-Veda, nor is it known that any other is in preparation; and only where such indexes exist can the inclusion of all that a text contains be assured. But I trust it will be found that the measure of completeness here attained is in general proportioned to the importance of the material: that it is the more indifferent forms and derivatives which, having been passed over by the Lexicon, have escaped my gleaning also. I expect to continue the work of verification and addition, and to make an eventual future edition perceptibly nearer to perfection in its details, and possessing such improvements in plan as my own experience and the criticisms of others may suggest.[2] It is unnecessary to add that

[1] The extant texts of which I have most painfully felt the lack are: The (Cashmere) Pāippalāda Atharva-Veda, which is in Professor Roth's hands alone; the latter half of the Māitrāyaṇī-Saṁhitā, as yet wanting in Schroder's edition, and the Kapiṣṭhala-Saṁhitā; and the unpublished Sūtras, as the Āpastamba (every new number of Garbe's edition of which brings valuable additional items of material) and the Çāñkhāyana.

[2] A conspectus of the work, with specimens, and with invitation of criticisms and suggestions, was published in the Proceedings of the American Oriental Society for May, 1882 (Journ. Am. Or. Soc., vol. xi., pp. cxvii ff.); and a leaf of specimens, with certain improvements, was sent out somewhat later to many Sanskrit scholars; but nothing was received in return.

corrections and additions of any kind will be welcomed by me, and duly acknowledged.

Of the verb-forms which, though not yet found — and, for the most part, destined never to be found — in recorded use, are prescribed or authorized by the Hindu grammarians, a liberal presentation is made under the different roots: such material being always distinguished from the other by being put in square brackets. It is in no part given at first hand, but only as reported by Western authorities: the Lexicon, Westergaard's *Radices*, and the various European grammars; all of these supplement rather than contradict one another; and any occasional disagreement among them is passed over, as relating to a matter of too little consequence to be worth reporting.

The periods in the life of the language which are acknowledged and distinguished by appropriate notation are six: the Veda (marked with V.), the Brāhmaṇa (with B.), the earlier or more genuine Upanishads (with U.), the Sūtras (with S.), the epics, Mahābhārata and Rāmāyaṇa (with E.), and the classical or common Sanskrit (with C.). This classification, however, is by no means an absolute one, and calls for certain explanations and limitations, as follows.

Under 'Veda' (V.) are included only the indexed texts of the Rig-Veda, Sāma-Veda, and Atharva-Veda. In strictness, certain passages of the Atharva-Veda should have been excluded, as being in prose and Brāhmaṇa-like; and, what is of much more importance, the older and better part of the *mantra*-material in the various *saṁhitā*'s of the Yajur-Veda, in the Brāhmaṇas, and even in the Sūtras, is quite as good Veda as most of the Atharvan, some of it even as parts of the Rik. In the present condition of things, however, it did not seem to me practicable to draw the division-line otherwise than in the partly arbitrary way in which I have drawn it. When the *mantra*-material is collected from all places and compared (as it by all means ought soon to be), it will be possible to use the term 'Veda' in a more exact sense, both inclusively and exclusively — though between what is genuinely old and what is in an artificially antique style a definite separation will probably never admit of being made.

It is further to be stated that in the following lists nothing is intended to be marked with simple V., as 'Vedic', that does not occur in the Rig-Veda; what is not Rig-Vedic though it may be found in both the other collections, is marked AV., or SV., or both, as the case may be. On the other hand, if anything occurring only in the Rik among the three Vedas is found also in later periods, the fact that it does not chance to be met with in the Atharvan or Sāman is too unimportant to notice, and (save perhaps in exceptional cases) it is marked V.B. or the like.

Between Brāhmaṇa, Āraṇyaka and Upanishad, again, the line of division is an evanescent one, and perhaps hardly worth the attempt at drawing. But I have followed the method of distinguishing by a U. the small number of these treatises that have an existence separate from Brāhmaṇa or Āraṇyaka, while not distinguishing the two latter from one another. The sign U. is the one of least importance and least frequency in the system adopted.

The division of Sūtras (S.) is a plainer one, except so far as these treatises contain *mantra*-material in their quoted verses (as already intimated) — and *brāhmaṇa*-material also in their quoted formulas. The proper language of the Sūtras themselves is a true continuator of that of the Brāhmaṇas.

As epic (E.) are reckoned only the two great poems, the Mahābhārata and Rāmāyaṇa. And in these it has, of course, been impossible to distinguish between the older and the more recent parts: although, beyond a question, a considerable part of both is in no manner distinguishable from the general later literature, except by a degree of archaizing neglect of the strict requirements of the native grammar.

Everything else that is Sanskrit falls under the head of classical (C.), or of the language as written under the domination of the native system of grammar. Here the only subdivision which one is tempted to make is to mark separately those forms and words which are found used only in the commentaries, and which are therefore open to a heightened suspicion of artificiality; but this I have not tried to do.

A *plus*-sign (+) indicates that the given formation is found to occur from the specified period onward, even to the latest or classical period.

Instead of a period, an individual text is sometimes referred to — yet not upon any very definite and consistent plan (except in the case of the Vedas, as explained above). A 'superior' figure (e. g. RV^1.) indicates the number of times a word or form has been met with — yet this, again, only in exceptional instances, and not in the case of every unique or very rare occurrence.

So far as the present-system is concerned, only so many specimen-forms are given as suffice to illustrate the mode of formation. It would have been space and time thrown away to instance in each case the various sub-formations — modes, participles, imperfect — that occur, since one form implies clearly enough the possible existence of the rest. The form taken as representative specimen is ordinarily the 3d singular, as being often more characteristic than the 1st; and that person is even occasionally given when, in verbs of infrequent use, it is not itself actually quotable. Irregular or exceptional forms, whether of the earlier or of the later language, are then added in parenthesis. Everywhere, an appended '*etc.*' means that other forms of the same make occur: yet I find on review that I have not used this sign consistently, and its absence must not be taken always as indicating more than that the variety of forms quotable is comparatively small. The various modes of present-formation are intended to be given in the order of their relative regularity or frequency; to each is prefixed in brackets the number belonging to it in the order of the conjugation-classes as given by the Hindu grammarians — since, however meaningless and unworthy of retention this may be, it is still widely used, not only in the grammars, but even by general writers on language.

In the other tense-systems, while in the main the same method is followed, the intention nevertheless is to give, on account of their greater infrequency and irregularity, a conspectus of the various tense and mode-formations from the same stem (not, of course, the participles, except for the aorist). Thus, for example, no quotable precative, either active or middle, is designedly omitted under the aorist to which it belongs; nor any quotable conditional under the first future; nor any pluperfect under the perfect. Moreover, in view of the rarity of the 2d sing. perfect active, and the useless prolixity of the native rules as to its formation, every example of it is given that has been found to occur. The order in which the aorists are presented is the systematic one, without reference to their frequency of use.

Among the verbal adjectives and nouns are included as belonging to the verbal conjugation only the passive participle, the infinitives, and the gerunds (along with that in *-am*, the distinction of which from an ordinary adverbially used accusative is not always easy to draw); the gerundives are quite too loosely attached to the conjugation-system to be worth treating as a part of it, and they are accordingly relegated to the list of derivatives.

Of the secondary or derivative conjugations, only examples enough are given to show the form of the stem — unless, indeed, some unusual or irregular forms are met with, in which case they are duly noted. To cite, for example, the innumerable futures and verbals of the causative conjugation, or even its perfects, all of them made upon precisely the same pattern, would have been wholly useless. The causative aorists, however, since they are made directly from the root, are of course put along with the other aorists, save in the exceptional cases where they actually come from the causative stem (as *atiṣṭhipat*, *bībhiṣas*, etc.). All the tertiary conjugations, not omitting even the common causative passives (any others are quite rare), are noted so far as found.

In the lists of derivatives are given not only those of genuinely primary character, but also those which have come to assume a primary aspect in the language, even though of incontestably secondary origin: such as the gerundives in *-tavya* and Vedic *-tva* (from *-tu*), and *-anīya* (from *-ana*), the *nomina agentis* in *-in*, and the various formations in *ya* (among which hardly any, if any, are really primary). These are in general placed next after the forms from which they are presumably derived. Apart from this, the order of arrangement intended to be pursued is in the main the alphabetic order of the suffixes, the radical stems or those without suffix standing at the head; but such an arrangement could not be very strictly carried out, nor does any particular importance belong to it, considering how easily the columns may be glanced over to verify the presence or absence of any given formation; and some inconsistencies will doubtless be found. Reduplicated stems are put after the others, and last of all the *quasi*-primitive formations from (secondary, or rarely primary or tertiary) conjugation-stems. Notation of the period of occurrence is made in the same way as for the verb-forms. A hyphen put before a stem indicates that it has not been found quotable otherwise than as posterior member of a compound: one following a stem (much more rarely) shows it to occur only as prior member of a compound, or in derivative stems or in denominative conjugation.

Throughout the whole work, accent-signs are applied only where the word is found actually so marked in accentuated texts.

It is, of course, impossible to draw the line everywhere between the derivatives of a root and words that do not belong to it; since etymology is from beginning to end a matter of balancing probabilities, and thick-set with uncertainties and chances of error. It has been my intention to err rather upon the side of liberality of inclusion than the opposite — and certainly I have in not a few cases put under certain roots words as to whose connection with those roots I have great misgivings; but doubtless also there are words omitted, by oversight or by failure of judgment, which ought to have been included. All such errors, it is hoped, will be viewed with a reasonable degree of indulgence, considering the novelty and the extreme laboriousness of the undertaking. Its main intent is to furnish the means of examining in their chronologic entirety the groups of words and forms that cluster about the so-called roots in Sanskrit, that they may be studied, and have their relations determined, with more complete understanding: and that intent will be gained in spite of minor omissions and inaccuracies. Regarding it as primarily an assemblage of materials for study, I have not hastened to anticipate the results of comparison by penetrating behind the aspect of things as shown in the Sanskrit language itself, or to reduce the materials to an Indo-European basis and form of statement. A few intimations as to the more obviously probable connections of certain roots are given in brief notes at the end of exposition of forms and derivatives.

The representative form of the roots is naturally that adopted in the grammar to which this work is a supplement. Although loath to differ from the Petersburg lexicon upon such a point, I cannot regret having adopted the *ṛ* instead of the *ar* or *ra*-form (e. g. *kṛ, kṛp*, instead of *kar, krap*) of the many roots exhibiting both elements in their forms and derivatives. So long as we speak of the Sanskrit root *vid*, and not *ved*, so long it seems to follow that we ought to speak of the root *vṛt*, and not *vart*, whatever may be the Indo-European value of the root in the one case or in the other. The meanings added after the roots by no means claim to be exhaustive; they are in general intended only to identify the root.

As a matter of course, not a few matters of doubtful classification present themselves in connection with the verb-forms, of which the scope of the work does not allow a discussion. Such are here and there noted by a question-mark. The classes of forms that contain the most puzzling problems are the reduplicated ones, and the present stems ending in **ya**: upon these no new light has been thrown since the publication of the author's Grammar, in which the difficulty of their treatment was noticed.

In the indexes of stems given at the end of the volume. a classification is adopted which is intended to facilitate the historical comprehension of the language, by distinguishing what belongs respectively to its older and to its later periods from that which forms a part of it throughout its whole history.

It may be added that the manuscript left the author's hands complete in July, 1884; the delay in its appearance is owing to his distance from the place of printing and publication.

I desire to express my obligation to Professor Lanman for kindly aiding the accuracy of the work by giving the proof-sheets an additional revision.

New Haven, July, 1885.

W. D. W.

ABBREVIATIONS.

AA. Āitareya-Āraṇyaka.
AB. Āitareya-Brāhmaṇa.
AÇS. Āçvalāyana-Çrāuta-Sūtra.
AGS. Āçvalāyana-Gṛhya-Sūtra.
AV. Atharva-Veda.
AVP. do. Pāippalāda-Text.
B. Brāhmaṇas.
BAU. Bṛhad-Āraṇyaka Upaniṣad
Bö. Böhtlingk's minor Lexicon.
BR. Böthlingk and Roth (Lexicon).
C. Classical Sanskrit.
ÇB. Çatapatha-Brāhmaṇa.
ÇÇS. Çāṅkhāyana-Çrāuta-Sūtra.
ÇGS. Çāṅkhāyana Gṛhya-Sūtra.
E. Epic Sanskrit.
GB. Gopatha-Brāhmaṇa.
GGS. Gobhilīya-Gṛhya-Sūtra.
JB. Jāiminīya-Brāhmaṇa.
JUB. Jāiminīya-Upaniṣad-Brāhmaṇa.
K. Kāṭhaka.
KB. Kāuṣītaki-Brāhmaṇa.
KÇS. Kātyāyana-Çrāuta-Sūtra.
LÇS. Lāṭyāyana-Çrāuta-Sūtra.
M. Mahābhārata.
MS. Māitrāyaṇī-Saṁhitā.
MU. Māitrī-Upaniṣad.
PB. Pañcaviṅça-Brāhmaṇa.
PU. Praçna-Upaniṣad.
R. Rāmāyaṇa.
RV. Rig-Veda.
S. Sūtras.
ṢB. Ṣaḍviṅça-Brāhmaṇa.
SV. Sāma-Veda.
SVB. Sāma-Vidhāna-Brāhmaṇa.
TA. Tāittirīya-Āraṇyaka.
TB. Tāittirīya-Brāhmaṇa.
TS. Tāittirīya-Saṁhitā.
U. Upanishads.
V. Vedas.
VS. Vājasaneyi-Saṁhitā.

For further explanations, see the Preface.

SANSKRIT ROOTS, VERB-FORMS, AND PRIMARY DERIVATIVES.

√ aṅh, 'be narrow or distressing'.

Such a root is inferable from the derivatives:

aṅhatí RV.	**aṅhú** V.B.	**áṅghri**? B.+	**áhi** V.+
áṅhas V.+	**aṅhīyas** B.S.	**aghá** V.+	**ahí** RV.

The verb-form **anāha** RV[1]. is of wholly doubtful meaning and connection.

√ 1 akṣ, 'attain'.

Present. [1.] **ákṣat** RV[1]., **akṣase** E[1].
Perfect. [**ānakṣa**,] **ākṣāṇá**? RV[1].
Aorist. [3. **ācikṣat**. —] 5. **ā́kṣiṣus** RV[1]
[*Future.* **akṣiṣyati, akṣyati; akṣitā, aṣṭā.**]
[*Verbal Adjectives and Nouns.* **aṣṭa; akṣitvā, aṣṭvā.**]
[*Secondary Conjugations: Passive*, **akṣya-**. — *Intensive.* — *Desiderative*, **ācikṣiṣa-**. — *Causative*, **akṣaya-**.]
Derivatives: **akṣiṣṭha**, JB.

A secondary root-form from √ 1 **aç, aṅç**, and occurring in a few isolated forms. Indra and Agni are called **akṣiṣṭhāu vahiṣṭhāu devānām** at JB. i. 304.

√ 2 akṣ, 'mutilate'.

Pres. [5.] **-akṣṇoti** *etc.* AV. ÇB.
Verb. **-aṣṭa** V.B.S.

Only used with prefix **nis**; does not appear to have anything to do with the preceding root.

√ aṅg, 'move'.

Pres. [1.] **aṅgatu** C[1].
[*Perf. etc.* **ānaṅga** *etc. etc.*]
[*Sec. Conj.: Caus.* **aṅgayati.**]

A single occurrence, doubtless artificial, in the Nalodaya.

√ ac, añc, 'bend'.

Pres. [1.] **añcati** *etc.* AV.+, **-te** B.; **ácati** *etc.* V.B., **-te** *etc.* AV.B.S.
Perf. [**ānañca**,] **acire** JB.
[*Aor etc.* **āñcīt; añciṣyati, añcitā.**]
Verb. **akná** B.S., **acita** E., **añcita** E.+ [**akta**]; **-ácya** V.B.; **-ā́cam** B.

Sec. Conj.: Pass. **acyáte** *etc.* V.+ [**añcyate.** — *Desid.* **añciciṣa-.**] — *Caus.* **añcayati** *etc.* C.

Deriv.:	**-añc** V.+	**aṅká** V.+	**áñcana** V.+	**aṅku-** V.+
	-añcin B.	**áṅkas** RV.	**-acana** S.+	**akṣṇá** B.S.
			-áñcas RV.	

√ aj, 'drive'.

Pres. [1.] **ájati -te** *etc.* V.+
Perf. **ajus**? RV[1]. [**ājitha** *etc.*]
Aor. 5. **ājiṣus** LÇS[1].
[*Fut.* **ajiṣyati, ajitā.**]
Verb. **-ajita**? ÇB.; **-ajya** S.; **-áje** RV.
Sec. Conj.: Pass. **ajyáte** *etc.* RV. [— *Desid.* **ajijiṣa-.**]

Deriv.:	**ágra**? V.+	**ajaka** C.	**ájman** V.	**-āja** B.+
	áj V.	**ájana** V.+	**-ájya** V.B.	**ājí** V.+
	-ája RV.	**ajirá** V.+	**ájra**? RV.	
	ajá V.+	**ájma** RV.	**ajvin** S.	

The form **ajus** only by very doubtful conjecture to RV. v. 6. 10; **ājiṣus** variant to AV. **āviṣus**; **ajita** in **-prajita**, possibly for **prājita** (or **pra-jita**, √ **ji**?).

√ añj, 'anoint'.

Pres. [7.] **anákti aṅkté** *etc.* V.+ — [1.] **añjet** S[1].
Perf. **ānañja** B. (**anajā anajyāt** RV.), **ānajé** *etc.* RV.
Aor. [1. **ajyāt**; **āñji.** — 3. **āñjijat.** —] 5. **āñjīs** TA.
[*Fut.* **aṅkṣyati añjiṣyati, aṅktā añjitā.**]
Verb. **aktá** V.+; **aṅktvā** S., **aktvā́** B. [**añjitvā**]; **-ájya** B.S.
Sec. Conj.: Pass. **ajyáte** *etc.* V.+ [— *Desid.* **añjijiṣa-.**] — *Caus.* **añjayati** *etc.* S.+

Deriv.:	**aṅga** C.	**-ajya**	**áñjana** V.+	**aktā́** RV.
	aṅgya C.	**-āja** E.+	**áñjas** V.+	**-akti** E.+
	añjaka C.	**ā́jya** V.+	**añjí** V.B.	**aktú** V.B.
	añjya C.			

√ aṭ, 'wander'

Pres. [1.] **aṭati -te** *etc.* E.+
[*Perf. etc.* **āṭa**; **āṭīt.**]
Fut. 1. **aṭiṣyati** E. [— 2. **aṭitā.**]
Verb. **aṭita** C.; **aṭitvā** C.
[*Sec. Conj.:* **aṭāṭya-**; **aṭiṭiṣa-**; **āṭaya-.**]

Deriv.:	**-aṭa** C.	**aṭavī**? C.	**āṭa** PB.+
	aṭana C.	**aṭyā** C.	

Apparently a modern form of the following root; **āṭa** in PB. is a proper name.

√ at, 'wander'.

Pres. [1.] atasi átant átamāna RV[4].
Verb. -atita C.; -atya S.
Deriv.: atasí RV. -áti? RV. átithi? V.+ atithín RV.C. átya RV.B.

√ ad, 'eat'.

Pres. [2.] átti *etc.* (ādat ādan) V.+, adāná RV. — [1.] adasva E.
[*Perf.* āda, āditha.]
Aor. 1. adyāsam JUB. [— 3. ādidat.]
Fut. 1. atsyati B.S. [— 2. attā.]
Verb. áttum V.+, -tave V., -tos B.; attvā́ya B.
Sec. Conj.: *Pass.* adyáte *etc.* B.+ — *Caus.* ādayati B.+, adayate *etc.* S.
Deriv.: -ád V.+ -ada AV.+ -adaka E.+ -adana B.+ adanīya C. attí B. attavya C. attṛ́ AV.+ áttra RV. attrá V. attrín RV. áttri (átri) V.+ ánna V.+ ádman V.B.S. -ádya V.+ -advan V. -advara ÇB. ā́dana RV. ādín V.+ ādyà AV.+

√ an, 'breathe'

Pres. [2.] ániti *etc.* (anánti anyā́t ā́nīt) V.+ — [1.] ánati (anet ana ānat ánant) *etc.* AV.B., -te JB. — [6.] anáti (3s.) AV.
Perf. āna V.
Aor. 5. āniṣus AV.
Fut. 1. aniṣyatí B. [— 2. anitā.]
Verb. anita B.; anitum B.; -anya B.; -ānam B.S.
Sec. Conj.: [*Desid.* aniniṣat-. —] *Caus.* ānayati *etc.* AV.+, -te E.
Deriv.: aná B.U. -ánana RV. -anátha VS. ánila B.+ āná V.+ ānana E.+

√ am, 'injure'.

Pres. [2.] amīṣi amīti amánti āmīt amāte amīṣva V.B. — [1.] áme *etc.* V.B.
Perf. āmire ÇB. [emāna] emuṣá? RV. (emūṣá ÇB.)
Aor. 3. āmamat *etc.* V.B.
Verb. [ānta, amita.]
Sec. Conj.: *Pass.* amyate MS. — *Caus.* āmáyati *etc.* V.B.
Deriv.: áma V.B. amáti V.B. ámati V.B. ámatra RV. -ámana ÇB. aminá RV. ámīva V.+ amla? E.+ āmá? V.+ ā́mana? AV.MS. -āmaya V.+ -ā́mis? RV. -āmayitnu V.

√ ay, *see* √ 1 i.

√ arc, ṛc, 'shine, praise'.

Pres. [1.] árcati *etc.* v.+, arce rv¹. — arcase (1*s.*) rv¹.
Perf. ānarca e.+, ānṛcús v., ānarcus e.+, ānṛce rv¹.
[*Aor.* ārcicat, ārcīt.]
Fut. arciṣyati c. (ārkṣyánt ? çb.)
Verb. arcita e.; arcitum e.; arcitvā e.; -arcya e.+; ṛcáse rv.
Sec. Conj.: *Pass.* ṛcyáte v. [— *Desid.* arciciṣa-.] — *Caus.* arcayati -te *etc.* v.+ (arcyate e.)

Deriv.:			
árc rv.	arcatra- rv.	arcí v.+	-ṛca av.+
arká v.+	arcátri rv.	arcín rv.	-ṛcas rv.
arcā́ b.+	arcana e.+	arcitṛ e.	-ṛkti? rv. (suv-)
arcaka c.	arcanīya e.+	arcís v.+	ṛkvá rv.
arcya e.+	arcanā́nas v.	ṛ́c v.+	ṛ́kvan v.

√ arj, *see* √ 1 ṛj, ṛñj.

√ art, *see* √ ṛt.

√ arh, 'deserve' etc.

Pres. [1.] árhati *etc.* v.+, -te *etc.* e.+
Perf. ānṛhús ts¹., arhire rv¹.
[*Aor. etc.* arhyāsam, ārhi, ārjihat, ārhīt; arhiṣyati, arhitā.]
Verb. arháse rv¹.
Sec. Conj.: [*Desid.* arjihiṣa-. —] *Caus.* arhayati *etc.* s.+

Deriv.:		
arghá v.+	-árha b.+	arháṇā v.+
-arghya c.	arhaṇa c.	arhaṇīya c.

√ av, 'favor'.

Pres. [1.] ávati *etc.* v.+
Perf. ā́va ā́vitha *etc.* v.+
Aor. 1. avyās -āt v.b.s. — 5. ā́vīt *etc.* (aviḍḍhi *etc.* aviṣat *etc.*) v.b.s.
Fut. 1. aviṣyáti v.b. — 2. avitā c.
Verb. -ūta rv.; ávitave v.b.; -ávya rv.
Sec. Conj.: *Caus.* ā́vayas -at v.b.u.

Deriv.:			
áva rv.	avitṛ́ v.b.s.	ávi? v.+	oma rv.
avana c.	-avitra b.s.	-avī? v.	óman v.b.
ávas v.b.	áviṣṭha rv.	ūtí v.+	omán v.+
avis-? rv.		ū́ma v.b.s.	

Common in v.; quite rare in later language.

√ 1 aç, aṅç, 'attain'.

Pres. [5.] açnóti açnuté *etc.* v.+ — [9?] açniyāt, açnīs m.
Perf. ānáṅça ānaçús *etc.* v.+, ānaçé *etc.* v.+ (ānāça ānaçma ānaçyām anáçāmahāi rv., ānaçadhve s.) — āçatus *etc.* āçāthe *etc.* rv.

Aor. 1. ā́ṣṭa ā́çata aṣṭa v.b., açyā́t açītá *etc.* v.b., aṣṭu b. [āçi.] — 2. açema rv., açemahi sv. [— 3. āçiçat.] — 4. ākṣi b., ákṣat rv. (*cf.* √ aks). [— 5. āçiṣṭa.]

Fut. 1. [açiṣyate] açnuviṣyāmahe çb[1]. [— 2. açitā, aṣṭā.]

Verb. aṣṭum k.; áṣṭave v.b., aṣṭavāi jb.s.; açitum e.; -aṣṭa v.b.

[*Sec. Conj.*: açāçya-; açiçiṣa-; āçaya-.]

Deriv.: áñça v.+	açana b.+	-açnuva ags.	-āça ççs.
áṣṭi v.+	açī- vs[1].	-açnuvín vs.	ā́çā v.+

Compare √ 1 akṣ and √ 2 naç (to which latter the forms ānaṭ *etc.* are here referred). Derivatives more doubtfully referable to this root are:

áçan rv.	áçman v.+	áçva v.+	āçú v.+
açáni v.+	áçri v.+	áṣṭrā v.+	ā́çīyas b.
áçna rv.	áçru v.+	āçiná rv.	ā́çiṣṭha v.b.u.

√ 2 aç, 'eat'.

Pres. [9.] açnā́ti (açāna) açnīte *etc.* v.+ — [1.] aça e[1].

Perf. ā́ça v.+ (-āçvāṅs b.)

Aor. [1. açyāt. — 3. āçiçat. —] 5. ā́çīt *etc.* v.+

Fut. 1. açiṣyáti *etc.* b.+ [— 2. açitā.]

Verb. açitá v.+; açitum u.; açitvā́ b.+; -áçya b.

Sec. Conj.: *Pass.* açyáte av.+ [— *Int.* açāçya-.] — *Desid.* áçiçiṣati *etc.* b.+ — *Caus.* āçayati b.+ (ā́çita rv.); açāpaya- mgs.

Deriv.: -áç av.	açitavyà b.+	áçna v.	āçi s.
-áçana v.+	açitṛ́ av.+	açni ta.	āçyà av.?+
açanā́ b.u.	açitra b.+	-āça e.+	áçiṣṭha b.
-açanīya s.+	açúṣa rv.	-āçaka b.	açiçiṣu s.
		-āçin b.+	āçayitavya b.

Doubtless ultimately the same with √ 1 aç.

√ 1 as, 'be'.

Pres. [2.] ásti sánti *etc.* (edhí) v.+ (sva sma smahe asate m., syāmahe c[1].)

Perf. ā́sa ā́sitha *etc.* v.+

Deriv.: ásu v.+ ásta v.+ -asti v.+ -āsa (itiha-) av.+ stí v.b.

√ 2 as, 'throw'.

Pres. [4.] ásyati *etc.* v.+, asyate *etc.* rv.b. — [1.] asati *etc.* rv[1]. (? asan) e.+

Perf. ā́sa *etc.* rv.+, āse rv[1].

Aor. 1. asyāt e[1].; āsi c[1]. — 2. āsthat *etc.* av[1].k[1].c. (? *see* √ sthā). [— 3. āsiṣat. — 5. āsiṣṭa.]

Fut. 1. asiṣyáti *etc.* rv.+ [— 2. asitā.]

Verb. asta v.+, asita e[1].; ástave b., -tavā́í b.; asitum e[1].; asitvā s.; -ásya v.+; -ā́sam b.s.u.

Sec. Conj.: *Pass.* asyate *etc.* av.+ [— *Desid.* asisiṣa-.] — *Caus.* āsayati *etc.* e.+

Deriv.:	**-ás** V.	**ásira** RV[1].	**astrá** V.+	**-āsa** AV.+
	ásana V.+	**áśiṣṭha** V.	**-asya** B.+	**-āsin** AV.+
	asanā́ RV.	**-asti** C.	**-asyā** E.+	**āsyà** AV.
	-asanīya C.	**-astavya** C.	**asrá** TB[1].	**-āsana** C.
	así? V.+	**ástṛ** V.B.		

√ ah, 'say'.

Perf. **āha āhús** V.+, **āttha āhatus** B.+

Deriv. **-āha**? PB[1].

If **nirāha** is from this root, then perhaps **svā́hā** V.+ is also to be referred to it.

√ āñch, 'tear'.

Pres. [1.] **āñchati** C.

Deriv. **āñchana** C.

Found only in the Suçruta, and doubtless artificial.

√ āp, 'obtain'

Pres. [5.] **āpnóti** *etc.* AV.+, **āpnute** E.

Perf. **ā́pa āpitha** *etc.* V.+, **āpiré āpāná** RV.

Aor. 1. **āpi** B.+ — 2. **ā́pat** *etc.* V.+ (**apeyam** AV.) — 3. **āpipan** ÇB. (**āpīpipat** BAU.) — 4. **āpsīs** E.

Fut. 1. **āpsyati** B.+, **-te** B.E. — 2. **āptā** B.

Verb. **āptá** V.+; **ā́ptum** B.+; **āptvā́** B.+; **-āpya** B.+

Sec. Conj.: Pass. **āpyáte** *etc.* B.+ — *Desid.* **ī́psati** *etc.* AV.+, **īpsate** *etc.* B.E. (**āipsīt** *etc.* B.) — *Caus.* **āpayati** *etc.* B.+, **-te** *etc.* E. (**āpipayiṣet** ÇB.)

Deriv.:	**-āpa** B.+	**-āpanīya** S.+	**-āptṛ** C.	**īpsā** E.+
	-āpaka E.+	**āpaneya** U[1].	**ā́pnāna**? RV.S.	**-īpsin** U.
	-āpin U.+	**āpí** V.+	**-āpayitavya** U.C.	**īpsu** S.+
	āpyà AV.+	**ā́pti** AV.+	**āpayitṛ** U.	**āpipayiṣu** E.
	āpana V.+	**āptavya** U.+		

To a more original form of the root (**āp** is perhaps **ā** + **ap**) doubtless belong also:

ápas V. **apás** V.B. **ápnas, apna-** RV. **-apta** (? **án-**) RV.

BR. regard **apás** at RV. iii. 6.7 as a verb-form from this simpler root.

√ ār, 'praise' (?).

Pres. [4.] **ā́ryanti** RV[2].

Verb. **āritá** RV.

Is perhaps a form of **ā** + **√ṛ**, 'resort to, have recourse to'; **ā́ryanti** in both occurrences is accented as if it contained a preposition.

√ ās, 'sit

Pres. [2.] **ā́ste** *etc.* (**ā́sīna**) V.+ (**āsāná** RV[2].), **āsti** B. — [1.] **āsati -te** *etc.* E.+ — [4.] **āsyati -te** *etc.* E.

Perf. āsā́ṁ cakre *etc.* B.+, āsāṁ cakāra E.
Aor. 5. āsiṣṭa *etc.* B.S.
Fut. 1. āsiṣyate *etc.* B.+, -yáti TS. [— 2. āsitā.]
Verb. āsitá B.+; āsitum B.+, āstum K.; āsitvā́ B.S.; -āsya C.
Sec. Conj.: Pass. āsyate E.+ [— *Desid.* āsisiṣa-.] — *Caus.* āsayati B.

Deriv.: āsá V.B.	-āsya U.+	-āsanīya C.	-āsti C.
-āsā U.	āsyā E.+	āsitavyà B.+	
-āsaka E.+	āsana AV.+	-āsitṛ E.	

√ 1 i, ī, ay, 'go'.

Pres. [2.] éti yánti *etc.* V.+, -ité -iyate *etc.* B.+ — [1.] áyate *etc.* V.+, ayati *etc.* AV[1].?+ — [4.] íyate *etc.* V.B.C. — [5.] *see* √ 2 i. — iye RV[1]. iyāte RV[1]., ímahe V.B., iyāná V.+, íyati RV[1]., -iyánt ÇB.M. (imi TA[1].; āitat AV[1].; yan RV[1].; īyāná SV[1].; īyámāna ÇB.; īmahi C.)
Perf. iyā́ya īyús *etc.* V.+ [iyayitha] (iyétha V.B., iyátha V.) — -ayāṁ cakre E.+
Aor. 1. īyāt *etc.* E.+ (iyāsam GGS.) [— 4. (adhy-) āiṣṭa. — 5. āyiṣṭa.]
Fut. 1. eṣyáti *etc.* AV.+, -te *etc.* B.+; ayiṣyati *etc.* B.+ — 2. etā́ *etc.* B.+
Verb. itá V.+, -īta C.; étum B.+, étave étavāí V.B., étos V.B.S.; itvā́ B.U.; -ítya V.+, -īya C.; -áyya B.; áyase, ityāí, iyádhyāi RV.; -ā́yam V.B.
Sec. Conj.: Pass. īyate C. — *Int.* īyāyate PU[1]. — [*Desid.* ayiyiṣate, iyiṣati. —] *Caus.* (praty-) āyayati *etc.* (-āyyate) C.; (adhy-) āpayati -te *etc.* TA.E.+ [āpipat.]

Deriv.: áya V.+	-it B.+	-etu RV.	-āpaka C.
ayátha RV.S.	íti V.+	etavyà B.+	-āpya C.
áyana V.+	ití V.B.	etṛ́ V.+	-āpana E.+
-āya V.+	-itya B.S.	éma VS.	-āpayitṛ C.
-āyin AV.+	ityā́ V.B.	éman RV.	
-āyana AV.U.	-ítvan V.	-eya E.+	-āyaka C.
āyú V.+	itvará RV.C.	éva V.B.	-āyana C.
ā́yu V.+	-itha RV.		-ǎyitavya C.
ā́yus V.+	īti E.+		
-āyuka B.	īya- RV.		

The last three derivatives only with **prati**; the four preceding, only with **adhi**.

The forms most distinctly calling for the admission of a root-form **ī** are, in the older language, **ímahe** V.B. (common in RV.), **īyām** and **īyāta** and **īyus** B.U., **īyāná** SV. (all single occurrences); in the later language, **-īta, īti, -īya** (all rare or sporadic). The present-stem **íya** is improperly called intensive.

√ 2 i, inv, in, 'send'.

Pres. [5.] inóti *etc.* (invire) RV. — [1.] ínvati *etc.* V. — [9.] inīmasi ? SV[1].
Verb. -inita ÇB.

Deriv.: **iná** RV.C. **-inva** V.B. **invaká** B.+ **enas** V.+
Doubtless the same with the preceding root.

√ iñg, 'stir'.

Pres. [1.] **iñgati -te** E.+
Verb. **iñgita** E.+
Sec. Conj.: Caus. **iñgáyati** *etc.* V.+ (**iñgyáte** ÇB.)
Deriv.: **iñga** E.+ **iñgana** S.+ **iñgya** C. **iñjanā** C.
Isolated forms as if from **īñg, iñk, iñj** are found in the Brāhmaṇas.

√ ich, *see* √ 1 iṣ.

√ iṭ.

A root **iṭ**, 'wander', is assumed by BR. on account of the proper name **iṭant** in KB., and the doubtful and obscure **iṭátas** at RV. x. 171. 1 — which latter, however, is shown by its accent to be no participle.

√ iḍ.

A root **iḍ** is perhaps to be assumed on account of the nouns **íḍ** V.+ and **íḍā** V.+

√ idh, indh, 'kindle'.

Pres. [1.] **inddhé indháte** *etc.* V.+ (**indhaté** RV., **índhāna** V.; **iñkṣva** AB.; **inttām** TA.)
Perf. **īdhé īdhiré** RV.ÇB. [— **indhāṁ cakre.**]
Aor. 1. **idhaté**?·RV[1]., **idhīmahi** V., **idhāná** V. — 5. **āindhiṣṭa** *etc.* B., **indhiṣīya** TS., **idhiṣīmahi** S.
Fut. 1. **indhiṣyant** S. [— 2. **indhitā.**]
Verb. **iddhá** V.+; **-idhya** S.+; **-ídham, -ídhe** RV.
Sec. Conj.: Pass. **idhyáte** *etc.* V.+ [— *Desid.* **indidhiṣa-.**] — *Caus.* **indhita** C.
Deriv.: **-idh** V.+ **-ídhya** TS. **édha** V.+ **índha** V.B.
-iddhi B. **-idhra**? V.+ **édhas** AV.+ **-indhaka** E.
idhmá V.+ **-eddhṛ** RV. **indhana** V.+

√ in, inv, *see* √ 2 i.

√ inakṣ, *see* √ 2 naç.

√ iyakṣ, *see* √ yaj.

√ irajy, *see* √ ṛj

√ iradh, *see* √ rādh.

√ **il**, 'be quiet'

Pres. [6.] **ilati** *etc.* C.
[*Perf. etc.* **iyela, āilīt, eliṣyati, elitā.**]
Sec. Conj.: Caus. **iláyati** *etc.* AV.B.S. (**āilayīt** AV.; **ilitá** ÇB.)
Deriv.: **-ilaya** B.S.
In TS., **īláyanti** is once read.

√ 1 **iṣ, ich**, 'seek, desire'.

Pres. [6.] **icháti -te** *etc.* V.+ — [1.] **-eṣati -te** *etc.* E.+ — [6.] **-iṣa -iṣant** E.+ — [4.] **-iṣyati** E.+
Perf. **iyeṣa īṣús, īṣe īṣire** *etc.* B.+
Aor. [3. **āiṣiṣat.** —] 5. **āiṣīt āiṣiṣus** *etc.* B.U.
Fut. 1. **eṣiṣyati** *etc.* B., **-te** B. [— 2. **eṣitā, eṣṭā.**]
Verb. **iṣṭá** V.+; **éṣṭum** B.+, **-ṭavāí** ÇB., **eṣitum** E.; [**iṣitvā, iṣṭvā;**] **-íṣya** V.+.
Sec. Conj.: Pass. **iṣyate** *etc.* E.+, **-ti** E. [— *Desid.* **eṣiṣiṣa-.**] — *Caus.* **eṣayati** *etc.*, **eṣita** C. (**ichayāmi** E[1].)

Deriv.:			
-ichaka E.+	**iṣirá** V.B.	**eṣaka** E.	**éṣaṇā** B.+
ichā E.+	**iṣṭí** V.B.	**eṣin** AV.+	**eṣaṇīya** C.
ichu S.+	**iṣmín** RV	**-eṣya** AB.	**eṣṭavyà** B.+
íṣ V.B.	**éṣa** V.+	**eṣyà** V.+	**eṣitavya** C.
-iṣa RV.	**eṣá** RV.	**éṣaṇa** V.+	**-eṣṭṛ** E.
iṣí V.			

Compare the roots 2 **iṣ** and **īṣ, eṣ**. The present-stems **eṣa, iṣa, iṣya** only later, unusual, and with certain prepositions.

√ 2 **iṣ**, 'send'.

Pres. [9.] **iṣṇáti** *etc.* (**iṣāṇa**) V.B.S. — [4.] **íṣyati -te** *etc.* V.+ — [6.] **iṣe** *etc.* RV.
Perf. **īṣáthus īṣus** RV., **īṣiré** AV.
Aor. 5. **prāiṣīt** E.+ (**aprāiṣīt** M.)
[*Fut.* **eṣiṣyati, eṣitā.**]
Verb. **iṣitá** V.+; [**iṣitvā;**] **-íṣya** B.+; **-éṣam** B.; **iṣádhyāi** RV.
Sec. Conj.: [*Desid.* **eṣiṣiṣa-.** —] *Caus.* **iṣáyati -te** *etc.* (**iṣayádhyāi** RV.) — **-eṣayati -te** *etc.* E.+ (**eṣyate** E.)

Deriv.:			
iṣáṇi RV.	**-eṣa** V.+	**-eṣya** B.+	**eṣitavya** B.C.
íṣu V.+	**-eṣaka** E.	**-eṣaṇa** E.+	**-eṣayitṛ** E.

Doubtless the same with √ 1 **iṣ**, with causative meaning. In later language, almost only **preṣaya**. The derivatives hardly occur except with **pra**.

√ **ī**, *see* √ 1 **i**.

√ **īkṣ**, 'see'.

Pres. [1.] **íkṣate** *etc.* V.+, **-ti** *etc.* B.+
Perf. **īkṣáṁ cakre** *etc.* B.+, **īkṣāṁ cakrus** E.

Aor. 1. āikṣi c. — [3. āicikṣat. —] 5. āikṣiṣi *etc.* b. (āikṣīt c.?)
Fut. 1. īkṣiṣyáte *etc.* b.+, -yáti b. [— 2. īkṣitā.]
Verb. īkṣitá b.+; īkṣitum e.+; īkṣitvā b.; -ī́kṣya b.+; -īkṣam b.s.
Sec. Conj.: *Pass.* īkṣyate *etc.* s.+ — *Desid.* īcikṣiṣa- (*in d.*). — *Caus.* īkṣáyati *etc.* v.+, -te av. (īkṣyate s.)
Deriv.: ī́kṣa b.+ īkṣin e.+ īkṣaṇa rv.? s.+ -īkṣitavyà b.+
īkṣā b.+ -īkṣya b.+ īkṣaṇīya e.+ īkṣitṛ c.
ī́kṣaka b.+ īkṣeṇyà rv. īcikṣiṣu c.

Only three occurrences in rv., but growing rapidly common. Active forms sporadic

√ īñkh, 'swing'.

Pres. [1.] īñkhati *etc.* c., -te aa.
Sec. Conj.: *Caus.* īñkháyati -te *etc.* v.+
Deriv.: -īñkha v.+ -īñkhana c. -īñkhaya rv.

The form eñkṣva ab. is false.

√ īj, *see* √ ej.

√ īḍ, 'praise'.

Pres. [2.] ī́ṭṭe ī́ḍate *etc.* (ī́ḍiṣva) v.b. — [1.] īḍāmahe v., īḍamāna s.
Perf. īḍé rv., īḍire e.+ [— īḍāṁ cakre.]
[*Aor. etc.* āiḍiṣṭa; īḍiṣyate, īḍitā.]
Verb. īḍitá v.+; īḍitum c.
Sec. Conj.: *Pass.* īḍyate c. [— *Desid.* īḍiḍiṣa-.] — *Caus.* āiḍayan c.
Deriv.: ī́ḍ rv. ī́ḍya v.+ īḍitavya b. īḍényа v.b. īḍitṛ́ av.

Only a few sporadic occurrences in the later language.

√ īr, 'set in motion'.

Pres. [2.] ī́rte ī́rate *etc.* v.b. (īráte b.) — [1.] āirat *etc.* rv., ī́rate (3*s.*) av.
Perf. īriré v. (erire rv.) [— īrāṁ cakre.]
[*Aor. etc.* āirirat, āiriṣṭa; īriṣyate, īritā.]
Verb. īrṇá b.+
Sec. Conj.: *Caus.* īráyati *etc.* v.+, -te *etc.* v.b. (īryate *etc.* b.+; īritá v.+; īryant m.; īrayádhyāi rv.)
Deriv.: īra b.+ īrya b. īrin e.+ īraṇa e.+ -īritṛ u.
-īraka c. īryā c. -īraṇīya c. īrmá v.b.

The form īryayati, doubtless false, is found once in çb.

√ īrṣy, 'be jealous'.

Pres. [1.] ī́rṣyati *etc.* b.s.
Verb. īrṣyita c.
Deriv.: īrṣyā́ av.+ īrṣyin c. īrṣyú av.+ īrṣyitavya c.
īrṣyaka c. īrṣyālu c.

Evidently a secondary root, but of doubtful origin (BR., from **irasy**). Not seldom written without the **y** in later works.

√ **īç**, 'be master'.

Pres. [2.] **īṣṭe íçate** *etc.* (2*s.* **íkṣe** RV., **íçiṣe** RV.S.; **íçe** 3*s.* V.B., **īçite** U.; **īçidhve** AV.) V.+ — [1.] **īçate īçata** V.B.U.
Perf. **íçire**? RV. [— **īçāṁ cakre.**]
[*Aor.* **āiçiṣṭa.**]
Fut. 1. **īçiṣyati** U., **-te** B. [— 2. **īçitā.**]
Verb. **īçita** U.
Deriv.: **íç** B. **īçā́** AV.+ **īçana** U. **īçitṛ** U.+ **īçvará** AV.+ **īçá** B.+ **īçin** U.+ **īçitavya** C. **-īçu** V.+

√ **īṣ, eṣ**, 'move'.

Pres. [1.] **íṣate** *etc.* V.B., **-ti** *etc.* V.B.U. — **éṣati** *etc.* AV.
Perf. **īṣé** RV. (**āíyes** *plpf.* RV[1].) [— **īṣāṁ cakre.**]
[*Aor. etc.* **āiṣiṣṭa; īṣiṣyate; īṣitā.**]
Verb. **-īṣita** V.B.
Deriv.: **īṣā́** ? RV. **eṣá** RV. **-eṣṭi** C. **eṣṭṛ́** B.S.

Doubtless ultimately one with √ 1, 2 **iṣ.**

√ **īh**, 'be eager'.

Pres. [1.] **íhate** *etc.* B.+, **-ti** E.+
[*Perf. etc.* **īhāṁ cakre; āijihat, āihiṣṭa; īhiṣyate, īhitā.**]
Verb. **īhita** E.+; **īhitum** C.
[*Sec. Conj.: Desid.* **ījihiṣa-.** — *Caus.* **īhaya-.**]
Deriv.: **-īha** C. **īhā** E.+ **-īhana** E. **ehá** AV. **-ehas** V.+

√ **u**, 'proclaim'.

Pres. [2.] **uve** RV[1]. — [5.] **unoti** RV[1]. [— 1. **avate.**]
[*Perf. etc. etc.* **ūve; āuṣṭa; oṣyate, otā; ūṣiṣa-, āvaya-.**]

Extremely doubtful root; **uvé** is possibly interjection (Bö.); **vyùnoti** is perhaps for **víyunoti**; and the pple **óta**, put here by BR., doubtless belongs to √ **vā**, 'weave'.

√ 1 **ukṣ**, 'sprinkle'.

Pres. [6.] **ukṣáti** *etc.* V.+, **-te** *etc.* V.+
[*Perf.* **ukṣāṁ cakāra.**]
Aor. 5. **āukṣiṣam** *etc.* B.
Fut. 1. **ukṣiṣyati** *etc.* B.S. [— 2. **ukṣitā.**]
Verb. **ukṣitá** V.+; **-úkṣya** B.+
Sec. Conj.: Pass. **ukṣyate** *etc.* B.+; *Caus.* **ukṣayati** *etc.* S.+

Deriv.: -ukṣ RV. úkṣaṇa AV.+ -ukṣitavya B.C. uṣṭṛ́ RV[1].
-ukṣa B.S. ukṣaṇīya JB. úṣṭṛ B.S. úṣṭra V.+
ukṣán V.+

Whether ukṣán and uṣṭṛ́ *etc.* belong here, is very doubtful.

√ 2 ukṣ, vakṣ, 'grow', *see* √ vakṣ.

√ uc, 'be pleased'.

Pres. [4.] ucyati *etc.* V.B.
Perf. uvócitha uvóca, ūciṣé RV.
[*Aor. etc.* āucīt; uciṣyati, ucitā.]
Verb. ucitá V.+ [ocitvā.]
Deriv.: -óka RV. okyà RV. ókas V.+ okivā́ṅs RV[1]. -ócana V.. -ocara AV.

√ uch, *see* √ 1 vas.

√ ujh, 'forsake'.

Pres. [6.] ujhati *etc.* E.+
Perf. ujhāṁ cakāra C.
Aor. 5. āujhīt C.
[*Fut.* ujhiṣyati, ujhitā.]
Verb. ujhita E.+; ujhitum C.; -ujhya C.
Deriv.: -ujha S.+ ujhana C. ujhiti PB.

A secondary root, coming from ud + √ hā (ujjahāmi *etc.*).

√ uñch, 'glean'.

Pres. [6?] uñchati *etc.* S.+
[*Perf. etc.* uñchāṁ cakāra; āuñchīt; uñchiṣyati, uñchitā.]
Verb. uñchitum C.; -uñchya C.
[*Sec. Conj.*. *Desid.* uñcichiṣa-. — *Caus.* uñchaya-.]
Deriv.: uñcha S.+ uñchana C.

√ ud, und, 'wet'.

Pres. [7.] unátti undánti *etc.* V.B.S., undáte (3*p.*) AV. — [6.] undati *etc.* B.S.
Perf. ūdus AV. [— undāṁ cakāra.]
[*Aor. etc.* āundidat, āundīt; undiṣyati, unditā.]
Verb. utta B., unna S.C.; -údya B.S.
Sec. Conj.: Pass. udyate RV. [— *Desid.* undidiṣa-. — *Caus.* undaya-.]
Deriv.: úd RV. udani- RV. -udra V.+ ódatī RV.
udaká V.+ -uditṛ C. útsa V.+ odaná V.+
udán, uda V.+ údman B. úndana B.+ ódman B.

√ ubj, 'force'

Pres. [6.] ubjáti *etc.* V.B.S.
]*Perf. etc.* ubjāṁ cakāra; āubjijat, āubjīt; ubjiṣyati, ubjitā.]

Verb. ubjitá AV.B.; -ubjya JB.
[*Sec. Conj. Desid.* ubjijiṣa-. — *Caus.* ubjaya-.]
Deriv.: -udga? B.+ ubja RV.? B.+ -ubji- PB.

√ ubh, umbh, 'confine'.

Pres. [9.] āubhnāt ubhnā́s RV. — [7.] unap RV., āumbhan TS. — [6.] umbhata (2*p.*) AV., āumbhat MS.[; ubhati.]
[*Perf. etc.* uvobha, umbhāṁ cakāra; āubhīt, āumbhīt; ubhiṣyati umbhiṣyati, ubhitā umbhitā.]
Verb. ubdhá RV.B., umbhita C.; -ubhya S.
**Deriv.* -úmbhana TS.

√ uṣ, 'shine', *see* √ 1 vas.

√ uṣ, 'burn'.

Pres. [1.] óṣati *etc.* V.+ — [9.] uṣṇán, uṣṇánt RV[1].
Perf. uvoṣa ÇB. [— oṣāṁ cakāra.]
Aor. 5. āuṣīt *etc.* B.S.
[*Fut.* 1. oṣiṣyati. — 2. oṣitā.]
Verb. uṣṭa B.S.; [oṣitvā;] -oṣya TS.; -uṣas K.; óṣam ÇB.
Sec. Conj.: Pass. uṣyate *etc.* C. [— *Desid.* oṣiṣiṣa-. — *Caus.* oṣaya-.]

Deriv.: úṣa? RV.	uṣṇá V.+	-uṣyá ÇB.	oṣá, -óṣa V.+
uṣā C.	-uṣṇi TA.	ūṣmán V.+	-óṣas RV.
		uṣman E.+	oṣiṣṭha B.

Apparently a differentiated form of √ 1 vas, which see.

√ 1 ūrṇu, *see* √ 1 vṛ.

√ 1 ūh, 'remove'.

Pres. [1.] ū́hati V.+, -te V.+
[*Perf.* ūhāṁ cakāra.]
Aor. 1. uhyāt ÇB.; ohi C. [— 3. āujihat.] — 5. āuhīt B.
Verb. ūḍha B.+, ūhita C.; ūhitum E.+, oḍhum E.+, -ūhitavāí B.; -ūhya B.+, -úhya B.+; -óham RV., -ū́ham MS.
Sec. Conj.: Pass. uhyate B.+, ūhyate C. — *Caus.* ūhayati C.

Deriv.: ūha AV.+	ūhyà B.+	ūhanīya S.+	ūḍhi C.
-ūhaka C.	ūhana S.+	ūhitavya C.	-oha RV.
			-oghas? RV.

Doubtless a differentiated form of √ vah, from which in some forms and meanings it is hardly to be separated.

√ 2 ūh, 'consider'.

Pres. [1.] óhate *etc.* V. — [2.] óhate (3*p.*) óhāna ohāná RV. — [1.] ūhati C., -te E. — ohiṣe (1*s.*) RV[1].
Perf. ūhé *etc.* V. [— ūhāṁ cakre.]
Aor. [3. āujihat. —] 5. āuhiṣṭa V.

[*Fut.* ūhiṣyate, ūhitā.]
Verb. ūhitum C.; -ūhya C.
Sec. Conj.: [*Desid.* ūjihiṣa-. —] *Caus.* ūhayati *etc.* E.
Deriv.: ūha E.+ ūhana C. ūhitavya C. óhas RV.
ūhya C. ūhanīya A. óha-? RV. óhasāna RV.
Probably 'bear in mind', and so originally identical with 1 ūh and **vah.**

√ ṛ, ṛch, 'go, send'.

Pres. [6.] ṛcháti *etc.* V.+, -te *etc.* ÇB.E.; archati *etc.* U.E. — [3.] íyarti *etc.* (iyárṣi) V.B. — [5.] ṛṇóti *etc.* ṛṇve *etc.* V. — ṛṇváti *etc.* RV. — [6.] rante ranta RV., rántī? SV. — [9. ṛṇāti.] — [2.] árti TS.
Perf. āra (ā́ritha) ārús *etc.* V.+; ānarchat M¹. [— arāṁ cakāra.]
Aor. 1. ārta ārata *etc.* (aryāt TS., arīta RV.; arāṇá RV.) V.B. — 2. ā́rat *etc.* V.B. (aranta arāmahi V.) [— 4. ārṣīt.]
Fut. 1. ariṣyati B. [— 2. artā.]
Verb. ṛtá V.+, arṇa C.; ártos B.; -ṛtvā́ AV.B.; -ṛ́tya AV.; -ā́ram RV.
Sec. Conj.: [*Pass.* aryate. —] *Intens.* álarti *etc.* RV. [arāryate *etc.* — *Desid.* aririṣa-.] — *Caus.* arpáyati *etc.* V.+, -te C. (arpipam AV.; arpayitā E.; arpitá árpita V.+; -árpya V.+; arpyate C.)
Deriv.:

ará, ára V.+	árṇa V.+	ā́rya V.+	rátha V.+
aryá, árya V.B.S.	árṇas RV.	iras- RV.	-arpaka C.
áraṇa V.+	ártha V.+	íriṇa V.+	-arpya C.
aráṇi V.+	-arman, árma V.+	írya V.	árpaṇa V.+
aratí RV.	árvan, -arva V.+	-ṛchā U.+	arpaṇīya C.
aráru V.B.	árvant V.B.	ṛtí, ṛ́ti V.+	-arpitṛ E.+
arí V.+	ārá V.+	ṛtú V.+	-arpayitṛ́ ÇB.
aritṛ́ RV.	-ārin B.	-ṛtha V.	-arpayitavya C.
arítra, áritra V.+	ā́ruka TA.	ṛṇá V.+	

√ ṛc, *see* √ arc.

√ ṛj, ṛñj, arj, 'direct, stretch, attain'.

Pres. [7.] ṛñjate (3*p.*) RV. — [6.] ṛñjáti -áte *etc.* RV. AA. — [4.] ṛ́jyant, ṛjyate RV. — ṛñjase (1*s.*) ṛñjasāná RV. — [1.] árjati B.U.C.
Perf. [ānarjus] ānṛjús AV¹.?
Aor. [3. ārjijat. — 5. ārjiṣṭa.]
[*Fut.* arjiṣyati, arjitā.]
Verb. ṛñjáse RV¹.
Sec. Conj.: [*Pass.* ṛjyate. — *Desid.* arjijiṣa-. —] *Caus.* arjayati -te *etc.* S.E.+
Deriv.:

arjaka C.	ṛjipyá RV.	ṛ́jīyas V.
-arjya C.	ṛjíçvan RV.	ṛjú V.+
arjana E.+	ṛjīpín RV.	ráji RV.
arjanīya C.	ṛjīṣá RV.	rájiṣṭha RV.B.
-arjayitṛ C.	ṛjūnas RV.	rajīyas JB.
	-ṛñga RV.	rāji AV.+

It seems impossible to divide these forms (generally distributed to two different roots) from one another. The root has three well-marked stages of development: **ṛj** or **ṛñj** in RV., **arj** in Brāh., and **arjaya** in the later language. Compare also √**rāj**, probably a derivative from it. With it is related, further, the anomalously formed stem **irajya** (**irajyáti -te** *etc.* RV., and **irajyú** RV.), 'direct, rule'.

√ 2 ṛj, 'shine'.

Inferable from the derivatives:

árjuna V.+ **-ṛjīká** V. **ṛ́jīti** RV. **ṛjrá** RV.

√ ṛt, art, 'pursue'.

Aor. 5. **artiḍhvam** PB[1].
Fut. **artiṣye** AV[1].
Deriv.: **artaná** VS[1]. **-artitṛ** V[1]. **ártuka** ÇB[1].

A very doubtful root; **ánvartiṣye** and **anvartitṛ́** apparent contractions for **anu-vart-**; and Bö. amends **artiḍhvam** to **arthi-** (but??). But **artana** and **artuka** seem to show that the thing had assumed the value of a root.

√ ṛd, ard, 'stir, dissolve'.

Pres. [6.] **ṛdantu ā́rdan** RV. — [1.] **árdati** *etc.* AV.+ [— 7. **ṛṇatti.**]
[*Perf. etc.* **ānarda; ārdidat, ārdīt; ardiṣyati, arditā.**]
Verb. **arṇṇa**? ÇB.
Sec. Conj.: [*Desid.* **ardidiṣa-.** —] *Caus.* **ardáyati** *etc.* ([**ārdayīt**] **ardyate ardita**) V.+
Deriv.: **-ardaka** C. **-ardin** C. **ardana** E.+

Of perplexing variety of meanings.

√ ṛdh, 'thrive'.

Pres. [5.] **ṛdhnóti** *etc.* V.+ — [7.] **ṛṇádhat ṛndhyām ṛndhánt** V. — [4.] **ṛdhyate -ti** V.+ (*Pass.*?).
Perf. **ānṛdhús** AV., **ānṛdhe** RV.ÇB.
Aor. 1. **ā́rdhma** B.S., **ṛdhā́the** RV., **ṛdhyā́m** *etc.* V.B.S., **ṛdhyā́sam** *etc.* AV.B.S., **ṛdhīmáhi** RV., **ṛdhánt** RV.; **ā́rdhi** B. — 2. **ṛdhet ṛdhema** AV.ÇB. — [3. **ārdidhat.** —] 5. [**ārdhīt**] **ārdhiṣṭa** MS.
Fut. 1. **ardhiṣyate** ÇB. — 2. **ardhitā** JB.
Verb. **ṛddha** AV.+ [**ṛddhvā, ardhitvā.**]
Sec. Conj.: *Pass.* **ṛdhyate** *etc.* V.+, **ṛdhyant** M. — *Desid.* **ī́rtsati** *etc.* (**ā́irtsīt** *etc.*) AV.ÇB. [**ardidhiṣa-.**] — *Caus.* **ardháyati** *etc.* AV.+
Deriv.:

árdha? V.+	**-ardhi** RV.	**-ṛ́dha** RV.	**ṛdhnuka** AGS.
ardhá? V.+	**árdhuka** B.S.	**ṛ́dhat, ṛ́dhak**? V.B.	**-īrtsā** AV.
árdhya RV.	**-ṛdh** V.S.	**ṛ́ddhi** AV.+	**-ardhayitṛ** U.S.

Compare roots **vṛdh** and **rādh**.

√ ṛç(?), 'harm'.

Perhaps to be inferred from the derivatives :

-arça RV. **árças** VS. + **ṛ́kṣa** V. + **ṛkṣī́kā** AV.B.
-arçani RV. **arçasānā́** RV. **-ṛkṣara** V.

√ ṛṣ, 'rush, push'.

Pres. [1.] **árṣati** *etc.* (**arṣase** AV.) V.B. — [6.] **ṛṣáti** *etc.* V.B.S.
Perf. **ānarṣat** TA.
[*Aor. etc.* **ārṣīt**; **arṣiṣyati**, **arṣitā**.]
Verb. **ṛṣṭa** V.B. [**arṣitvā**.]
[*Sec. Conj.*: **arṣiṣiṣa-**; **arṣaya-**.]
Deriv.: **-arṣa** B. **-árṣu** RV. **ṛṣabhá** V.+ **ṛṣṭí** V. +
-árṣaṇa B. **arṣṭṛ́** B. **ṛ́ṣi** V.+ **ṛṣvá** V.B.
arṣaṇī́ AV. **ṛṣú** RV.

Hardly calls for the usual division into two roots. Some of the derivatives doubtful.

√ ej, īj, 'stir'.

Pres. [1.] **ījate**, **ī́jamāna** RV.; **éjati** *etc.* V. +
[*Perf. etc.* **ejāṁ cakāra**; **āijijat**; **ejiṣyati**, **ejitā**.]
Sec. Conj.: [*Desid.* **ejijiṣa-**. —] *Caus.* **ejayati** ÇB., **-te** C.
Deriv.: **ejáthu** AV. **-ejaya** V. +

√ edh, 'thrive'.

Pres. [1.] **édhate** *etc.* V.+, **-ti** *etc.* B.+
Perf. **edhire** C. — **edhā́ṁ cakrire** ÇB., **edhām babhūvire** C.
Aor. [3. **āididhat**. —] 5. **edhiṣīyá** *etc.* AV.B.
[*Fut.* **edhiṣyate**, **edhitā**.]
Verb. **edhita** E.+; **édhitum** B.+
Sec. Conj.: *Desid.* **edidhiṣa-** (*in d.*). — *Caus.* **edhayati** *etc.* S. +
Deriv.: **-edha**? B.S. **edhatú** V.B. **-edhana** E. **edhas** S.E. **edidhiṣu-** VS.

Perhaps related with **ṛdh**.

√ katth, 'boast'.

Pres. [1.] **katthate** *etc.* E. +, **-ti** *etc.* E.
[*Perf. etc.* **cakatthe**; **akatthiṣṭa**; **katthiṣyate**, **katthitā**.]
Verb. **katthita** E. +; **katthitum** E.
Sec. Conj.: *Caus.* **katthayati** E.
Deriv.: **-kạtthā** E. **katthaka** C. **-katthin** E.+ **katthana** E.+ **katthitavya** C.

A secondary prakritized root, but of unclear derivation.

√ kad, 'destroy'

Only in the deriv. **kadana** E.+, and in **cakāda kadanam** R., where **cakāda** is a misreading for **cakāra**.

√ kan, kā, 'be pleased, enjoy'

Pres. [4.] kā́yamāna RV¹.
Perf. cākana cākánas *etc.* cākanyāt cākandhi *etc.* cā̆kánanta cākán RV.; caké cakāná V.B.S.
Aor. 5. akāniṣam kā́niṣas RV.

Deriv.:	kanā́ RV.	kaniṣṭhá V.B.	kanī́na V.+	kanyā̀ V.+
	kanaka? E.+	kániṣṭha B.+	kánīyas V.+	-kāti RV.
				-kāyyà RV.

Doubtless the same with the following root, **kam**. The stem **cākán**, on account of its accent, rather perfect than intensive.

√ kam, 'love'.

Perf. cakamé *etc.* V.+
Aor. 3. [acakamata] acīkamata *etc.* B. [— 5. kamiṣiṣṭa.]
Fut. 1. kamiṣyate *etc.* B. — 2. kamitā B.
Verb. kāṁta E.+; [kāṁtvā, kamitvā;] -kamas B.; -kā́mam ÇB.
Sec. Conj.: [*Intens.* caṅkam-. — *Desid.* cikamiṣa-. —] *Caus.* kāmáyate *etc.* V.+, -ti *etc.* E.

Deriv.:	kám? V.+	kamitṛ C.	kā́mya V.+	kā́muka B.+
	kama-? V.	kamra C.	-kāmyā́ AV.+	kāṁti E.+
	kamana C.	kā́ma V.+	-kāman RV¹.	kāmayitavya
	kamanīya C.	kāmín V.+	kāmana S.+	C.

Doubtless the same with the preceding.

√ kamp, 'tremble'.

Pres. [1.] kampate *etc.* U.+, -ti *etc.* E.
Perf. cakampe *etc.* E.
[*Aor. etc.* acakampat, akampiṣṭa; kampiṣyate, kampitā.]
Verb. kampita E.+ [kapita]; kampitum E., -tos B.; -kampya S.+
Sec. Conj.: [*Int.* caṅkamp-. — *Desid.* cikampiṣa-. —] *Caus.* kampayati *etc.* B.+, -te *etc.* U.+ (kampyate C.)

Deriv.:	kampa E.+	kampin E.+	kampanā E.+	kapanā́? RV.
	-kampā E.+	kampya E.+	-kampanīya C.	kapí? V.+
	-kampaka E.+	kampana E.+	kampra S.+	képi? RV.

√ kal, 'drive, produce', etc.

[*Pres. etc.* kalate, cakale, *etc.*]
Sec. Conj.: Caus. kālayati *etc.* S.+, -te *etc.* B.+ (kālyate *etc.* S.+) — kalayati *etc.* E.+, -te *etc.* C.

Deriv.:	kalā́? B.+	-kalya C.	-kalanīya C.	-kālaka C.
	-kalikā C.	kalana S.+	-kalayitṛ C.	-kālana S.+

Divided by BR. and Bö. into two roots: 2 **kal (kālay)**, 'drive'; and 1 **kal (kalay)**, 'drive etc. etc.'

√ **kaṣ**, 'scratch'.

Pres. [1.] **kaṣati** *etc.* AV. +, **-te** *etc.* B. +
[*Perf. etc.* **cakāṣa; akāṣīt.**]
Fut. 1. **kaṣiṣyati** TS. [— 2. **kaṣitā.**]
Verb. **kaṣita** C.; **-kāṣam** S. +
Deriv.: **kaṣa** E. + **kaṣaṇa** C. **-kāṣa** B. + **-kāṣin** C.

√ **kas**, 'open'.

Pres. [1.] **kasati** *etc.* AV.C.
Perf. **cakase** C.
Aor. 3. **acīkasat** C.
[*Fut.* **kasiṣyati, kasitā.**]
Verb. **kasta** V.B.S., **kasita** S. +
Sec. Conj.: [*Int.* **canīkas-.** — *Desid.* **cikasiṣa-.** —] *Caus.* **kāsayati** *etc.* C. (**kāsyate** C.)
Deriv.: **kasanā?** C. **-kasti** TS. **-kāsa** E. + **-kāsin** S. + **-kāsanīya** C. **-kasuka** AV. + **-kasvara** C. **-kāsaka** C. **-kāsana** C.

√ **kā**, *see* √ **kan.**

√ **kāṅkṣ**, 'desire'.

Pres. [1.] **kāṅkṣati -te** *etc.* B. +
Perf. **cakāṅkṣa** E. +
[*Aor. etc.* **acakāṅkṣat, akāṅkṣīt; kāṅkṣiṣyati, kāṅkṣitā.**]
Verb. **kāṅkṣita** E. +
Sec. Conj.: [*Int.* **cākāṅkṣya-.** — *Desid.* **cikāṅkṣiṣa-.** —] *Caus.* **kāṅkṣayate** E.
Deriv.: **-kāṅkṣa** C. **kāṅkṣin** E. + **-kāṅkṣaṇa** C. **kāṅkṣā** E. + **-kāṅkṣya** C. **kāṅkṣaṇīya** C. **-kāṅkṣitavya** C.

Perhaps a desiderative formation from √ **kan** or **kam.**

√ **kāç**, 'appear, make a show'.

Pres. [1.] **kāçate** *etc.* B. +, **-ti** *etc.* E.
Perf. **cakāçe** *etc.* E. + [— **kāçāṁ cakre.**]
[*Aor. etc.* **acakāçat, akāçiṣṭa; kāçiṣyate, kāçitā.**]
Verb. **kāçita** E.; **-kā́çya** B.
Sec. Conj.: *Int.* **cākaçīti** *etc.* V.B.U., **cākaçyáte** *etc.* B.S. [— *Desid.* **cikāçiṣa-.**] — *Caus.* **kāçayati** AV. +, **-te** U. + (**kāçyate** E.)
Deriv.: **kā́ça** V. + **-kāçin** E. + **-kāçanīya** C. **-kāçaka** E. + **-kāçya** C. **-caṅkaça** AV. **-kāçana** E. + **-kāçayitavya** C.

√ **kās**, 'cough'.

Pres. [1.] **kāsate** *etc.* C., **-ti** C.
[*Perf. etc.* **kāsāṁ cakre; acakāsat, akāsiṣṭa; kāsiṣyate, kāsitā; cākās-, cikāsiṣa-, kāsaya-.**]
Deriv.: **kā́s** AV. **kāsā́** AV.C. **kāsā** AV. **kā́sikā** AV. **-kāsana** C.
Verb-forms only in the medical literature, and probably denominative, from **kā́s** or **kāsā́**.

√ **ku**, *see* √ **kū**.

√ **kuc, kuñc**, 'shrink, curl'.

Pres. [1.] **kuñcate** *etc.* C. — [6.] **kucati** *etc.* S[1].C.
Perf. **cukoca** C. [**cukuñca.**]
[*Aor. etc.* **akocīt, akuñcīt; kociṣyati kuñciṣyati, kocitā kuñcitā.**]
Verb. **kucita** E.+, **kuñcita** E.+
Sec. Conj.: *Pass.* **kucyate** C. — [*Int.* **cokucya-.** — *Desid.* **cukuñciṣa-.** —]
Caus. **kuñcayati** *etc.* E.+; **kocayati** *etc.* E.+
Deriv.: **kuca** E.+ **kuñcana** C. **-kocaka** C.
-kucana C. **kuñci** C. **-kocin** C.
-kuñcaka C. **koca** E.+ **-kocana** E.+
Given by the grammarians as two distinct roots, and not without some justification.

√ **kuñj**, 'rustle'.

Pres. [1.] **kuñjati** C.
A single occurrence, in the Harṣacarita. If not a false reading, is probably an artificial word.

√ **kuṭṭ**, 'divide, crush'.

Sec. Conj.: *Caus.* **kuṭṭayati** *etc.* C. (**kuṭṭita** C., **-kuṭṭya** E.+)
Deriv.: **-kuṭṭa** E.+ **-kuṭṭaka** C. **kuṭṭana** C.
Perhaps a prakritized form of 1 **kṛt.** The forms **avakuṭya** and **prakuṭya** (BR. √ 2 **kuṭ**) are only the usual and permitted abbreviations of **-kuṭṭya.**

√ **kuṇṭh**, 'dull'.

Doubtless only a denominative from **kuṇṭha** E.+, 'dull'. The participle **kuṇṭhita** C., and the derivatives **kuṇṭhaka** E.+, **-kuṇṭhana** E.+, occur.

√ **kuth**, 'stink'.

Verb. **kuthita** C.
Sec. Conj.: *Caus.* **kothayati** *etc.* C.
Deriv.: **kotha** C. **-kothaka** B.
Except the n. pr. **nikothaka**, found only in Suçruta: no proper root.

√ **kup**, 'be angry'.

Pres. [4.] **kupyati** *etc.* E.+, **-te** *etc.* E.
Perf. **cukopa** *etc.* U[1].E.
Aor. [2. **akupat**. — 3. **acūkupat**. —] 5. **kopiṣṭhās** E.
[*Fut.* **kopiṣyati, kopitā.**]
Verb. **kupita** RV[1]. E. + (**kupta** C[1]. ?)
Sec. Conj.: [*Int.* **cokup-**. — *Desid.* **cukupiṣa-, cukopiṣa-**. —] *Caus.* **kopáyati** *etc.* RV. ÇB. E. +, **-te** E. (**cukopayiṣa-** *in d.*)
Deriv.: **kupá** B.S. **kupāyú** AV.? **kopin** E.+ **-kopitṛ** E.
kupana? C. **-kupya** E. **kopya** E. **kopayiṣṇu** E.
kúpaya RV. **kopa** E.+ **kopana** E.+ **cukopavisu** E.

√ **kuṣ**, 'tear'.

Pres. [9.] **kuṣṇāti** *etc.* C. — [6.] **kuṣati** *etc.* C.
[*Perf. etc.* **cukoṣa; akoṣīt, akukṣat; koṣiṣyati kokṣyati, koṣitā koṣṭā; cokuṣ-, cukuṣiṣa- cukoṣiṣa-, koṣaya-.**]
Verb. **kuṣita** C.; **-kúṣya** MS.
Deriv.: **koṣá** (? *n. pr.*) ÇB. **-koṣaṇa** S.C.

The occurrence in MS. hardly a genuine one.

√ **kū**, 'design'.

Pres. [6.] **kuvate** ÇB[2].
Verb. **-kūta** AV.+; **-kā́vam** TS.
Deriv.: **-kūti** V.+ **kaví** V.+ **kávīyas** SV.

Used only with **ā**, except in **niṣkā́vam**, the belonging of which is doubtful (as is also that of **kaví**). RV. has **-kava, kavatnú, kavā́rí**, 'stingy', of questionable relationship. The grammarians set up roots 1 **ku**, 2 **ku** or **kū**, 'shout', giving them a full set of forms; and Nir. once uses their intens. **kokūyate.**

√ **kūj**, 'hum'.

Pres. [1.] **kū́jati** *etc.* AV.+, **-te** *etc.* E.
Perf. **cukūja -je** *etc.* C.
Aor. 1. **akūji** C.
[*Fut.* **kūjiṣyati, kūjitā.**]
Verb. **kūjita** E.+; **kūjitvā** C.
[*Sec. Conj.:* **cokūj-, cukūjiṣa-, kūjaya-.**]
Deriv.: **kūja** E.+ **kūjana** E.+ **kūjitavya** E.

√ **kūḍ, kūl**, 'burn'.

Sec. Conj.: *Caus.* **kūḍayati** *etc.* RV[1]. AB[1].+, **kūlayati** *etc.* S.+ (**kūlita** C., **-kūḍya** S.C.)

√ kūṇ, 'shrink'.

Pres. [1.] kūṇati c[1].
Sec. Conj.: Caus. kūṇayati *etc.* c.

√ kūrd, 'leap, exult'.

Pres. [1.] kūrdati -te *etc.* E.+
Perf. cukūrda *etc.* c. [-de.]
[*Aor. etc.* akūrdiṣṭa; kūrdiṣyate, kūrditā.]
Verb. kūrdita c.
Deriv.: kūrda s. kūrdana c. -kroda? TS. -krodin? MS.
Compare √ gūrd, which is doubtless the same with this.

√ 1 kṛ (skṛ), 'make'.

Pres. [5.] kṛṇóti kṛṇuté *etc.* V.B.S. — [8.] karóti kuruté *etc.* RV[3]. AV.+ — [2.] kárṣi AV[1]., kṛthás kṛtha kṛṣé RV. — [1.] karanti *etc.* RV. — kurmi E. — kṛṣe (1s.) RV[1].
Perf. cakā́ra cakré *etc.* (cakártha cakṛṣé *etc.*) V.+ (cakriyās acakrat *etc.* acakriran RV.)
Aor. 1. ákaram ákar ákran *etc.* akri ákṛta ákrata *etc.* V.B.S. (kárati -te *etc.* V.B.S., kriyāma RV., kriyāsam -āsma V.B.S., kṛdhí *etc.* V.+, kṛṣvá *etc.* RV., kránt krāṇá RV.; kránta RV.; akat ÇB.); ákāri V.+ — 2. ákarat *etc.* AV.B.S. — 3. acīkarat c. — 4. akārṣīt *etc.* B.+, akṛṣi *etc.* B.C.
Fut. 1. kariṣyáti *etc.* V.+, -te *etc.* B.C. (akariṣyat *etc.* B.+) — 2. kartā S.+
Verb. kṛtá V.+; kártum AV.+, -tave V.B., -tavāí B.S., -tos V.B.S.; kṛtvā́ AV.+, -tvī́ V.B., -tvā́ya B.; -kṛ́tya V.+; -kā́ram B.+
Sec. Conj.: Pass. kriyáte *etc.* V.+ — *Int.* karikṛ- carikṛ- V.B. — *Desid.* cíkīrṣati *etc.* AV.+, -te *etc.* S.+ (acikīrṣīs ÇB.; cikīrṣayati C.). — *Caus.* kārayati -te *etc.* B.+ (kāryate *etc.* E.+; cikārayiṣa- *in d.*)

Deriv.:

kará V.+	kártṛ RV.	kāruka B.+	-kṛtha RV.
karaṇá RV.	kartṛ́ V.+	-kūrmi, -in RV.	-kra RV.
kárana V.+	kártra AV.	-kṛt V.+	krátu V.+
karaṇīya B.+	kárman V.+	-kṛ́tya *n.* V.+	kriyā KÇS. E.+
-karaṇi? E.	kárvara V.	-kṛtya *a.* V.+	cákri RV.
káras RV.	-kāra V.+	kṛtyā́ V.+	-karikra B.
káriṣṭha RV.	kāraka E.+	kṛ́ti V.+	-cikīrṣ C.
-kariṣṇu S.+	kārin AV.+	kṛ́tu (-tvas) V.+	cikīrṣā E.+
karúṇa V.B.	kāryà AV.+	kṛ́tvya RV.	cikīrṣu E.+
kártva V.	kāraṇa S.+	kṛtnú V.	kārayitṛ B.E.
kartavyà B.+	-kāraṇīya C.	kṛtríma V.+	kārayitavya E.+
	kāru E.+	kṛ́tvan V.	cikārayiṣu C.
		kṛ́tvarī AV.	-ciṣkārayiṣu E.

The root-form skṛ is found especially after sam and pari; but also the AOR. nír askṛta RV., and pple upaskṛta E.+. In V. occur only saṁskṛta and **pariṣkṛta** RV. AV., and **pariṣkṛṇvánti** and **-vánt** RV. (against **sám akṛṇvan** *etc.* RV.). But from B. on, forms with **sk** after **sam** are frequent, almost to the exclusion of those with simple **k**; even such as **sam askurvata, saṁ caskāra, saṁ skariṣyanti, saṁskārayām āsa, saṁciṣkārayiṣu.** Of the derivatives, there are found with **saṁ** only: **skaraṇa** S.+, **skartavya** C., **skartṛ** E.+, **skāraka** E.+, **skārya** E.+, **skṛti** B.+; also **skriyā** with **saṁ** C. and **pari** C.; **skāra** with **saṁ** S.+, **pari** E.+, and **upa** C.; and **skara** with **apa** C., **upa** E.+, **pari** E., and **vi** (?) E.+; finally, **áskra** RV., which is doubtful.

√ 2 kṛ, kir, 'scatter'.

Pres. [6.] **kiráti** *etc.* V.+, **-te** *etc.* V.+
Perf. **cakāra cakre** E. [**cakarus.**]
Aor. 1. **kīryāt** C. — 4. **akīrṣata** PB. — 5. **kāriṣat** RV.
Fut. 1. **kariṣyati** *etc.* E. [**karīṣyati.** — 2. **karitā.**]
Verb. **kīrṇa** B.+; **-kīrya** S.+
Sec. Conj.: *Pass.* **kīryáte** *etc.* B.+ (**kīryet** E.) — [*Int.* **cākar-, cekīrya-.** — *Desid.* **cikariṣa-.** —] *Caus.* [**kārayati,**] **kīrayet** E.

Deriv.:	**kara** V.? B.+	**-kāra**? S.+	**-kira** C.	**-kīrya** C.
	-karaka E.	**-kāraka** C.	**kiráṇa** V.+	**-kula**? E.+
	-karitṛ B.	**-kir** C.	**-kiri** B.	

One or two late forms occur with prefixed **s**: **apaskiramāṇa, praticaskare**; others are authorized by the grammarians; in derivatives, **viṣkira** S.+

√ 3 kṛ, 'commemorate'.

Pres. **cakránt**? RV.
Aor. 4. **akārṣam** AV. — 5. **akāriṣam ákārīt** RV.
Sec. Conj.: *Int.* **carkarmi carkṛdhi** *etc.* **carkirāma -ran** **cárkṛṣe** (3s.) RV. AV[1].

Deriv.:	**kārá** RV.	**kārú** V.	**kīrtí** V.+	**carkṛtí** RV.
	kārín RV.	**kīrí, -ín** RV.	**-keru** RV.	**carkṛ́tya** V.

Cakránt is anomalous and altogether questionable.

√ 1 kṛt, 'cut'.

Pres. [6.] **kṛntáti** *etc.* V.+, **-te** *etc.* B.E. — [1.] **kartati** *etc.* E.
Perf. **cakarta** *etc.* (**cakartitha, cakartus**) V.+, **cakartire** E.
Aor. 2. **ákṛtas** RV. (**kṛtant-** RV.) — 3. **acīkṛtas** TB. [**acakartat.**] — 5. **kartīs** B.
Fut. 1. **kartsyati** AV.; **kartiṣyati** C. [— 2. **kartitā.**]
Verb. **kṛttá** V.+; **-kṛ́tya** V.+; **-kártam** ÇB.
Sec. Conj.: *Pass.* **kṛtyáte** *etc.* AV.+ — [*Int.* **carīkṛt-.** —] *Desid.* **cikartiṣa-** (*in d.*) [**cikṛtsa-.**] — *Caus.* **kartayati** *etc.* S.+, **kṛntayati** LÇS.

Deriv.:	kartá V. +	-kartin C.	kṛ́tā RV.	kṛntana S. +
	gárta? B. +	karttavya E.	kṛtí RV.	kṛntátra V.B.
	kartya C.	-karttṛ E. +	kṛ́tti? V. +	cikartiṣā C.
	kartana V. +	kartarī C.	-kṛnta B.	cikartiṣu C.

Saṁskṛtatrá V[1]. is doubtless not referable to this root.

√ 2 kṛt, 'spin'.

Pres. [7.] kṛṇátti *etc.* V.B.S.
Sec. Conj.: *Caus.* kartita kartya C.
Deriv. karttṛ E.

√ kṛp, 'lament'.

Pres. [1.] kṛ́pate *etc.* V.
Perf. cakṛpánta RV.
Aor. 1. akṛpran V. — 5. akrapiṣṭa RV.
Sec. Conj.: *Caus.* kṛpáyati *etc.* RV. (kṛpayánt RV[1].), -te *etc.* JB.
Deriv.: kṛpā E. + kṛpáṇa V. + kṛpaṇá AV. +

√ kṛç, 'be lean'.

Pres. [4.] kṛ́çyati ÇB.
Perf. cakárça AV.
[*Aor. etc.* akṛçat; karçiṣyati, karçitā.]
Verb. kṛçita AB. [kṛçitvā, karçitvā.]
Sec. Conj.: *Caus.* karçáyati *etc.* V. +
Deriv.: karçana V. + kṛçá V. + kráçīyas C.

√ kṛṣ, 'drag, plough'.

Pres. [1.] kárṣati *etc.* V. +, -te *etc.* B. + — [6.] kṛṣáti -te *etc.* V. +
Perf. cakarṣa *etc.* (cakarṣatus) B. +
Aor. 3. acīkṛṣam RV. [acakarṣat. — 4. akārkṣīt, akrākṣīt.] — 7. akṛkṣat *etc.* B. (akṛkṣathās ÇB.)
Fut. 1. krakṣyánt S., krakṣye B., [karkṣyati] karṣiṣyánt B. [— 2. karṣṭā, kraṣṭā.]
Verb. kṛṣṭá AV. +; kraṣṭum E. +; kṛṣṭvā́ B. +; -kṛṣya S. +
Sec. Conj.: *Pass.* kṛṣyáte *etc.* B. + — *Int.* cárkṛṣati *etc.* V.B. [carīkṛṣ-. — *Desid.* cikṛkṣa-.] — *Caus.* karṣayati *etc.* E. +

Deriv.:	karṣa S. +	karṣū́ B. +	kā́rṣi, -ṣín B.	kṛṣya S. +
	karṣaka E. +	karṣaṇa E. +	kā́rṣman RV.	kṛṣṭí V. +
	karṣin, -ṣí B. +	karṣaṇīya C.	kṛṣí V. +	kraṣṭavya C.
				-kraṣṭṛ C.

It does not seem worth while to divide this root, evidently one, into two nearly related ones, as is often done.

√ kḷp, 'be adapted'.

Pres. [1.] **kálpate** *etc.* v. + (**kálpant**? av.)
Perf. **cākḷpé** *etc.* v., **-pus** av. (**-pat** v.); **cakḷpe** c.
Aor. [2. **akḷpat.** —] 3. **acīkḷpat** *etc.* v. + [— 4. **akḷpta.** — 5. **akalpiṣṭa.**]
Fut. 1. **klapsyate** ab., **kalpiṣyate** c. [**kalpsyati.** — 2. **kalpitā, kalptā.**]
Verb. **kḷptá** v. +
Sec. Conj.: [*Int.* **calkḷp-, calīkḷp-.** — *Desid.* **cikḷpsati, cikalpiṣate.** —]
Caus. **kalpáyati -te** *etc.* v. + (**kalpyáte** b. +; **cikalpayiṣati** ab.)
Deriv.: **kálpa** v. + **kalpana** u. + **kalpitavya** c. **-kalpayitṛ** çb.
kalpaka e. + **kalpanā** e. + **kḷ'pti** b. + **kalpayitavya** b. +
kalpya e. + **kalpanīya** u. +
With this root are apparently related **kṛ́p** v.b., **kṛpa** v. +

√ knū, 'wet'.

[*Pres. etc.* **knūyate, cuknūye, aknūyīt, knūyiṣyati, knūyitā.**]
Verb. **-knū́yam** çb.
Sec. Conj.: *Caus.* [**knopayati**] (**-knopam** c.)
Deriv. **-knopana** c.

√ krakṣ, 'crash'.

Pres. [1.] **krákṣamāṇa** rv[1].
Deriv.: **-krakṣa** rv[1]. **-krakṣin** rv[1].
Apparently an onomatopoetic root.

√ krath, 'be jubilant'.

[*Pres. etc.* **krathati** *etc.*]
Sec. Conj.: *Caus.* **krātháyati** tb[1].
Deriv.: **kratha** e. + **krathana** e. + **krātha** e. **-krāthin** e. **krāthana** c.
A very doubtful group of derivatives, in meaning and connection.

√ krand, kland, 'cry out'.

Pres. [1.] **krándati** *etc.* v. +, **-te** *etc.* e. — **klandate** c[1].
Perf. **cakranda** c., **cakradé** rv. (**cakradat** *etc.* rv.)
Aor. 2. **kradas** rv. — 3. **acikradat** *etc.* v.b. — 4. **ákrān** v.b. — 5. **akrandīt** c.
[*Fut.* **krandiṣyati, kranditā.**]
Verb. **krandita** c.; **kranditum** c.
Sec. Conj.: *Int.* **kánikrand-, kánikrad-, kanikradyá-** v.b. [**cākrand-.** — *Desid.* **cikrandiṣa-.**] — *Caus.* **krandáyati** *etc.* v. +
Deriv.: **kránda** v. + **klandá** av. **krandanú** rv.
-krandin c. **krándana** v. + **krándas** v.
krándya v.b. **-krandanīya** c. **kanikradá** b.

√ kram, 'stride'.

Pres. [1.] krā́mati *etc.* krámate *etc.* v. + (kramati *etc.* RV.? E.+, krāmate *etc.* U.E.) [— 4. krāmyati.]
Perf. cakrā́ma cakramús *etc.*, cakramé *etc.* v. + (cákramanta RV.)
Aor. 1. akran ákramus *etc.* RV. — 2. akramat -man AV.B. [— 3. acikramat.] — 4. akraṁsta -sata *etc.* V.B.S. (kraṁsate RV.) — 5. ákramīt *etc.* V.B.U., krámiṣṭa (3s.) RV. (akramīm RV., akrāmīt ÇB.)
Fut. 1. kraṁsyáti -te AV.B.E.; kramiṣyati -te B.+ (akramiṣyat U.) [— 2. kramitā, kraṁtā.]
Verb. krāṁtá AV.+; krámitum B.+, -tos B., krāṁtum E.+; kramitvā E.+, krāṁtvā́ B.+ [kraṁtvā]; -krámya V.+; -kráme RV.; -krā́mam AV.+
Sec. Conj.: Pass. kramyate *etc.* S.+. — *Int.* caṅkram- V.+, caṅkramyáte B.+ — *Desid.* cikramiṣati *etc.* B.U. [cikraṁsa-.] — *Caus.* kramayati *etc.* B.+; krāmayati *etc.* B.+ (krāmyate C.)
Deriv.:

kráma V.+	-kramaṇīya E.+	-krāmya C.	-krāṁtṛ E.
-kramin E.+	-kramitavya E.	-krāmaṇa C.	caṅkrama AV.+
kramya C.	-krāma B.	-krā́muka B.	caṅkramaṇa S.+
krámaṇa V.+	-krāmin AV.B.	-krāṁti B.+	-krāmayitavya C.

The aor. akran is by some referred to √krand.

√ krī, 'buy'.

Pres. [9.] krīṇā́ti krīṇīté *etc.* V.+
Perf. cikrāya S. [cikriye.]
[*Aor.* akrāiṣīt, akreṣṭa.]
Fut. 1. kreṣyati -te *etc.* B.S. [— 2. kretā.]
Verb. krītá V.+; kretum E.+; krītvā́ AV.+; -krī́ya B.+
Sec. Conj.: Pass. krīyáte *etc.* B.+ [— *Int.* cekrī-.] — *Desid.* cikrīṣate C. [— *Caus.* krāpayati, acikrapat.]

Deriv.:				
	krayá AV.+	krayya B.+	-krāyaka E.+	kretavya E.+
	-krayaka E.	kráyaṇa B.+	-krī AV.+	kretṛ E.+
	-krayin E.+	krayaṇīya S.	-krīti B.	kreya E.+

√ krīḍ, 'play'.

Pres. [1.] krī́ḍati -te *etc.* V.+
Perf. cikrīḍa -ḍe *etc.* B.+
[*Aor.* acikrīḍat, akrīḍīt.]
Fut. 1. krīḍiṣyati C. [— 2. krīḍitā.]
Verb. krīḍita E.+; krīḍitum C.; -krīḍya E.
Sec. Conj.: [*Int.* cekrīḍ-. —] *Desid.* cikrīḍiṣa- (*in d.*). — *Caus.* krīḍayati *etc.* S.+ (krīḍāpayati E.)

Deriv.: **krīḍá** v. + **krīḍā́** b. + **krīḍín** v. + **krīḍana** e. + **krīḍí** rv.b. **krīḍitṛ** c. **krīḍú** rv. **cikrīḍiṣā** c. **cikrīḍiṣu** c.

√ **kru**, 'be rough or raw'.

Such a root appears to be assumable for the derivatives:

kravaṇá rv. **kravís, -vi** v. **kraviṣṇú** v. **kravyá** v.+ **-kru** rv. **krūrá** av.+

√ **krudh**, 'be angry'.

Pres. [4.] **krúdhyati** *etc.* av. +, **-te** *etc.* e. +
Perf. **cukrodha cukrudhus** *etc.* b. +
Aor. 2. **krudhat** *etc.* av. + — 3. **ácukrudhat** *etc.* rv.
[*Fut.* **krotsyati, kroddhā.**]
Verb. **kruddhá** v. +; **kroddhum** e.; **kruddhvā** s.
Sec. Conj.: [*Int.* **cokrudh-.** — *Desid.* **cukrutsa-.** —] *Caus.* **krodháyati** *etc.* av. + (**krodhyate** m.)
Deriv.: **krudh** c. **krudhmí** rv. **kródha** av.+ **krodhana** e.+ **krodhanīya** e.

√ **kruç**, 'cry out'.

Pres. [1.] **króçati** *etc.* v. +, **-te** *etc.* rv.e.
Perf. **cukroça** *etc.* e. [**cukruçe.**]
Aor. 7. **akrukṣat** *etc.* v.b.
[*Fut.* **krokṣyati, kroṣṭā.**]
Verb. **kruṣṭa** b. +; **kroṣṭum** e.; **-kruçya** e. +
Sec. Conj.: *Pass.* **kruçyate** e. — [*Int.* **cokruç-.** — *Desid.* **cukrukṣa-.** —] *Caus.* **kroçya** e. +
Deriv.: **-kroça** v. + **-kroçaka** b. + **-kroçin** c. **-kroçya** s. **klóça** rv. **kroçaná** v. + **kroṣṭu** c. **kroṣṭṛ́** v. + **-kroçayitṛ** c.

√ **krūḍ**, 'thicken' (?).

Sec. Conj.: *Caus.* **akrūḍayat, krūḍyamāna, cukrūḍāyati** b.
All in a single passage of the Kāṭhaka. Possible derivative, **kroḍá** av. +

√ **klath**, 'turn' (?).

Pres. [1.] **kláthan** b.
A single occurrence, in vs.; no derivatives.

√ **kland**, *see* √ **krand.**

√ **klam**, 'be weary'.

Pres. [4.] **klāmyati** c.
Perf. [**caklāma,**] **caklame** c.
[*Aor. etc.* **aklamīt; klamiṣyati, klamitā.**]

Verb. klāṁtá E. +
Sec. Conj.: Caus. klāmayati C.
Deriv.: klama E. + klāṁti C.
Compare √ çram.

√ klav, 'stammer'.

Verb. klavita C.
Probably artificial and false, inferred from viklava E. +, viklavita C.

√ klid, 'be wet'.

Pres. [4.] klidyati -te *etc.* E. + — [1.] klindant C[1].
[*Perf. etc.* cikleda; aklidat, aciklidat; kledişyati kletsyati, kleditā klettā.]
Verb. klinna S. + [kliditvā, klittvā.]
Sec. Conj.: [*Int.* ceklid-. — *Desid.* cikledişa-, ciklidişa-, ciklitsa-. —]
Caus. kledayati *etc.* S. +
Deriv.: -klíndu AV. -kledin C. kledana C.
kleda E. + -kledya E. -kledīyas AV.

√ kliç, 'distress'.

Pres. [9.] kliçnāti *etc.* E. + — [4.] kliçyate *etc.* E. +, -ti *etc.* E. +
Perf. cikleça *etc.* C.
[*Aor. etc.* kliçyāt akleçi, acikliçat, akleçīt, aklikṣat; kleçişyati klekṣyati, kleçitā kleṣṭā.]
Verb. kliṣṭa E. + [kliçita]; kleṣṭum E.; [kliçitvā, kliṣṭvā;] -klíçya ÇB. +
Sec. Conj.: [*Int.* cekliç-. — *Desid.* cikleçişa-, cikliçişa-, ciklikṣa-. —]
Caus. kleçayati *etc.* E. +
Deriv.: kleça U. + -kleçaka C. kleçin C. kleçana C. kleṣṭṛ E.

√ kvaṇ, 'sound'.

Pres. [1.] kvaṇati C.
[*Perf. etc.* cakvāṇa; akvāṇīt; kvaṇişyati, kvaṇitā.]
Verb. kvaṇita C.
Sec. Conj.: Caus. kvaṇayati *etc.* C.
Deriv. -kvaṇana C.

√ kvath, 'boil'.

Pres. [1.] kvathati -te *etc.* B. +
[*Perf. etc.* cakvātha; akvathīt; kvathişyati, kvathitā.]
Verb. kvathita C.
Sec. Conj.: Caus. kvāthayati *etc.* S. + (kvāthyate *etc.* E. +)
Deriv.: kvatha C. kvathana C. kvātha C. kvāthayitavya C.

√ kṣad, 'divide'.

Pres. [1.] kṣádate *etc.* V. B.
Perf. cakṣadé *etc.* RV.
Deriv.: kṣattṛ́ V. -kṣad RV. kṣádman RV.

√ kṣan, 'wound'.

Pres. [8.] **kṣaṇóti kṣaṇuté** *etc.* B. +
[*Perf.* **cakṣāṇa cakṣaṇe.**]
Aor. [1. **akṣata.** —] 5. **kṣaṇiṣṭhās** AV. [**akṣaṇīt.**]
[*Fut.* **kṣaṇiṣyati -te, kṣaṇitā.**]
Verb. **kṣata** V. +; **kṣaṇítos** ÇB.
[*Sec. Conj.*: **caṅkṣaṇ-; cikṣaṇiṣa-; kṣāṇaya-.**]
Deriv.: **kṣaṇana** C. **kṣati** E. +

√ kṣap, 'be abstinent'.

Pres. [1.] **kṣapati** E. +, **kṣápate** V.S.
Verb. **kṣapitum** C.
Deriv. **kṣapaṇa** E. +

The words **kṣáp** V., **kṣapā́** V. + do not appear to be connected with this root.

√ kṣam, 'endure'.

Pres. [1.] **kṣámate** *etc.* V. +, **-ti** *etc.* E. + (**kṣā́mat** AV. ?). — [4.] **kṣamyate** *etc.* E. + [**kṣāmyati.**]
Perf. **cakṣame** *etc.* B. + (**cakṣamīthās** RV.)
[*Aor.* **akṣamat, acikṣamat, akṣaṁsta, akṣamiṣṭa.**]
Fut. 1. **kṣaṁsyati** *etc.* E., **kṣamiṣyati** B. + [— 2. **kṣaṁtā, kṣamitā.**]
Verb. **kṣā́ṁta** E. +, **kṣamita** E.; **kṣaṁtum** E. +
Sec. Conj.: *Pass.* **kṣamyate** E. + — [*Int.* **caṅkṣam-.** — *Desid.* **cikṣaṁsa-, cikṣamiṣa-.** —] *Caus.* **kṣamayati** *etc.* E. + (**kṣāmaye** M., **kṣamāpaya-** C.)
Deriv.: **kṣám, kṣā́** V. **kṣamá** AV. + **kṣamā** E. + **kṣamaṇīya** E. **kṣaṁtavya** E. + **kṣamitavya** E. **kṣaṁtṛ** E. **kṣāmya** E. **kṣā́man** V. **kṣā́mi** SV. **kṣā́ṁti** E. + **kṣmā́** V. + **cākṣmá** ? RV. **kṣamāpaṇa** C[1].

√ kṣar, 'flow'.

Pres. [1.] **kṣárati** *etc.* V. +, **-te** *etc.* E.
Perf. **cakṣāra** C.
Aor. **ákṣār** (3s.) RV.
[*Fut.* **kṣariṣyati, kṣaritā.**]
Verb. **kṣarita** B.; **kṣáradhyāi** RV.
Sec. Conj.: [*Int.* **cākṣar-.** — *Desid.* **cikṣariṣa-.** —] *Caus.* **kṣārayati** *etc.* B. +
Deriv.: **kṣara** V. + **kṣaraṇa** C. **kṣāraṇa** C. **kṣīrá** ? V. +

√ kṣal, 'wash'.

Sec. Conj.: *Caus.* **kṣālayati** *etc.* B. + (**kṣālāpayīta** S.)
Deriv.: **kṣāla** E. + **-kṣālaka** E. + **-kṣālya** C. **-kṣālana** S. +

Doubtless the same with the preceding root.

√ kṣā, 'burn'.

Pres. [4.] kṣā́yati *etc.* B.S.
Verb. kṣāṇa? B.S.
Sec. Conj.: *Caus.* kṣāpáyati *etc.* AV. B.S.
Deriv.: -kṣā́ṇa B. kṣātí RV. kṣāma B.+ kṣāra E.+

√ 1 kṣi, 'possess'.

Pres. [2.] kṣéti *etc.* V.B. (kṣyánt TS., kṣiyánt V.). — [6.] kṣiyáti *etc.* AV. B. — [1.] kṣáyati *etc.* V.
[*Perf.* cikṣāya.]
Aor. 4. kṣeṣat RV.
Fut. kṣeṣyánt RV.
Sec. Conj.: *Caus.* kṣayáya RV., kṣepayat RV.
Deriv.: kṣáya V. kṣayaṇá VS. -kṣit V.+ -kṣetṛ RV.
kṣā́? V. kṣatrá? V.+ kṣití V.+ kṣétra V.+
-kṣas? RV. kṣéma V.+

√ 2 kṣi, kṣī, 'destroy'.

Pres. [9.] kṣiṇā́ti *etc.* V.B. — [5.] kṣiṇoti *etc.* AV.+ — [1.] kṣayati B. — [4.] kṣī́yate *etc.* V.B. — [2.] kṣidhí SV[1].
[*Perf.* cikṣāya.]
Aor. 1. [kṣīyāt;] kṣāyi B.S. — 4. kṣeṣṭhās kṣeṣṭa AV. B.S.U.
Fut. 1. akṣeṣyata (3s.) ÇB.; kṣayiṣyāmi E. [— 2. kṣetā.]
Verb. kṣitá V.+, kṣīṇa AV.+; -kṣetos B.; [kṣītvā;] -kṣīya ÇB.
Sec. Conj.: *Pass.* kṣīyáte V.+. — [*Int.* cekṣi-. —] *Desid.* cikṣīṣati B. — *Caus.* kṣayayati *etc.* E.+; kṣapayati *etc.* E.+
Deriv.: kṣaya E.+ -kṣayaṇa AV.B.S. kṣeṣṇú B. -kṣapayitṛ C.
kṣayin E.+ kṣayiṣṇu U.C. kṣapaṇa E.+ kṣapayiṣṇu C.
kṣayya B.+ -kṣit B. kṣapitavya C. kṣayayitavya E.
kṣíti AV.+

√ kṣip, 'throw'.

Pres. [6.] kṣipáti *etc.* V.+, -te *etc.* E.+
Perf. cikṣepa *etc.* E.+, cikṣipe E.
Aor. [1. kṣipyāt; akṣepi. —] 3. cikṣipat *etc.* V. [— 4. akṣāipsīt, akṣipta.]
Fut. 1. kṣepsyati *etc.* E.+, -te E. [— 2. kṣeptā.]
Verb. kṣiptá V.+, kṣipita S.; kṣeptum E.+, -tos B.; kṣiptvā C.; -kṣipya E.+; -kṣepam E.
Sec. Conj.: *Pass.* kṣipyate E.+ (-yant M.) — [*Int.* cekṣip-. —] *Desid.* cikṣipsa- (*in d.*). — *Caus.* kṣepayati *etc.* E.+
Deriv.: kṣíp RV. kṣipti C. kṣepya C. kṣeptavya E.+
-kṣipa C. kṣiprá V.+ kṣepan B. kṣeptṛ E.+
kṣípā RV. kṣepa E.+ kṣepaṇa S.+ kṣepnú RV.
kṣipaṇí RV. kṣepaka E.+ kṣépiṣṭha B. -cikṣipsu C.
kṣipaṇú RV. -kṣepin C. kṣépīyas B.+

√ kṣu, 'sneeze'.

Pres. [2.] **kṣāuti kṣuvánti** *etc.* B. +
Perf. **cukṣāva** *etc.* B., **cukṣuve** C.
[*Aor. etc.* **akṣāvīt; kṣaviṣyati, kṣavitā.**]
Verb. **kṣuta** E. +; **kṣutvā** B. +
Sec. Conj.: *Desid.* **cukṣūṣati** JB. [— *Desid.-Caus.* **cukṣāvayiṣati.**]
Deriv.: **kṣava** AV. **kṣavathu** C.

√ kṣud, 'crush'.

Pres. [1.] **kṣódati -te** RV. [— 7. **kṣuṇatti kṣuntte.**]
Perf. **cukṣudus** E.
[*Aor. etc.* **akṣudat, akṣāutsīt akṣutta; kṣotsyati -te, kṣottā.**]
Verb. **kṣuṇṇa** E. +; **-kṣudya** C.
Sec. Conj.: *Caus.* **kṣodayati** *etc.* RV. C.
Deriv.: **kṣudrá** V. + **kṣoda** E. + **kṣódas** RV. **kṣódiṣṭha** B.
kṣodya E. **kṣodīyas** B. +

√ kṣudh, 'be hungry'.

Pres. [4.] **kṣúdhyati** *etc.* V. +
[*Perf.* **cukṣodha.**]
Aor. 2. **kṣudhat** AV.
[*Fut.* **kṣotsyati, kṣoddhā.**]
Verb. **kṣudhita** U. + [**kṣudhitvā.**]
Deriv.: **kṣúdh** V. + **kṣudhā** E. + **-kṣudhya** AV. **kṣudhi** C. **kṣódhuka** B.S.

√ kṣup, 'be startled' (?).

Pres. [6.] **akṣupat** R[1]. (*Aor.* 2 ?).
Deriv.: **kṣupa** E. + **kṣúmpa** RV.

Not a genuine root. The only verbal form in a single punning etymology.

√ kṣubh, 'quake'.

Pres. [4.] **kṣubhyati -te** *etc.* E. + — [1.] **kṣobhate** U[1]. — [5.] **kṣubhnuyus** JB. [— 9. **kṣubhnāti.**]
Perf. **cukṣobha** C., **cukṣubhe** AV. +
[*Aor. etc.* **kṣubhyāt akṣobhi, akṣubhat, acukṣubhat, akṣobhīt -bhiṣṭa; kṣobhiṣyati -te, kṣobhitā.**]
Verb. **kṣubdha** B. +, **kṣubhita** E. +; **-kṣobdhos** ÇB. [**kṣobhitum; kṣubdhvā, kṣubhitvā.**]
Sec. Conj.: [*Int.* **cokṣubh-.** — *Desid.* **cukṣubhiṣa-, cukṣobhiṣa-.** —] *Caus.* **kṣobhayati -te** E. + (**kṣobhyate** E. +, **cukṣobhayiṣa-** *in d.*)
Deriv.: **kṣúbh** RV. **kṣobha** B. + **-kṣobhin** C. **kṣóbhaṇa** V. +
kṣubhā E. + **kṣobhaka** C. **kṣobhya** E. + **kṣobhayitṛ** C.
cukṣobhayiṣu E.

√ **kṣṇu**, 'whet'.

Pres. [2.] **kṣṇāumi** RV., **kṣṇāuti** S., **kṣṇuvāná** AV.
[*Perf. etc.* **cukṣṇāva**; **akṣṇāvīt**; **kṣṇaviṣyati**, **kṣṇavitā**.]
Verb. **kṣṇutá** B.; **-kṣṇutya** B.
Deriv.: **-kṣṇut** B.S. **kṣṇótra** RV.

√ **kṣmā**, 'tremble'.

[*Pres. etc.* **kṣmāyate**, **cakṣmāye**, *etc.*]
Sec. Conj.: *Caus.* **kṣmāpayati** C.
No genuine root. The single example in Nirukta.

√ **kṣviḍ**, 'hum'.

Pres. [1.] **kṣveḍati** *etc.* E.+
Verb. **kṣveḍita** E.+
Sec. Conj.: *Caus.* **kṣveḍayati** E.
Deriv.: **kṣveḍa** E.+ **kṣveḍana** E.+
A later form of the root next following.

√ **kṣvid**, 'hum'.

Pres. [1.] **kṣvedati** *etc.* B.
Verb. **kṣviṇṇa** C.; **-kṣvídas** B.
Apparently onomatopoetic.

√ **kṣvel**, 'play'.

Pres. [1.] **kṣvelati** *etc.* R.
Verb. **kṣvelita** E.+
Deriv.: **kṣvelana** C. **kṣveli** C.

√ **khac**, 'show through'.

Pres. [1.] **khacati** *etc.* C.
Verb. **khacita** E.+

√ **khañj**, 'limp'.

Pres. [1.] **khañjati** *etc.* C.
[*Perf. etc.* **cakhañja** *etc. etc.*]
Deriv.: **khañja** C. **khañjana** C.

√ **khad**, 'be hard'.

Pres. **-khadánt**? ÇB.
[*Perf. etc.* **cakhāda** *etc. etc.*]
Deriv.: **khadā** S. **khadirá** V.+
Very doubtful root; the occurrence in ÇB. perhaps a false reading.

√ **khan, khā**, 'dig'.

Pres. [1.] **khánati -te** *etc.* v.+
Perf. **cakhā́na cakhnus** *etc.* av.+ [**cakhne.**]
Aor. [1. **khanyāt, khāyāt.** — 3. **acīkhanat.** —] 4. **khān** b. [— 5. **akhănīt, akhaniṣṭa.**]
Fut. 1. **khaniṣyati** *etc.* b.+ [— 2. **khanitā.**]
Verb. **khātá** v.+; **khánitum** b.+; **khanitvā** c., **khātvā** b.+, **-tvī́** b.; **-khāya** b.+; **-khānam** s.
Sec. Conj.: Pass. **khāyate** *etc.* b.+, **khanyate** *etc.* e.+ [— *Int.* **caṅkhan-, cākhā-.** — *Desid.* **cikhaniṣa-.**] — *Caus.* **khānayati** *etc.* s.+ (**khanaya-** e.?)

Deriv.:			
khá v.+	**khanana** c.	**khanítra** v.+	**khānya** s.
khā v.+	**khananīya** c.	**khara** v.+	**khāni** c.
khaná av.	**khaní** av.+	**khātṛ** c.	**-khu** v.+
khanaka e.	**khanitṝ́** v.+	**khānaka** c.	**-kheya** c.

√ **khārj**, 'creak'.

Pres. [1.] **kharjati** s.
Deriv.: **khargálā** v.+ **kharjū́ra** b.+

√ **khall**, 'be relaxed'

Pres. [1.] **khallate** c.
Verb. **khallita** c.
Deriv. **khalla** c.

√ **khā**, *see* √ **khan.**

√ **khād**, 'chew'.

Pres. [1.] **khā́dati** *etc.* v.+
Perf. **cakhā́da** *etc.* v.+
[*Aor.* **acakhādat; akhādīt.**]
Fut. 1. **khādiṣyate** e. [**-ti.** — 2. **khāditā.**]
Verb. **khāditá** b.+; **khāditvā** b.u.
Sec. Conj.: Pass. **khādyate** c. [— *Int.* **cākhād-.**] — *Desid.* **cikhādiṣati** e.+ — *Caus.* **khādayati** *etc.* e.+

Deriv.:			
khādá v.+	**khādya** e.+	**khā́das-** rv.	**cikhādiṣu** e.+
khādaka s.+	**khādana** e.+	**khāditavya** c.	
khādin e.+	**khādanīya** c.	**khāditṛ** c.	

√ **khid**, 'tear'.

Pres. [6.] **khidáti** *etc.* v.+. [— 7. **khintte.**] — [4.]? *see Pass.*
[*Perf. etc.* **cikheda; acīkhidat, akhāitsīt; khetsyati, khettā.**]
Verb. **khinna** e.+; **-khídya** b.s.; **-khídam** av.
Sec. Conj.: Pass. **khidyate** *etc.* e.+, **-ti** *etc.* e.+ — [*Int.* **cekhid-.** — *Desid.* **cikhitsa-.** —] *Caus.* **khedayati -te** e.+

Deriv.: -khida B. khidvāṅs RV. khedin C. kheditavya E.
khidrá RV. khédā V.+ khedana C. khedayitavya C.

√ khud, '*futuere*'.

Pres. [6.] khudáti *etc.* V.
Sec. Conj.: *Int.* canīkhudat S. (kánīkhunat TB.)
Deriv. khódana AV.

√ khel, 'stagger'.

Pres. [1.] khelati *etc.* E.+
Verb. khelita C.
Sec. Conj.: *Caus.* khelayati *etc.* C.
Deriv.: khelá V.+ khelana C. kheli C.

√ khyā, 'see'.

Pres. [2.] khyāsi khyāti khyāhi khyāta E.+
Perf. cakhyāu cakhyus *etc.* V.+
Aor. [1. akhyāyi; khyāyāt, khyeyāt. —] 2. ákhyat *etc.* V.B.S., akhyata *etc.* V.B. — 4. khyeṣam B.S. [khyāsīṣṭa.]
Fut. 1. khyāsyáti *etc.* B.+, -te E.+ [— 2. khyātā.]
Verb. khyātá AV.+; khyā́tum B.+; -khyā́ya V.+; -khyāí V.B.; -khyā́yam B.
Sec. Conj.: *Pass.* khyāyate *etc.* B.+ (khyāyiṣyate B.) — [*Int.* cākhyā-. —] *Desid.* cikhyāsita C. — *Caus.* khyāpayati -te *etc.* B.+ ([acikhyapat;] khyāpyate *etc.* C.; cikhyāpayiṣa- *in d.* C.)
Deriv.: -khya B.+ -khyātṛ V.+ -khyeya AV.+ khyāpana E.+
-khyā V.+ khyā́na B.+ khyāpaka C. khyāpanīya C.
khyāti B.+ -khyāyaka E.+ khyāpin C. -cikhyāsu C.
-khyātavya E.+ -khyāyin S.+ khyāpya E. cikhyāpayiṣā C.

√ gach, *see* √ gam.

√ gad, 'say'.

Pres. [1.] gadati *etc.* S.+
Perf. jagāda jagade *etc.* E.+
Aor. 1. agādi C. [— 5. agādīt.]
Fut. 1. gadiṣyate E. [— 2. gaditā.]
Verb. gadita E.+; gaditum C.; -gadya S.
Sec. Conj.: *Pass.* gadyate *etc.* E.+ — *Int.* jāgadyate C. — *Desid.* jigadiṣati E. — *Caus.* gādayati S.
Deriv.: gada B.+ gadana B.+ -gādin C. gadgada C.
gadya E.+ gadi C. -gādya C.
ví gada in AV. (V. 22. 6) is doubtless a vocative, vígada.

√ gadh, 'attach' (?).

Verb. -gadhita RV[2].
Deriv. gádhya RV.
A root of doubtful meaning and relations.

√ gabh, *see* √ gāh.

√ gam, gach, 'go'.

Pres. [1.] gáchati *etc.* V.+, -te *etc.* V.+. — gámanti RV., -ntu V. — [2.] gathá RV[1].

Perf. jagā́ma (jagantha [jagamitha]) jagmús *etc.* jagmé *etc.* V.+ (jaganma RV.; jaganvā́ṅs V.+, jagmivāṅs B.+; jagamyāt *etc.* V.; ájagan *etc.* ajagmiran V.)

Aor. 1. ágamam ágan ágman *etc.* ágata áganmahi agmata *etc.* V.B.S. (gámat *etc.* V.B., gamāmahāi RV.; gamyā́t *etc.* V.B.S., gmīya B.; gahi gantu *etc.* V.B.S.; gmánt V.); agāmi RV., agami C. — 2. agamat *etc.* B.+ (gamét *etc.* V.B.S., gamemahi V.S.) — 3. ajīgamat *etc.* V.B. — 4. agaṁsi agaṁsmahi *etc.* S.+ (agasmahi *etc.* V.B.) [gaṁsīṣṭa, gasīṣṭa.] — 5. gamiṣṭam RV., gmiṣīya VS.

Fut. 1. gamiṣyati *etc.* AV.+, -te *etc.* E. (agamiṣyat U.) — 2. gaṁtā́ *etc.* B.+

Verb. gatá V.+; gáṁtum B.+, -tave V.B., -tavāí V., -tos V.B.; gatvā́ AV.+, -tvā́ya V.B., -tvī́ RV.; -gátya V.+, -gamya U.S.+; gámadhyāi RV., -dhye TS.; -gámas MS.

Sec. Conj.: Pass. gamyáte *etc.* AV.+ — *Int.* gánīgam- V.B., jaṅgam- (*in d.*), jāgam- AV.? — *Desid.* jígamiṣati -te *etc.* B.+, jigāṁsati *etc.* AV.+, -te *etc.* S.+ — *Caus.* gamáyati *etc.* V.+, -te *etc.* S.+ (gāmaya RV[1].)

Deriv.:	gacha C.	gamiṣṇú B.	-gátvan RV.	gamayitṛ B.+
	-gama V.+	-gat V.	gatvara C.	gamayitavya B.C.
	gamaka C.	gáti V.+	-gāmin E.+	jágat V.+
	-gamin C.	-gaṁtva S.	-gāmuka B.+	jágmi RV.
	gamya U.+	gaṁtavyà B.+	gmā́ RV.	jigatnú V.
	gámana V.+	gáṁtṛ V.+	-gman RV.	jaṅgama U.+
	gamanīya E.+	-gatha V.B.	jmā́ RV.	jaṅgamana C.
	gámiṣṭha V.S.	gatnú AV.	jmán V.	-jigamiṣu C.
				jigāṁsu C.

√ garj, 'roar'.

Pres. [1.] garjati *etc.* E.+, -te *etc.* E.+
Perf. jagarja *etc.* E.+
[*Aor. etc.* agarjīt; garjiṣyati, garjitā.]
Verb. garjita E.+; garjitvā E.; -garjya C.

Deriv.:	garja C.	-garjin C.	garjana E.+	garji C.

√ **gard**, 'exult' (?).

Pres. [1.] **agardat** PB.
Deriv. **gárda** TS.
Perhaps the same with √ **gūrd.**

√ **garh**, 'chide'.

Pres. [1.] **garhate** *etc.* RV.S.E.+, **-ti** *etc.* E.+
Perf. **jagarha -he** *etc.* E.+
[*Aor. etc.* **agarhiṣṭa; garhiṣyate, garhitā.**]
Verb. **garhita** S.+; **garhitum** E.; **-garhya** C.
Sec. Conj.: Pass. **garhyate** *etc.* C. — [*Int.* **jāgarh-**. — *Desid.* **jigarhiṣa-**. —]
Caus. **garhayati -te** *etc.* U.+
Deriv.: **garhā** E.+ **garhya** S.?+ **garhaṇa** E.+ **garhitavya** E.
garhin E.+ **garhaṇīya** E.+

√ **gal**, 'drop'.

Pres. [1.] **galati** *etc.* C.
[*Perf. etc.* **jagāla; agālīt;** *etc.*]
Verb. **galita** E.+
Sec. Conj.: Int. **galgalīti** VS., **galgalyate** C. — *Caus.* **gālayati** *etc.* C.
Deriv.: **galana** C. **gālana** C.

√ **galbh**, 'dare'.

Pres. [1.] **galbhate** *etc.* C.
Perf. **jagalbhe** C.
Deriv. **-galbha** B.+
With **pra**, and doubtless in reality a denominative of **pragalbhá.**

√ 1 **gā**, 'go'.

Pres. [3.] **jígāti** *etc.* V.B. [— 2. **gāte.**]
Perf. **jagāyāt** RV.[1], (**adhi-**) **jage** *etc.* E.+
Aor. 1. **ágāt águs** *etc.* V.+ (**gāni gātá** *etc.* V.; **agan** 3*p.* C.) [**agāyi.**] —
3. (**adhy-**) **agīṣṭa ágīṣata** *etc.* B.+ [**agāsta**]; **geṣam -ṣma** AV.B.S.
[*Fut.* **gāsyate,** (**adhy-**) **agīṣyata; gātā.**]
Verb. **gā́tave** RV[1].
Sec. Conj.: [*Pass.* **gīyate.** — *Int.* **jegīya-.** —] *Desid.* **jigīṣati** *etc.* SV[1].C[1].
[**jigāsa-.** — *Caus.* **gāpayati, ajīgapat.**]
Deriv.: **-gā** V.+ **gā́tra** V.+ **-gāya** V. **gáṅgā**? V.+
-ga V.+ **-gāna** RV. **-gū**? B.
gātú V.B. **-gāman** RV. **geṣṇa**? U.

√ 2 **gā**, 'sing'.

Pres. [4.] **gā́yati** *etc.* V.+, **-te** *etc.* V.+ — [1.] **gāti** KB[1]., **gā́nti** M. — **gāyiṣe**
(1*s.*) RV[1].

Perf. jagāu *etc.* B.+, jage *etc.* C.
Aor. [1. geyāt; agāyi. —] 4. gāsi (1*s.*) RV. — 6. agāsīt -siṣus *etc.* V.B.U. (gāsiṣat RV.)
Fut. 1. gāsyati *etc.* B.+ (agāsyat *etc.* B.U.) [— 2. gātā.]
Verb. gītá V.+; gātum B.+; gītvā B.+; -gāya AB., -gī́ya ÇB.C.
Sec. Conj.: Pass. gīyáte *etc.* V.+ (gīyant M.) — *Int.* jegīyate *etc.* E.+ [jāgā-.] — *Desid.* jigāsati *etc.* B. — *Caus.* gāpayati *etc.* B.+, -te B. [ajīgapat]; gāyayeyus JUB.

Deriv.:			
-gā V.+	gāyatrá V.+	gātṛ V.+	gīti S.+
-ga AV.+	gāyana S.+	gāthá V.+	gī́tha AV.+
-gāya C.	-gā́yas RV.	gā́thā V.+	geya B.+
gāyaka B.+	gātú RV.	gāna U.S.+	-geṣṇa AB.
-gāyin C.	gātavya C.	-gāman RV.	-jigītha, -ta B.U.
			-gāpana S.

√ gāh *etc.*, 'plunge'.

Pres. [1.] gā́hate *etc.* V.+, -ti *etc.* E.
Perf. jagāha C. (jigāhire S[1].)
[*Aor.* ajīgahat; agāḍha, agāhiṣṭa.]
Fut. 1. gāhiṣyate E.+ [— 2. gāḍhā, gāhitā.]
Verb. gāḍha S.+, gāhita E.+; gāhitum E.; -gāhya S.+
Sec. Conj.: Pass. gāhyate *etc.* E.+ — *Int.* jáñgahe V. [jāgāh-. — *Desid.* jigāhiṣa-, jighākṣa-.] — *Caus.* gāhayati *etc.* C.

Deriv.:			
-gáha RV.	gāhá V.+	gámbhan B.	gabhvara C.
gáhana RV.E.	-gāhin C.	gambhára RV.	gādhá V.+
gah-, gañhmán B.	-gāhya E.+	gámbhiṣṭha B.	gādhana C.
gáhvara AV.+	gāhana S.+	gabhīrá V.+	
	gāhanīya C.	gambhīrá V.+	

The connection of these derivatives is probable, but not beyond question.

√ gir, gil, *see* √ 2 gṛ.

√ gu, 'sound'.

[*Pres. etc.* gavate; juguve; agoṣṭa; goṣyate, gotā; guta.]
Sec. Conj.: Int. jóguve jóguvāna V.B.
Deriv.: -gut? RV. jogū́ RV.

√ guñj, 'hum'.

Pres. [1.] guñjati *etc.* C.
[*Perf. etc.* juguñja; aguñjīt; guñjiṣyati, guñjitā.]
Verb. guñjita C.
Deriv.: guñja C. -guñjin C.

√ **guṇṭh**, 'cover up'.

Sec. Conj.: Caus. **guṇṭhayati** *etc.* C. (**guṇṭhita** E.+, **-guṇṭhya** S.+)
Deriv. **guṇṭhana** C.

Probably a denominative formation.

√ **gup**, 'protect'.

Pres. [1.] **gopant**? C[1].
Perf. **jugopa jugupus** *etc.* V.+
Aor. 3. **ajūgupat** *etc.* B.S. (**ajugupa-** B.) [— 4. **agāupsīt.** — 5. **agopīt.**]
Fut. 1. **gopsyati** *etc.* AV.+ [**gopiṣyati.** — 2. **goptā, gopitā.**]
Verb. **gupitá** V., **guptá** AV.+; **goptum** B., **gopitum** C.
Sec. Conj.: Pass. **gupyate** *etc.* B. [— *Int.* **jogup-.**] — *Desid.* **jugupsate** *etc.* B.+, **-ti** *etc.* E.+, **jugupiṣa-** (*in d.*) [**jugopiṣa-.**] — *Caus.* **gopayati** *etc.* E.+, **-te** *etc.* E. (**gopyate** E.)

Deriv.:			
-gup E.+	**gopya** E.+	**goptavya** E.	**jugupsā** E.+
-gupya B.	**gópana** AV.+	**goptṛ́** AV.+	**jugupsu** S.+
gúpti AV.+	**-gopanīya** C.	**gópiṣṭha** B.	**jugupiṣu** E.

Perhaps ultimately a denominative from **gopā́**, but assuming the aspect of a root even in the Veda.

√ **guph, gumph**, 'twine'.

Pres. [1.] **gumphati** *etc.* C.
Verb. **gumphita, guphita** C.
Sec. Conj.: Caus. **gumphayati** *etc.* C.
Deriv.: **gumpha** C. **-gumphaka** C. **gumphana** C.

√ **gur**, 'greet'.

Pres. [6.] **guráte** *etc.* V.+, **-ti** *etc.* C.
Perf. [**jugure**] **jugurat -ryās -ryā́t** RV.
Aor. 1. **gūrta** RV. [— 5. **aguriṣṭa.**]
[*Fut.* **guriṣyate, guritā.**]
Verb. **gūrtá** V.+, **gūrṇa** S.+; **-gū́rya** V.+, **-gurya** C.
Sec. Conj.: Int. **járgurāṇa** RV. — *Caus.* **gūraya-** (*in d.*).

Deriv.:			
-gur B.S.	**gūraṇa** C.	**-goraṇa** C.	**jugurváṇi** RV.
-guraṇa C.	**gūrtí** RV.	**-gūrayitṛ** C.	

Doubtless a secondary form of √ 1 **gṛ**.

√ **gulph**, 'bunch'.

Sec. Conj.: Caus. **gulphayeyus** S[1]., **gulphita** S.
Deriv. **gulphá** AV.+

A very doubtful case.

√ guh, 'hide'.

Pres. [1.] gū́hati -te *etc.* V.+
Perf. jugūha C., juguhe jugūhire E.
Aor. [1. agūhi. —] 2. guhas guhant- guhámāna RV. [— 3. ajūguhat. — 4. agūḍha. — 5. agūhīt, agūhiṣṭa.] — 7. aghukṣat *etc.* V.B. [aghukṣata.]
[*Fut.* gūhiṣyati -te, ghokṣyati -te; gūhitā, goḍhā.]
Verb. gūḍhá V.+; gūhitum E.+; [gūhitvā, gūḍhvā,] gūḍhvī́ RV.; -guhya E.+, -gūhya ? E.
Sec. Conj.: *Pass.* guhyáte *etc.* V.+ [— *Int.* joguh-.] — *Desid.* jugukṣati RV. [jughukṣa-.] — *Caus.* gūhayati *etc.* S.+
Deriv.: gúh RV. guha E.+ gúhā V.+ gúhya V.+ -gūha C. gūhana S.+ gūhitavya E. -gūhitṛ C. góha V.B.S. -gohana RV. -gohya RV.S.

√ gūrd, 'exult' (?).

Pres. [1.] agūrdan JB.
Deriv. gūrda B.+
Compare roots kūrd, gard, and gūrdh. See J.A.O.S., vol. xi., p. cxlvii.

√ gūrdh, 'exalt' (?).

Sec. Conj.: *Caus.* gūrdhaya RV[1].
Perhaps the same with the preceding.

√ 1 gṛ, 'sing'.

Pres. [9.] gṛṇā́ti gṛṇīté *etc.* V.+ (gṛṇé 3s. V., gṛṇā́ta 2p. AV.) — [6.] (sam-)girate *etc.* C., -ti C. — gṛṇīṣé (1s.) V.
Perf. jagā́ra TA.
[*Aor.* gīryāt; agārīt.]
Fut. 1. gariṣyati S. [garīṣyati. — 2. garītā.]
Verb. [gīrṇa;] -gī́rya B.; gṛṇīṣáṇi RV.
Deriv.: -gara AV.+ -garaṇa C. -garitṛ B.S. gír V.+ -gira C. -gīrya B.
Compare roots gur and 2 jṛ.

√ 2 gṛ, gir, gil, 'swallow'.

Pres. [6.] giráti *etc.* AV.+, -te *etc.* E.+ (gírāmi AV[1].); gilati *etc.* B.+ — [9.] gṛṇā́ti *etc.* AV.S.
Perf. jagāra V.+
Aor. 1. (*or* 2.) garat -ran V. [gīryāt.] — 3. ajīgar RV[1].? [— 4. agīrṣṭa.] — 5. gārīt RV.
Fut. 1. gariṣyati B.C. [garīṣyati. — 2. garītā.]

Verb. gīrṇá v.+, gilita c.; giritum c.; -gī́rya AV.+
Sec. Conj.: *Pass.* gīryate *etc.* E. — *Int.* járgurāṇa RV., jalgulas RV. [jāgṛ-, jegilya-. — *Desid.* jigariṣa-.] — *Caus.* girayati c. [gārayati.]

Deriv.:			
garā AV.+	-gāra E.+	-gila AV.+	gárgara? v.+
gala E.+	-gārin E.+	-giraṇa c.	-jīgarta? B.+
-garaṇa c.	-gir V.B.S.	gilana c.	jígarti RV.
garas? B.S.	-gira AV.	-gra, -gri RV.	

√ 3 gṛ, jāgṛ, 'wake'.

Aor. 3. ájīgar RV.; jigṛtám -tá RV.
Sec. Conj.: *Int.* jāgarti jā́grati *etc.* v.+ (jāgarāsi *etc.*, jāgṛyāt *etc.*, jāgṛhí *etc.*; jā́grat; ájāgar; jāgā́ra *etc.*; jāgariṣyáti -te; jāgaritá; jāgaráyati *etc.*). *Irreg.*, *as* √ jāgṛ: jāgṛmi M.; jāgrati, -te *etc.* S.E., jāgarati M.; jajāgāra E.+, jāgarām āsa c.; [jāgaryāt, ajāgāri, ajāgarīt.]

Deriv.:			
jāgara B.+	jāgaraṇá B.+	jāgarū́ka RV.C.	jāgṛtavya E.
jāgaraka c.	jāgariṣṇu c.	jāgartavya E.	jā́gṛvi v.+

√ gṛdh, 'be greedy'.

Pres. [4.] gṛ́dhyati *etc.* v.+
Perf. jagṛdhus B.C. (jāgṛdhús RV.)
Aor. 2. ágṛdhat *etc.* V.B.U.
Fut. 1. gardhiṣyati B. [— 2. gardhitā.]
Verb. gṛddha E.+; gṛddhvā c. [gṛdhitvā.]
[*Sec. Conj.*: jarīgṛdh-; jigardhiṣa-; gardhayati.]

Deriv.:			
gṛ́tsa? V.B.	gṛdhna E.	gṛ́dhya AV.	gṛ́dhra v.+
gardha c.	gṛdhnú v.+	gṛdhyā E.	
gardhin v.+		gṛdhyin E.	

√ grath, granth, 'tie'.

Pres. [9.] grathnā́ti *etc.* B.+ — [7.] gṛṇatti? AV. [— 1. granthati, grathati.]
[*Perf. etc.* jagrantha jagranthus grethus; grathyāt, ajagranthat, agranthīt.]
Fut. 1. granthiṣyati B. [— 2. granthitā.]
Verb. grathitá v.+; [granthitvā, grathitvā;] -grathya B.+; -grantham B.
Sec. Conj.: *Pass.* grathyate c. — [*Int.* jāgranth-, jāgrathya-. — *Desid.* jigranthiṣa-. —] *Caus.* granthayate E., grathayati c.

Deriv.:			
grathín RV.	grathana c.	grathna's.	granthana S.+
grathya c.	grathanīya c.	grantha B.+	granthí v.+
	grathitavya c.	granthín RV.	

√ grabh, grah, 'seize'.

Pres. [9.] gṛbhṇā́ti gṛbhṇīté *etc.* v.b.; gṛhṇā́ti gṛhṇīté *etc.* (gṛhāṇá) v.+ — [1.] gṛhṇati *etc.* e., -te u. — gṛhīthās e., -ītá ms.c., -īṣva b., agṛhītām e.

Perf. jagrā́bha jagṛbhus jagṛbhré *etc.* v. (jagṛbhma jagṛbhyāt v., jagṛbhriré rv.; ajagrabham *etc.* v.b.s.u.); jagrā́ha jagṛhus jagṛhe *etc.* v.+ (jagṛhmá sv.: jagrāhatus m.).

Aor. 1. agrabham v.b., agṛbhran rv.; grabhat ab., gṛbhāṇá ms. [gṛhyāt; agrāhi.] — 2?. gṛhe (3*s.*) ms., gṛhate (3*p.*) gṛhāmahi rv. — 3. ajigrabhat ms. (ajīgṛbham k.), ajigrahat c. — [4. aghṛkṣata. —] 5. agrabhīt agrabhīṣus *etc.* agrabhiṣṭa *etc.* v.b. (agrabhīm ts.); agrahīt *etc.* agrahīṣṭa *etc.* av.+ (agrahāiṣam ab.)

Fut. 1. grahīṣyati -te b.+ (agrahīṣyat *etc.* b.+, agrahāiṣyat b.u.; gṛhīṣyati, grahiṣyati e.) — 2. grahītā e.

Verb. gṛbhītá v.b., gṛhītá av.+; gráhītum b.+, -tavāi b., -tos b.; gṛbhītvā́ av., gṛhītvā́ av.+; -gṛ́bhya v., -gṛ́hya v.+; -grábhe rv., gṛbhé rv., -graham jb.: gṛhaye k.; -grā́ham b.+

Sec. Conj.: Pass. gṛhyáte *etc.* av.+ — [*Int.* jāgrah-, jarīgṛhya-. —] *Desid.* jighṛkṣati -te *etc.* b.+. jigrahīṣa- kb. (ajagrabhāiṣan? ab.) — *Caus.* gṛbháyant rv.; grāhayati -te b.+ (grāhyate *etc.* c.)

Deriv.:	grábha rv.	-grahiṣṇu s.	grāhyà v.+	gṛ́bhi v.
	gráha v.+	grahītavya b.+	grā́hi v.	gṛhú rv.
	-grahin e.	grábhītṛ av.b.	grā́huka b.	-gṛhīti b.+
	gárbha v.+	grahītṛ av.+	gṛ́bh v.b.	jighṛkṣā e.+
	grábhaṇa v.s.	grābhá v.b.s.	-gṛh c.	jighṛkṣu e.+
	gráhaṇa av.+	grāha av.+	gṛbhá rv.	
	grahaṇīya e.	grāhaka e.+	gṛhá v.+	
	-gráhi b.+	grāhin e.+	gṛ́hya av.+	

Compare √ glah. There seems to be no good reason why the root should not be given as gṛbh, gṛh.

√ gras, 'devour'.

Pres. [1.] grasati *etc.* e.+, grásate v.b.

Perf. jagrasāná jagrasīta rv.

Aor. 5. agrasīt c.

Fut. 1. grasiṣyati -te *etc.* e.+ [— 2. grasitā.]

Verb. grasitá rv., grasta e.+; grasitvā́ b.; -grāsam c.

Sec. Conj.: Pass. grasyate *etc.* e. — [*Int.* jāgras-. — *Desid.* jigrasiṣa-. —] *Caus.* grāsayati *etc.* b.s.

Deriv.:	grasya e.	grásiṣṭha v.b.	grasti c.	grāsa s.+
	grasana c.	grasiṣṇu e.	grastṛ c.	-grāsaka c.

√ grah, *see* √ grabh.

√ glap, *see* √ glā.

√ glah, 'gamble'.

Pres. [1.] glahate *etc.* E.
[*Perf. etc.* jaglahe; aglahīṣṭa.]
Fut. 1. aglahīṣyat E. [— 2. glahitā, glāḍhā.]
Deriv.: gláha AV.+ gláhā AV. gláhana AV.
Doubtless from √ grah.

√ glā, 'be weary'.

Pres. [4.] glā́yati *etc.* AV.+, -te *etc.* S.E. — [2.] glāti E.
[*Perf.* jaglāu.]
Aor. [1. glāyāt, gleyāt. — 4. glāsīṣṭa. —] 6. (*or* 4.) glāsīs E.
[*Fut.* glāsyati, glātā.]
Verb. glāná B.+ (glānta M.)
Sec. Conj.: [*Int.* jāglā-. — *Desid.* jiglāsa-. —] *Caus.* glāpáyati *etc.* V.+ glapayati *etc.* E.+, -te E. [ajiglapat] (glapet M[1].)
Deriv.: -glā? GB. glāvín VS. -glā́pana B.
glāni E.+ glāsnu S.+ glapana C.

√ ghaṭ, 'strive'.

Pres. [1.] ghaṭate *etc.* E.+, -ti E.+
Perf. jaghaṭe C.
[*Aor.* ajīghaṭat, aghaṭiṣṭa.]
Fut. 1. ghaṭiṣyate C. [— 2. ghaṭitā.]
Verb. ghaṭita C.; ghaṭitum C.
Sec. Conj.: *Int.* jāghaṭīti C. — [*Desid.* jighaṭiṣa-. —] *Caus.* ghaṭayati *etc.* (ghaṭyate) E.+, -te C.; ghāṭayati *etc.* (ghāṭyate) E.+
Deriv.: ghaṭa E.+ ghaṭanā C. -ghāṭin C. -ghāṭi RV.
ghaṭaka C. -ghāṭa AV.+ -ghāṭana C. ghaṭayitavya C.
ghaṭana C. -ghāṭaka C. -ghāṭanīya E.+

√ ghaṭṭ, 'rub' *etc.*

[*Pres.* 1. ghaṭṭate.]
Perf. jaghaṭṭire E.
Fut. [1. ghaṭṭiṣyati. —] 2. ghaṭṭitā M.
Verb. ghaṭṭita E.+
Sec. Conj.: *Caus.* ghaṭṭayati *etc.* E.+ (ghaṭṭyate C.)
Deriv.: ghaṭṭa E.+ -ghaṭṭin C. ghaṭṭana E.+ ghaṭṭitṛ E.

√ ghar, *see* √ ghṛ.

√ ghas, 'eat'.

[*Pres.* 1. ghasati.]
Perf. jaghā́sa jakṣus jakṣivā́ṅs *etc.* V.B. (jakṣīyā́t RV.)
Aor. 1. ághas (2, 3*s.*) ákṣan *etc.* V.B.S. (aghat 3*s.* B.S., ághastām 2*d.*, aghasta 2*p.* B.; ghásas -sat RV.S.; ghástām *impv.* B.), gdha? RV¹. — 2. aghasat? JB. — 3. ajīghasat MS.
[*Fut.* ghatsyati, ghastā.]
Verb. -gdha- TS.
Sec. Conj.: *Desid.* jíghatsati *etc.* AV.+

Deriv.:	kṣú V.	ghasmara E.+	ghāsá AV.+	-gdhi B.
	ghasa AV.+	ghasra C.	-ghāsin VS.	jighatsā B.+
	ghasana C.	ghasvara C.	-ghāsyà B.	jighatsú AV.+
		ghasí VS.	ghāsí RV.	

Compare √ 1 jakṣ, which is a reduplicated form of this. The anomalous participle gdha occurs only in agdhā́d, and gdhi in ságdhi.

√ ghuṭ, 'turn' (?).

[*Pres. etc.* ghuṭati, ghoṭate; jughoṭa jughuṭe; aghuṭat, aghoṭiṣṭa; ghoṭisyati -te, ghuṭitā ghoṭitā.]
Verb. ghuṭita C., ghoṭita E.; -ghuṭya C.
Deriv. ghoṭa S.
No proper root.

√ ghuṣ, 'sound'.

Pres. [1.] ghóṣati -te *etc.* V.+ — [4.] ghuṣyant C¹.
Perf. jughoṣa JB.
Aor. 1. ghóṣi RV. [— 2. aghuṣat. — 3. ajūghuṣat. — 5. aghoṣīt.]
[*Fut.* ghoṣiṣyati, ghoṣitā.]
Verb. ghuṣṭa E.+ [ghuṣita]; -ghúṣya RV.C.
Sec. Conj.: *Pass.* ghuṣyate *etc.* E.+ — [*Int.* joghuṣ-. — *Desid.* jughuṣiṣa-, jughoṣiṣa-. —] *Caus.* ghoṣáyati *etc.* V.+ (ghoṣyate C.)

Deriv.:	-ghuṣa AV.	ghóṣa V.+	ghoṣaṇa E.+	ghóṣi RV.
	ghuṣya E.	-ghoṣaka C.	ghoṣaṇā C.	ghoṣṭṛ B.
		ghoṣín AV.+	ghoṣaṇīya C.	

One or two RV. forms (including the anomalously accented ghóṣayas) are referred by BR. to a root 2 ghuṣ, 'crush'; but hardly with sufficient reason.

√ ghūrṇ, 'waver'.

Pres. [6, 1.] ghūrṇati -te E.+
Perf. jughūrṇa -ṇe E.+
[*Aor. etc.* aghūrṇīt; ghūrṇiṣyati, ghūrṇitā.]
Verb. ghūrṇita E.+
Sec. Conj.: *Caus.* ghūrṇayati *etc.* (ghūrṇyate) C.
Deriv.: ghūrṇa S.+ ghūrṇana C.

√ ghṛ, ghar, 'drip'.

Pres. [3.] jígharti *etc.* V.B. (jiharti S[1].) [— 1. gharati.]
[*Perf. etc.* jaghāra; aghārṣīt;ghariṣyati, ghartā.]
Verb. ghṛtá V.+; -ghāram GB.
Sec. Conj.: Pass. ághriyata MS. — *Caus.* ghārayati *etc.* AV.+ (ghāryate S.)
Deriv.: -ghāra B.S. -ghāraṇa S. gharmá V.+ ghṛṇā́ RV.
-ghārin AV. jághri RV. ghṛṇá RV. ghṛ́ṇi V.

Gharmá etc. are referred to a second root ghṛ, 'be hot'; but the two are probably ultimately identical.

√ ghṛṣ, 'rub'.

Pres. [1.] gharṣati *etc.* E.+, -te *etc.* E.
Perf. jagharṣa C.
[*Aor. etc.* agharṣīt; gharṣiṣyati, gharṣitā.]
Verb. ghṛṣṭa E.+; ghṛṣṭvā C.; -ghṛṣya S.+
Sec. Conj.: Pass. ghṛṣyate *etc.* C. (-ti *etc.* E.+) — *Caus.* gharṣita R.
Deriv.: gharṣa E.+ gharṣaṇa E.+ ghṛ́ṣu RV. ghṛ́ṣvi RV.
-gharṣin C. -ghṛṣṭi E. -ghṛ́ṣva TA.

The relation to this root of the last three derivatives is doubtful.

√ ghrā, 'smell'

Pres. [3.] jíghrati (3*p.*) AV.MS., jighrāṇa E., jighratī C. — [1.] jíghrati *etc.* V.+, -te *etc.* S.E. — [2.] ghrāti KB.E.
Perf. jaghrāu C.
Aor. 1. [aghrāt,] ghrāyāt S. [ghreyāt, aghrāyi. — 6. aghrāsīt.]
[*Fut.* ghrāsyati, ghrātā.]
Verb. ghrātá B.+ [ghrāṇa; ghrātvā,] jighritvā C.; -ghrāya S.+, -jighrya S.+; -ghrā́yam B.S.
Sec. Conj.: Pass. ghrāyate C. — [*Int.* jāghrā-, jeghrīya-. — *Desid.* jighrāsa-. —] *Caus.* ghrāpayati *etc.* B.+ [ajighrapat -ghripat.]
Deriv.: -ghra S. ghrāti B.+ ghrātṛ́ B.+ -jighra AV.+
ghrā́ṇa B.+ ghrātavyà B.+ ghréya E.+ -jighraṇa S.+
-ghrāpaṇa S.

√ cak, 'quake'.

Pres. [1.] cakanti C[1].
Verb. cákita C.

√ cakās, 'shine'.

Pres. [2.] cakāsti -sati *etc.* C. (cakāçat C., cakāçete? E.)
[*Perf. etc.* cakāsāṁ cakāra; acacakāsam, acīcakāsam.]
Sec. Conj.: Caus. cakāsayām āsatus C.

√ cakṣ, 'see'.

Pres. [2.] cáṣṭe cákṣate *etc.* v.+, cakṣi cakṣus rv. — [1.] cakṣate -ṣante *etc.* rv.e.+, cakṣati *etc.* e.
Perf. cacakṣé *etc.* b.+, cacákṣa rv. (acacakṣam rv.)
Verb. caṣṭum c.; -cákṣya v.+; -cákṣe rv., -cákṣi v.; cákṣase v.
Sec. Conj.: Pass. cakṣyate *etc.* e.+ — *Caus.* cakṣayati *etc.* v.b.
Deriv.: -cakṣ rv. cákṣya v.b. cakṣáṇi rv. cákṣus v.+
-cakṣā çb. cákṣan av. cákṣas v.b.s.
-cakṣin avp. cákṣaṇa v.+ cákṣu v.u.

√ cañc, 'dance'.

Pres. [1.] cañcati c.
A late and doubtless derivative root (perhaps from cañcala?).

√ caṭ, 'go' (?).

Pres. [1.] caṭati *etc.* c.
Perf. cacāṭa c.
Verb. caṭita c.
Sec. Conj.: Caus. cāṭayati *etc.* c.
Deriv.: -cāṭa c. -cāṭana c. -cāṭanīya c.
Also a late root, perhaps a form of cat; caṭaka e.+, caṭu c., cāṭu c. probably have nothing to do with it.

√ cat, 'hide' (?).

Pres. [1.] cátant rv.
[*Perf.* cacāta cete.]
Aor. 3. acīcatam -te ta. [— 5. acatīt, acatiṣṭa.]
[*Fut.* catiṣyati -te; catitā.]
Verb. cattá v.
Sec. Conj.: Caus. cātayati -te v.b.
Deriv.: -cát rv. catín rv. -cā́tana v. -catnuka? ab.
The words cātaka c., catura c., cattra or cāttra c. probably do not belong to this root.

√ can, 'be pleased'.

Aor. 5. caniṣṭám rv., cániṣṭhat? rv.
Deriv.: cánas v.b. cániṣṭha rv. cā́ru v.+
Compare √ kan. The form cániṣṭhat is plainly corrupt.

√ cand, *see* √ çcand.

√ cam, 'sip'.

Pres. [1.] cā́mati b.+; camanti *etc.* c. [— 5. camnoti.]
Perf. cacāma cemus e.
[*Aor. etc.* acāmi, acamīt; camiṣyati, camitā.]

Verb. cāṁta s.+; -camya b.+
Sec. Conj.: [*Int.* cañcam-. — *Desid.* cicamiṣa-. —] *Caus.* cāmayati *etc.* b.+ (-camayya çgs[1].)

Deriv.: camaka? *n. pr.* c.	camana s.+	camū́? v.+
-cāma s.+	camasá v.+	-cāṁti c.

Always with prep. ā, except in Nirukta.

√ car, 'move'.

Pres. [1.] cárati -te *etc.* v.+
Perf. cacā́ra (cacartha c.) cerús *etc.* av.+, cere c.
Aor. 3. ácīcarat *etc.* av.+ — 4. acārṣam b.s. — 5. acārīt *etc.* v.b.u.s. (cacārīt? u.)
Fut. 1. cariṣyati *etc.* b.+, -te b. (acariṣyat m.) [— 2. caritā.]
Verb. caritá v.+, cīrṇa u.+; cáritum b.+, -tave v., -tavāí b., -tos b.s., cartum e.+; caritvā́ b.+, cartvā m., cīrtvā m.; -cárya b.+; caráse rv.; carádhyāi rv.; -cā́ram b.
Sec. Conj.: *Pass.* caryáte *etc.* b.+ — *Int.* carcarīti *etc.* av.b.; carcūryá- v.+ — *Desid.* cicariṣati *etc.* çb.; cicarṣati kb. — *Caus.* cāráyati -te *etc.* b.+ (cāryate b.+)

Deriv.: cara v.+	-caraṇīya c.	carṣaṇí v.+	céru rv.
carā́ rv.	-caréṇya rv.	cāra av.+	cacará rv.
cáraka b.+	caritavya b.+	cāraka e.+	cárcara rv.c.
-cárya av.+	cartavya e.	cārin v.+	carācará v.b.
-caryā s.+	-caritṛ u.	-cāryà b.+	-cārayitavya c.
carátha rv.	carítra v.+	cāraṇa e.+	-cārayitṛ c.
cáraṇa v.+	cariṣṇú v.+	cāraṇīya c.	cicariṣu b.
caráṇi rv.	-cárṣaṇa? rv.	-cāruka b.	

Compare √ cal.

√ carc, 'repeat'.

Sec. Conj.: *Caus.* carcayati c., carcita e.+

Deriv.: carcā c.	carcaka c.	-carci s.
	carcana c.	-carcī c.

Probably in reality a denominative of carcā, and this a frequentative formation, perhaps from √ car.

√ carv, 'chew'.

[*Pres. etc.* carvati *etc.*]
Verb. carvita c., cūrṇa s.+; carvitum c.
Sec. Conj.: *Pass.* carvyate *etc.* c. — *Caus.* carvayati *etc.* c.
Deriv.: carvya c. carvaṇa c. carvaṇā c. cūrṇi c.

√ cal, 'stir'.

Pres. [1.] calati *etc.* av.+, -te *etc.* e.
Perf. cacāla celus *etc.* e.+

[*Aor.* calyāsam; acālīt.]
Fut. 1. caliṣyati E.+ [— 2. calitā.]
Verb. calita E.+; calitum E.+
Sec. Conj.: Int. calcalīti MS., cācalat AV. — *Desid.* cicaliṣa- (*in d.*). — *Caus.* calayati *etc.* C.; cālayati E.+, -te E. (cālyate E., -ti M.)
Deriv.: cala E.+ -calaka C. -calāka B.+ calana E.+ -calī AV.+ -calū B.S. calitavya E. cāla C. -cālin C. cālya E.+ cālana E.+ -cācala AV. -cācali RV. cañcala E.+ calācalá V.E. cicaliṣu C.

A later variation of √ car.

√ cāy, 'note, observe'.

Pres. [1.] cā́yati *etc.* B., cā́yamāna RV.
Perf. cikyus AA. [cacāya -ye.] -cāyāṁ cakrus JB.
Aor. 5. acāyiṣam AV. [acāyiṣṭa.]
[*Fut.* cāyiṣyati -te; cāyitā.]
Verb. citá B.; cāyitvā́ AV.; -cā́yya V.B.U.
Sec. Conj.: Pass. cāyyate TS.
Deriv.: cāyanīya C. cāyitṛ C. cāyú RV. -citi B.

A form, but an early specialized one, of √ 2 ci. The meanings 'reverence, be in awe' are rare and secondary.

√ 1 ci, 'gather'.

Pres. [5.] cinóti cinuté *etc.* V.+ — cinvati (3*s.*) C. — [2.] ceti RV. — [1.] cayat cáyema RV.
Perf. cikā́ya *etc.* cikye -yire *etc.* V.+ [cicāya cicetha, cicye.]
Aor. 1. acet citana ciyántu RV. [cīyāt.] — 4. acāiṣam *etc.* B. [aceṣṭa.] — 5. cayiṣṭam RV.
Fut. 1. ceṣyáti -te *etc.* B.+ — 2. cetā *etc.* E.
Verb. citá V.+; cetum B.+, -tavāi B.; citvā́ B.+, cayitvā E.; -cítya C., -cīya M.
Sec. Conj.: Pass. cīyáte *etc.* B.+ (-cīyant M.) — [*Int.* ceci-. —] *Desid.* cikīṣate *etc.* B.+; cicīṣati C. — *Caus.* cāyayate C. [cāpayati.]
Deriv.: kāya VS.? E.+ caya S.+ cáyana AV.+ cayanīya C. cayitavyà MS. -cayiṣṭha RV. -cāya B. -cāyin E.+ -cāyyà B. cít B. cítya AV.B. -cityā B.+ cíti B.+ cītí AV. cetavyà B. -cetṛ B. ceya E.+ -cicīṣā C.

See √ 2 ci.

√ 2 ci, 'note, observe'.

Pres. [3.] cikéṣi *etc.* V.B. (cikīhi AV., ciketu TS., cikéthe RV., cikitām AV., cíkyat V., acikayus B.) — [5.] cinoti cinute E.+ — [1.] cayate *etc.* V.B.
Perf. cikāya *etc.* V.+

Aor. 1. ácet ácidhvam RV. — 4. aceṣṭa C.
Fut. ceṣyati E.
Verb. citá V.+; cetum B.+; -citya E.+
Sec. Conj.: Pass. cīyate *etc.* C. — *Desid.* cikīṣati -te *etc.* V.B.S.
Deriv.: -caya V.+ -cāyin E.+ -cetavya E.+ -ceya B.
-cayana C. -cít RV. cetṛ́ V.B. -cira RV.
cāyaka C. citi B.+

Compare √ cāy, which appears to be an early specialized form of this root; cay (BR. 3 ci) is another. The forms and derivatives of 2 ci are not everywhere well separable from those of 1 ci, and there is reason to suspect the two roots of being ultimately one; words with the prefixes nis and vi, especially, are probably best referred to 1 ci, with the meaning 'take apart', and so 'resolve, decide'.

√ cit, 'perceive, know, appear'.

Pres. [1.] cétati *etc.* cétante RV.
Perf. cikéta cikitus *etc.* cikité -tré *etc.* V.B.S. (cíketa; cíketati *etc.* cíketat *etc.*; cikiddhi; aciket, acikitat, cikitas; cikitrire) [ciceta.]
Aor. 1. áceti céti RV., cité? RV., citántī? RV., cítāna V.B. (-cetāna RV.) — [3. acīcitat. —] 4. acāit RV. [— 5. acetīt.]
[*Fut.* cetiṣyati, cetitā.]
Verb. cittá V.+; cité? RV.; citáye VS.
Sec. Conj.: Int. cékite *etc.* -tat RV.C. — *Desid.* cíkitsati *etc.* V.+, -te E.+ (acikitsīs AV., cikitsyate *etc.* E.+) — *Caus.* citáyati *etc.* -te *etc.* RV.; cetáyati *etc.* -te *etc.* V.+
Deriv.: kéta V.+ cétya RV. cetyā́ RV. cikitsā B.+
ketana E.+ cétana V.+ cikít RV. cikitsaka B.+
ketú V.+ cetanā E.+ cíkiti SV. cikitsya E.+
cít V.+ cétas V.+ cikitú V. cikitsana E.+
citi C. cétiṣṭha V.B. cikitván RV. -cikitsanīya C.
cítti V.+ cetú RV. cikitvít RV. cikitsú AV.+
cittí RV. -cetúna RV. -ciketas U. cetayitavya U.+
citrá V.+ céttṛ V.B. cikita S. cetayitṛ B.+

Compare roots 2 ci and cint. The grammarians give two separate roots, kit and cit, each with full sets of forms — which are not all reported here.

√ cint, 'think'.

Sec. Conj.: Caus. cintayati *etc.* -te *etc.* B.+ ([acicintat;] cintyate *etc.* U.+; cintayita C.)
Deriv: cintā E.+ -cintin C. cintana E.+ -cintitṛ E.
cintaka E.+ cintya U.+ cintanīya C. cintayitavya C.

Perhaps the denominative of a nasalized derivative of √ cit.

√ cud, 'impel'.

Pres. [1.] códati -te *etc.* v.
Aor. 3. acūcudat E. — 5. codīs RV.
Verb. cudita M.
Sec. Conj.: *Caus.* codáyati *etc.* -te *etc.* v.+ (codyate *etc.* s.+)
Deriv.: codá RV.C. códa RV. codaka s.+ -codin C. codya E.+ códana v.+ codanā s.+ codanīya B. -codas RV. coditṛ́ RV. códiṣṭha RV. codayitavya C. codayitṛ́ RV.C.

√ cup, 'stir'.

Pres. [1.] copati M[1].
[*Perf. etc.* cucopa; acopīt; copiṣyati, copitā.]
Verb. cupita C.
Deriv. -cumpuna? V.B.

√ cumb, 'kiss'.

Pres. [1.] cumbati *etc.* E.+, -te C.
Perf. cucumba *etc.* E.+
[*Aor. etc.* acumbīt; cumbiṣyati, cumbitā.]
Verb. cumbita C.; cumbitum C.; -cumbya C.
Sec. Conj.: *Pass.* cumbyate *etc.* C. — *Desid.* cucumbiṣati C. — *Caus.* cumbayitum C.
Deriv.: cumbā C. cumbaka C. cumbin C. cumbana C.

√ cur, 'steal'.

Aor. 3. acūcurat C.
Sec. Conj.: corayati *etc.* E.+, -te E.+ (coryate C.)
Deriv: corá TA.+ coraka C. corayitavya C.

√ culump, 'suck in'.

A single occurrence of a form from this bastard root, with ud, is referred to in Böhtlingk's Lexicon, as found in the Mahāvīracarita.

√ cūṣ, 'draw, suck'.

[*Pres. etc.* cūṣati; cucūṣa; acucūṣat, acūṣīt; cūṣiṣyati, cūṣitā.]
Sec. Conj.: *Pass.* cūṣyate C. — *Caus.* cūṣayati C.
Deriv.: cūṣin C. cūṣya E.+ cūṣaṇa C. coṣa C. coṣya E.+. coṣaṇa C.

√ cṛt, 'bind'.

Pres. [6.] cṛtáti *etc.* V.B.S. [— 1. cartati.]
Perf. cacarta AV.

[*Aor. etc.* acīcṛtat, acacartat, acartīt; cartiṣyati, cartsyati, cartitā.]
Verb. cṛttá V.S.; -cṛtya B.S.; -cṛ́tam AV.
Sec. Conj.: Pass. cṛtyáte B. [— *Int.* carīcṛt-. — *Desid.* cicartiṣa-, ci-cṛtsa-. — *Caus.* cartayati.]
Deriv.: -cartya B. -cartana B. -cṛt V.+ -cṛtya B.

√ ceṣṭ, 'stir'.

Pres. [1.] céṣṭati *etc.* AV.+, -te *etc.* B.+
Perf. ciceṣṭa *etc.* E.
[*Aor. etc.* aciceṣṭat acaceṣṭat, aceṣṭīt; ceṣṭiṣyati, ceṣṭitā.]
Verb. ceṣṭita E.+; ceṣṭitum E.+; ceṣṭitvā́ B.
Sec. Conj.: Caus. ceṣṭayati *etc.* B.+, -te *etc.* S.+
Deriv.: -ciṣṭu? B. (á-) ceṣṭa C. ceṣṭana E.+ ceṣṭayitṛ E.
ceṣṭā S.+ ceṣṭitavya E.

√ cyu, 'move, stir'.

Pres. [1.] cyávate *etc.* V.+, -ti *etc.* RV.? E.+
Perf. cucyuvé RV. (cicyuṣé RV.)
Aor. 1. cyávāna? RV. — 3. acucyavat -van -vus V.B. (-vīt -vītana cu-cyavat -vīrata cucyuvīmáhi RV.) [acicyavat.] — 4. acyoṣṭa *etc.* V.B.U.
Fut. 1. cyoṣyate B. [— 2. cyotā.]
Verb. cyutá V.+; cyavitum E., cyótos ÇB.
Sec. Conj.: [*Int.* cocyu-. — *Desid.* cucyūṣa-. —] *Caus.* cyāváyati *etc.* V.+, -te *etc.* V.+ [cicyāvayiṣa-, cucyāvayiṣa-]; cyavayati PB[1].
Deriv.: -cyava V.+ -cyavīyas RV. -cyāvuka B. cyāutná RV.
cyávana V.+ cyāva E. -cyut V.+ cyāvayiṣṇú AV.
-cyávas RV. cyāvana E.+ cyuti V.+ cyāvayitavya B.

The RV. forms here grouped under the reduplicated aorist are of difficult and doubtful classification.

√ cyut, 'drip'.

Pres. [1.] cyotati *etc.* S.C.
[*Perf. etc.* cucyota; acyutat, acucyutat, acyotīt; cyotiṣyati, cyotitā.]
Sec. Conj.: [*Int.* cocyut-. — *Desid.* cucyotiṣa-, cucyutiṣa-. —] *Caus.* cyo-tayati C.
Only a blundering *varia lectio* for √ çcut, which see.

√ chad, 'cover'.

[*Pres.* 1. chadati -te.]
Verb. channa B.+
Sec. Conj.: Caus. chādáyati *etc.* V.+, -te *etc.* E.+ (chādyate *etc.* S.+ [cichā-dayiṣa-.])

Deriv.: -chad v.+ chada s.+ -chadin c. chadana e.+ chadi b.+ chadíś v.+ chattra s.+ chadman s.+ chala? e.+ -chāda b.+ -chādaka c. -chādin c. chādya c. chādana s.+

√ chand, chad, 'seem, please'.

Pres. [2.] chantsi -ntti RV.MS. — [1.] chandati B.E.
Perf. cachanda RV. (cachadyāt RV.)
Aor. 3. acachadat c. — 4. achān -ntta -ntsus RV. (chantsat RV.)
Sec. Conj.: *Caus.* chadáyati *etc.* V.B.; chandayati *etc.* B.+, -te *etc.* RV. (chandyate *etc.* E.+)
Deriv.: -chad RV. chánda v.+ chandá RV. chandaka E.+ chándya RV. chandana c. chándas v.+ chándu RV.

Of very questionable relationship to √ chad 'cover', although the two are not separated by the Hindu grammarians.

√ chā, 'cut up'.

Pres. chyati *etc.* AV.B. — chāyáti? TB. — chayet c.
[*Perf. etc.* cachāu; achāt, achāsīt; chāsyati, chātā.]
Verb. chāta s., chitá ÇB.C.; chayitvā c.; -chā́ya ÇB.
Sec. Conj.: [*Int.* cāchā-, cāchi-. — *Desid.* cichāsa-. —] *Caus.* chāyayati B.U.
Deriv.: chavī́ -vi? B.+ -chāna c.

√ chid, 'cut off'.

Pres. [7.] chinátti chindánti *etc.* v.+ (— chindeta c.; achinam M.)
Perf. cicheda cichide *etc.* B.+
Aor. 1. chedma RV.; [chidyāt;] áchedi V.B.S. — 2. achidat *etc.* AV.+ — 3. acichidas E. — 4. achāitsīt *etc.* B.+ (chetsīt *etc.* B.+), chitsi *etc.* AV.+ (chetsi *etc.* B.U.).
Fut. 1. chetsyati -te *etc.* B.+ (achetsyat M.) [— 2. chettā.]
Verb. chinná v.+; chettum B.+, -ttavāí B.S.; chittvā́ B.+; -chídya AV.+
Sec. Conj.: *Pass.* chidyáte *etc.* v.+ (chidyati *etc.* E.) — [*Int.* cechid-. —] *Desid.* cichitsati -te JB. — *Caus.* chedayati *etc.* s.+
Deriv.: -chid v.+ chidā c. chidura c. -chitti B.+ chidrá v.+ cheda AV.+ -chedaka c. -chedin E.+ chedya E.+ chedana B.+ chedanīya c. chettavya E.+ chettṛ B.+ cichitsu E.

√ chuṭ, chuḍ, 'wrench'.

Sec. Conj.: *Caus.* choḍayati *etc.* c., choṭita c.
Deriv. choṭikā c.

All very late and questionable forms.

√ chur, 'scatter'.

[*Pres. etc.* **churati; cuchora; achorīt;** *etc.*]
Sec. Conj.: Caus. **churayati** *etc.* C., **churita** E.+; **chorayati** *etc.* C.
Deriv. **-churaṇa** C.

√ chṛd, 'spue, eject'.

Pres. [7.] **chṛṇatti** *etc.* B. [**chṛntte.** — 1. **chardati.**]
Perf. **cacharda** C. [**-de.**]
[*Aor. etc.* **achṛdat, acachardat acichṛdat, achārdīt, achṛtta; chardiṣyati -te, chartsyati -te, charditā.**]
Verb. **chṛṇṇá** B. [**charditvā, chṛttvā.**]
Sec. Conj.: [*Int.* **carīchṛd-.** — *Desid.* **cichardiṣa-, cichṛtsa-.** —] *Caus.* **chardayati -te** *etc.* B.+ [**cichardayiṣa-.**]
Deriv.: **chardana** S.+ **chardi** S.+ **chardis** C. **chardayitavya** C. **chardanīya** C.

√ 1 jakṣ, 'eat'.

Pres. [2.] **jakṣiti jagdhi** C., **ajakṣus** KB., **jakṣat** (*pple*) U.C. — [1.] **jakṣati** *etc.* U.C.
[*Perf. etc.* **jajakṣa; ajajakṣat, ajakṣīt; jakṣiṣyati, jakṣitā.**]
Verb. **jagdhá** V.+; **jagdhum** C.; **jagdhvā́** AV.+, **jagdhvā́ya** RV.
[*Sec. Conj.:* **jājakṣ-; jijakṣiṣa-; jakṣaya-.**]
Deriv. **jágdhi** B.+

A reduplicated form of √ **ghas.** The present forms found later only in the Bhāgavata-Purāṇa.

√ 2 jakṣ, 'laugh'.

Pres. [2.] **jákṣat** (*pple*) RV.ÇB.

A reduplicated form of √ **has.**

√ jagh, 'eat, devour'.

Pres. [5.] **jaghnuyāt**? C.

Found only in Vasiṣṭha (i. 23); but Bühler appears to read **jahnuyāt**; he renders it 'offend'.

√ jajh.

Pres. **jájhatī** RV[1].

This is a ἅπ. λεγ., of doubtful character and meaning.

√ jañj.

Pres. **jáñjatī** RV[1].

This is of the same character as the preceding.

√jan, jā, 'give birth, be born'.

Pres. [1.] jánati -te *etc.* V.B. — [4.] jā́yate *etc.* V.+, -ti *etc.* E.+ — [2.] jániṣva RV.B. [— 3. jajanti.]

Perf. jajā́na jajñús *etc.* jajñé *etc.* V.+ (jajanús RV., jajánat B.)

Aor. 1. ajan (3*s.*) S., ajñata (3*p.*) B.; ájani jáni V.B., jáni RV.; jāyāt E.+ — 3. ájījanat -nata *etc.* V.+ — 5. ájaniṣṭa *etc.* V.+, jániṣṭām RV. (janiṣīya -ṣīṣṭa -ṣīmahi V.B.S.; janiṣeyam -ya K.; jániṣṭhat? SV.)

Fut. 1. janiṣyáti -te *etc.* V.+ (ajaniṣyata *etc.* B.), jāsyati *etc.* E. — 2. janitā́ B.+

Verb. jātá V.+; jánitos V.B.S.; janitvī́ RV.

Sec. Conj.: [*Pass.* janyate. — *Int.* jañjan-, jājā-. —] *Desid.* jíjaniṣate ÇB. — *Caus.* janáyati -te *etc.* V.+ (jijanayiṣet ÇB.)

Deriv.:

gnā́ V.B.S.	jánī V.+	janitṛ V.+	jénya RV.
-jana C.	-janu,-nū AV.B.	janítra V.+	jā́nuka B.
jána V.+	janús V.B.	jánman V.+	jájñi B.
janaka E.+	jantú V.+	jániman V.	jánayati B.S.
jánya V.+	jántva RV.	jániṣṭha? V.B.	janayitavya C.
jánana V.+	jánitva V.	-janiṣṇu B.	janayitṛ B.+
jánas V.+	janitavyà AV.	janiṣya E.	janayiṣṇu E.
			-jijanayiṣitavyà ÇB.
jā́ V.+	jā́tu? V.+	jā́ni V.+	jāyā́ V.+
-ja V.+	jātū́ RV.	-jā́man V.	-jāyin E.+
jāti B.+	jātṛ AV.?	jāmā E.	-jā́van RV.
	jā́na V.B.U.	jāmí V.+	-jā́vara B.

√jap, 'whisper'.

Pres. [1.] jápati *etc.* B.+, -te *etc.* S.+

Perf. jajāpa jepus *etc.* E.

Aor. [3. ajījapat. —] 5. ajapīt GB. [ajāpīt.]

Fut. 1. japiṣyáti B. [— 2. japitā.]

Verb. japita S.+, japta E.+; japitum E.; japitvā B.+, japtvā S.+

Sec. Conj.: *Pass.* japyate E. — *Int.* jañjapyáte ÇB. [— *Desid.* jijapiṣa-. — *Caus.* jāpayati.]

Deriv.:

japá B.+	japana E.	jāpa E.+	jāpya E.+
japin C.	japanīya C.	jāpaka E.+	-jañjapa C.
jápya B.+	japtavya E.+	jāpin C.	jañjapūka C.

√jam.

[*Pres.* 1. jamati.]

Sec. Conj.: *Int.* jājamat M.

Artificially made forms, to frame a derivation for the name **jamadagni.**

√ **jambh, jabh,** 'chew up, crush'.

[*Pres.* 1. **jambhate, jabhate.**]
Aor. 3. **ajījabham** AV. [**ajajambhat.** —] 5. **jambhiṣat** RV.
Verb. **jabdha** AV.; **jabhitum** C.
Sec. Conj.: *Int.* **jáñjabhāna** AV.S., **-bhat** S.; **jañjabhyáte** *etc.* B.+ — *Caus.* **jambháyati** *etc.* V.B.
Deriv.: **jámbha** V.+ **jambhá** AV.+ **jámbhaka** B.+ **jabhya**? AV. **jámbhana** AV.+

√ **jar,** *see* √ **jṛ.**

√ **jalp,** 'murmur, speak'.

Pres. [1.] **jálpati** *etc.* B.+, **-te** *etc.* C.
Perf. **jajalpa** *etc.* E. (**jalpire** C.)
[*Aor. etc.* **ajalpīt; jalpiṣyati, jalpitā.**]
Verb. **jalpita** E.+
Sec. Conj.: *Pass.* **jalpyate** C.
Deriv.: **jalpa** E.+ **jalpaka** C. **jalpin** E. **jalpya** E. **-jalpana** C. **jálpi** V. **jalpitṛ** E. **-jarjalpa**? VS.

√ **jas,** 'be exhausted'.

Pres. [1.] **jásamāna** RV. — [4.] **jasyata** (2*p.*) RV.
Perf. **jajāsa** AV.
Aor. 3. **ajījasata** (3*s.*) ÇB. (**jajastám** RV.)
Sec. Conj.: *Caus.* **jāsayati** *etc.* B.+ (**jāsyate** E.)
Deriv.: **jásu** RV. **jásuri** RV. **-jasra** V.+ **jásvan** RV.

√ **jah,** *see* √ **hā.**

√ **jā,** *see* √ **jan.**

√ **1 ji,** 'conquer'.

Pres. [1.] **jáyati -te** *etc.* V.+ — [2.] **jéṣi jitam** RV.
Perf. **jigā́ya** *etc.* (**jigetha** RV.; **jigīvā́ṅs** V., **jigivā́ṅs** B.+) **jigye** *etc.* V.+ — **-jayām āsa** C.
Aor. 1. [**ajāyi, jīyāt**] **jayyāt** JUB.M. — 3. **ajījayat** M. — 4. **ajāiṣīt** *etc.* V.+ (**ajāis -āit jeṣam jes jéṣma** V.B.S., **jéṣat** *etc.* RV.), **jeṣi** TB. (**ajāiṣṭa** M.) — 5. **ajayit** TS., **ajayiṣata** (3*p.*) C.
Fut. **jeṣyati** *etc.* V.+, **-te** *etc.* E.; **jayiṣyati** JB.E., **-te** E. — 2. **jetā́** *etc.* B.E.
Verb. **jitá** V.+; **jétum** B.+, **-tave** B.; **jitvā́** B.+; **-jítya** AV.+; **jiṣé** RV.
Sec. Conj.: *Pass.* **jīyate** *etc.* E.+ (**jīyeyam** M.) [— *Int.* **jejīya-.**] — *Desid.* **jígīṣati -te** *etc.* V.+ — *Caus.* **jāpayati** *etc.* B.S. (**ajījapata -jipata** B.)

Deriv.: jayá V.+ jayin E.+ jayyà B. -jayana E.+ jayús RV. -ji AV. -jit V.+ -jityā B. jíti V.+ -jítvan V.B. -jitvara C. jina C. jiṣṇú V.+ jayiṣṇu U.E. jétva V.B. jetavya E.+ jetṛ V.+ jayitṛ B.E. jéman RV. jemán B. jeya E.+ jeṣá V.B.S. -jeṣin B. jāyin B.+ jāyú RV. jā́yuka MS. jigyú RV. jigīṣā́ V.+ -jigīṣin GB.E. jigīṣú V.+ -jāpayitṛ B.

√ 2 ji, jinv, 'quicken'.

Pres. [5.] jinóṣi RV.TS., ajinot JB., jinvé RV. — [1.] jínvati *etc.* V.B.S., -te RV.

Perf. jijinváthus RV.

[*Aor.* ajinvīt.]

Fut. 1. jinviṣyati AB. [— 2. jinvitā.]

Verb. jinvitá AV.

Deriv.: jīrá V.B.S. jīrí RV. -jinva RV.

√ jīv, 'live'.

Pres. [1.] jívati *etc.* V.+, -te *etc.* E.+

Perf. jijīva *etc.* B.+, -ve R.

Aor. 1. jīvyā́sam -yāsma AV.B.S. [— 3. ajījivat, ajijīvat.] — 5. ajīvīt *etc.* AV.+

Fut. 1. jīviṣyati *etc.* B.+ (ajīviṣyam U.), -te M. [— 2. jīvitā.]

Verb. jīvitá V.+; jívitum B.+, -tavāí AV.; jīvitvā JB.; -jīvya E.+; jīváse V.B.M[1].

Sec. Conj.: Pass. jīvyáte *etc.* B.+ [— *Int.* jejīvya-.] — *Desid.* jijīviṣati B.+, -te C.; jújyūṣati *etc.* ÇB. (jijyūṣita AB.) — *Caus.* jīváyati *etc.* V.+ (jīvāpayati *etc.* E.+; jijīvayiṣa- *in d.*)

Deriv.: jīvá V.+ jīvaka S.+ jīvin B.+ jīvya E.+ jívana V.+ jīvanī́ya AV.+ jīvás V.B.E. jīvā́tu V.+ jīvātṛ (*in d.*) C. jīvitavya C. -jīvitṛ C. jijīviṣā E. jijīviṣu E. -jijīvayiṣu E

√ jur, *see* √ jṛ.

√ juṣ, 'enjoy'.

Pres. [6.] juṣáte *etc.* V.+, -ti *etc.* RV.E.+ — [2.] jóṣi V.

Perf. jujóṣa *etc.* V.+, jujuṣé *etc.* V.C. (jújoṣati *etc.* jújoṣat *etc.* RV.; jújoṣate RV., jujóṣate SV.; jujuṣṭana V.; ajujoṣam K.)

Aor. 1. ajuṣran RV. (joṣati jóṣat jóṣā RV., joṣase AV.; juṣāṇá V.B.C.); juṣyāt C. [— 3. ajūjuṣat.] — 5. jóṣiṣat RV.

[*Fut.* joṣiṣyate, joṣitā.]

Verb. júṣṭa V., juṣṭá V.+; juṣṭví RV.

Sec. Conj.: [*Int.* jojuṣ-. — *Desid.* jujuṣiṣa-, jujoṣiṣa-. —] *Caus.* joṣáyate *etc.* V.+, -ti E.

Deriv.: -jus V.+, -juṣa B., júṣṭi V., jóṣa V.+, jóṣya RV., joṣaṇa B.+, -jóṣas V.B., joṣṭṛ V.B.S., joṣayitavya C., jóṣayitṛ B.

√ jū, 'be swift'.

Pres. [9.] junā́ti *etc.* RV. — [1.] jávate *etc.* RV.B.

Perf. jūjuvus -vat -vā́ṅs -vāná RV.

[*Aor.* 3. ajījavat.]

Verb. jūtá V., javita E.+; -jávam TS.

Sec. Conj.: *Caus.* jāvayati C. [jijāvayiṣa-.]

Deriv.: javá V.+, javín V.+, jávana V.+, jávas V., jáviṣṭha V.+, jávīyas RV.B.U., júvas RV., jū́ V.B., jūtí V.B.U.

Related with √ jīv, and perhaps with √ ji jinv; javita is more probably denominative from java.

√ jūrv, 'consume'

Pres. [1.] jū́rvati *etc.* V.

Aor. 5. jūrvīt RV.

Doubtless a secondary formation (u- or eighth class) from √ jṛ jur.

√ 1 jṛ, jur, 'waste away'.

Pres. [1.] járati *etc.* jaranta RV. (járant V.+) — [6.] juráti *etc.* RV. — [4.] jī́ryati *etc.* AV.+, -te *etc.* E.+; jū́ryati *etc.* RV.

Perf. jajāra AV. [jajarus, jerus]; jujurvā́ṅs RV.

Aor. [1. jīryāt. — 2. ajarat. — 3. ajījarat. —] 5. jāriṣus RV.

[*Fut.* jarīṣyati, jarītā.]

Verb. jīrṇá AV.+, jūrṇá RV. [jarītvā.]

Sec. Conj.: *Pass.* jīryate *etc.* C. — [*Int.* jājṛ-, jejīrya-. — *Desid.* jijarīṣa-, jijīrṣa-. —] *Caus.* jaráyati -te *etc.* V.+ (jāráyant RV.)

Deriv.: jára V.+, jarā́ V.+, jaraṇá V.+, jaraṇi RV., jarás V.+, jarimán V.B., járūtha? RV., jā́ra RV., jāraṇa C., jírvi AV., jívri? RV, -jīrti C., jírṇi B., -jur RV., -jurya V.B., jū́rya RV., jūrṇí RV., jáguri RV., jarjara B.+, jarayitṛ C., -jarayu RV., jarā́yu? V.+

Compare √ jūrv and jvar.

√ 2 jṛ, 'sing'.

Pres. [1.] járate *etc.* V.

Verb. jarádhyāi RV.

Deriv.: jaráṇā? RV., jarā́ RV., jaritṛ́ V.S., jū́rṇi? RV.

A secondary form of √ 1 gṛ. BR. ascribe a few of the forms to a third √ jṛ (jar), 'approach'.

√ jṛmbh, 'gape'.

Pres. [1.] **jṛ́mbhate** *etc.* v.+, **-ti** *etc.* b.+
Perf. **jajṛmbhe** *etc.* e.+
[*Aor. etc.* **ajṛmbhiṣṭa; jṛmbhiṣyate, jṛmbhitā.**]
Verb. **jṛmbhita** e.+; **jṛmbhitvā** s.
Sec. Conj.: Int. **jarījṛmbhate** c. — *Caus.* **jṛmbhayati** *etc.* c.
Deriv.: **jṛmbha** e.+ **jṛmbhaka** e.+ **-jṛmbhin** c. **jṛmbhaṇa** e.+ **jṛmbhā** c.

√ jeh, 'loll, pant'.

Pres. [1.] **jéhamāna** v.
[*Perf. etc.* **jijehe; ajijehat, ajehiṣṭa; jehiṣyate, jehitā; jehayati.**]
If, as seems probable, **jihmá** v.+ belongs here, the root should be written **jih.** It is perhaps a secondary reduplicated formation from √ **hā.**

√ jñā, 'know'.

Pres. [9.] **jānā́ti -nīté** *etc.* v.+ (**jānīma jānithās** m.) — 1. **jānati -te** *etc.* u.e. — **jña** (2*s. impv.*) c.
Perf. **jajñāú jajñé** *etc.* v.+
Aor. 1. **ajñāyi** v.+; **jñeyā́s** rv. [**jñāyāt.**] — 4. **ájñāsam ajñāsthās** av.b., **jñeṣam** av.b. — 6. **ajñāsiṣam** *etc.* av.+
Fut. 1. **jñāsyati -te** *etc.* b.+ (**ajñāsyat** m.) — 2. **jñātā** b.
Verb. **jñātá** v.+; **jñā́tum** b.+, **-tos** b.; **jñātvā́** b.+; **-jñā́ya** b.+; **-jñā́yam** b.
Sec. Conj.: Pass. **jñāyáte** *etc.* v.+ —[*Int.* **jājñā-.** —] *Desid.* **jijñāsate** *etc.* av.+, **-ti** *etc.* e.+ (**jijñāsiṣi** b., **jijñāsyate** *etc.* e.+) — *Caus.* **jñapayati** *etc.* av.+, **-te** u. (**ajijñipat** ts., **ajijñapat** *etc.* c.; **jñaptá** b.+ [**jñapita**], **jñaptum** e.+; **jñapyáte** çb. [**jñīpsa-**]); **jñāpayati** *etc.* b.+, **-te** *etc.* e.+ (**jñāpyate** *etc.* e.+, **ajñāpiṣyat**? u.)

Deriv.:

-jānaka? e.	**jñātṛ́** v.+	**-jñapya** c.	**-jñāpayitavya** c.
-jñā v.+	**jñātra** b.	**-jñapana** av.	**jijñāsā** b.+
jñá b.+	**-jñāya** v.b.	**jñapti** c.	**jijñāsyà** b.+
jñā́s rv.	**jñeya** b.+	**jñāpaka** e.+	**jijñāsana** c.
jñā́na v.+	**-jajñi** v.b.	**jñāpya** e.+	**-jijñāsenya** b.
jñātí v.+	**jijñu** e.	**jñāpana** c.	**-jijñāsitavya** u.
jñātavya u.+		**jñāpanīya** c.	**jijñāsu** e.+

√ jyā, jī, 'overpower, injure'.

Pres. [9.] **jinā́ti** *etc.* v.b.s. — 4. **jīyate** rv.çb.
Perf. **jijyāú** b.
Aor. [1. **jīyāt.** —] 6. **ajyāsiṣam** *etc.* b.
Fut. 1. **jyāsyati -te** b. [— 2. **jyātā.**]
Verb. **jītá** av. [**jīna; jītvā; -jyāya.**]
Sec. Conj.: Pass. **jīyáte** av.ms. — [*Int.* **jājyā-, jejīya-.** —] *Desid.* **jíjyāsati** *etc.* v.b. [— *Caus.* **jyāpayati, ajijyapat.**]

Deriv.: -jīti V.B.S. jyā́ V.B. -jya AV. jyā́na B. jyānī́ AV.B. -jyāya MS. -jyeya B.U. -jyéya *n.* AV. jyāyukā JB. jyā́yas V.+ jyeṣṭha V.+ jyāyiṣṭha E.+

Related with √ ji.

√ jyut, 'shine'.

Pres. [1.] jyótati MS., -te M.?
Verb. -jyótya B.S.
Sec. Conj.: *Caus.* jyotáya AV. (jyotyámāna ÇB.)
Deriv.: jyuti E. jyotā VS. -jyotana S. jyotaya? AV. jyótis V.+ jyótsnā B.+

A differentiated form of √ dyut.

√ jri, 'go'.

Pres. [1.] jrayati RV[1].
[*Perf. etc.* jijrāya; jrīyāt, ajijrayat, ajrāiṣīt; jreṣyati, jretā; jejrī-, jijrīṣa-, jrāyaya-.]
Deriv.: -jráya RV. jráyas RV. jrayasāná RV. -jri RV.

√ jvar, 'be hot'.

Pres. [1.] jvarati *etc.* U.+
[*Perf. etc.* jajvāra; ajijvarat, ajvārīt.]
Fut. 1. jvariṣyati E. [— 2. jvaritā.]
Sec. Conj.: *Pass.* jvaryate C. [— *Int.* jājvarya-, jājūr-. — *Desid.* jijvariṣa-.] — *Caus.* jvarayati *etc.* C.
Deriv.: jvara AV.+ -jvāra RV.C.

Another form of √ jval, and apparently related with jṛ, jur, jūrv.

√ jval, 'burn, flame'.

Pres. [1.] jválati *etc.* B.+, -te *etc.* E.+
Perf. jajvāla *etc.* B.+
Aor. [3. ajijvalat. —] 5. ajvālīt B.U., ajvalīt C.
Fut. 1. jvaliṣyati B.+ [— 2. jvalitā.]
Verb. jvalita B.+; -jvalya S.
Sec. Conj.: *Int.* jājvalīti C. (-lati -lant E.), -lyate E. — [*Desid.* jijvaliṣa-. —] *Caus.* jvalayati *etc.* B.+, -te ÇB.; jvālayati *etc.* S.+ (jvālyate B.+)
Deriv.: jvala E.+ jvalana B.+ jvalitṛ C. jvāla S.+ jvālā E.+ jvālin E.+ -jvālana C.

Compare √ jvar, of which this is another form.

√ jhaṭ, 'confuse'.

Only in ujjhaṭita, in a single doubtful occurrence (C.). Given a full set of forms by the grammarians.

√ jhaṇ, 'sound'.

A single occurrence, **jhaṇati,** in the Harṣacarita (Bö.).

√ jhar, 'fall'.

Pres. [1.] **jharant** c[1].
Deriv.: **jhara** E.+ **-jharaṇa** C.
A very questionable root.

√ ṭaṅk, 'cover' (?).

[*Pres. etc.* **ṭaṅkati, ṭaṭaṅka.**]
Aor. 1. **aṭaṅki** C.
Verb. **ṭaṅkita** C.
Sec. Conj.: Caus. **ṭaṅkayati** C.
Deriv. **ṭaṅka** E.+
Most probably a denominative of **ṭaṅka,** rather.

√ ṭal, 'be confused'.

Pres. [1.] **ṭalati** C.
A single late occurrence, doubtless artificial.

√ ṭīk, 'trip'.

Pres. [1.] **ṭīkate** C.
A single late and doubtless artificial occurrence. Bö. gives also **uṭṭīkita,** but without statement of authority.

√ ṭup, 'swell'.

Bö. suggests such a root as origin of **(ā-) ṭopa** E.+

√ ḍam, 'sound'.

A single doubtful (onomatopoetic?) occurrence, **ḍamant** C.

√ ḍamb, 'mock'.

Pres. [1.] **ḍambate**? C.
Sec. Conj.: Caus. **ḍambayati** *etc.* C. (**ḍambyate** C.)
Deriv.: **-ḍamba** C. **-ḍambaka** C. **-ḍambin** C. **-ḍambya** C. **-ḍambana** C.
All forms only with prefix **vi.**

√ ḍī, 'fly'

Pres. [4.] **ḍīyate** C.? — [1.] **ḍayate** C.?
[*Perf. etc.* **ḍiḍye; aḍīḍayat, aḍayiṣṭa; ḍayiṣyate, ḍayitā.**]
Verb. **ḍīna** E.+; **-ḍīya** C.
Sec. Conj.: Pass. **ḍīyate** C. — [*Int.* **ḍeḍī-.** — *Desid.* **ḍiḍayiṣa-.** —] *Caus* **ḍāyayati** C.
Deriv.: **-ḍayana** C. **-ḍīyana** E. **ḍītara**? ÇB **-ḍīyāna** C.
A later form of √ **dī,** and rare, except in **ḍīna.**

√ ḍval, 'mix'.

Sec. Conj.: *Caus.* **ḍvālayati** *etc.* C.
Deriv. **-ḍvālana** C.
Only used by one scholiast; no proper root.

√ ḍhāuk, 'approach'

Pres. [1.] **ḍhāukate** *etc.* C.
Perf. **ḍuḍhāuke** C.
[*Aor. etc.* **aḍuḍhāukat, aḍhāukiṣṭa; ḍhāukiṣyate, ḍhāukitā.**]
Verb. **ḍhāukita** E.+
Sec. Conj.: [*Int.* **ḍoḍhāuk-.** — *Desid.* **ḍuḍhāukiṣa-.** —] *Caus.* **ḍhāukayati** *etc.* C.
Deriv. **ḍhāukana** C.

√ taṅs, tas, 'shake'.

[*Pres.* 1. **taṅsati -te.**]
Perf. **tatasré** RV.
Aor. 2. **átasat** AV.B. — 3. **átataṅsatam** RV.
Sec. Conj.: *Int.* **tantasāíte** RV. [**tantasyate.**] — *Caus.* **taṅsayati** VS., **-te** RV. (**taṅsayádhyāi** RV.)
Deriv.: **-taṅsa** B.+ **taṅsu**? E.+ **tásara** V.B. **-tantasāyya** RV. **-taṅsana** C. **-tasti**? B.+ **títaü**? RV.S.+

√ tak, 'rush'.

Pres. [2.] **takti atakta** RV. [— 1. **takati.**]
[*Perf. etc.* **tatāka; atăkīt; takiṣyati, takitā.**]
Verb. **taktá** RV.; **-táṅkam** AV.
Deriv.: **-takana** C. **tákavāna** RV. **takvá** RV. **-tákvarī** AV. **táku** RV. **-takri**? RV. **tákvan** V.B.
Probably not to be separated from √ **tac**, which with prefix **ā** has won a special meaning.

√ takṣ, 'fashion'.

Pres. [2.] **tāṣṭi** AB., **tákṣati** (3*p.*) *etc.* RV. — [5.] **takṣṇuvánti** *etc.* B.S. — [1.] **tákṣati** *etc.* V.+, **-te** *etc.* E.+
Perf. **tatákṣa** *etc.* V.+ (**takṣathus takṣus** V.B.), **tatakṣé** *etc.* V.E.
Aor. [3. **atatakṣat.** —] 5. **atakṣiṣus** RV. (**takṣiṣat** S.)
[*Fut.* **takṣiṣyati, takṣyati; takṣitā, taṣṭā.**]
Verb. **taṣṭá** V.+; **-takṣya** C.
[*Sec. Conj.*: **takṣya-; tātakṣ-; titakṣiṣa-, titakṣa-; takṣaya-.**]
Deriv.: **takṣa** S.+ **tákṣya** RV. **takṣaṇa** S.+ **taṣṭi** C. **takṣaká** AV.+ **tákṣan** V.+ **táṣṭṛ** RV.

√ tañc, tac, 'coagulate'.

Pres. [7.] **tanákti** *etc.* B.S.
[*Perf. etc.* **tatañka; atāñkṣīt, atañcīt; tañkṣyati tañciṣyati, tañktā tañcitā.**]
Verb. [**takta;**] [**taktvā, tañcitvā;**] **-tácya** B.
[*Sec. Conj.:* **tātañc-, tātacya-; titañkṣa-, titañciṣa-; tañcaya-.**]
Deriv.: **-tañka** E.+ **-táñcana** B.S. **takmán** AV. **takra** E.+ **-tañkyà** B.S.
See √ **tak.** Only used with **ā.**

√ taṭ, 'clatter'.

A single form, **taṭati,** in Adbh. Brāh., doubtless an onomatopoetic formation.

√ taḍ, 'beat'.

Pres. [2.] **tāḍhi**? RV[1].
Perf. **tatāḍa** C.
[*Aor.* 3. **atītaḍat.**]
Sec. Conj.: *Caus.* **tāḍayati** *etc.* E.+ (**tāḍyate** E.+)
Deriv.: **taḍít** V.+ **tāḍaka** E.+ **tāḍya** E.+ **tāḍanīya** C. **tā́ḍa** AV.+ **-tāḍin** C. **tāḍana** E.+ **tāḍayitṛ** C.

√ 1 tan, tā, 'stretch'.

Pres. [8.] **tanóti tanuté** *etc.* V.+
Perf. **tatā́na** *etc.* V.+ (**tatántha** V.B. [**tenitha**]), **tenus** *etc.* E.+ (**tatánat** *etc.* **tatananta tatanyus** RV.); **tené** *etc.* AV.+ (**tatane** RV., **tatne** *etc.* V., **tate** RV.)
Aor. 1. **atan** RV., **átata** *etc.* (**atathās atnata**) V.B.; **atāyi** B. — 2. **atanat** *etc.* RV. [— 3. **atītanat.**] — 4. **atāṅsīt** B. (**atān** V.), **atasi ataṅsmahi** B. — 5. **atānīt** MS. [**atanīt, ataniṣṭa.**]
Fut. 1. **taṅsyáte** B. [**taniṣyati -te.**] — 2. [**tanitā,**] **tāyitā** C.
Verb. **tatá** V.+; **tantum** B.; **tatvā** B., **tatvā́ya** B. [**tanitvā**]; **-tátya** B.+, **-tāya** C.
Sec. Conj.: *Pass.* **tāyáte** *etc.* V.+, **tanyate** *etc.* C. — [*Int.* **tantan-.** — *Desid.* **titāṅsa-, titaniṣa-.** —] *Caus.* **tānayati** AV.C.
Deriv.: **tán** V. **tána** RV. **tanā́** AV. **tánaya** V.+ **tánas** RV. **-táni** V.+ **tániman** B.+ **tániṣṭha** B.S. **tánīyas** B. **tanú** V.+ **tanū́** V.+ **tanus** E. **tantí** V.+ **-tati** B.+ **tántu** V.+ **-tanitṛ** C. **tántra** V.+ **-tatnī̆** AV.B. **-tatnu** AV. **-tā** RV. **tā́na** V.+ **-tānaka** C. **-tānuka**? C. **-tāyitṛ** C. **tatanúṣṭi** RV. **tena**? C.

Compare √ **tāy.**

√ 2 tan, 'roar'.

Pres. [4.] tanyati RV.
Deriv.: tanyatá̄ RV. tanyatú V. tanyú RV. tanayitnú RV.
Appears to be an abbreviated form of √ stan.

√ tand, 'be weary'.

Pres. [1.] tandate RV[1]. (tandrat? RV[1].)
Deriv.: tandra V.+ tandri E.+ tandrī́ AV.+

√ tap, 'heat'.

Pres. [1.] tápati -te *etc.* V.+ — [4.] tápyati *etc.* B.+, -te *etc.* B.+
Perf. tatā́pa tepé *etc.* V.+ (tatápate RV.)
Aor. 1. tapāná SV.; átāpi V.B. — 3. atītapat E., -pe RV. (tītapāsi AV.) — 4. atāpsīt *etc.* V.B.S., atapthās? AV.
Fut. 1. tapsyáti *etc.* B.+ (atapsyat M.), -te *etc.* E.; tapiṣyati *etc.* E. — 2. taptā E.
Verb. taptá V.+, tapita C.; taptum E.+, táptos ÇB.; taptvā B.+; -tápya V.+
Sec. Conj.: *Pass.* tapyáte *etc.* V.+ — *Int.* tātapyate *etc.* E.+ [— *Desid.* titapsa-.] — *Caus.* tāpáyati *etc.* -te *etc.* AV.+ (tāpyate B.E.; tāpitā *fut.* E.)

Deriv.:	-tap RV.S.	tápu RV.	tápiṣṭha V.	-tāpin B.+
	tapa V.+	tápus V.	tapiṣṇu E.	-tāpya B.
	tapya E.	tápuṣi V.B.	tapīyas C.	tāpana E.+
	tápana V.+	tapti C.	tapyatú V.B.	-tāpitṛ? E.
	tapaná,-nī V.B.	taptavya E.	tāpa AV.+	tāpayitṛ C.
	tápas V.+	taptṛ E.	-tāpaka C.	tāpayiṣṇú RV.

√ tam, 'faint'.

Pres. [4.] tā́myati *etc.* B.+, -te *etc.* E.+
Perf. tatāma B.
Aor. [1. atā̆mi. —] 2. tamat *etc.* RV.B.S.
[*Fut.* tamiṣyati, tamitā.]
Verb. tāṁtá B.+; támitos B.S.
Sec. Conj.: *Caus.* tamáyati *etc.* B.S.

Deriv.:	tamaka C.	tamī C.	tāṁti C.	tāma C.
	tamana S.	támiṣīci V.	-tameru VS.	-tāmaka C.
	támas V.+	támisra V.+	tamrá RV.	tāmī S.
				tāmrá AV.+

√ tark, 'think'.

Sec. Conj.: *Caus.* tarkáyati -te *etc.* E.+ (tarkyate *etc.* E.+)

Deriv.:	tarka S.+	tarkaka E.	-tarkya B.+	tarkaṇīya E.
	tarkā E.	tarkin C.	tarkaṇa E.+	tarkuka? E.

Probably a denominative formation.

√ **tarj**, 'threaten'.

Pres. [1.] **tarjati** *etc.* E.+, **-te** E.
[*Perf. etc.* **tatarja; atarjīt; tarjiṣyati, tarjitā.**]
Verb. **tarjita** E.+; **-tarjya** E.
Sec. Conj.: Caus. **tarjayati** *etc.* E.+, **-te** E. (**tarjyate** *etc.* E.)
Deriv.: **tarjaka** C. **tarjana** E.+ **tarjanā** E.+

√ **tas**, *see* √ **taṅs.**

√ **tā**, *see* √ **tan.**

√ **tāy**, 'stretch'.

[*Pres.* 1. **tāyate.**]
Perf. [**tatāye**] **tāyāṁ cakre**? JB.
[*Aor. etc.* **atāyi, atāyiṣṭa; tāyiṣyate, tāyitā.**]
Sec. Conj.: Pass. **tāyyámāna** VS.

Very questionable forms. The JB. manuscript reads (iii. 177) **anusaṁtāyāyāṁ cakre.** Belongs probably in some way to √ **tan, tā.** The Bhāgavata-Purāna has once **tāyitā**(periph. fut.), which is given above under √ **tan.**

√ **tāv.**

Pres. [1.] **tā́vati** AV.

Probably a false reading.

√ **ti**, 'crush'.

Pres. [5.] **tinoti** C[1].

A single occurrence, and most probably a false reading.

√ **tij**, 'be sharp'.

Pres. [1.] **téjate** *etc.* RV.ÇB.
Perf.? **titigdhi** B.S.
Verb. **tiktá** V.+
Sec. Conj.: Int. **tétikte** *etc.* V.B. — *Desid.* **tī́tikṣate** *etc.* V.+, **-ti** *etc.* E.+ (**titikṣmahe** M.) — *Caus.* **tejayati** *etc.* E.+
Deriv.: **-tikti** RV. **tīkṣṇá** V.+ **téjana** V.+ **téjīyas** RV.C.
tigitá RV. **tegá**? VS. **téjas** V.+ **titikṣā** E.+
tigmá V.+ **teja** C. **téjiṣṭha** V.B.S. **titikṣú** AV.+

√ **tim**, 'be quiet'.

Pres. [4.] **timyant** C[1]. [**tīmyati.**]
[*Perf. etc.* **titema** *etc.*; **tetimya-.**]
Verb. **timita** R.
Deriv.: **timi**? E.+ **timira**? E.+

Apparently related with √ **tam**; the participle, with that of √ **stim.**

√ **tir**, *see* √ **tṛ**.

√ **til**.

Accepted by BR. in VS. xxiii. 24 **prátilāmi** (TS. TB. **prásulāmi**); but an unintelligible and probably false reading.

√ **tu**, 'be strong'.

Pres. [2.] **tavīti** RV. [**tāuti**.]
Perf. **tūtāva** RV. (**tūtos -ot** RV.)
Sec. Conj.: *Int.* **távītuat** RV.
Deriv.: **tavā-**? RV. **tavás** V. **távyas** RV. **tuví-** V.VS.
távya RV. **taviṣá** V. **tīvrá** V.+ **túvis-** V.B.
tavyà TS. **táviṣī** RV. **túmra**? RV. **tū́ya** V.
távas V.B.S. **távīyas** V. **turá** V.+ **tūtumá**? RV.

√ **tuc**, 'impel, generate'.

A root or root-form (see √ **tuj**) inferable from the following derivatives:
túc RV. **-túka**? RV. **toká** V.+ **tókman, -ma** V.+

√ **tuj**, 'urge, thrust'.

Pres. [7.] **tuñjánti tuñjáte** (3*p*.) *etc.* RV. — [1.] **túñjamāna** RV. — [6.] **tujánt tujete** RV. [— 1. **tojati**.]
Perf. **tūtujāná** (*and* **tū́tujāna**) **tutujyāt** RV. [**tutoja**.]
[*Aor. etc.* **atojīt**; **tojiṣyati, tojitā**.]
Verb. **tujáse** RV., **-túje** RV., **tujáye**? V.
Sec. Conj.: *Pass.* **tujyáte** *etc.* RV. — *Caus.* **tujáyant** *etc.* V.
Deriv.: **túj** V. **túji** RV. **túgra** RV. **tuñga**? E.+
tújya RV. **tuñjá** RV. **túgvan** RV. **tūtuji** RV.

This and the preceding are probably two forms of the same root. For the connection of meaning, compare the roots **su, sū**.

√ **tud**, 'push, thrust'.

Pres. [6.] **tudáti** *etc.* V.+, **-te** E. — [7?] **tundāná** AV., **tundate** RV. (— **tudāyáti** AV.)
Perf. **tutóda** V.+ [**tutude**.]
[*Aor. etc.* **atūtudat, atāutsīt atutta**; **totsyati -te, tottā**.]
Verb. **tunná** V.+; [**tuttvā**;] **-tudya** E.
Sec. Conj.: *Pass.* **tudyate** *etc.* E.+ — *Int.* **totudyate** S. [— *Desid.* **tututsa-**.] — *Caus.* **todayati** *etc.* E.+ (**todyate** E.+)
Deriv.: **-tud** S.E. **tunda**? C. **-todin** V.+ **todana** C.
-tuda AV.+ **todá** V.+ **todya** C. **tóttra** B.+

√ **tur**, *see* √ **tṛ**.

√ turv, tūrv, 'overcome'.

Pres. [1.] tū́rvati *etc.* RV.B.
Deriv.: turvá RV. turván RV. turvī́ti RV. tū́rvi RV. turváṇi RV.

A specialized form of √ tṛ, tur, to which the derivatives might in part with equal propriety be referred.

√ tul, 'lift, weigh'.

[*Pres.* 1. tolati.]
Sec. Conj.: Caus. tolayati *etc.* E.+ (tolyate C.); tulayati *etc.* E.+, -te *etc.* E.+
Deriv.: tula C. tulya S.+ tolaka C. tolana E.+ tulā́ B.+ tulana C. tolya C.

√ tuç, 'drip'.

Pres. [1.] toçate *etc.* V. (toçé RV.)
Sec. Conj.: Caus. toçaya RV.
Deriv.: toçá RV. -tóçana RV. toçás RV.

BR. refer two or three of the forms to a root 2 tuç = tuṣ.

√ tuṣ, 'be content'.

Pres. [4.] tuṣyati *etc.* S.+, -te C.
Perf. tutoṣa *etc.* E.+
[*Aor. etc.* atuṣat, atūtuṣat; tokṣyati, toṣṭā.]
Verb. tuṣṭa E.+; toṣṭum E.; -tuṣya C.
Sec. Conj.: [*Int.* totuṣ-. — *Desid.* tutukṣa-. —] *Caus.* toṣayati *etc.* JB.+ (toṣyate C.); tuṣáyantī RV.
Deriv.: tuṣṭi E.+ -toṣaka C. toṣaṇa E.+ toṣayitavya E. tūṣṇī́m? V.+ toṣin E.+ toṣaṇīya E.+ toṣayitṛ C. toṣa E.+ toṣya E. toṣṭavya C.

√ tūrv, *see* √ turv.

√ tṛ, tir, tur, 'pass'.

Pres. [1.] tárati *etc.* V.+, -te *etc.* V.+ — [6.] tiráti -te *etc.* V.B.S.; turáti -te *etc.* V.B. — [3.] titarti *etc.* RV.C. [tutorti.] — [8.] tarute RV¹. — [2?] turyā́ma RV. — [4.] tī́ryatī? AV.; tūrya RV¹. — táruṣema -ṣante -ṣanta RV.
Perf. tatāra V.+ (tatarúṣas RV.), terus E.+, tatare C.; titirus titirvā́ṅs RV.; tuturyā́t -yāma RV.
Aor. 1. atāri V.B. [tīryāt.] — 3. atītaras AV. — 4. atārṣīt *etc.* S.+ — 5. átārīt *etc.* V.B.S. (átārima RV.; tāriṣat *etc.* V.B.S.; tāriṣīmahi RV.)
Fut. 1. tariṣyati *etc.* S.+, -te *etc.* E.+ [tarīṣyati. — 2. taritā.]

Verb. **tīrṇá** v.+, **tūrtá** ÇB., **tūrṇa** s.+; **tartum** E.+, **taritum** E.+, **tarītum** E.+; **tīrtvā́** AV.U.; **-tīrya** E.+, **-tū́rya** RV.; **-tíram -tíre** RV.; **tarádhyāi** RV.; **tarīṣáṇi** RV.

Sec. Conj.: Pass. **tīryate**? E. — *Int.* **tartṛ-** RV., **táritṛ-** RV., **tártur-** RV. [**tātṛ-.**] — *Desid.* **titīrṣati** *etc.* B.+, **-te** *etc.* E., **tū́tūrṣati** RV. [**titarĭṣa-.**] — *Caus.* **tāráyati** *etc.* AV.+, **-te** *etc.* s.+ (**tāryate** *etc.* E.+); **turáyant** v., **-yante** RV.

Deriv.:

tára v.+	**táras** v.+	**tartavya** E.	**tārá** AV.+
tarín? AV.	**tarás** SV.	**taritavya** s.+	**tāraka** E.+
tárya RV.	**tárīyas** RV.	**-tárītu**? V.B.	**tārin** RV.E.+
tarĭ E.+	**táru**? RV.	**-tarītṛ** v.	**tāryà** AV.E.+
táraṇa v.+	**táruṇa**? v.+	**tarutṛ** v.	**tāraṇa** E.+
taraṇīya E.+	**tárus** RV.	**tárutra** RV.	**-tāraṇīya** C.
taráṇi v.+	**táruṣa** v.	**-taritra**? B.	**-tārayitṛ** B.
-taratha? C.	**tárūṣas** RV.	**-tárman** RV.	
-tira AV.B.	**tirás**? v.+	**tíra** B.+	**titīrṣā** C.
		tīrthá v.+	**titīrṣu** E.+
túr RV.B.	**turas-** RV.	**-tūrti** V.B.	**táturi** V.B.S.
túra RV.	**turí** RV.	**tū́rṇi** V.B.	**-tartura** RV.
turáṇa RV.	**turyā́** TS.	**-tū́rya** V.B.S.	**tuturváṇi** RV.
		toraṇa? E.+	

Compare roots **tur** (oftener given as a separate root), **turv**, **tvar**, and **trā**.

√ tṛd, 'split, bore'.

Pres. [7.] **tṛṇátti** *etc.* V.B.U., **tṛntte** ÇB. (**atṛṇam** KBU.) [— 1. **tardati.**]

Perf. **tatárda** *etc.* V.C. (**tatárditha** RV.), **tatṛdāná** RV.

Aor. 1. **tárdas** RV., **tṛdyus** s. [— 3. **atatardat, atītṛdat.** — 5. **atardīt.**]

[*Fut.* **tardiṣyati -te, tartsyati -te; tarditā.**]

Verb. **tṛṇṇá** B.S.U.; **-tṛ́dya** B.S.; **-tṛ́das** v.

Sec. Conj.: [*Int.* **tarītṛd-.** —] *Desid.* **títṛtsati** *etc.* V.B. [**-te; titardiṣati -te.**] — *Caus.* **tardayati** s.

Deriv.:

tardá AV.+	**-tardi**? E.	**-tṛd** RV.	**tṛdilá** RV.
tradá RV.	**tárdman** AV.B.S.	**-tṛtti** B.	**tṛ́tsu**? RV.
tardana v.+		**tṛ́ṇman**? AV.	

√ tṛp, 'be pleased'.

Pres. [4.] **tṛ́pyati** *etc.* AV.+, **-te** *etc.* E.+ — [5.] **tṛpṇoti** *etc.* V.B. (**tṛpnoti** *etc.* C.) — [6.] **tṛmpáti** *etc.* V.B.S. — [1.] **tarpanti** E.

Perf. **tatarpa** *etc.* E. (**tātṛpus -pāṇá** v.)

Aor. 1. **tṛpyāsma** TS. — 2. **átṛpat** *etc.* V.B. (**tṛpánt** RV.) — 3. **atītṛpat** *etc.* **-panta** AV.+ [**atatarpat.** — 4. **atārpsīt, atrāpsīt.** — 5. **atarpīt.**]

Fut. 1. **atrapsyat** B. [**tarpsyati, tarpiṣyati.** — 2. **tarpitā, tarptā, traptā.**]

Verb. **tṛptá** AV.+.

Sec. Conj.: [*Int.* tarītṛp-. —] *Desid.* títṛpsati v. [titarpiṣa-.] — *Caus.* tarpáyati *etc.* v.+, -te *etc.* v.+ (tarpyate *etc.* e.; titarpayiṣati b.s.)

Deriv.:	-tarpaka c.	tárpaṇa av.+	-tṛpa rv.c.	tṛprá? v.b.s.
	-tarpya e.	tarpaṇīya u.	tṛpála rv.	-tṛpsu ta.
	tálpa? av.+	-tṛp rv.	tṛ́pti v.b.	tā́tṛpi rv
			tṛptí rv.	tarpayitavyà b.

Some accept a √ 2 tṛp 'steal' for asutṛ́p v.c. and paçutṛ́p rv.

√ tṛṣ, 'be thirsty'.

Pres. [4.] tṛ́ṣyati *etc.* v.b.
Perf. tātṛṣús -ṣāṇá tatṛṣāṇá rv.
Aor. 2. tṛṣat *etc.* av.b., tṛṣāṇá rv. — 3. atītṛṣāma *etc.* v.b.
[*Fut.* tarṣiṣyati, tarṣitā.]
Verb. tṛṣitá v.+, tṛṣṭá? *adj.* v. [tṛṣitvā, tarṣitvā.]
Sec. Conj.: *Caus.* tarṣáyati *etc.* b. (tarṣita e.+)

Deriv.:	tarṣa e.+	tarṣaṇa c.	tṛṣ e.+	tṛṣú rv.
	tarṣyā́- rv.	tarṣula e.	tṛṣā c.	tṛ́ṣṇā v.+
			tṛṣyā́ v.	tṛṣṇáj rv.

√ tṛh, 'crush'.

Pres. [7.] tṛṇeḍhi tṛṇéḍhu tṛṅhanti *etc.* v.b. [tṛṇehmi. — 6. tṛhati, tṛṅhati.]
Perf. tatarha av.
Aor. [1. tṛhyāt; atarhi. —] 2. atṛham av. [— 3. atatarhat, atītṛhat. — 5. atarhīt. — 7. atṛkṣat.]
[*Fut.* tarhiṣyati, tarkṣyati; tarhitā, tarḍhā.]
Verb. tṛḍhá rv.; tṛḍhvā́ av. [tarhitvā]; -tárham av.
Sec. Conj.: *Pass.* tṛhyáte *etc.* av. [— *Int.* tarītṛh-. — *Desid.* titarhiṣa-, titṛkṣa-. — *Caus.* tarhaya-.]
Deriv. tárhaṇa v.

√ tyaj, 'forsake'.

Pres. [1.] tyajati *etc.* s.+, -te *etc.* e.+
Perf. tatyāja tatyaje *etc.* e.+ (tityā́ja rv., tityagdhi? k.)
Aor. [1. tyajyāt; atyāji. — 3. atityajat. —] 4. atyākṣīt *etc.* e.+
Fut. 1. tyakṣyati -te *etc.* e., tyajiṣyati -te *etc.* e.+ [— 2. tyaktā.]
Verb. tyaktá b.+, tyajita c.; tyaktu- e.; tyaktvā e.+; -tyájya b.+
Sec. Conj.: *Pass.* tyajyate *etc.* e.+ [— *Int.* tātyaj-.] — *Desid.* tityakṣa- c. — *Caus.* tyājayati *etc.* e.+ (tyājyate c.)

Deriv.:	-tyaj v.+	tyajana avp.	tyaktavya e.+	tyājaka c.
	-tyaja e.+	tyájas rv.	tyaktṛ e.+	tyājya e.+
	tyajya e.+	tyajás v.	tyāgá v.+	-tyājana c.
			tyāgin e.+	

√ trap, 'be abashed'.

Pres. [1.] **trapate** *etc.* E.+, **-ti** *etc.* E.
[*Perf. etc.* **trepe; atrapta, atrapiṣṭa; trapsyate trapiṣyate, traptā trapitā.**]
Sec. Conj.: [*Int.* **tātrap-.** — *Desid.* **titrapsa-, titrapiṣa-.** —] *Caus.* **trapayati** *etc.* C. [**trāpayati.**]
Deriv.: **tṛprá**? V.B.S. **trapa** E.+ **trapā** E.+ **-trapaṇa** C. **-trapaṇīya** C. **trápu**? AV.+

√ tras, 'be terrified'.

Pres. [1.] **trásati** *etc.* V.+, **-te** *etc.* E. — [4.] **trasyati** *etc.* E.+, **-te** *etc.* C.
Perf. **tatrāsa tatrasus** *etc.* E.+, **tresus** E.+ (**treṣus** M[1].), **tatrasire** E.
Aor. 3. **atitrasan** AV. — 5. **trāsīs** ÇB. [**atrasīt.**]
Fut. 1. **trasiṣyati** E. [— 2. **trasitā.**]
Verb. **trastá** B.+; **-trasas** K.
Sec. Conj.: *Int.* **tātrasyate** JB. [— *Desid.* **titrasiṣa-.**] — *Caus.* **trāsayati** *etc.* AV.+, **-te** *etc.* E. (**trāsyate** E.)
Deriv.: **trasa** V.+ **trasana** S. **trasara** C. **trasnu** B.+ **trāsa** AV.+ **trāsaka** C. **trāsin** E. **trāsana** E.+ **trāsanīya** C. **-trāsuka** B.

√ trā, 'rescue'.

Pres. [4.] **trā́yate** *etc.* V.+ — [2.] **trā́sva trā́dhvam** RV., **trāti trāhi** *etc.* E.+
Perf. **tatré** V.B.
Aor. 4. **atrāsmahi** ÇB. (**atrāsatām** ÇB., **trāsate trā́sāthe -sīthām** RV.)
Fut. 1. **trāsyate** *etc.* B.+, **-ti** E. [— 2. **trātā.**]
Verb. **trāta** B.+ [**trāṇa**]; **trātum** E.+; **trātvā** C.
Sec. Conj.: *Pass.* **trāyate** *etc.* C.
Deriv.: **trā́** V.+ **-tra** V.+ **trāṇa** U.+ **trātavya** E.+ **trātṛ́** V.+ **trātra** RV.C. **trā́man** V.+ **-trā́van**? AV. **trayayā́yya** RV.

A secondary root, from √ tṛ.

√ truṭ, 'come to pieces'.

Pres. [6.] **truṭati** *etc.* C. — [4.] **truṭyati** *etc.* C. (**truḍyeyus** C.)
Perf. **tutroṭa** C.
Verb. **truṭita** C.
Sec. Conj.: *Caus.* **troṭayati** *etc.* C.
Deriv.: **truṭi** E.+ **troṭaka** C.

Probably a denominative formation from **truṭi.**

√ **tvakṣ**, 'fashion'.

Pres. [2.] **tvakṣāṇá** RV[1]. [— 1. **tvakṣati.**]
[*Perf. etc.* **tatvakṣa; atvakṣīt; tvakṣiṣyati, tvakṣitā, tvaṣṭā.**]
Deriv.: **-tvákṣaṇa** RV. **tvákṣas** RV. **tvákṣīyas** RV. **tvaṣṭi** C. **tváṣṭṛ** V.+

Compare √ **takṣ.**

√ **tvañg**, 'leap'.

Pres. [1.] **tvañgati** *etc.* C.
Late and probably artificial.

√ **tvac**, 'cover'.

Such a root is assumed by some for **tvác** V.+ 'skin', and **ātúc** RV. 'dimness'.

√ **tvar**, 'hasten'.

Pres. [1.] **tvárate** *etc.* B.+, **-ti** *etc.* E.+
Perf. **tatvare** E.+
Aor. 3. **atitvarat** E. [**atatvarat.** — 5. **atvariṣṭa.**]
[*Fut.* **tvariṣyate, tvaritā.**]
Verb. **tvarita** E.+
Sec. Conj.: [*Int.* **tātvarya-, totur-.** — *Desid.* **titvariṣa-.** —] *Caus.* **tvaráyati** *etc.* AV.+, **-te** *etc.* E. (**tvaryate** E.); **tvāraya-** C.
Deriv.: **tvara** C. **tvarā** S.+ **tvaraṇá** AV. **tvaraṇīya** E.
A secondary root-form from √ **tṛ, tur,** under which are here placed the derivatives with **tūr-** (**tūrta, tūrti, tūrṇa**).

√ **tviṣ**, 'be stirred up'.

Pres. [2.] **atviṣus** RV. — [6.] **atviṣanta** RV. — [4.] **tviṣyant** C[1]. [— 1. **tveṣati -te.**]
Perf. **titviṣé** *etc.* RV. (**átitviṣanta** RV.) [**titviṣus.**]
[*Aor. etc.* **atitviṣat, atvikṣat -kṣata; tvekṣyati -te, tveṣṭā.**]
Verb. **tviṣitá** RV.; **tviṣé** RV.
[*Sec. Conj.*: **tetviṣ-; titvikṣa-; tveṣaya-.**]
Deriv.: **tvíṣ** V.+ **tvíṣi** V.B.S. **tveṣín** RV. **tveṣátha** RV. **tviṣā** C. **tveṣá** V.B. **tveṣyà** RV. **tveṣás** RV.

√ **tsar**, 'approach stealthily'.

Pres. [1.] **tsárati** *etc.* V.B.S.
Perf. **tatsāra** RV.
Aor. 4. **atsār** RV. — 5. **atsāriṣam** ÇB.
[*Fut.* **tsariṣyati, tsaritā.**]
Verb. **-tsárya** ÇB.
Deriv.: **tsarā** C. **tsáru** V.+ **-tsāra** V.+ **tsārín** V.B.

√ thurv ?

Pres. [1.] **thūrvant** MS.

Probably a false reading; the edition has **tūrvant**, with one of the manuscripts (and the parallel texts).

√ daṅç, daç, 'bite'.

Pres. [1.] **dáçati** *etc.* V.+, **-te** *etc.* E.+ — **daṅçati** C[1].
Perf. **dadaṅçus** E. (**dadaçvā́ṅs** RV.)
[*Aor.* **daçyāt, adadaṅçat, adāṅkṣīt.**]
Fut. 1. **daçiṣyati** E. [**daṅkṣyati.** — 2. **daṅṣṭā.**]
Verb. **daṣṭá** AV.+; **daṅṣṭvā** B.; **-daçya** E.
Sec. Conj.: Pass. **daçyate** *etc.* E. — *Int.* **dándaçāna** RV. (**dandaçayitvā** C.)
[— *Desid.* **didaṅkṣa-.**] — *Caus.* **daṅçayati** *etc.* S.+ (**daṅçita** *adj.* E.+)

Deriv.:

daṅça AV.+	**daṅçana** E.+	**dáṅṣṭrā̆** V.+	**daçā**? B.+
daṅçaka C.	**dáṅçuka** B.	**dáṅçman** AV.S.	**daçana** E.+
-daṅçin AV.	**daṅṣṭṛ́** AV.	**daṅkṣṇú** B.	

√ daṅs, 'be wondrous'.

Sec. Conj.: Caus. **daṅsáyas** RV[1].

Deriv.:

-dáṅsa RV.	**dáṅsas** V.B.	**dáṅsu** RV.	**dasmá** V.
daṅsánā̆ RV.S.	**dáṅsiṣṭha** RV.	**dasmánt** RV.	**dasrá** V.+

√ dakṣ, 'be able'.

Pres. [1.] **dákṣate** *etc.* V.B., **-ti** RV.
Perf. **dadakṣe** B.
Aor. 3. **adadakṣat** B. [— 5. **adakṣiṣṭa.**]
Fut. 1. **dakṣiṣyate** B. [— 2. **dakṣitā.**]
Sec. Conj.: Caus. **dakṣayati** *etc.* B.

Deriv.: **dákṣa** V.+ — **dákṣas** V. — **dakṣā́yya** RV. — **dákṣiṇa** V.+

√ dagh, 'reach to'.

Pres. [5.] **daghnuyāt** B.
Aor. 1. **dhak dhaktam daghma daghyās** RV. — 2? **daghat** B.
Fut. 1. **daghiṣyante** JUB.
Verb. **-dághas** B., **-dághos** ÇB.

Deriv.: **-dagh** S. — **-daghna** V.+ — **-daghvan** V.B.

√ dad, *see* √ 1 dā.

√ dadh, *see* √ 1 dhā.

√ dan, 'straighten' (?).

Pres. **dán dánas** RV.

Very doubtful forms.

√ dabh, dambh, 'harm'.

Pres. [1.] **dábhati** *etc.* V.B. — [5.] **dabhnoti** *etc.* V.B.
Perf. **dadā́bha debhus** RV.; **dadámbha** AV. (**dadabhanta** RV.)
Aor. 1. **dabhús** RV. [— 3. **adadambhat.** — 5. **adambhīt.**]
[*Fut.* **dambhiṣyati, dambhitā.**]
Verb. **dabdhá** V.; **dabdhum** B.; [**dambhitvā, dabdhvā;**] **-dábhe** RV.
Sec. Conj.: Pass. **dabhyate** RV. [— *Int.* **dādambh-, dādabh-.**] — *Desid.* **dípsati** *etc.* V.B.; **dhīpsati** JB. [**dhipsa-, didambhiṣa-.**] — *Caus.* **dambháyati** *etc.* V.B.

Deriv.:	**dábha** V.	**dabdhi** B.S.	**dābhya** V.+	**dambhin** E.+
	dábhya RV.	**-dabhna**? AV.	**dambha** E.+	**-dámbhana** V.+
	dabhíti RV.	**dabhrá** V.+	**dambhaka** C.	**dipsú** V.
		dābha V.B.		

√ dam, 'control'.

Pres. [4.] **dā́myati** ÇB.
[*Aor.* **adamīt.**]
Verb. **dāṁtá** B.+; [**dāṁtvā,**] **damitvā** E.; **-damya** E.?
Sec. Conj.: Caus. **damáyati** *etc.* V.+

Deriv.:	**dám** V.+	**damaka** E.+	**-damatra** S.+	**damitṛ́** RV.
	dáma V.+	**damin** E.	**damana** V.+	**damayitṛ** E
	damá B.	**-damya** E.		

√ day, 'share'.

Pres. [1.] **dáyate** *etc.* V.+, **dayāmasi** AV.
Perf. **dayām āsa** C.
[*Aor. etc.* **adayiṣṭa; dayiṣyate, dayitā.**]
Verb. **dayita** E.+
Sec. Conj.: [*Int.* **dandayya-, dādayya-.** —] *Caus.* **dayayet** C.
Deriv.: **dayā́** V.+ **dayitnu** S.

A secondary form of √ 2 dā 'divide', from which it is hardly worth separating.

√ daridrā, *see* √ 1 drā.

√ dal, 'burst'.

Pres. [1.] **dalati** *etc.* E.+
[*Perf.* **dadāla.**]
Aor. 5. **adalīt** C. [**adālīt.**]
Fut. 1. **daliṣyati -te** *etc.* C. (**adaliṣyat** C.)
Verb. **dalita** E.+
Sec. Conj.: Caus. **dalayati** *etc.* C.; **dālayati** *etc.* E.+ (**dalyate** C., **dālyate** C.)

Deriv.: dala B.+ -dāla B.+ dālana C. dāli C.
dalana C. -dālaka B.+ -dālya C. dalayitṛ C.

A secondary root-form from √ 1 dṛ.

√ das, dās, 'waste'.

Pres. [4.] dásyati *etc.* V.B.S. — [1.] dā́sati *etc.* V.B.S.
Perf. dadasvā́ṅs RV. [dadāsa.]
Aor. 2. dasat *etc.* V.B.S. (dásamāna? RV.) — 5. dāsīt RV.
[*Fut.* dasiṣyati, dasitā; dāsiṣyati, dāsitā.]
Verb. dasta B.+
Sec. Conj.: *Caus.* dasaye TS., -yanta RV.; dāsayati *etc.* AV.B.
Deriv.: dása RV. -dasvant AV. dāsá V.+ dāsanu B.
-dasya V.S. dásyu V.+ -dāsin S.+ -dāsuka B.

Usually classed as two roots, das and dās; dā́sati *etc.* only with abhi.

√ dah, 'burn

Pres. [1.] dáhati *etc.* V.+, -te *etc.* E.+ — [4.] dahyati E. — [2.] dhákṣi RV.
Perf. dadā́ha *etc.* B.+, dehe C.
Aor. 1. dahyāt M.? — 3. adīdahat C. — 4. adhākṣīt *etc.* V.+ (adhāk V.B.S., dhákṣant dákṣant RV.)
Fut. 1. dhakṣyáti *etc.* V.+, -te *etc.* S.+ (dhakṣyet adhakṣyam M.); dahiṣyati E.+ [— 2. dagdhā.]
Verb. dagdhá V.+; dágdhum B.+, -dhos B.; dagdhvā́ B.+; -dáhya B.+; -dáhas B.; -dāham C.
Sec. Conj.: *Pass.* dahyáte *etc.* AV.+, -́ti *etc.* S.+ — *Int.* dandahīti *etc.* C., dandahyate *etc.* C. — *Desid.* didhakṣati *etc.* E.+, -te *etc.* E.; dhíkṣate ÇB. — *Caus.* dāhayati *etc.* E.+ (dāhyate U.)
Deriv.: dah V.S. dakṣí RV. -dāgha AV. dāhana E.
dahati E. dákṣu RV. dāha AV.+ dā́huka B.S.
dáhana AV.+ dhákṣu RV. dāhaka C. didhakṣā E.+
-dagdhavya E. dakṣús RV. dāhin S.+ didhakṣu E.+
dagdhṛ V.+ dāhya E.+

√ 1 dā, dad, 'give'.

Pres. [3.] dádāti dátte *etc.* V.+ (dehí V.+, daddhí V.) — [1.] dádati -te *etc.* V.+ (dadīyam U., dadāyant U.) — [4.] dāyamāna M. — [2.] dā́ti dātu RV.; dadmi E.+
Perf. dadāú dadé *etc.* V.+ (dadātha dadrire RV.; dadivā́ṅs dadāvā́ṅs AV., dadvā́ṅs RV.) [dadade.]
Aor. 1. ádāt *etc.* V.+, deyām RV.; adi MS., adithās adita adimahi B., dīṣva B.; dāyi V.B. [adādi.] — 2. ádat *etc.* V.B. — [3. adīdadat. —] 4. adiṣi adiṣata AV.B.C. (dāsat dā́sathas RV.; deṣam deṣma B.S.) [dāsīṣṭa.] — 5. adadiṣṭa SV.

Fut. 1. dāsyáti *etc.* AV.+ (adāsyat M.), -te *etc.* B.+; dadiṣye K. — 2. dātā́ *etc.* B.E. [daditā.]

Verb. -dāta RV., dattá V.+, -tta V.+, -dita B.+ [dadita]; dā́tum V.+, -tave V., -tavāí RV., -tos V.B.; dattvā́ AV.+, -tvā́ya RV.; -dā́ya V.+, -dádya AV.; -dā́m B., -dāí RV.; dāváne RV.; -dā́yam B.+

Sec. Conj.: Pass. dīyáte *etc.* V.+; dadyámāna RV. — [*Int.* dādā-, dedīya-, dādad-.] — *Desid.* dítsati *etc.* V.+, -te *etc.* C.; dídāsant RV., didāsitha B.S. [didadiṣa-.] — *Caus.* dāpayati *etc.* AV.+ [adīdapat.]

Deriv.:	dā́, -da V.+	dāyá V.+	-di JB.+	dadí V.
	dā́ti V.	dāyaka E.+	díya RV.	ditsā C.
	-tti V.B.	dāyin AV.+	déṣṭha RV.	ditsú V.+
	dātavya B.+	-dā́van V.S.	deṣṇá V.+	diditsu M.
	dātṛ V.+	dāván RV.	-dád AV.	dāpin C.
	dātrá? V.B.	dā́nu? V.	-dada C.	-dāpya S.C.
	dā́na V.+	-déya *n.* V.B.	datti C.	-dāpana S.
	dāná? RV.	déya *gdve.* V.+	dátra? V.	dāpanīya C.
	dā́man RV.E.	-dās? V.+	dāda M.	dāpayitavya C.
	dāmán RV.	-das V.B.	daditṛ́ VS.	-dāpayitṛ B.

√ 2 dā, 'divide, share'.

Pres. [1.] dā́ti *etc.* V.B.S. — [6?] dyáti *etc.* AV.B.S.

Perf. dadire B.

Aor. 1. [adāt, deyāt;] adimahi B. (adīm- VS.K.). — 4. diṣīya RV.

Fut. 1. dāsyati S. [— 2. dātā.]

Verb. diná V.B., dita C., [dāta,] -tta B.+; -dāya B.+, -ditya? C.

Sec. Conj.: Pass. dīyate *etc.* AV.+ — [*Int.* dādā-, dedi-. — *Desid.* ditsa-, didāsa-, dīdāṅsa-. —] *Caus.* dāpayīta S.

Deriv.:	-tti B.	dā́tṛ RV.C.	-dā́na AV.B.S.	dāyá? RV.
	dā́tu RV.	dā́tra RV.	-dānīya B.S.	díti? RV.
	-dātavya C.	dāná? RV.	dā́nu V.	-deya C.

A form of this root is **day**, given above separately.

√ 3 dā, di, 'bind'.

Pres. [6?] dyati *etc.* V.B. — [2?] dīṣva VS.

Aor. 5. adiṣi AV.?

Verb. dita V.+; -dāya S.+

Deriv.:	-dātṛ RV.C.	dā́man V.+	-dāya C.	díti? V.+
	-dā́na V.+	dāmán RV.	-di AV.	dīná? V.+

Not recognized by the native grammarians as separate from the preceding, and of somewhat doubtful character.

√ 4 dā, 'clear'.

Pres. [4?] dāyamāna C[1].

[*Perf. etc.* dadāu; dāyāt, adāsīt; dāsyati, dātā.]

Verb. **dāta** TA.E.+
[*Sec. Conj.:* **dāya-; dādā-; didāsa-; dāpaya-.**]
Deriv. **-dāna** C.

Only with **ava**; certainly no separate root, and probably a specialization of meaning of the particle of √ 2 **dā.**

√ dāç, 'make offering'.

Pres. [1.] **dā́çati** *etc.* V. — [2.] **dāṣṭi** RV. — [5.] **dāçnóti** RV.
Perf. **dadā́ça** *etc.* V. (**dádāçati -ças -çat** RV.; **dadāçvā́ṅs** RV.B., **dāçvā́ṅs** V., **dāçivā́ṅs** SV.)
[*Aor. etc.* **adāçīt; dāçiṣyati, dāçitā.**]
Sec. Conj.: [*Int.* **dādāç-.** — *Desid.* **didāçiṣa-.** —] *Caus.* **adāçayat** ÇB[1].
Deriv.: **dā́ç** V. **-dā́ça** AV.+ **dāçú** V. **dā́çuri** V.

√ dās, *see* √ das.

√ div, 'play', *see* √ 1 dīv.

No root √ **div** 'shine' exists as such in the language, except so far as it may be inferable from the noun **dív** or **dyú** V.+, **divít** RV., and the (in that case, secondary) root **dyut.** With all these the root **dīv** 'play' has nothing to do.

√ diç, 'point'.

Pres. [6.] **diçáti** *etc.* V.+, **-te** *etc.* RV.B.+ — [3.] (*Perf.?*) **dideçati dideṣṭu** *etc.* **didiṣṭa** RV. — [4.] **diçyati** M[1].
Perf. **didéça** *etc.* AV.+, **didiçe** C.
Aor. [3. **adīdiçat.** —] 4. **adikṣi ádiṣṭa** RV. — 7. **adikṣat** ÇB.C.
Fut. 1. **dekṣyati** *etc.* S.+, **-te** C. [— 2. **deṣṭā.**]
Verb. **diṣṭá** V.+; **deṣṭum** E.+; **-díçya** B.+; **-díçe** RV.
Sec. Conj.: *Pass.* **diçyate** *etc.* E.+ — *Int.* **dédiçat** *etc.* **dédiṣṭe** *etc.* RV., **dediçyate** AV.VS. — *Desid.* **didikṣati** C. — *Caus.* **deçayati** *etc.* B.+, **-te** C.
Deriv.: **díç** V.+ **deçaka** C. **-deçana** B.+ **deṣṭṛ** V.+
diṣṭi V.+ **deçin** S.+ **deçanā** C. **deṣṭrá** RV.
deçá AV.+ **deçya** AV.+ **deṣṭavya** E.+ **-didikṣā** C.
-didikṣu C.

√ dih, 'smear'.

Pres. [2.] **degdhi dihanti ádihan** *etc.* V.+ (**déhat** RV.) [**digdhe.**]
Perf. **didihe** B. [**dideha.**]
Aor. [1. **adehi.** — 3. **adīdihat.** — 4. **adigdha.** —] 7. **adhikṣus** JB. [**adhikṣat -ṣata.**]
[*Fut.* **dhekṣyati -te; degdhā.**]
Verb. **digdhá** AV.+; **-dihya** S.+

Sec. Conj.: Pass. dihyate *etc.* c. — [*Int.* dedih-. — *Desid.* didhikṣa-. —]
Caus. dehayati -te E.+

Deriv.: -dih V.Ś. -degha B. dehī́ RV. -dehya C.
deha B.+ dehikā C. dehalī S.+

√ 1 dī, 'fly'.

Pres. [4.] dī́yati *etc.* RV., dī́yase SV.
Sec. Conj.: Int. dédīyitavā́í ÇB.

Represented later by √ ḍī. From it may possibly come didyú V.B.

√ 2 dī, dīdī, 'shine'.

Pres. dīdyati (3*p.*) *etc.* ádīdet *etc.* dīdye *etc.* V.B.S. (dī́dayat RV., dīdāyat dīdayante AV., dīdihí V.B.S., didīhí RV.; dīdyāsam B.S.)
Perf. dīdā́ya V.B.S. (dīdaya ÇB.S., dīdétha dīdiyus RV.; dīdivā́ṅs V.B.; dīdáyasi *etc.* dīdáyat *etc.* V.B.; dīdidā́ya? AÇS.; dīdidāsi dīdyasva S.

Deriv.: -dīti RV. -dīditi RV. dī́di- RV. dī́divi RV. dīdhiti S.+

Compare √ dīp. Some confusion of forms is made between dīdī and dīdhī.

√ dīkṣ, 'be consecrated'.

Pres. [1.] dīkṣate *etc.* B.+
Perf. didīkṣé *etc.* B., -ṣus PB.C.
Aor. 3. adidīkṣas B. — 5. adīkṣiṣṭa *etc.* B.
Fut. 1. dīkṣiṣyáte *etc.* B.+ [— 2. dīkṣitā.]
Verb. dīkṣitá AV.+; dīkṣitvā́ B.U.; -dīkṣya S.
Sec. Conj.: Desid. didīkṣiṣate *etc.* B. — *Caus.* dīkṣayati *etc.* B.+, -te E. (dīkṣāpaya E.)

Deriv.: dīkṣā́ AV.+ dīkṣaka C. (*n. pr.*) dīkṣaṇa S.+ dīkṣayitṛ B.

BR. suggest a derivation from √ dakṣ.

√ dīdhī, *see* √ dhī.

√ dīp, 'shine'.

Pres. [4.] dī́pyate *etc.* AV.+, -ti *etc.* E.+
Perf. didīpe C.
Aor. [1. adīpi. —] 3. adidīpat *etc.* RV.C.; adīdipat *etc.* B.E. [— 5. adīpiṣṭa.]
[*Fut.* dīpiṣyate, dīpitā.]
Verb. dīpta U.+
Sec. Conj.: Int. dedīpyate *etc.* E.+ (-yantīm E.) — [*Desid.* didīpiṣa-. —]
Caus. dīpáyati *etc.* V.+, -te *etc.* S.E. (dīpyáte TB.E.)

Deriv.: dīpa U.S.+ dīpaka E.+ dīpana S.+ dī́pti B.+
dīpin C. dīpra C.

Probably related with √ 2 dī.

√ 1 dīv, 'play'.

Pres. [4.] **dī́vyati** *etc.* V.+. **-te** *etc.* B.+ (**divyati** *etc.* M.?)
Perf. **didéva** AV.
Aor. [3. **adīdivat.** —] 5. **adevīt** *etc.* E.
Fut. 1. **deviṣyati** *etc.* E.+ (**adeviṣyat** M.) [— 2. **devitā.**]
Verb. **dyūtá** AV.+ [**dyūna**]; **devitum** E.+; [**devitvā, dyūtvā**;] **-dī́vya** RV.
Sec. Conj.: [*Int.* **dedīv-.** — *Desid.* **didevisa-, dudyūṣa-; dudyūṣaya-.** —]
Caus. **devayati** *etc.* C.
Deriv.: **dī́v, dyū́** V. **dīvitṛ**? **devin** AV.+ **devitṛ** E.+
-dī́van V. **-deva** B. **devitavya** E. **-dyūtyà** RV.
dīvana C. **dévana** V.+

Proper form, **dīū**; and it has nothing to do with the so-called root **div** 'shine', which is **diu.**

√ 2 dīv (dev), 'lament'.

Pres. [1.] **devati** E.+ [**-te.**]
[*Perf. etc.* **dideva; adidevat, adeviṣṭa; deviṣyate, devitā.**]
Verb. **dyūna** B.+; **devitum** E.
Sec. Conj.: *Caus.* **devayati** *etc.* E.+, **-te** E.+
Deriv.: **-deva** E. **-devaka** C. **-devin** E. **-devana** C.

Only with **pari** (unless in **ādyūna**); hence perhaps a peculiar specialization of meaning of √ 1 **dīv** (**paridyūna** 'played out'?). At any rate, rather **dīv** than **div**, on account of the long **ū** in **dyūna.**

√ du, dū, 'burn'.

Pres. [5.] **dunóti** *etc.* AV.+ — **dunvasva** M.
[*Perf. etc.* **dudāva; dūyāt, adāuṣīt; doṣyati, dotā.**]
Verb. **dūná** AV.+, **duta** AA.? C[1].
Sec. Conj.: *Pass.* **dūyate** *etc.* U.S.+, **-ti** *etc.* E.+ — [*Int.* **dodu-.** — *Desid.* **dudūṣa-.** —] *Caus.* **dāvayati** C.
Deriv.: **dava** C. **davathu** C. **dāvá** AV.+ **dūyana** C.
-davyà B.S. **-dāvyà** AV.B. **doman** AV.

For the form **daviṣāṇi** RV., BR. assume a √ 2 **du** = 1 **dīv** 'play'.

√ dudh, 'stir up'.

Pres. **dódhat** V.
Verb. **dúdhita** RV.
Deriv.: **dúdhi** RV. **dudhrá** RV. **dodhaka**? C.

Probably a reduplicated form of √ **dhū.**

√ dul, 'raise'.

Sec. Conj.: *Caus.* **dolayati** *etc.* C.
Deriv.: **dulā́**? TS. **dola** E.+

Doubtless another form of √ **tul**; as verb, denominative of **dola.**

√ duṣ, 'spoil'.

Pres. [4.] **duṣyati** *etc.* B.+, **-te** *etc.* E.+ (**dūṣyant** C[1].)
[*Perf.* **dudoṣa.**]
Aor. 2. **duṣat** B. — 3. **adūduṣat** *etc.* V. — 5. **doṣiṣṭam** ÇB.
[*Fut.* **dokṣyati, doṣṭā.**]
Verb. **duṣṭa** S.+
Sec. Conj.: [*Int.* **doduṣ-.** — *Desid.* **dudukṣa-.** —] *Caus.* **dūṣayati** *etc.* V.+, **-te** *etc.* E.+ (**dūṣyate** *etc.* E.+) [**doṣayati.**]
Deriv.: **dus-** V.+ **dūṣin** E.+ **doṣa** U.S.+ **doṣya** MS.
dúṣṭi AV.C. **dūṣya** E.+ **doṣā́** V.+ **doṣás** AV.
dūṣa E.+ **dū́ṣaṇa** AV.+ **doṣin** C. **-dūṣayitṛ** C.
dūṣaka E.+ **dū́ṣi** AV.

√ duh, 'milk, derive'.

Pres. [2.] **dógdhi duhánti** *etc.* V.+, **dugdhé duháte** *etc.* V.+ (**duhé** 3*s.* V.B., **duhaté** RV., **duhrate -hré** V.B.; **dúhāna** V., **duhāná dúghāna** RV.; **duhā́m** 3*s.* V.B., **duhrā́m duhratām** 3*p.* AV., **dhuṅgdhvam** AÇS.; **dohat dóhate** *etc.* RV.; **duhīyát -yán** RV.; **duhús** RV., **áduhan** B., **-hran** AV.B.) — [6.] **duhet** *etc.* E.+, **aduhat** V.B.E.+ — [4.] **duhyati** *etc.* C., **-te** M.
Perf. **dudóha duduhé** *etc.* V.+ (**dudóhitha** V.+, **duduhré** V.B., **-hrire** V.; **dudūhus** C.)
Aor. [1. **adohi.** —] 3. **adūduhat** *etc.* C. — 4. [**adugdha,**] **ádhukṣata** (3*p.*) RV., **dhukṣīmáhi** B. — 7. **ádhukṣat -ṣata** *etc.* V.+ (**dhukṣásva aduk-ṣat** *etc.* **dukṣata** RV.)
Fut. 1. **dhokṣyate** C. [— 2. **dogdhā.**]
Verb. **dugdhá** V.+; **dogdhum** E., **dógdhos** B.; **dugdhvā** B.+; **duhádhyāi** RV.; **doháse** RV.; **-doham** C.
Sec. Conj.: *Pass.* **duhyáte** *etc.* V.+ [— *Int.* **doduh-.**] — *Desid.* **dudhukṣati** C. (**dúdukṣati** RV.) — *Caus.* **doháyati** *etc.* B.+, **-te** S. (**dohyáte** B.)
Deriv.: **-duh** V.+ **dóha** V.+ **dóhana** B.+ **dogdhavya** B.E.
-dugh S. **dógha** RV. **dohána** RV. **dogdhṛ́** AV.+
-duha E. **-dohaka** C. **dóhas** V.B.S. **dogdhra** S.
dúgha V. **-dohin** E. **dohás** RV. **dudhukṣu** E.
duhitṛ́ V.+ **dohya** C.

√ dū, *see* √ du.

Another root **dū** seems inferable from the derivatives:
dáviṣṭha V. **dávīyas** V.B. **dūtá** V.+ **dūrá** V.+ **dūr?** ÇB.

√ 1 dṛ, 'pierce, split'.

Pres. [2.] **dárṣi adar dárt** RV. — [9.] **dṛṇīyā́t** ÇB.
Perf. **dadā́ra** *etc.* V.+ (**dadṛvā́ṅs** RV.) [**dadaritha dadaratus dadratus**], **dadre** S.+

Aor. 1. dīryāt C. [— 2. adarat.] — 3. adīdarat *etc.* E.+ [adadarat.] — 4. darṣasi dárṣat darṣate darṣīṣṭa RV. [— 5. adārīt.]

[*Fut.* darīṣyati, darītā.]

Verb. dīrṇá B.+, dṛta E.; -dīrya B.+; -dāram C.

Sec. Conj.: *Pass.* dīryáte *etc.* B.+, dīryati *etc.* E.+ — *Int.* dárdṛ- RV.TS. (dardirat adardirus RV.); dādṛhí RV. [dedīrya-. — *Desid.* didarīṣa-, didīrṣa-.] — *Caus.* dārayati *etc.* B.+, -te *etc.* C. (dāryate *etc.* E.+); daráyati *etc.* RV.C.

Deriv.:	dara V.+	dartnú RV.	dāraṇa E.+	dṛ́ti V.+
	daraṇa S.+	darmán RV.S.	-dāri E.+	dṛván? VS.
	-daraṇīya C.	darmá RV.	dārú RV.	drá? AV.
	-dari RV.C.	dāra AV.+	dāruṇá? B.+	-driya RV.
	dárīman RV.	-dāraka E.+	-dir ÇB.	dadru C.
	dartṛ RV.	dārin V.+	durá? RV.	-dardira RV.

Compare √ dal.

√ 2 dṛ, 'heed'.

[*Perf.* dadre.]

Aor. 1. adṛthās *etc.* B. — [3. adīdarat. —] 4. dṛḍhvam B.

[*Fut.* dariṣyate, dartā.]

Verb. dṛta E.+: -dṛ́tya B.+

Sec. Conj.: *Pass.* driyáte *etc.* B.+, -ti *etc.* E.+ [— *Int.* dardṛ-, dedrīya-. — *Desid.* didariṣa-. — *Caus.* dāraya-.]

Deriv.:	-dara U.? C.	-daraṇa S.+	-dartavya C.	-duri RV.
	-darin C.	-daraṇīya C.	-dāra V.B.S.	-dṛtya B.

Only with prefix ā, and with passive present-system, suggesting a specialization from √ 1 dṛ.

√ dṛp, 'rave'.

Pres. [4.] dṛpyati *etc.* V.+ — [1.] darpati S.

[*Perf.* dadarpa.]

Aor. 2. adṛpat B. [— 4. adrāpsīt, adārpsīt. — 5. adarpīt.]

Fut. 1. drapsyati ÇB., darpiṣyati JB. [— 2. draptā, darptā, darpitā.]

Verb. dṛpta V.+, dṛpita RV

Sec. Conj.: *Caus.* darpayati *etc.* E.+

Deriv.: darpa E.+ darpaka C. darpin C. darpaṇa E.+ -dṛ́pti RV.

√ dṛbh, 'bunch'.

Pres. [6.] dṛbháti *etc.* B. — [1.] dṛbhmas? B.

Verb. dṛbdha B.+

Sec. Conj.: *Caus.* darbhita C.

Deriv.: darbhá V.+ dṛ́bhīka? RV. dṛbdhi? darbhaṇa S.?

√ dṛç, 'see'.

Pres. [4.] paçyati *etc.*, *see* √ paç.
Perf. dadárça dadṛçé *etc.* V.+ (dádṛçe dádṛçre dádṛçāna RV., dadṛçrām AV., -çrire TB., dadṛçivāṅs U., darçivāṅs E.+) [dadarçitha dadraṣṭha.]
Aor. 1. adarçam *etc.* B.+ (adarçma TS., adṛçma JB., adarçus B.; adarças -çat B.S.; darçati *etc.* V., dárçat *etc.* V.B.), ádṛçran V.B. (adṛçram dṛçānā́ dṛ́çāna RV.), ádarçi dárçi V. — 2. dṛçan V., ádṛçan B., dṛçéyam *etc.* V.B. — 3. adīdṛçat *etc.* B.+ [adadarçat.] — 4. adrākṣīt *etc.* B.+ (ádrāk B.), adṛkṣata RV. (dṛ́kṣase RV.) [drakṣīran.] — 7. dṛkṣam K.
Fut. 1. drakṣyáti *etc.* B.+, -te *etc.* E.+ — 2. draṣṭā *etc.* E.
Verb. dṛṣṭá V.+; dráṣṭum AV.+; dṛṣṭvā́ AV.+, -ṭvā́ya RV.; -dṛ́çya V.+; dṛçé V.B.; dṛçáye V.; -darçam C.
Sec. Conj.: Pass. dṛçyáte *etc.* V.+, -ti *etc.* E.+ — *Int.* darīdṛçyate C. [dardṛç-.] — *Desid.* dídṛkṣate *etc.* V.+, -ti E. — *Caus.* darçáyati *etc.* AV.+, -te *etc.* S.+ (didarçayiṣa- S.+)

Deriv.:				
	dárça V.+	darçanī́ya B.+	dṛçīkú B.S.	draṣṭṛ́ AV.+
	darçá AV.+	dṛ́ç V.+	dṛçénya RV.	-dreçya U.
	darçaka E.+	-dṛ́ça V.+	dṛ́ṣṭi V.+	didṛkṣā E.+
	-darçin E.+	dṛ́çya V.+	-dṛçna TS.	didṛ́kṣu V.+
	dárçya RV.	dṛçatí RV.	-dṛçvan C.	didṛkṣéya RV.
	darçatá V.B.	dṛçí V.+	-dṛkṣa B.+	didṛkṣéṇya V.B.
	dárçana V.+	dṛçīka V.	draṣṭavyà B.+	darçayitṛ E.+

√ dṛh, dṛṅh, 'make firm'.

Pres. [1.] dṛ́ṅhati *etc.* -te *etc.* V.B. — [6.] dṛṅhántam AV., dṛṅhéthe RV. — [4.] dṛ́hya dṛ́hyasva RV. [— 1. darhati.]
Perf. [dadarha, dadṛṅha] dādṛhāṇá adadṛhanta RV.
Aor. [3. adadarhat, adīdṛhat. —] 5. adṛṅhīt *etc.* B. [adarhīt.]
[*Fut.* darhiṣyati, darhitā; dṛṅhiṣyati, dṛṅhitā.]
Verb. dṛḍhá V.+
Sec. Conj.: [*Int.* darīdṛh-, dardṛh-; darīdṛṅh-, dardṛṅh-. — *Desid.* didarhiṣa-, didṛṅhiṣa-. —] *Caus.* [darhaya-;] dṛṅhayati *etc.* V.S.

Deriv.:			
dṛh B.+	-dṛṅha AV.	dṛṅhitṛ́ V.B.	d ṛ́h V.
	dṛ́ṅhaṇa AV.B.S.	drahyát? RV.	

Divided by the Hindu grammarians into two roots, dṛṅh 'fix', and dṛh 'grow', from the latter of which are then derived dīrghá V.+ and the related words drā́ghīyas V.B.S., drā́ghiṣṭha RV., drāghmán V.B., drāghimán B. (drāghuyā́ TS.).

√ dev, *see* √ 2 dīv.

√ dyu, 'attack'.

Sāyaṇa has once **pra dyāuti,** apparently an artificial formation, on the authority of the occurrence of a root **dyu** in the Dhātupāṭha.

√ dyut, 'shine'.

Pres. [1.] **dyótate** *etc.* V.+, **-ti** *etc.* E.
Perf. **didyute** *etc.* V.+, **didyóta** AV., **didyutus** TS.
Aor. 1. **dyutant- dyutāná** V.B., **dyútāna** RV. — 2. **adyutat** *etc.* B.+ — 3. **ádidyutat** *etc.* V.B. — 4. **ádyāut dyāut** V.B. [— 5. **adyotiṣṭa.**]
Fut. 1. **dyotiṣyati** B. [— 2. **dyotitā.**]
Verb. **dyuttá** AV.ÇB. [**dyutita; dyutitvā, dyotitvā;**] **-dyutya** AB.
Sec. Conj.: *Int.* **dávidyut-** V.B. [**dedyut-.** — *Desid.* **didyutiṣa-, didyotiṣa-.**] — *Caus.* **dyotayati** *etc.* V.+ (**dyotyate** C.); **dyutayanta** RV.

Deriv.:	**dyút** V.+	**dyota** AV.+	**dyótana** V.+	**-dyótman** RV.
	-dyuta E.	**dyotaka** C.	**dyotaná** RV.	**didyút** V.B.
	dyuti E.+	**dyotin** C.	**dyotaní** V.	**-dyotayitavya** U.
		dyotya C.	**dyotis** C.	

Compare √ **jyut** and √ **div.** BR. set off a few of the forms to a √ 2 **dyut** 'break'.

√ dram, 'run'.

[*Pres. etc.* **dramati; dadrāma; adramīt; dramiṣyati, dramitā.**]
Sec. Conj.: *Int.* **dandramyate** U. [— *Desid.* **didramiṣa-.** — *Caus.* **dramayati.**]

Apparently another form of √ 1 **drā.**

√ 1 drā, 'run'.

Pres. [2.] **drāhi drā́tu drāntu** V.
Perf. **dadrus** *etc.* V.C., **dadrāṇá** RV.
Aor. [1. **drāyāt, dreyāt.** —] 4. **drāsat** RV. [— 6. **adrāsīt.**]
[*Fut.* **drāsyati, drātā.**]
Verb. **drāṇa** U.+
Sec. Conj.: *Int.* **dáridrāti** *etc.* TS.C. [**dādrā-.** — *Desid.* **didrāsa-.**] — *Caus.* **drāpayati** ÇB. ([**adidrapat**] **dídrāpayiṣati** ÇB.)

Deriv.:	**drá?** AV.	**drāk?** C.	**drāpi?** B.	**dáridra** B.+

Compare roots **dram** and **dru.** The intensive stem **daridrā** is reckoned by the Hindu grammarians as a root, and artificially furnished with a set of verb-forms and primary derivatives.

√ 2 drā, 'sleep'.

Pres. [2.] **drāti** *etc.* B.+ — [4.] **drāyate** *etc.* E.+
Perf. **dadrāu** C.
Aor. 4. (*or* 6.) **adrāsīt** B.

Fut. drāsyáti B.
Verb. drāṇa AV.B.+, drita? C.
Sec. Conj.: Desid. didrāsati C.
Deriv.: -drā V.+ -didrāsu C.

√ drāḍ, 'split'.

A single doubtful occurrence, uddrāḍayan C.

√ dru, 'run'.

Pres. [1.] drávati *etc.* V.+, -te *etc.* E.+
Perf. dudrāva *etc.* B.+ [dudrotha, dudruma], dudruve *etc.* E.
Aor. [1. drūyāt; adrāvi. —] 3. adudruvat B.+ (adudrot dudrávat RV.) [adudravat, adidravat.]
Fut. 1. droṣyati B. [— 2. drotā.]
Verb. drutá B.+; drotum C.; drutvā́ B.; -drútya B.+
Sec. Conj.: Int. dodru- (dodrāva TS.) [— *Desid.* dudrūṣa-.] — *Caus.* drāváyati *etc.* V.+, -te *etc.* E. (drāvyate E.); dravayanta RV.

Deriv.:	dravá V.+	draví RV.	-drāva VS.	-dru V.+
	dravya? U.S.+	dravitṛ́ RV.	-drāvin S.+	druti C.
	drávaṇa B.+	dravitnú V.	-drāvya E.	drāvayitnú RV.
	dravará RV.	dráviṇa *etc.*? V.+	drāvaṇa E.+	

√ druh, 'be hostile'

Pres. [4.] drúhyati *etc.* B.+, -te *etc.* E.+
Perf. dudróha *etc.* V.B. (dudróhitha AV.), dudruhe C.
Aor. [1. druhyāt; adrohi. —] 2. druhas -han V.E. [— 3. adudruhat.] — 4. drogdhās M. — 7. adrukṣas B.
Fut. 1. dhrokṣyati MS. [drohiṣyati. — 2. drogdhā, droḍhā, drohitā.]
Verb. drugdhá V.+ [drūḍha]; drogdhavāi K.; [drugdhvā, drohitvā, druhitvā;] -drúhya MS.E.
Sec. Conj.: [*Int.* dodruh-. —] *Desid.* dudrukṣat K. [dudrohiṣa-, dudruhiṣa-, dudhrukṣa-. — *Caus.* drohaya-.]

Deriv.:	drúh V.+	druhyú RV.	drógha V.	drogdhavyà B.+
	druhya C.	druhiṇa C.	droha V.+	drogdhṛ E.+
	druhú AV.	drúhvan V.	drohin E.+	dudhrukṣu C.

√ drū, 'hurl' (?).

Pres. [9.] drūṇāti MS., drūṇāná RV.
Only two occurrences, of which that in MS. does not appear connectible with √ dru.

√ dvar ?

Such a root perhaps to be recognized in dvará RV., dvarín RV., -dvaras? RV., and in dvā́r or dúr V.+ 'door'.

√ dviṣ, 'hate'.

Pres. [2.] **dvéṣṭi dviṣánti** *etc.* V.+, **dviṣṭe dviṣáte** *etc.* AV.+ — [6.] **dviṣati** *etc.* M., **-te** *etc.* S.U.+
Perf. **didveṣa** ÇB. [**didviṣe.**]
Aor. [1. **adveṣi.** — 3. **adidviṣat.** —] 7. **dvikṣat dvikṣata** (3*s*.) AV.
[*Fut.* **dvekṣyati -te; dveṣṭā.**]
Verb. **dviṣṭa** V.+; **dveṣṭum** E., **dvéṣṭos** ÇB.
Sec. Conj.: [*Int.* **dedviṣ-.** — *Desid.* **didvikṣa-.** —] *Caus.* **dveṣayati** C.
Deriv.: **dvíṣ** V.+ **-dviṣṭi** C. **dveṣin** E.+ **dveṣaṇīya** C.
dviṣa C. **dvéṣa** V.+ **dvéṣya** AV.+ **dvéṣas** V.B.
-dviṣeṇya RV. **-dveṣaka** E. **dvéṣaṇa** V.+ **dveṣṭṛ** E.+

√ dhan, 'run'.

[*Pres.* 3. **dadhanti.** — 1. **dhanati.**]
Perf. **dadhánat dadhanyus dadhanváṅs** RV.
Sec. Conj.: *Caus.* **dhanáyan -yante -yanta** RV.
Deriv. **dhániṣṭha** RV.
Compare roots **dhanv, dhav, dhāv, dhū.**

√ dhanv, 'run'.

Pres. [1.] **dhánvati** *etc.* V.B. (**dhaniva** SV.)
Perf. **dadhanvé -viré** RV.
Aor. 5. **ádhanviṣus** V.B.
Deriv. **dhánutṛ** RV.

Seems to be a secondary root-form, from the preceding. Its **v** has value as **u** in half the RV. cases (in the present-system).

√ dham, dhmā, 'blow'

Pres. [1.] **dhámati** *etc.* V.+, **-te** *etc.* U.E. — [2.] **dhmānt** C.
Perf. **dadhmāu** *etc.* **dadhmire** E.
Aor. [1. **dhmāyāt dhmeyāt; adhmāyi.**] — 6. **adhmāsīt** C.
Fut. 1. **dhamiṣyati** *etc.* E.+ [**dhmāsyati.** — 2. **dhmātā.**]
Verb. **dhamitá** RV., **dhmātá** V.+; **-dhmāya** B.+
Sec. Conj.: *Pass.* **dhamyate** *etc.* V.+, **-ti** E.; **dhmāyáte** *etc.* B.+, **-ti** *etc.* ÇB.E.+ — *Int.* **dādhmāyate** C. [**dedhmīya-.** — *Desid.* **didhmāsa-.** —] *Caus.* **dhmāpayati** *etc.* E.+ (**dhmāpyate** E.) [**adidhmapat.**]
Deriv.: **-dhama** AV.+ **dhamitra** C. **-dhmānīya** C. **dhmāpana** C.
-dhamana C. **-dhmā̆** B.+ **dhmātavya** C.
dhamáni V.+ **dhmā́na** AV.+ **dhmātṛ** RV.

√ dhav, 'flow'

Pres. [1.] **dhavate** *etc.* RV.
Deriv. **dhávīyas** RV.

√ 1 dhā, dadh, 'put'.

Pres. [3.] dádhāti dhatté *etc.* V.+ — [1.] dádhati -te *etc.* V.+ — [2.] dhāti RV³. — [4.] dhāyeta MU., adhāyata M.

Perf. dadhāú dadhé *etc.* V.+ (dadhā́tha V., dadhidhvé -iṣvá -idhvam RV., dadhre RV.)

Aor. 1. ádhāt adhus *etc.* V.+ (adhītām RV.; dheyām -yus [-yāsus] RV.; dhā́tu *etc.* V.; dhetana RV.TB.), adhithās adhita *etc.* V.+ (ahita hita AV.TA.; adhīmahi dhīmahi dhīmahe V.; dhāmahe RV.; dhiṣe dhire dhéthe dhāithe RV.; dhiṣvá RV.); ádhāyi dhā́yi V.+ — 2. adhat SV., dhat RV. — 4. dhāsus dhāsathas -tha RV., adhiṣi -ṣata B.+ (dhiṣīya B.S., dheṣīya MS.) — 5? dhāyīs RV.

Fut. 1. dhāsyati -te *etc.* B.+ (adhāsyat C.) — 2. dhātā *etc.* B.

Verb. hitá V.+, -dhita V.C.; dhā́tum B.+, -tave V.B., -tavāí AV., -tos V.B., -dhitum C.; dhitvā́ B. [hitvā]; -dhā́ya AV.+; -dhā́m AV.; dhiyádhyāi RV.; [-dhāyam.]

Sec. Conj.: Pass. dhīyáte *etc.* V.+ — [*Int.* dedhīyate. —] *Desid.* dhítsati *etc.* V.+, -te *etc.* V.+ (dhitsyate C.); dídhiṣati *etc.* -te *etc.* RV. (dídhiṣāṇa RV.) — *Caus.* dhāpayati *etc.* V.+, dhāpayīta S. (dhāpyate C.)

Deriv.:

-dhā̆ V.+	dhāya S.	-dhi V.+	-dadhus MS.
-dhā́na V.+	-dhāyaka C.	-dhiti V.B.S.	dadhiṣú AV.
dhānā́? V.+	-dhāyin C.	-hiti V.+	didhiṣú V.+
-dhānīya C.	dhāyyà B.S.	dheya B.+	didhiṣā́yya RV.
dhā́tu V.+	dhā́yu RV.	-dhéya *n.* V.+	-dhitsā E.+
-dhātavya B.+	dhāsí RV.	dhéṣṭha V.B.	-dhitsu S.+
dhātṛ V.+	-dhas V.+	-dadha B.S.	-dhāpana S.
dhā́man V.+		dádhi V.B.	-dhāpayitavya C.

√ 2 dhā, 'suck'.

Pres. [4?] dháyati *etc.* V.+

Perf. dadhús RV.

Aor. 1. adhāt AV. [dheyāt. — 3. adadhat. — 6. adhāsīt.]

Fut. 1. dhāsyati E. [— 2. dhātā.]

Verb. dhītá V.B.; dhā́tave V.; dhītvā́ ÇB.; -dhī́ya ÇB. [-dhāya.]

Sec. Conj.: [*Pass.* dhīyate. — *Int.* dādhā-, dādhī-, dedhīya-. — *Desid.* dhitsa-. —] *Caus.* dhāpayate *etc.* RV., -ti ÇB. [adīdhapat.]

Deriv.:

-dhā V.+	-dhāyin C.	dhārú AV.	dhénā V.
-dhaya B.+	dhā́yas V.	dhāsí RV.S.	dhenú V.+
dhā́tu RV.S.	dhāyú RV.	dhāsyú AV.	dadhán, dádhi V.+

Related with √ dhi. The connection of some of the derivatives by no means beyond question.

√ 1 dhāv, 'run'.

Pres. [1.] dhā́vati *etc.* -te *etc.* V.+

[*Perf.* dadhāva -ve.]

Aor. [1. dhāvyāsam. —] 3. adadhāvat RV. [adīdhavat.] — 5. adhāvīt B. [adhāviṣṭa.]

Fut. 1. dhāviṣyati C. [-te. — 2. dhāvitā.]

Verb. dhāvita E.+; dhāvitvā C.; -dhāvya C.

Sec. Conj.: [*Int.* dādhāvya-. — *Desid.* didhāviṣa-. —] *Caus.* dhāváyati etc. V.+

Deriv.: dhāvaka E. dhāvin C. dhāvana E.+ dhāvitṛ E. dhā́rā? V.+

Compare roots dhan, dhanv, dhav. It is reckoned by the grammarians as filling up the defective conjugation of √ sṛ.

√ 2 dhāv, 'rinse'.

Pres. [1.] dhā́vati *etc.* -te *etc.* V.+

Perf. [dadhāva] dadhāvire C.

Aor. 5. adhāviṣṭa (3s.) RV.

Verb. dhāutá SV.+; dhāutvā? C.; -dhāvya S.

Sec. Conj.: *Pass.* dhāvyate C. — *Caus.* dhāvayati *etc.* -te *etc.* B.+

Deriv.: dhāva C. -dhāvin C. dhāutí RV. dhā́rā? V.+ dhāvaka E. dhā́vana B.+

Perhaps rather related with √ dhū than with √ 1 dhāv.

√ dhi, dhinv, 'nourish'.

Pres. [5.] dhinoti dhinvanti *etc.* B.+

[*Perf.* didhinva.]

Aor. 5. adhinvīt PB.

[*Fut.* dhinviṣyati, dhinvitā.]

Perhaps only another form of √ 2 dhā, with causative value. Some of the derivatives given under √ 2 dhā might be put as properly here.

√ dhī, dīdhī, 'think'.

Pres. [2.] dhīmahi B.+ — [3?] dīdhayas dī́dhayan dīdhyat *etc.* dī́dhyat adīdhet *etc.* dī́dhye dīdhyāthām dīdhīthām dī́dhyāna adīdhīta *etc.* V.B.

Perf. dīdhaya -dhima (-mas SV.) -dhiyus -dhyus dīdhire V.B.

Verb. dhītá V.+

Sec. Conj.: *Int.* dedhyat TS. — *Desid.*? dhī́ṣamāṇa RV[1].

Deriv.: dhī́ V.+ dhī́ra V.+ dhiyasāná RV. -dīdhayu RV. dhītí V.B. dhī́van AV.[1] dī́dhiti V.+

Compare √ dhyā. The form dhīmahi belongs here only as thus used later, with a false apprehension of its proper meaning.

√ dhukṣ, 'kindle'.

Pres. [1.] dhukṣate E[1].

[*Perf. etc.* dudhukṣe; adudhukṣat, adhukṣiṣṭa; dhukṣiṣyate, dhukṣitā.]

Sec. Conj.: [*Int.* **dodhukṣ-**. — *Desid.* **dudhukṣiṣa-**. —] *Caus.* **dhukṣayati** *etc.* E.+ (**dhukṣyate** C.)

Deriv. **-dhukṣaṇa** E.+

Occurring only with the prefix **sam**.

√ dhū, dhu, 'shake'.

Pres. [5.] **dhūnóti dhūnuté** *etc.* V.+; **dhunoti dhunute** *etc.* JB.S.+ — [2.] **dhuváte** (3*p.*) ÇB., **dhuvāná** TS. — [6.] **dhuvati** *etc.* AV.B. (**dhūvet** K.) — [9.] **dhunīyāt dhunāna dhūnāna** C. — **dhunet**? M[1].

Perf. **dudhāva** *etc.* E.+, **dudhuve** AV. (**dudhuvīta dūdhot** RV.)

Aor. 4. **adhūṣṭa -ṣata** RV.S. [**adhoṣṭa**. — 5. **adhāvīt adhuvīt, adhaviṣṭa**.]

Fut. 1. **dhaviṣyati** B.S., **-te** B. [**dhoṣyati -te**. — 2. **dhavitā, dhotā**.]

Verb. **dhūtá** V.+, **dhuta** E.+ [**dhūna; dhavitum**;] **dhūtvā** AB.; **-dhū́ya** AV.+

Sec. Conj.: *Pass.* **dhūyáte** *etc.* AV.+ (**dhūyant** M.) — *Int.* **dodhavīti** *etc.* V.E., **dodhūyate** *etc.* E.+ (**dodhūyat** *pple.* E.+); **davidhu-** RV. (**davidhāva** RV.) — [*Desid.* **dudhūṣa-**. —] *Caus.* **dhūnayati -te** *etc.* E.+ [**dhāvayati**.]

Deriv.: **-dhu** V.	**-dhāva** B.	**dhuvaka** JB.	**-dhuti** C.
-dhava RV.	**dhavitavyà** ÇB.	**dhúvana** B.S.	**dhúni**? V.B.
-dhavana B.S.	**ḍhavítra** B.S.	**dhū́ti** RV.	**dhūnana** E.+

Compare √ 2 **dhāv**.

√ dhūrv, 'injure'.

Pres. [1.] **dhū́rvati** *etc.* V.B.

[*Perf.* **dudhūrva**.]

Aor. 5. **adhūrvīt** ÇB.

[*Fut.* **dhūrviṣyati, dhūrvitā**.]

Verb. **dhū́rvitum** ÇB.

A secondary root-form from √ **dhvṛ dhur**.

√ dhṛ, 'hold'.

Pres. [1.] **dhareran** AÇS[1].; **adhāram** R[1].

Perf. **dadhāra** *etc.* (**dadhartha**) JB.E.+; **dādhā́ra** V.B. (**dādhártha** RV.TA.); **dadhré** *etc.* V.+

Aor. 1. **dhṛthās** AV.; **adhāri** C. — 3. **ádīdharat** *etc.* V.B.S. (**dīdhar, didhṛtam -tá** RV.), **-rata** (3*s.*) ÇB. [— 4. **adhārṣīt**.]

Fut. 1. **dhariṣyati** *etc.* E.+, **-te** *etc.* AV.+ — 2. **dhartā** C.

Verb. **dhṛtá** V.+; **dhartum** C. **-tavāi** KB.; **dhṛtvā́** B.+; **-dhṛtya** B.; **dhartári** RV.; **-dhāram** S.

Sec. Conj.: *Pass.* **dhriyáte** *etc.* V.+, **-ti** *etc.* E.+ — *Int.* **dardharṣi adardhar** RV.; **dādharti dādhrati dādhartu** B. (**dadhartu**? AVP.; **dādhārayati** JB.) — *Desid.* **didhīrṣa-** (*in d.*) [**didhariṣate**.] — *Caus.* **dhāráyati -te** *etc.* V.+ (**dhāryáte** B.+; **didhārayiṣa-** S.C.)

Deriv.:	dhára v.+	dharmán RV.	-dhāri C.	dhruvás RV.
	dháraṇa AV.+	dhárman V.+	dhīra E.+	dhruví V.B.
	-dharaṇīya C.	dhárma AV.+	dhúr V.+	dā́dhṛvi RV.
	dharaṇi E.+	dhariman C.	dhura E.+	dṛdhrá? RV.
	dharúṇa V.B.	dhárīman RV.	-dhṛt V.+	didhīrṣā C.
	-dhártu RV.	dhárīyas B.S.	-dhṛk E.+	-didhīrṣu C.
	-dhárītu RV.	-dhā́ra V.+	dhṛ́ti V.+	-dhāraya V.+
	dhartṛ́ V.B.	dhā́raka B.+	-dhṛtvan B.	dhārayú RV.
	dhartrá B.S.	dhārin U.S.+	-dhra V.+	dhārayitavya U.+
	dháritṛ B.+	dhārya E.+	-dhri? V.+	dhārayitṛ B.+
	dharṇasí V.B.	dhā́raṇa V.+	dhruvá V.+	dhārayiṣṇu C.
	dharṇí RV.	-dhāraṇīya C.		-didhārayiṣā C.

√ dhṛṣ, 'dare'.

Pres. [5.] dhṛṣṇóti *etc.* V.+ — [1.] dhárṣati *etc.* VS.B. — [2?] dhṛṣánt RV., dhṛṣāṇá AV.

Perf. dadhárṣa *etc.* V.B. (dādhṛṣus AV.; dadhárṣat -ṣati dadharṣīt RV.; dadhṛṣate dádhṛṣanta AV.

Aor. 2. adhṛṣas ÇB. (dhṛṣámāṇa? RV.) — [3. adīdhṛṣat, adadharṣat. —] 5. adharṣiṣus TA.

[*Fut.* dharṣiṣyati, dharṣitā.]

Verb. dhṛṣṭá V.+, dhṛṣitá V.; -dhṛṣya B.+; -dhṛ́ṣe V.B., -dhṛ́ṣas RV.

Sec. Conj.: [*Int.* darīdhṛṣ-. — *Desid.* didharṣiṣa-. —] *Caus.* dharṣayati *etc.* B.+

Deriv.:	dhárṣa V.+	dharṣaṇa E.+	dhṛ́ṣṭi B.+	dadhṛṣá RV.
	-dharṣaka E.+	dharṣaṇīya E.+	dhṛṣṇú V.+	dā́dhṛṣi V.
	-dharṣin C.	-dhṛṣ V.	dhṛṣya V.+	dadhṛṣváṇi RV.
	-dharṣya AV.	dhṛṣáj RV.		-dharṣayitavya C.

√ dhmā, *see* √ dham.

√ dhyā, 'think'.

Pres. [4.] dhyā́yati *etc.* B.+, -te *etc.* E.+ (dhyāyīta U.) — [2.] dhyāti *etc.* B.+ (dhyāyāt B.S.)

Perf. dadhyāu *etc.* B.+

Aor. 4. dhyāsus M. — 6. ádhyāsiṣam ÇB.

Fut. 1. dhyāsyati E. — 2. dhyātā JUB.

Verb. dhyāta B.+; dhyātvā B.+; -dhyāya E.+; dhyāyam C.

Sec. Conj.: *Pass.* dhyāyate C. — [*Int.* dādhyā-. —] *Desid.* didhyāsate ÇB. [— *Caus.* dhyāpayati.]

Deriv.:	dhyā́ V.+	dhyāna U.+	dhyātṛ C.	-didhyāsana C.
	-dhyāyin B.+	dhyātavya C.	dhyeya E.+	-didhyāsitavya B.
				-didhyāsu C.

Compare √ dhī, of which this is a later secondary form.

√ dhraj, dhrāj, 'sweep'.

Pres. [1.] dhrájati *etc.* RV.; dhrā́jamāna MS.
Aor. 5. dhrājiṣīya MS.
Deriv.: -dhrajati RV. dhrájas RV. dhrā́j MS. dhrā́ji V.B. dhráji- RV. dhrājá MS. dhrājí MS.

√ dhvaṅs, dhvas, 'scatter'.

Pres. [1.] dhvaṅsati -te *etc.* B.+
Perf. dadhvaṅsus U., dadhvaṅsire E.; dadhvasé V.B.
Aor. 2. dhvasán RV. [— 3. adadhvaṅsat. — 5. adhvaṅsiṣṭa.]
[*Fut.* dhvaṅsiṣyate, dhvaṅsitā.]
Verb. dhvasta B.+; -dhvasya E.+
Sec. Conj.: *Pass.* dhvasyate C., -ti GB. [— *Int.* danīdhvaṅs- -dhvasya-. — *Desid.* didhvaṅsiṣa-.] — *Caus.* dhvaṅsáyati *etc.* B.+, -te *etc.* JB.; dhvasáyati *etc.* RV.
Deriv.:
-dhvasa E.+ dhvasánti *n. pr.* RV. dhvasmán RV. dhvaṅsin E.+
dhvasán *n. pr.* ÇB. dhvasirá RV. dhvasrá RV.B. dhváṅsana B.+
dhvasáni V. dhvasti C. dhvaṅsá AV.+ dhvaṅsi S.
-dhvaṅsaka C.

√ dhvan, 'sound'.

Pres. [1.] dhvanati *etc.* C.
Perf. dadhvanus C.
Aor. [3. adidhvanat adadhvanat. —] 5. ádhvanīt RV.
[*Fut.* dhvaniṣyati, dhvanitā.]
Verb. dhvanita C., dhvāntá B.+
Sec. Conj.: *Int.* dandhvan- (*in d.*). — *Caus.* dhvanayati B. (dhvanayīt RV.); adhvānayat RV. (dhvānita C.)
Deriv.: dhvana TA. dhvaní AV.C. dhvāna S.+ dandhvana E. dhvanyà RV. dhvanana S.+ dhúni? V.B.

The RV. forms are set off by BR., perhaps rightly, to a separate √ dhvan 'cover', to which then dhvāntá RV.E.+ 'dark' is also referred.

√ dhvṛ, dhur, dhru, 'injure'.

Pres. [1.] dhvárati *etc.* B.
[*Perf.* dadhvāra.]
Aor. 4. [adhvārṣīt,] ádhūrṣata (3*p.*) RV. [dhvṛṣīṣṭa. — 5. dhvariṣīṣṭa.]
[*Fut.* dhvariṣyati, dhvartā.]
Verb. dhūrta E.+, dhruta TB.; dhū́rvane RV.
Sec. Conj.: [*Int.* dādhvarya-. —] *Desid.* dúdhūrṣati *etc.* AV.ÇB. [— *Caus.* dhvārayati.]

Deriv.: dhúr ÇB.MS. -dhru? RV. dhvarā́ MS. -dhvartavya TS.
dhūrtí RV. -dhrut RV. dhvarás RV. -dhvṛt RV.
-dhoraṇa? C. dhrúti RV.

Compare √ dhūrv, which is a secondary form (u-class) of this root.

√ **naṅç**, *see* √ 2 naç.

√ **nakṣ**, 'attain'.

Pres. [1.] nákṣati -te *etc.* V.B.
Perf. nanakṣús -kṣé RV.
[*Aor. etc.* anakṣīt; nakṣiṣyati, nakṣitā.]
Deriv.: nákṣatra? V.+ nakṣya RV.

A secondary form of √ 2 naç. Compare also inakṣ, under √ 2 naç.

√ **naṭ**, 'dance, play'.

Pres. [1.] naṭati C.
Sec. Conj.: *Caus.* nāṭayati *etc.* C.
Deriv.: naṭa E.+ naṭana C. nāṭa C. nāṭin C.
naṭanīya C. nāṭaka C. nāṭayitavya C.

A prakritized formation from √ nṛt.

√ **nad**, 'sound'.

Pres. [1.] nádati *etc.* AV.+, -te *etc.* E.+
Perf. nanāda nedus E.+, nedire E.
[*Aor. etc.* anīnadat, anādīt; nadiṣyati, naditā.]
Verb. nadita C.; -nadya E.+
Sec. Conj.: *Pass.* nadyate E. — *Int.* nā́nadati (3p.) *etc.* V.E., nāṇadyate *etc.* JB.E. — [*Desid.* ninadiṣa-. —] *Caus.* nadáyati -te *etc.* RV.E.; nādayati -te *etc.* E.+ (nādyate E.+)
Deriv.: nadá V.+ -nadathu U. nādá V.+ -nādana E.
nadī́? V.+ nadanú RV. nādín AV.+ nānada B.S.
-nadin E. nadanimán AV. nādi S.

Compare the next root.

√ **nand**, 'rejoice'.

Pres. [1.] nándati *etc.* V.+, -te *etc.* E.+
Perf. nanandus *etc.* E.+
[*Aor.* ananandat, anandīt.]
Fut. nandiṣyate E. [-ti. — 2. nanditā.]
Verb. nandita E.+; -nandya E.+
Sec. Conj.: *Pass.* nandyate *etc.* C. — [*Int.* nānand-. — *Desid.* ninandiṣa-. —] *Caus.* nandayati -te *etc.* U.+

Deriv.:

nánda v.+	**nándana** av.+	**nandáthu** b.+	**nánāndṛ**? v.
nandaka e.+	**-nandanīya** c.	**nāndaná** sv.u.	**-nandayitavya** u.+
nandin av.+	**nándi** b.+	**nāndī́** rv.e.+	**-nandayitṛ** c.
-nandya c.	**nanditṛ** e.	**nānduka** c.	

Doubtless the same with the preceding root.

√ nabh, 'burst'.

Pres. [1.] **nábhate** *etc.* v. [— 9. **nabhnāti.** — 4. **nabhyati.**]
[*Perf. etc.* **nanābha nebhe,** *etc.*]
Sec. Conj.: Caus. **anabhayan** ab.; **nambhaya** ts.s.

Deriv.:

nábh rv.	**nabhanyà** rv.	**nabhāka** rv.b.	**nā́bh** rv.
nabhanú, -ū́ rv.	**nábhas** v.+	**nábhya** v.b.s.	**nā́bhi** v.+

The connection of part of the derivatives with this root is quite questionable.

√ nam, 'bend, bow'.

Pres. [1.] **námati -te** *etc.* v.+ (**namāna** r.)
Perf. **nemus** c. (**nānāma nanámas** rv.), **neme** rv. (**nanāmire** m.)
Aor. 3. **anīnamat** *etc.* rv.c. — 4. **anān** k., **anaṁsata** (*3p.*) b. (**naṁsāi náṁsante** rv.) — 6. **anaṁsīt** c.
Fut. 1. **naṁsyati** b., **namiṣyati** c. [— 2. **naṁtā.**]
Verb. **natá** v.+; **naṁtum** c., **namitum** c.; **natvā** c.; **-nátya** b., **-namya** e.+; **-námam -náme** rv.
Sec. Conj.: Pass. **namyatē** u.+ — *Int.* **nánnamīti** *etc.* v.b. (**nannamus** b.), **-māna** (**námnate anamnata** rv.); **nannamyate** s. — *Desid.* **ninaṁsa-** (*in d.*) — *Caus.* **namayati** *etc.* v.+; **nāmayati** *etc.* u.s.+ (**nāmyate** *etc.* e.+, **-ti** *etc.* c.)

Deriv.:

-nam av.	**námī**? rv.	**-nāma** e.+	**nemí** v.+
náma rv.? e.+	**nati** av.+	**-nāmaka** c.	**-nannama** rv.
namana c.	**náṁtva** rv.	**nāmin** v.+	**-ninaṁsu** c.
namanīya c.	**naṁtṛ** c.	**nāmya** e.+	**namayitavya** c.
námas v.+	**namrá** v.+	**nāmana** c.	**-namayitṛ** c.
namasāná v.		**-nāmuka** b.	**namayiṣṇu** rv.

√ nard, 'bellow'.

Pres. [1.] **nardati** *etc.* b.+, **-te** *etc.* e.+
Perf. **nanarda** e.
[*Aor. etc.* **anardīt; nardiṣyati, narditā.**]
Verb. **nardita** e.+; **-nardam** e.
Sec. Conj.: Int. **nānardyamāna** c. — *Caus.* **-nardayati** gb.
Deriv.: **-narda** s.+ **-nardin** u. **nardana** c.

√ 1 **naç**, 'be lost'.

Pres. [4.] **náçyati** *etc.* V.+, **-te** *etc.* E. — [1.] **náçati -te** *etc.* V.E.+
Perf. **nanāça** V.E., **neçus** B.+
Aor. 2. **anaçat** E.+ — 3. **aneçat** *etc.* V.B.; **anīnaçat** *etc.* V.+ (**nīnaçus** E.)
Fut. 1. **naçiṣyati** AV.+; **nañkṣyati -te** *etc.* E.+ (**anañkṣyata** M.) — 2. **naçitā** E. [**nañṣṭā**.]
Verb. **naṣṭá** V.+ [**naṣṭum, nañṣṭum; naṣṭvā, nañṣṭvā**.]
Sec. Conj.: [*Int.* **nānaç-**. — *Desid.* **ninaçiṣa-, ninañkṣa-**. —] *Caus.* **nāçáyati** *etc.* V.+, **-te** *etc.* E.+ (**nāçayádhyāi** RV.; **ināçayiṣa-** C.)
Deriv.: **-naç** RV.B. **naṣṭi** B.+ **nāçin** B.+ **nāṣṭrā́** AV.B.
-nañçin V.S. **naçvara** C. **nāçya** E.+ **nāçayitṛ́** VS.
naçana B.+ **nāça** B.+ **nā́çana** AV.+
nañçuka K. **nāçaka** E.+ **nā́çuka** TS.

The forms from the stem **naça** are perhaps to be classed as of aorist 2.

√ 2 **naç, nañç**, 'attain'.

Pres. [1.] **náçati -te** *etc.* V.
Aor. 1. **ā́naṭ** V.B. (**naṭ** V.; **anaṣṭām nak nakṣi** *impv.* **náñçi naçīmahi** RV.)
Verb. **-náçe** RV.VS.
Sec. Conj.: *Desid.* **ínakṣati** *etc.* RV.
Deriv.: **náñça** RV. **-náñçana** RV. **-náça** V. **-nā́ça** RV.S.

The form **ā́naṭ** is by some referred to √ 1 **aç**. Compare √ **nakṣ**.

√ **nas**, 'unite'.

Pres. [1.] **násate** *etc.* RV.
Aor. 1. **nasīmahi** RV.

√ **nah**, 'tie'.

Pres. [4.] **náhyati -te** *etc.* V.+ (**nahyus** AB.) — [1.] **nahet** M.
[*Perf. etc.* **nanāha** (**nanaddha nehitha**) **nehe; anīnahat, anātsīt anaddha; natsyati -te, naddhā**.]
Verb. **naddhá** V.+; [**naddhvā**;] **-náhya** B.+
Sec. Conj.: *Pass.* **nahyate** C. [— *Int.* **nānah-**. — *Desid.* **ninatsa-**.] — *Caus.* **nāhayati** *etc.* S.+
Deriv.: **-nah** (**nádh**) V.+ **náhus** V.+ **nāha** AV.+ **-nāhana** C.
náhana V.+ **-naddhi** B. **-nāhya** B.S. **-nāhuka**? AB.
náhas? C. **-naddhavya** E.+

√ **nāth, nādh**, 'seek aid'.

Pres. [1.] **nāthate** *etc.* B.+, **-ti** *etc.* E.+; **nā́dhamāna** V.
[*Perf. etc.* **nanātha, nanādhe; anāthīt, anādhiṣṭa; nāthiṣyati, nādhiṣyate; nāthitā, nādhitā**.]

Verb. nāthitá V.+, nādhitá RV.; nāthitum C.; -nāthya C.
Sec. Conj.: Pass. nāthyate C.
Deriv: nāthá V.+ -nādha B. nā́dhas RV.

√ niṅs, 'kiss'.

Pres. [2.] níṅsate niṅsata níṅsāna RV.
[*Perf. etc.* niniṅse; aniṅsiṣṭa; niṅsiṣyate, niṅsitā.]
Deriv. -niṅsin C.

√ nikṣ, 'pierce'.

Pres. [1.] níkṣati *etc.* AV.
[*Perf. etc.* ninikṣa; anikṣīt; nikṣiṣyati, nikṣitā.]
Verb. -níkṣe V.
Deriv.: -nikṣaṇa C. nī́kṣaṇa? RV. nékṣaṇa AV.S.

Is perhaps a desiderative formation from √ 1 naç.

√ nij, 'wash'.

Pres. [2?] nije C., nijāná RV. — [3.] ninikta (2*p.*) RV.
[*Perf.* nineja, ninije.]
Aor. 2. anijam -jan AV.S. [— 3. anīnijat.] — 4. anāikṣīt nikṣi AV.
[*Fut.* nekṣyati -te, nektā.]
Verb. niktá V.+; niktvā́ B.+; -níjya B.+; -níje RV.
Sec. Conj.: Pass. nijyate *etc.* E.+ — *Int.* nénekti nenikté *etc.* V.+ [— *Desid.* ninikṣa-.] — *Caus.* nejayati *etc.* B.+
Deriv.: -nij V.S. -neka S.C. -neja C. néjana V.+
-nikti C. -nega B.S. nejaka C. -nektṛ S.
-nejya PB.

The intensive is regarded by the grammarians as the present-stem of this root.

√ nind, nid, 'revile'.

Pres. [1.] níndati *etc.* V.+, -te *etc.* E.+
Perf. nininda E.+ (nindima ninidús RV.)
Aor. 1. nindyāt U., ni dāná RV. — 5. ánindiṣus RV.S. (níndiṣat AV.)
Fut. [1. nindiṣyati. —] 2. ninditā E.
Verb. ninditá V.+; -nindya E.
Sec. Conj.: Pass. nidyáte RV.; nindyate C. — *Desid.* nínitsati RV., -te S.
Deriv.: níd RV. nindā́ AV.+ níndya V.+ ninditṛ́ RV.
nídā RV. nindaka E.+ nindana C. ninitsú RV.
-nedya RV. nindin C. nindanīya C.

√ nī, 'lead'.

Pres. [1.] náyati -te *etc.* V.+ — [3?] ninīthás ninīyāt RV., ninetu MS. — [2.] néṣi V.S., nethá RV., ánītām RV.

Perf. ninā́ya ninyus *etc.* V.+ (ninétha RV., nīnima TS.), ninye B.+ — -nayām āsa M., -nayāṁ cakre B.

Aor. [1. anāyi. — 3. anīnayat. —] 4. anāiṣīt *etc.* V.+ (nāis anāit B.S.; neṣati *etc.* RV., néṣat V.B., neṣa AV.), aneṣṭa *etc.* V.B. — 5. anayīt AV., anayīṣṭa (2*p.*) S. — anāyiṣata (*pass.*) C.

Fut. 1. neṣyati *etc.* AV.+, -te *etc.* B.+ (aneṣyathās M.); nayiṣyati *etc.* JB.E.+ (anayiṣyat JB.), -te *etc.* E. — 2. netā E., nayitā E.

Verb. nītá V.+; nétum B.+, -tavāí B.S., -tos B., nayitum B.+; nītvā́ B.+, nayitvā E.+; -nī́ya AV.+; neṣáṇi RV.; -nāyam JB.

Sec. Conj.: Pass. nīyáte *etc.* V.+ — *Int.* nenīyáte *etc.* V.+ — *Desid.* nínīṣati *etc.* V.+, -te *etc.* U.S.+ — *Caus.* nāyayati *etc.* E.+, -te E.

Deriv.:	-nī V.+	-nāyya C.	netrá AV.+	néṣa RV.
	naya V.+	-nāyana C.	nīthá V.+	néṣṭṛ V.+
	-nayin E.+	nīti V.+	nī́thā V.	-nenī RV.
	nayana U.S.+	netavya E.+	neman-? RV	ninīṣā E.+
	nāyá RV.C.	nayitavya E.+	-nī́ya B.	ninīṣu E.+
	nāyaka E.+	netṛ V.+	neya S.+	-ninīṣeṇya B.
	-nāyin E.	-nayitṛ E.	náyiṣṭha RV.	

√ nīḍ, 'nest'.

May be mentioned on account of nīḍá V.+ and nīḍí RV.

√ 1 nu, nū, 'praise'.

Pres. [2.] nāuti nuvánti *etc.* V.+ (anāvan RV.) — [1.] návate -ti *etc.* V. [— 6. nuvati.]

Perf. nunāva C.

Aor. 3. [anūnavat] ánūnot *etc.* RV. — 4. [anāuṣīt,] ánūṣi *etc.* V.B. — 5. [anāvīt anuvīt,] anaviṣṭa RV.

[*Fut.* naviṣyati, nuviṣyati; navitā, nuvitā.]

Verb. nuta C. [nūta; navitum, nuvitum;] -nutya S.; -nāvam B.

Sec. Conj.: Pass. nūyate *etc.* E.+ — *Int.* nónavīti nonumas *etc.* V., nonuvanta RV. (nónāva nonuvus RV.); návīnot RV. [— *Desid.* nunūṣa-. — *Caus.* nāvayati (nunāvayiṣa-).]

Deriv.:	-nava B.+	navana C.	nāvá RV.	nonuva C.
	návya RV.	náviṣṭi RV.	nuti C.	

√ 2 nu, 'move'

Pres. [1.] návate *etc.* RV. — [2.] nāuti S.

Verb. nūta? PB.

Sec. Conj.: Caus. nāvayati *etc.* B.

√ nud, 'push'.

Pres. [6.] nudáti -te *etc.* V.+

Perf. nunoda C., nunude *etc.* V.+

Aor. 1. nudyāt E.+ — [3. anūnudat. —] 4. [anāutsīt,] ánutta *etc.* V.B. — 5. nudiṣṭhās AV.

Fut. 1. notsyati E., -te B.E. [— 2. nottā.]

Verb. nuttá V.+, nunna SV.E.+, nudita M.; -nudya S.+; -núde RV., -nudas K.; -nódam V.

Sec. Conj.: Int. anonudyanta B. — *Desid.* nunutsa- (*in d.*). — *Caus.* nodayati *etc.* U.+ (nodyate E.+)

Deriv.:	-nud V.+	noda V.+	nodya C.	-nunutsu C.
	-nuda E.+	-nodaka C.	nodana C.	-nodayitavya C.
	nutti B.+	-nodin C.	-nottavya B.	

√ nṛ, 'sport'.

To be recognized with probability in the derivatives:
narúṇa TA. naríṣṭā AV.VS. nariṣyant E.+ narmá VS. narman E.+ also in sūnára V.B. and sūnṛ- (sūnṛ́tā V.+). Compare also √ nṛt.

√ nṛt, 'dance'.

Pres. [4.] nṛ́tyati *etc.* V.+, -te *etc.* E.+

Perf. nanarta nanṛtus E.+

Aor. 1. nṛtus RV. (*perf.*?) — 2. nṛtámāna? RV. [— 3. anīnṛtat, ananartat.] — 5. anartiṣus V.

Fut. 1. nartiṣyati C. [nartsyati. — 2. nartitā.]

Verb. nṛttá AV.+; nartitum C., narttum C.; nartitvā C.; -nartam B.

Sec. Conj.: Pass. nṛtyate C. — *Int.* narīnartti *etc.* C., narīnṛtyate C. -ti? C. — *Desid.* ninartiṣa- (*in d.*) [ninṛtsa-]. — *Caus.* nartáyati *etc.* V.+, -te *etc.* E.+

Deriv.:	nṛ́t AV.	-nartin VS.	nṛtú RV.	nartayitṛ E.
	nṛtya U.+	nartana S.+	nṛtū́ RV.	ninartiṣā C.
	-narta E.+	nṛ́ti? AV.	-nṛtti B.	
	nartaka E.+	nṛtí V.	nartitavya C.	

Compare roots naṭ and nṛ.

√ ned, 'flow'.

Pres. [1.] nedati *etc.* B., -te U.

[*Perf. etc.* nineda, ninede ninide; anedīt, -diṣṭa; nediṣyati, -te; neditā.]

Deriv. -neda MS.

√ pac, 'cook'.

Pres. [1.] pácati -te *etc.* V.+ (pacāna M.) — [4.] pácyate *etc.* RV.ÇB.

Perf. papā́ca pecus *etc.* V.B. [papaktha, pecitha], pece pecire *etc.* V.+ (ápeciran AV.)

Aor. [1. pacyāt; apāci. — 3. apīpacat.] — 4. [apākṣīt, apakta] pákṣat RV.

Fut. 1. **pakṣyati -te** *etc.* B. + (**apakṣyat** C.)— 2. **paktā́** B.
Verb. (**pakvá**;) **páktave** AV.B.; **paktvā́** AV.E.
Sec. Conj.: *Pass.* **pacyáte** *etc.* V.+, **-ti** M. — *Int.* **pāpacyate** *etc.* C. — [*Desid.* **pipakṣa-**. —] *Caus.* **pācayati -te** *etc.* B.+ (**pācyate** E.)
Deriv.: **pac**? C. **-paca** B.+ **-pacya** AV. **pácana** V.+ **pacatá** V.B. **pacatyà** RV. **paktí** RV. **pákti** VS.+ **paktavya** E. **paktṛ́** AV.+ **paktrima** C. **pakthá** RV.B. **pakthín** RV. **pakvá** V.+ **pacelima** C. **pāka** V.+ **pākin** C. **pākya** U.S.+ **pācaka** E.+ **-pācin** C. **pācya** U. **pācana** C. **-pācayitṛ** C.

√ paj, 'start' (?).

Perf. **pā́paje** RV[1].
Deriv.: **pajrá** V.S. **pā́jas** V.B.

The connection of form and meaning among these words is altogether questionable.

√ paṭ, 'tear'.

Pres. [1.] **paṭati** C[1].
Sec. Conj.: *Caus.* **pāṭayati** *etc.* U.+, **-te** *etc.* E. (**pāṭyate** C.)
Deriv.: **pāṭa** E.+ **pāṭaka** B.+ **-pāṭin** C. **pāṭya** C. **pāṭana** E.+ **pāṭanīya** C.

√ paṭh, 'read'.

Pres. [1.] **paṭhati** *etc.* TA.+, **-te** *etc.* E.+
Perf. **papāṭha** C.
[*Aor. etc.* **apīpaṭhat, apāṭhīt; paṭhiṣyati, paṭhitā.**]
Verb. **paṭhita** S.+; **paṭhitvā** C.
Sec. Conj.: *Pass.* **paṭhyate** *etc.* E.+ — *Int.* **pāpaṭhīti** *etc.* C., **pāpaṭhyate** C. — [*Desid.* **pipaṭhiṣa-**. —] *Caus.* **pāṭhayati** *etc.* C. (**pāṭhyate** C.)
Deriv.: **paṭhaka** E. **paṭhana** C. **paṭhanīya** C. **paṭhitavya** C. **paṭhiti** C. **pāṭha** S.+ **pāṭhaka** E.+ **pāṭhin** E.+ **pāṭhya** E.+ **pāṭhana** C.

√ paṇ, 'bargain'.

Pres. [1.] **paṇate** *etc.* B.+, **-ti** *etc.* E.+
[*Perf. etc.* **peṇe; apīpaṇat, apaṇiṣṭa; paṇiṣyate, paṇitā.**]
Verb. **paṇita** E.; **paṇitvā** S.
Sec. Conj.: *Pass.* **paṇyate** *etc.* E. [— *Int.* **pampaṇ-**. — *Desid.* **pipaṇiṣa-**. —] *Caus.* **paṇayati** *etc.* C. [**pāṇayati.**]
Deriv.: **paṇa** AV.+ **-paṇin** C. **páṇya** B.+ **páṇana** B.+ **paṇí** V.+ **paṇāyya** B. **vaṇíj**? V.+ **paṇitṛ** C. **-pāṇa** AV. **pāṇí**? V.+ **paṇayitṛ** C.

√ 1 pat, 'fly, fall'.

Pres. [1.] pátati *etc.* V.+, -te *etc.* E.+
Perf. papā́ta petús *etc.* V.+ (paptima paptús paptivā́ṅs RV.; papatyāt AV.)
Aor. 1. apāti B. — 3. apaptat *etc.* V.B.S.; apīpatat *etc.* V.
Fut. 1. patiṣyáti *etc.* AV.+, -te E. (apatiṣyat B.+) — 2. patitā M.
Verb. patitá AV.+; pátitum B.; patitvā́ AV.B.; -pátya B.+; -pā́tam B.+
Sec. Conj.: *Int.* pā́patīti *etc.* RV. [panīpat-.] — *Desid.* pipatiṣati *etc.* AV. ÇB.; pitsa- (*in d.*). — *Caus.* pātáyati *etc.* V.+, -te *etc.* E.+ (pātyate *etc.* E.+); patáyati *etc.* V.B.S., -te RV.

Deriv.:	-pat RV.	pátman V.B.	pāta AV.+	-paptani RV.
	pata- V.+	-patya B.	pātaka S.+	patāpata S.
	pátana V.+	pátvan V.B.S.	pātin AV.+	pipatiṣu E.+
	-ptu? MS.	patará RV.	pātya E.+	-pitsu C.
	patāka S.+	patáru RV.	pātana S.+	patayālú AV.
	-patitavya C.	pátiṣṭha V.B.	pātanīya C.	patayiṣṇú V.
	páttra V.+	-patiṣṇu B.+	pā́tuka B.E.	pātayitṛ C.
	pátatra V.C.	patīyas B.		

√ 2 pat, 'rule'.

Pres. [4.] pátyate *etc.* V.B.
Doubtless only a denominative of páti.

√ path, 'go' (?).

Pres. [1.] páthati *etc.* S.
[*Perf. etc.* papātha, apathīt; pathiṣyati, pathitā.]
Sec. Conj.: *Caus.* pāthayati B.S.
Deriv.: páth pathí pánthan V.+ pánthā V. páthan- B. pā́thas V.+ pā́this B.

No real root; the present forms doubtless bad readings for patati etc.; the causative a denominative of the stem path.

√ pad, 'go'.

Pres. [4.] pádyate *etc.* V.+, -ti *etc.* AB.E. — [2?] padyām R[1]., patsva M[1].
Perf. papāda pedus *etc.* V.+, pede *etc.* B.+
Aor. 1. apadmahi VS. -dran RV. (padāti -dāt V.; padīṣṭá V.); ápādi pā́di V.+ — 3. apīpadat AV.B. — 4. apatsi *etc.* V.B.U. (patthās AV.)
Fut. 1. patsyati *etc.* B.+ (patsyantu C.), -te *etc.* U.+ [— 2. pattā.]
Verb. panná AV.+; páttum B.+, -tave RV., -tos B.; -pádya V.+; -pádas V.B.; -pā́dam B.+
Sec. Conj.: *Int.* panīpadyate C. — *Desid.* pitsati B., -te C. — *Caus.* pādáyati *etc.* V.+, -te *etc.* AV.+ (pādyate *etc.* B.+; pipādayiṣati B.+)

Deriv.: -pad v.+ pā́d v.+ padá v.+ -padana B.U.S. padanī́ya B.+ -pádi RV[1]. pattí AV.+ -pattavya E.+ -pattṛ C. -padva? C. -pāda B.+ -pādaka E.+ -pādin C. -pā́dya B.+ -pādana E.+ -pādanīya C. pādú? RV.MS. pā́duka B. -pitsā C. -pitsu C. -patsu C. -pādayitavya C. -pādayitṛ C. -pipādayiṣā C. -pipādayiṣu C.

√ pan, 'admire'.

Pres. [1.] pánanta RV.
Perf. papana papné RV.
Aor. 5. paniṣṭa (3s.) RV.
Verb. panitá RV.
Sec. Conj.: *Pass.* panyáte RV. — *Int.* pánipnat V.B. — *Caus.* panáyati -te etc. RV.
Deriv.: pana- RV. pánya RV.K. panā́yya RV.AB. panas- RV. panú RV. panitṛ́ RV. paniṣṭama SV. pániṣṭi SV. pániṣṭha V.B. pánīyas V. pányas RV. -panyā RV. -panyu RV. panayā́yya RV.

The words paṇya S., paṇā́yya ÇB. seem to belong in meaning to this root.

√ pard, '*pedere*'.

Not quotable either in verb-forms or derivatives [parda, pardin, pardana].

√ 1 paç, spaç, 'see'.

Pres. [4.] páçyati -te etc. V.+
Perf. paspaçé etc. V.
Aor. 1. áspaṣṭa (*pres.*?) RV. [— 3. apaspaçat.]
Verb. spaṣṭa V.+
Sec. Conj.: *Caus.* spāçayate etc. V.B., -ti S.
Deriv.: páç? RV. paçya V.+ paçyin C. paçyata AV. -paçyana C. spáç V.B. spaça B.+ -spā́çana AV. paspaçā C.

The stem paçya is regarded as supplying the deficient present of √ dṛç.

√ 2 paç, 'bind'.

Regarded as inferable from paçú V.+, pā́ça V.+

√ 1 pā, 'drink'.

Pres. [1.] píbati -te etc. V.+ — [2.] pānti RV[1]., pāthás AV[1]. — [3.] pipatu K., pipīte pipate pipīya apipīta B., pipāná RV., pípāna AV.
Perf. papāú etc. V.+ (papātha RV., papīyāt RV.), pape etc. V.
Aor. 1. apāt etc. V.+ (pāhí pātám pātá pā́nt V.); peyās (3s.) RV.; ápāyi RV. — [3. apīpyat. —] 4. pāsta AV.

Fut. 1. pāsyati -te *etc.* B.+ [— 2. pātā.]
Verb. pītá V.+; pātum C., pā́tave V.B., -tavāi B., -tos KB.; pītvā́ V.B.S., -tvī́ RV.; -pā́ya AV.S., -pīya E.+; -pāí? RV.; píbadhyāi RV. [pāyam.]
Sec. Conj.: *Pass.* pīyáte *etc.* AV.+ — *Int.* pepīyate *etc.* U.C. [pāpā-.] — *Desid.* pipāsati *etc.* V.+; pípīṣati *etc.* RV. (√ pī?) — *Caus.* pāyáyati *etc.* V.+, -te C. (pāyyate S.; pipāyayiṣet K.)
Deriv.: -pā̆ V.+ pānta RV. pitú? V.B. -piba AV.C.
pā́na V.+ -pāyaka E. pītí V.B.S. papí RV.
pānīya E.+ -pāyin B.+ -pītha V.+ pipāsā́ B.+
pātavya B.+ -pā́yya RV.C. -péya V.+ pipāsu E.+
pātṛ V.+ pāyána V.+ pipīṣu RV.
pā́tra V.+ -pā́van V.B. pāyayitavyà MS.
Compare √ 3 pā.

√ 2 pā, 'protect'.

Pres. [2.] pā́ti *etc.* V.+ (pāná RV[1].)
[*Perf.* papāu.]
Aor. 4. pāsati *etc.* RV. — 6. apāsīt C.
[*Fut.* pāsyati, pātā.]
Verb. [pāta;] pātum E.
[*Sec. Conj.*: pāyate; pāpā-; pipāsa-; pālayati.]
Deriv.: -pā̆ V.+ pātṛ́ V.C. pāla V.+ pitṛ́? V.+
-pā́na AV.+ pā́tra? RV[1]. -pā́van V.B. -pīti RV.
pātavya C. pāyú V. páti? V.+ -pītha V.
-pā́yya RV. -pī́thya RV.

√ 3 pā, 'rise against'.

BR. refer to such a root certain forms from the reduplicated middle stem pipī with prefix ud. Since, however, such forms occur with the unquestionable meaning 'drink', and, on the other hand, forms from ut-piba (ÇB.) with the meaning given to 3 pā, it seems probable that we have here only a curiously specialized use of √ 1 pā + ud.

√ pāy, '*cacare*'.

Pres. [1.] pāyate? U.
Deriv. pāyú B.+
A single very doubtful occurrence (see BR.).

√ pi, pī, 'swell, fatten'.

Pres. [1.] páyate RV. — [2?] píyāna RV. — [3?] pīpihí V.B., pipyatam *etc.* pīpáyat *etc.* pīpaya ápīpet *etc.* (-payat -pema -pyan) pīpáyanta pí̄pyāna RV. — [5.] pinvánt -vatí AV., pinvire pinvāná RV., pinvāte apinvātām JB.

Perf. pīpā́ya *etc.* (pīpetha pipyathus -yus pīpivā́ṅs pipyúṣ-) pipye? (pīpyānā́) RV.
Verb. pīnā́ AV.+

Deriv.:	-paya? RV.	-pit RV.	pī́va AB.	pīvara E.+
	páyas V.+	pitú V.B.	pī́van V.+	pī́vas V.B.
	-pyasa? AV.	pīyū́ṣa V.+	pīvā́ṅs M.	pī́viṣṭha ÇB.

The roots pinv and pyā (given for convenience separately) are extensions of this. The classification of the reduplicated forms is difficult and questionable.

√ pinv, 'fatten'.

Pres. [1.] pínvati -te *etc.* V.B.S.
Perf. pipinváthus RV.
[*Aor. etc.* apinvīt; pinviṣyati, pinvitā.]
Verb. pinvitá ÇB.
Sec. Conj.: Caus. pinvayati ÇB.
Deriv.: -pinva RV. pínvana B.S.

A secondary root-form, from stem [5.] pinu of √ pī, from which stem a few regular forms are also made in the older language.

√ pibd, 'be firm' (?).

Pres. [1.] píbdamāna V.B.
Deriv. pibdaná V.

√ piç, 'adorn'.

Pres. [6.] piṅçáti -te *etc.* V.B.
Perf. pipéça pipiçus pipiçé -çre V.
Aor. 1. piçānā́ RV. [— 3. apīpiçat. — 5. apeçīt.]
[*Fut.* peçiṣyati, peçitā.]
Verb. piṣṭá V.B., piçitá AV.+
Sec. Conj.: Pass. piçyáte AV. — *Int.* pépiçat -çāna V.B. [— *Desid.* pipiçiṣa- pipeçiṣa-. — *Caus.* peçaya-.]

Deriv.:	píç V.	piçācá V.+	peça V.+	péças V.+
	piçá V.	piçā́ci RV.	peçī B.+	peçitṛ́ VS.
	piçáṅga V.+	píçuna? V.+	péçana V.	

√ piṣ, 'crush'.

Pres. [7.] pináṣṭi piṅṣánti *etc.* V.+ (piṇák RV.), piṅṣe M. — [6.] piṅṣá AV.?, apiṅṣat M.; piṣeyam piṣantī apiṣan E, ápīṣan AV.
Perf. pipéṣa pipiṣe *etc.* V.+
Aor. 1? apiṣṭām (3*d.*) C[1]. — 3. apīpiṣat E. — 7. apikṣan ÇB. [apikṣātām.]
Fut. 1. pekṣyati U. [— 2. peṣṭā.]
Verb. piṣṭá V.+; péṣṭum B.+, -ṭavāí B.; piṣṭvā́ B.; -piṣya S.+; -péṣam B.+

Sec. Conj.: Pass. **piṣyáte** *etc.* B.+ [— *Int.* **pepiṣ-**. — *Desid.* **pipikṣa-**.] — *Caus.* **peṣayati** *etc.* S.+

Deriv.: **peṣa** E.+ **peṣya** C. **péṣaṇa** B.+ **péṣṭra**? AV. **peṣaka** C. **péṣī** RV. **peṣṭṛ** C. **pípiṣvant**? RV.

Doubtless we are to read **apiṅṣṭām** for **apiṣṭām** (Bhāg. Pur.).

√ pis, 'stretch' (?).

Pres. [4.] **pisyati** ÇB.

Perf. **pipisus** ÇB.

Deriv. **pésuka** ÇB.

√ 1 pī, *see* √ pi.

√ 2 pī, *see* √ pīy.

√ pīḍ, 'press'.

Perf. **pipīḍé** RV.

Sec. Conj.: Caus. **pīḍayati** *etc.* AV.+, **-te** E. (**pīḍyate** *etc.* B.+; **-pīḍam** C.)

Deriv.: **-pīḍa** E.+ **-pīḍaka** C. **pīḍanīya** E. **-pīlana** C. **pīḍā** S.+ **-pīḍin** C. **pīḍayitavya** E. **pipīla**? AV.+ **pīḍana** U.+

√ pīy, 'abuse'.

Pres. [1.] **píyati** *etc.* V.B.

Deriv.: **píyāru** V. **píyaka** AV. **pīyatnú** RV. **pīyú** V.B.

√ puṭ, 'scale' etc.

Pres. [6.] **puṭati** C.

[*Perf. etc.* **pupoṭa**; **apoṭīt**; **poṭiṣyati**, **poṭitā**.]

Verb. **puṭita**? C.

Sec. Conj.: Pass. **puṭyate** C. [— *Caus.* **puṭayati**, **poṭayati**.]

Deriv.: **puṭa** B.+ **puṭana** C. **-poṭa** C. **-poṭana** C. **-puṭaka** C. **-poṭaka** C.

A late and bastard root, probably denominative of **puṭa**.

√ puth, 'crush'.

[*Pres. etc.* **puthyati**; **pupotha**; **apothīt**; **pothiṣyati**, **pothitā**.]

Sec. Conj.: Caus. **pothayati** *etc.* E.+, **-te** E.+

Deriv.: **potha** E. **pothaka** E.

√ puṣ, 'thrive'.

Pres. [4.] **púṣyati** *etc.* V.+, **-te** *etc.* E.+ — [9.] **puṣṇāti** *etc.* E.+ — [1.] **poṣati** C[1].

Perf. pupóṣa *etc.* V.+ (pupuṣyās RV.)
Aor. 1. puṣyāsam -sma B., -yāt C. [apoṣi.] — 2. [apuṣat] (puṣeyam -ema V.B.S., puṣa S.) [— 3. apūpuṣat. — 5. apoṣīt.]
[*Fut.* poṣiṣyati, pokṣyati; poṣitā, poṣṭā.]
Verb. puṣṭá V.+; puṣyáse RV.
Sec. Conj.: *Pass.* puṣyate *etc.* C. — [*Int.* popuṣ-. — *Desid.* pupoṣiṣa-, pupuṣiṣa-, pupukṣa-. —] *Caus.* poṣayati *etc.* V.+

Deriv.:			
-puṣ RV.C.	pūṣa C.	póṣa V.+	-poṣas RV.
puṣya V.+	pūṣán V.+	poṣaka E.+	poṣuka B.
púṣka- V.+	pūṣaṇá RV.E.	poṣin RV.C.	poṣṭṛ E.+
púṣpa V.+	pūṣaryà RV.	póṣya V.+	poṣitṛ C.
puṣṭí V.		poṣaṇa E.+	poṣayitnú RV.
púṣṭi AV.+		poṣaṇīya C.	poṣayiṣṇú AV.

√ pū, 'cleanse'.

Pres. [9.] punā́ti punīté *etc.* V.+ (punāhí SV., punaté RV.) — [1.] pávate *etc.* V.B.S. (pávamāna V.+), pava RV^1., pavant C^1. — punīṣé (1s.) RV^1.
Perf. pupuvus B.S., -ve *etc.* B. (apupot RV.MS.)
Aor. [3. apīpavat. —] 5. apāviṣus RV., apaviṣṭa *etc.* RV.MS.
[*Fut.* paviṣyati -te; pavitā.]
Verb. pūtá V.+ [pavita, pūna;] pavitum JB.; [pavitvā,] pūtvā́ AV., pūtví RV.; -pū́ya B.S.; -pāvam S.
Sec. Conj.: *Pass.* pūyáte *etc.* V.+ [— *Int.* popu-. — *Desid.* pupūṣa-, pipaviṣa-.] — *Caus.* paváyati *etc.* B.S., -te AA.; pāvayati *etc.* E.+, -te E. (pāvyate *etc.* C.)

Deriv.:			
-pū V.B.	pávyā RV.	potṛ V.+	-pāva V.+
-pu AV.	pávana V.+	potrá V.+	pāvaká V.+
-pvā? V.	pū́ti B.+	pavītṛ́ RV.	pāvana E.+
pava C.	pūtríma AV.	pavitṛ́ AV.+	-puna E.+
pavā́ RV.		pavítra V.+	pavayitṛ́ B.

√ pūj, 'reverence'.

Pres. [1.] apūjan? M^1.
Perf. pupūjire M^1.
[*Aor.* apūpujat.]
Sec. Conj.: *Caus.* pūjayati *etc.* S.+, -te *etc.* E. (pūjyate *etc.* E.+)

Deriv.:			
pūjā S.+	pūjya E.+	pūjana RV.E.+	pūjayitṛ E.
pūjaká E.+		pūjanīya E.+	pūjayitavya C.

√ pūy, 'stink'.

Pres. [1.] pū́yati *etc.* B.S. [-te.]
[*Perf. etc.* pupūye; apūpuyat, apūyiṣṭa; pūyiṣyate, pūyitā.]
Verb. [pūta,] pūyita (*caus.*?) ÇB.
[*Sec. Conj.*: popūy-, popū-; pupūyiṣa-; pūyaya-.]
Deriv.: pū́ya B.+ pū́ti AV.+

√ pūr, *see* √ 1 pṛ.

√ 1 pṛ, pṛṇ, pūr, 'fill'.

Pres. [3.] píparti píprati *etc.* V.C. (ápiprata 3*s.* RV.; pipīpṛhi C¹.) — [9.] pṛṇā́ti *etc.* V.B.S. — [6.] pṛṇáti -te *etc.* V.B. — [5.] pṛṇuyāt S¹. — [4.] pū́ryamāṇa RV¹.

Perf. pupūre -rire C. (pupūryās RV.); [papāra, paparus paprus] papṛvā́ṅs? MS.

Aor. 1. pūrdhí RV.; apūri C.; priyāsam AV. [pūryāt.] — 3. apūpuram ÇB. (pūpurantu RV.); pīparat RV¹. — 5. [apārīt,] pūriṣṭhās TA.

[*Fut.* parīṣyati, parītā.]

Verb. pūrṇá V.+, pūrtá V.+, pṛta S¹. [pūrita]; pūritum E.; [pūrtvā;] -pūrya E.+; -puras K.; pṛṇádhyāi RV.; -pūram S.

Sec. Conj.: Pass. pūryáte *etc.* B.+, -ti *etc.* E. (*or pres.* 4.) — [*Int.* pāpṛ-, popūr-. — *Desid.* pipariṣa-, pupūrṣa-. —] *Caus.* [pārayati;] pūráyati *etc.* AV.+, -te *etc.* E.+ (pūryate *etc.* E.+)

Deriv.: púr V. — -paraṇa C. — párus V.+ — párvan V.+ — purú V.+ — párīṇas RV. — párīman RV. — páreman SV. — púrīṣa? V.+ — pūrtí V.+ — pūra E.+ — pūraka E.+ — -pūrin E. — -pū́rya B.E. — pū́raṇa B.+ — pūraṇīya C. — -pṛṇa V.B.S. — pápri RV. — pápuri RV. — púpuri SV. — púraya? RV. — pūrayitṛ E. — pūrayitavya C.

See also √ prā, which is a secondary form of this root.

√ 2 pṛ, 'pass'.

Pres. [3.] píparti píprati *etc.* V.B.S.C. (pīpṛhi S¹.C¹.) — [1.] para VS¹.? — [2.] párṣi RV.

Aor. 3. ápīparat *etc.* V.B. (pī́parat V.B., pīpárat RV¹.) — 4. párṣati *etc.* RV., párṣat V.B., parṣa V. — 5. pāriṣat RV.

Verb. parṣáṇi RV.

Sec. Conj.: Caus. pāráyati *etc.* V.+, -te *etc.* E.+ (pāryate C.)

Deriv.: -páraṇa V. — partṛ́ RV. — parṣá? RV. — -parṣin? ÇB. — parṣáṇi RV. — párṣiṣṭha RV. — pārá V.+ — -pārin AB. — pā́raṇa V.+ — pāraṇīya E.+ — perú V. — pápri V. — pípru? V. — -pāraya RV. — pārayitṛ́ B. — pārayiṣṇú V.+

The aorist stem parṣ has almost won the value of a secondary root.

√ 3 pṛ, 'be busy'.

Pres. [5.] pṛṇoti C¹., pṛṇvāṇa C¹.

Verb. pṛta B.+

Sec. Conj.: Pass. priyate E.+ — *Caus.* pārayati *etc.* C.

Deriv.: -pra? RV. — -pāra E.+

Only with **ā** and (especially) **vyā**; hence in all probability a specialized use of 1 or 2 **pṛ** (1 **pṛ** 'be filled up or occupied', or 2 **pṛ** with **vi-ā**, 'made to pass to and fro, kept in motion').

√ pṛc, 'mix'.

Pres. [7.] **pṛṇákti pṛñcánti** *etc.* V.B., **pṛṅkté** *etc.* V.B. — [1.] **pṛñca pṛ́ñcatī** AV. — [3.] **pipṛgdhi** V.B., **pipṛkta** RV.
Perf. **papṛcus** B. (**papṛcāsi** RV., **-cyāt** *etc.* V.). **papṛcāná** RV.
Aor. 1. **párcas** RV., **pṛcīya** *etc.* RV.S., **pṛcāná** RV. — 4. **aprāk** AV., **apṛkṣi -kta** *etc.* V.B.S. [— 5. **aparcīt, aparciṣṭa.**]
[*Fut.* **parciṣyati -te, parcitā.**]
Verb. **pṛktá** V.+, **-pṛgṇa**? RV¹.; **-pṛ́ce** RV., **-pṛ́cas** V.B.S.
Sec. Conj.: *Pass.* **pṛcyáte** *etc.* V.+ [— *Int.* **parīpṛc-**. — *Desid.* **piparciṣa-**. — *Caus.* **parcaya-**.]
Deriv.: **-pṛc** V.B. **parka** AV.+ **pṛ́kṣ**? RV. **prakṣá**? V. **-párcana** V. **pṛkṣá**? RV.

√ pṛṇ, *see* √ 1 pṛ.

√ pṛt, 'fight'.

Inferable from the derivatives **pṛ́t** RV., **pṛ́tanā** V.+

√ pṛç, pṛṣ (?).

Under this heading may be grouped a number of words of doubtful relations, in part perhaps connected with √ **spṛç**:

pṛ́çana RV. **pṛçaní** RV. **pṛ́çni** V.+ **pṛ́ṣant** V.+ **pṛṣatá** B.+ **pṛṣṭá** V.B. **pṛṣṭí** V.B. **pṛṣṭhá** V.+ **párçu** V.+ **párçāna** V.

√ pyā, 'fill up'.

Pres. [4.] **pyā́yate** *etc.* V.+
Perf. **pipye**? RV. [**papye.**]
Aor. [1. **apyāyi.** —] 4. **apyāsam** AA. — 5. **pyāyiṣīmahi** S. — 6. **pyāsiṣīmahi** AV.B.S.
[*Fut.* **pyāsyate, pyāyiṣyate; pyātā, pyāyitā.**]
Verb. **pyāta** TS. [**pyāna.**]
Sec. Conj.: *Caus.* **pyāyáyati** *etc.* AV.+, **-te** *etc.* C. (**pyāyayiṣṭhās** U.; **pyāyyáte** *etc.* B.+)
Deriv.: **-pyāya** C. **-pyāyya** E. **-pyā́yana** B.+ **-pyāyayitṛ** B. **-pyāyin** C.

Is a secondary root-form from √ **pī**.

√ prach, 'ask'.

Pres. [6.] pṛcháti -te *etc.* v.+
Perf. papracha paprachus b.+
Aor. [3. apaprachat. —] 4. áprākṣīt *etc.* v.+ (áprāṭ rv.), aprașṭa c. (pṛkṣase? rv.)
Fut. 1. prakṣyati *etc.* b.+ (aprakṣyat b.u.) [— 2. praṣṭā.]
Verb. pṛṣṭá v.+; práṣṭum v.+; pṛṣṭvā e.+; -pṛchya e.+; -pṛ́cham -che rv.
Sec. Conj.: Pass. pṛchyáte *etc.* v.+ — [*Int.* parīpṛch-. —] *Desid.* pipṛchiṣa- (*in d.*). — [*Caus.* prachaya-.]
Deriv.: -pṛch rv. prāch- e.+ pṛchā c. pṛchaka b.+ pṛ́chya rv.c. praṣṭavya e.+ praṣṭṛ u.+ praçná v.+ -praçnya b. pipṛchiṣu c. papṛkṣéṇya rv.

The rv. form papṛkṣé is also referred hither by BR.

√ prath, 'spread'.

Pres. [1.] práthate *etc.* v.+, -ti *etc.* v.+
Perf. paprathé *etc.* v.+, -thatus c.
Aor. 1. prathāná rv. — 3. (*perf.*?) papráthat *etc.* -thanta rv. — 5. aprathiṣṭa *etc.* rv.
[*Fut.* prathiṣyate, prathitā.]
Verb. prathita b.+
Sec. Conj.: Caus. pratháyati *etc.* v.+, -te *etc.* v. (práthayi tb.s.)
Deriv.:

-pṛth? rv.	pṛ́thī̆ v.b.	práthana b.+	práthiṣṭha v.b.
pṛthá b.+	pṛthú v.+	práthas v.b.	práthīyas b.s.
pṛ́thak v.+	pṛthivī́ v.+	prathu e.+	prathasnu? tb.
pṛ́thavāna rv.	prathā c.	prathimán rv.c.	prathayitṛ c.

√ prā, 'fill'.

Pres. [2.] prā́si rv.
Perf. paprāú *etc.* v. (paprā́tha rv.; paprā rv.), papre *etc.* v.
Aor. 1. aprāt *etc.* v.b.; aprāyi av. — 4. aprās (3*s.*) rv.b.
Verb. prātá rv.
Deriv.: -prā rv. -pra av.b.s. -prā́ṇa (api-) rv. -prā́van rv.

A secondary root-form, from √ 1 pṛ.

√ prī, 'please'.

Pres. [9.] prīṇā́ti -ṇīté *etc.* v.+ — [4. (*or pass.*)] prīyate *etc.* u.+, -ti *etc.* e.+ (priyanti e[1].)
Perf. pipriyé -yāṇá rv.; apipres *etc.* b.s. (piprāyat *etc.* -áyasva piprīhí rv.)
Aor. 1. prīyāt c. — 4. aprāiṣīt *etc.* b. (préṣat rv.) [apreṣṭa.]

[*Fut.* **preṣyati -te, pretā.**]
Verb. **prītá** v.+; **prītvā́** çb.
Sec. Conj.: [*Int.* **peprī-.** —] *Desid.* **píprīṣati** rv. — *Caus.* **prīṇayati** *etc.* s.+

Deriv. **-prī** v.b.s.	**prīti** s.+	**premán** v.+	**piprīṣā** e.+
priyá v.+	**pretṛ́** rv.s.	**préyas** v.+	**piprīṣu** e.+
práyas v.b.	**preṇí** v.	**préṣṭha** v.+	**prīṇana** b.+

The so-called causative is, of course, a denominative, apparently of a pple **prīṇa,** not occurring independently.

√ pru, 'flow'.

Pres. [1.] **právate** *etc.* rv.b.s.
Perf. **pupruve** *etc.* b.
Aor. 4. **proṣṭhās** s.
Verb. **prutá** rv.
Deriv.: **pravá** rv. **pravaṇá**? v.+ **-prut** v.b.
A side-form to the much more common √ **plu.**

√ pruth, 'snort'.

Pres. [1.] **próthati** *etc.* v.b., **-amāna** rv.
[*Perf. etc.* **puprotha, -othe; aprothīt, -thiṣṭa; prothiṣyati -te, prothitā.**]
Verb. **-prúthya** rv., **prothya** s.
Sec. Conj.: *Int.* **pópruthat** rv. — *Caus.* **prothayitvā** s.
Deriv.: **protha** b.+ **prothátha** rv.

√ pruṣ, 'sprinkle'.

Pres. [5.] **pruṣṇuvánti -ṇávat -ṇute** rv. — [9.] **pruṣṇánt** b. — [6.] **pruṣa** rv., **-ṣánt**? av. — [4.] **ápruṣyat** çb.
[*Perf. etc.* **puproṣa; aproṣīt.**]
Fut. 1. **proṣiṣyánt** ts. [— 2. **proṣitā.**]
Verb. **pruṣitá** rv.
Deriv.: **-pruṣ** v.+ **-prūṣ** ts. **pruṣvā** av.b. **pṛ́ṣvā**? ts.
Compare √ **pluṣ.**

√ plī (?).

The isolated form **vi plīyante** occurs at svb. iii. 9. 1.

√ plu, 'float'.

Pres. [1.] **plávate** *etc.* v.+, **-ti** *etc.* b.+ — [2?] **pluvīta** s., **apluvan** e.
Perf. **pupluve** b.+, **-vus** e.+
Aor. 3. [**apuplavat,**] **ápiplavam** çb. — 4. **aploṣṭa** *etc.* b.
Fut. 1. **ploṣyati -te** *etc.* b.
Verb. **plutá** av.+; **-plutya** s.+, **-plū́ya** çb.k.

Sec. Conj.: Int. **poplūyate** *etc.* B.+ [— *Desid.* **puplūṣa-.**] — *Caus.* **plāvayati** *etc.* B.+, **-te** *etc.* E.+ (**plāvyate** C.); **plavayati** C[1].

Deriv.: **plavá** V.+ **plavana** S.+ **plāva** B.+ **plāvya** E.+ **plavaka** E. **plavitṛ** E. **-plāvaka** C. **plāvana** B.+ **-plavin** C. **pluti** S.+ **plāvin** B.+ **plāvayitṛ** E.

Compare √ **pru.**

√ **pluṣ,** 'burn'.

Pres. [1.] **ploṣati** C[1]. [**pluṣyati, pluṣṇāti.**]

[*Perf. etc.* **puploṣa; aploṣīt; ploṣiṣyati, ploṣitā.**]

Verb. **pluṣṭa** E.+

Sec. Conj.: Pass. **pluṣyate** C.

Deriv.: **plúṣi** V.B. **ploṣa** C. **ploṣin** C. **ploṣaṇa** C.

Compare √ **pruṣ.**

√ **psā,** 'devour'.

Pres. [2.] **psā́ti** *etc.* AV.B.

[*Perf. etc.* **papsāu; psāyāt, pseyāt, apsāsīt; psāsyati, psātā.**]

Verb. **psātá** B.; **-psā́ya** B.

Sec. Conj.: Pass. **apsīyata** JB. [— *Int.* **pāpsā-.** — *Desid.* **pipsāsa-.** — *Caus.* **psāpaya-.**]

Deriv. **psānīya** C.

Doubtless a secondary root-form, from √ **bhas.**

√ **phakk,** 'swell' (?).

Pres. [1.] **phakkant** C[1].

[*Perf. etc.* **paphakka; apaphakkat, aphakkīt; phakkiṣyati, phakkitā; phakkyate, pāphakk-, piphakkiṣa-, phakkaya-.**]

The single occurrence doubtless artificial.

√ **phaṇ,** 'spring'.

Pres. [1.] **phaṇati** C.

[*Perf. etc.* **paphāṇa paphaṇus pheṇus; aphaṇīt aphāṇīt; phaṇiṣyati, phaṇitā.**]

Sec. Conj.: Int. **pánīphaṇat** RV., **pamphaṇat** S. — [*Desid.* **piphaṇiṣa-.** —] *Caus.* **phāṇayati** *etc.* RV.LÇS. [**phaṇayati.**]

Deriv.: **phaṇá** B.+ **phāṇṭa** B.+ **phéna**? V.+

√ **phar,** 'scatter' (?).

Sec. Conj.: Int. **parpharat** RV[1].

Deriv.: **-pharvī** V.B. **phárvara** RV. **phā́riva** RV. **parpharī́ka** RV.

All the derivatives of doubtful meaning and connection.

√ 1 **phal**, 'burst'.

Pres. [1.] **phalati** *etc.* E. +
Perf. **paphāla** E. [**phelus.**]
[*Aor. etc.* **apīphalat, aphālīt; phaliṣyati, phalitā.**]
Verb. **phalita** E. +
Sec. Conj.: [*Int.* **pamphul-.** — *Desid.* **piphaliṣa-.** —] *Caus.* **phālayati** *etc.* E.
Deriv.: **phálaka** B. + **phalin** C. **phā́la** V. + **phulla** E. +

See √ 2 **phal**. The pple **phullant** M[1]. is doubtless a denominative formation from **phulla**.

√ 2 **phal**, 'fruit'.

Pres. [1.] **phalati** *etc.* E. +, **-te** E.
Perf. **phelire** C.
Fut. **phaliṣyati** *etc.* E. +
Verb. **phalita** E. +
Deriv.: **phála** V. + **phalitavya** E.

Doubtless in reality a denominative of **phála**, which from √ 1 **phal**.

√ **baṅh**, 'make firm'.

[*Pres. etc.* **baṅhate; babaṅhe; abaṅhiṣṭa; baṅhiṣyate, baṅhitā.**]
Verb. **bāḍha** V. +
Sec. Conj.: *Caus.* **baṅhayate** *etc.* B.
Deriv.: **bahala** C. **bahú** V. + **báṅhiṣṭha** V. + **bāhú**? V. +
báṅhīyas MS.

√ **bandh**, 'bind'.

Pres. [9.] **badhnā́ti** *etc.* V. + (**badhāna** AV. +, **bandhāna** E., **badhnīhi** C.), **-nīté** *etc.* V.B.S. — [1.] **abandhat** C., **-dhata** (3s.) E., **abadhnanta** E.
Perf. **babándha** AV. +, **bedhús** AV., **babandhus** E. +; **bedhe -dhiré** *etc.* AV. [**babandhe.**]
[*Aor.* **badhyāt, ababandhat, abhāntsīt.**]
Fut. 1. **bhantsyati** *etc.* B.S., **bandhiṣyati -te** E. + [— 2. **banddhā.**]
Verb. **baddhá** V. +; **banddhum** E. +, **baddhum**? E., **bandhitum** E.; **baddhvā́** AV. +, **-dhvā́ya** B.; **-bádhya** B. +; **-bádhe** AV.; **-bandham** C.
Sec. Conj.: *Pass.* **badhyáte** *etc.* V. +, **-ti** C. — [*Int.* **bābandh-, bābadhya-** — *Desid.* **bibhantsa-.** —] *Caus.* **bandhayati** *etc.* B. +
Deriv.:

bandhá V. +	**bándhana** V. +	**-baddhavya** C.	**badhirá** V. +
bandhaka E. +	**bandhanīya** E. +	**-banddhṛ** C.	**bandhayitṛ** C.
bandhin E. +	**bándhu** V. +	**banddhra** AV.	
bandhya E. +	**-bándhuka** B.		

√ bal, 'whirl' (?).

Sec. Conj.: Int. **balbalīti** çb[1].

It is not probable that this solitary verb-form has anything to do with the common derivatives (from a √ **bal** 'be strong') **bála** v.+, **bálīyas** av.+, **báliṣṭha** b.+, **baliman** u., **bālá**? s.+

√ bādh, 'oppress'.

Pres. [1.] **bā́dhate** *etc.* v.+, **-ti** *etc.* e.+
Perf. **babādhé** v.+, **-dha**? m.
Aor. [3. **ababādhat.** —] 5. **bādhiṣṭa** v. (**bādhithās** ta.); **bādhiṣṭām** ta.
Fut. 1. **bādhiṣyati** c., **-te** e. [— 2. **bādhitā.**]
Verb. **bādhitá** v.+; **bādhitum** e.; **-bā́dhya** rv.; **bā́dhe** rv.
Sec. Conj.: Pass. **bādhyate** *etc.* e.+ — *Int.* **bābadhe bā́badhāna, badbadhé -dhāná** rv.b. — *Desid.* **bībhatsate** *etc.* v.+; **bibādhiṣate** çb. — *Caus.* **bādhayati** *etc.* av.+

Deriv.:

bādh rv.	**-bādhin** b.c.	**bādhanīya** c.	**bībhatsa** s.+
bādhá, -ā v.+	**bādhyà** b.+	**-bā́dhas** rv.	**bībhatsā́** b.
bādhaka e.+	**bādhana** e.+	**bādhitavya** e.+	**bībhatsú** v.+
		bādhitṛ e.+	

Compare √ **vadh, badh.** The reference of **bībhatsa-** to this root is not beyond question.

√ budh, 'know, wake'.

Pres. [4.] **búdhyate** *etc.* v.+, **-ti** *etc.* e.+ — [1.] **bódhati** *etc.* v.+, **-te** *etc.* e.+
Perf. **bubudhé** *etc.* v.+, **bubodha** e. (**búbodhati** *etc.* **bubodhas** rv.)
Aor. 1. **bodhi** (*impv.*) rv.; **abudhran -ram** rv., **budhāná** rv.; **ábodhi** v.+ — 2. **budhánta** rv., **budhéma** av.? — 3. **abūbudhat** v. — 4. **ábhutsi** *etc.* v.b., **abuddha** c. [**bhutsīṣṭa.**] — 5. **bódhiṣat** rv., **abodhiṣata** c.
Fut. 1. **bhotsyati** b., **-te** b. [— 2. **boddhā.**]
Verb. **buddhá** v.+; **boddhum** e.+; **buddhvā** c.; **-budhya** b.+; **-búdhe** b., **budhí** rv.
Sec. Conj.: Pass. **budhyate** c. — *Int.* **bobudhīti** *etc.* b.c. — *Desid.* **bubhutsati -te** *etc.* c. [**bubodhiṣa-.**] — *Caus.* **bodháyati** *etc.* v.+, **-te** b. (**bodhyate** e., **bubodhayiṣa-** *in d.*)

Deriv.:

-budh v.b.	**bodhin** e.+	**buddhi** s.+	**bodhayitavya** c.
budha b.+	**bodhya** e.+	**boddhavya** u.+	**bodhayitṛ́** rv.c.
-budhya rv.	**bódhana** v.+	**bodhitavya** c.	**bodhayiṣṇu** e.
búdhan- tb	**bodhanīya** e.+	**boddhṛ** e.+	**bubodhayiṣu** e.+
bodhá v.+	**bodhi** e.+	**bubhutsā** c.	**bibodhayiṣu** e[1].
bodhaka e.+	**bodhít-** rv.	**bubhutsu** e.+	

√ bul, 'submerge'.

Sec. Conj.: Caus. **bolayati** C.

The single occurrence in a commentary is doubtless artificial.

√ bṛṅh, vṛṅh, 'roar', *see* √ vṛṅh.

√ 1 bṛh, 'make big or strong'.

Pres. [1.] **bṛṅhati -te** *etc.* ÇB. — [6.] **bṛhati** *etc.* AV.B.

Perf. **babarha** AV., **babṛhāṇá** RV.

Verb. **bṛḍha** ÇB., **vṛḍha** ÇB.C.

Sec. Conj.: Int. **bárbṛhat barbṛhi** RV. — *Caus.* **barhaya** V.; **bṛṅhayati** *etc.* (*or* **vṛṅh-**) E.+, **-te** E.

Deriv.: **bṛh-** V.+ **-barha** S.+ **-bárhaṇa** V.+ **barháṇā** RV. **bṛhánt** V.+ **-bárhas** V.B. **bárhiṣṭha** V.+ **barhís**? V.+ **bráhman** V.+ **brahmán** V.+ **-bṛṅhin** C. **bṛṅhaṇa** E.+ **bṛṅhaṇīya** C. **bṛṅhayitavya** C.

Compare the following root.

√ 2 bṛh, vṛh, 'tear', *see* √ vṛh.

The relations of the two roots **bṛh**, and the connection of some of their derivatives, are not wholly clear.

√ brū, 'say'.

Pres. [2.] **brávīti bruvánti** *etc.* **brūté bruváte** *etc.* V.+ (**brūmi** R., **bravīhi** E.+, **abrūvan** U., **abravat**? M.) — [6.] **abruvam** U.E., **bruvadhvam** M., **bruvamāṇa** C.

Aor. 1. **brūyāsta** M[1].

Deriv.: **-brava** V. **-bruva** AV.+

√ blī, *see* √ vlī.

√ bhakṣ, 'partake of, eat'.

Pres. [1.] **bhakṣati -te** *etc.* E.+

Aor. 1. **abhakṣi** C. — 3. **ababhakṣat** ÇB.

Verb. **bhakṣitum** E.+; **-bhakṣam** S.

Sec. Conj.: Desid. **bibhakṣiṣati** E.? — *Caus.* **bhakṣáyati** *etc.* V.+, **-te** *etc.* B.+ (**bhakṣyáte** *etc.* B.+; **bibhakṣayiṣati** E.+)

Deriv.:
bhakṣá V.+ **bhakṣaka** C. **bhakṣin** S.+ **bhakṣya** E.+ **bhákṣaṇa** V.+ **bhakṣaṇīya** B.C. **bhakṣitavya** C. **bhakṣitṛ** E. **bhakṣiván** B.S. **bhakṣayitṛ** E.+ **bhakṣayitavya** B.+ **bibhakṣayiṣā** C. **bibhakṣayiṣu** E.+

Secondary root-form, from √ **bhaj** (as denominative of **bhakṣá**); the non-'causative' forms only sporadic.

√ **bhaj**, 'divide, share'.

Pres. [1.] **bhájati -te** *etc.* v.+ — 2. **bhakṣi** RV.

Perf. **babhā́ja bhejus** *etc.* v.+ (**babhakṭha** ÇB. [**bhejitha**]), **bhejé -jiré** *etc.* v.+

Aor. 3. **abībhajus** ÇB. — 4. **abhākṣīt** *etc.* v.+ (**abhāk** V.B., **bhakṣat** RV.), **ábhakṣi -kta** *etc.* v.+ (**bhakṣīṣṭa** *etc.* V.B.S., **-ṣīta** SV.)

Fut. 1. **bhakṣyati -te** *etc.* B. (**abhakṣyan** M.); **bhajiṣyati -te** *etc.* E.+ [— 2. **bhaktā**.]

Verb. **bhaktá** v.+; **bhaktum** B.+, **bhajitum** E.; **bhaktvā́** AV.+, **-tvā́ya** RV.; **-bhajya** B.+; **-bhā́jam** (*inf.*) B.

Sec. Conj.: *Pass.* **bhajyáte** *etc.* AV.+ — [*Int.* **bābhaj-**. —] *Desid.* [**bibhakṣa-**;] **bhikṣa-** (*see* √ **bhikṣ**). — *Caus.* **bhājayati** *etc.* v.+, **-te** C. (**bhājyáte** *etc.* AV.B.)

Deriv.:	**bhāj** v.+	**bhajanīya** E.+	**bhāgá** v.+	**bhājaka** C.
	bhága v.+	**bhajenya** C.	**bhāgin** B.+	**bhājin** U.+
	bhajin C.	**bhaktí** v.+	**-bhāgya** S.	**bhājya** C.
	-bhajya C.	**bhajitavya** E.	**bhāgīyas** C.	**bhā́jana** B.+
	bhajana C.	**bhaktṛ** RV.	**-bhāja** S.	**bhājayú** RV.

Compare the derivative root-forms **bhakṣ** and **bhikṣ**; compare also √ **bhañj**.

√ **bhañj**, 'break'.

Pres. [7.] **bhanákti** *etc.* v.+ (**abhanas** AV.)

Perf. **babhañja** *etc.* v.+, **-jire** C.

Aor. 1. **abhāji** C. [**abhañji**; **bhajyāt**. — 3. **ababhañjat**.] — 4. **abhāṅkṣīt** *etc.* E.+

Fut. 1. **bhaṅkṣyati** E. — 2. **bhaṅktā** M.

Verb. **bhagna** S.+; **bhaṅktvā** E.+, **bhaktvā** E.; **-bhajya** E.+; **-bhañjam** C.

Sec. Conj.: *Pass.* **bhajyáte** *etc.* AV.+, **-ti** *etc.* E.+ [— *Int.* **bambhañj-**, **bambhajya-**. — *Desid.* **bibhaṅkṣa-**. — *Caus.* **bhañjaya-**.]

Deriv.:	**bhaṅgá** v.+	**bhaṅgi** C.	**bhañjana** AV.+	**bhaṅktṛ** C.
	bhaṅgin RV.C.	**bhañjaka** C.	**-bhañjanu** RV.	**bhaṅgurá** v.+

√ **bhaṭ**, 'hire'.

This so-called root (**bhāṭayati** *etc.* C.) is only a denominative of **bhaṭa** E.+ doubtless a prakritized form of **bhṛta**.

√ **bhaṇ**, 'speak'.

Pres. [1.] **bhaṇati** *etc.* JB.C.

Perf. **babhāṇa** C. [**babhaṇitha**.]

Aor. 1. **abhāṇi** C. [— 3. **abībhaṇat**, **ababhāṇat**. — 5. **abhāṇīt**.]

[*Fut.* **bhaṇiṣyati**, **bhaṇitā**.]

Verb. **bhaṇita** C.; **bhaṇitvā** C.

Sec. Conj.: Pass. **bhaṇyate** c. — *Desid.* **bibhaṇiṣa-** (*in d.*) [— *Caus.* **bhāṇayati.**]

Deriv.: **-bhaṇa** c. **bhaṇana** c. **bhaṇiti** c. **bhāṇaka** c. **bhaṇanīya** c. **bhāṇa** c. **bibhaṇiṣu** c.

A later form of √ **bhan.**

√ bhan, 'speak'.

Pres. [1.] **bhánati** *etc.* **-nanta** RV.

Probably related with √ **bhā.** Compare √ **bhaṇ,** the later form.

√ bhand, 'be bright'.

Pres. [1.] **bhándate** *etc.* RV.

[*Sec. Conj.: Caus.* **bhandayati.**]

Deriv.: **bhandána** V.B. **bhándiṣṭha** V.S. **bhadrá** V.+

√ bharts, 'revile'.

Pres. [1.] **bhartsati** *etc.* AV.? KB. E.

Sec. Conj.: Caus. **bhartsayati** *etc.* E. +, **-te** c[1]. (**bhartsyate** *etc.* E.+)

Deriv. **bhartsana** E.+

The form **bhartsyā̃mi** AV. is certainly a false reading.

√ bharv, 'devour'.

Pres. [1.] **bhárvati** *etc.* RV.

Deriv.: **-bharva** ? RV. **bhārvará** ? RV.

√ bhal, 'perceive'.

[*Pres. etc.* **bhalate** *etc.*]

Sec. Conj.: Caus. **bhālayati -te** *etc.* U.C.

√ bhaṣ, 'bark'.

Pres. [1.] **bhaṣati** *etc.* E.+, **-te** *etc.* E.

[*Perf. etc.* **babhāṣa; abhāṣīt; bhaṣiṣyati, bhaṣitā.**]

Verb. **bhaṣitum** E.

Deriv.: **bhaṣá** VS. **bhaṣaka** C. **bhaṣaṇa** C. **-bhāṣ** ? AB.

√ bhas, 'devour'.

Pres. [3.] **bábhasti bápsati** *etc.* V.B. (**babhasat** RV., **babdhām** C[1].) — [1 ?] **bhásat bhasáthas** RV.

Verb. **bhasita** C.

Deriv.: **bhas** C. **bhástrā** ? B. + **-psu** RV. **babhasa** U. **-bhasa** ? E. **bhásman** V. +

Compare the derived root **psā.** The nouns **bhasád** V.B.S., **bháṅsas** V. hardly belong here.

√ **bhā**, 'shine'

Pres. [2.] **bhāti** *etc.* v.+
Perf. **babhāu** *etc.* E.+
[*Aor.* **bhāyāt, abhāsīt.**]
Fut. 1. **bhāsyáti** B.+ [— 2. **bhātā.**]
Verb. **bhāta** U.+
[*Sec. Conj.*: *Pass.* **bhāyate.** — *Int.* **bābhā-.** — *Desid.* **bibhāsa-.** — *Caus.* **bhāpaya-, abībhapat.**]
Deriv.: **bhā́** v.+ **bhāna** E.+ **bhānú** v.+ **-bhā́van -varī** v.+
bha S.+ **bhāti** C. **bhā́ma** v. **bhā́s** v.+
Compare roots **bhan** and **bhās.**

√ **bhām**, 'be angry'.

[*Pres. etc.* **bhāmate; babhāme; abhāmiṣṭa; bhāmiṣyate, bhāmitā.**]
Verb. **bhāmitá** RV.TS.
[*Sec. Conj.*: *Int.* **bābhāmya-.** — *Caus.* **bhāmaya-.**]
Deriv. **bhā́ma** V.B.
In reality, the solitary form **bhāmitá** is doubtless *quasi*-pple from **bhāma** (√ **bhā**).

√ **bhāṣ**, 'speak'.

Pres. [1.] **bhāṣate** *etc.* B.+, **-ti** *etc.* E.+
Perf. **babhāṣe** *etc.* B.+
Aor. [1. **abhāṣi.** — 3. **ababhāṣat, abībhaṣat.** —] 5. **abhāṣiṣi** C.
Fut. 1. **bhāṣiṣyate** C. [— 2. **bhāṣitā.**]
Verb. **bhāṣita** E.+; **bhāṣitum** U.+, **bhāṣṭum** E.; **bhāṣitvā** E.; **-bhāṣya** E.+
Sec. Conj.: *Pass.* **bhāṣyate** *etc.* E.+ — [*Int.* **bābhāṣ-.** — *Desid.* **bibhāṣiṣa-.** —]
Caus. **bhāṣayati** *etc.* E.+, **-te** *etc.* B.E.
Deriv.: **-bhāṣ** AB. **bhāṣaka** C. **bhāṣaṇa** E.+ **bhāṣitavya** E.
-bhāṣa E.+ **bhāṣin** E. **-bhāṣaṇīya** C. **bhā́ṣitṛ** B.+
bhāṣā S.+ **bhāṣya** S.+
Related with roots **bhā, bhās, bhan.**

√ **bhās**, 'shine'.

Pres. [1.] **bhā́sati** *etc.* AV.+, **-te** *etc.* E.+
Perf. **babhāse** *etc.* E.+
[*Aor. etc.* **ababhāsat abībhasat, abhāsiṣṭa; bhāsiṣyate, bhāsitā.**]
Verb. **bhāsita** C.
Sec. Conj.: [*Int.* **bābhās-.** — *Desid.* **bibhāsiṣa-.** —] *Caus.* **bhāsayati** *etc.* U.+, **-te** E. (**bhāsyate** C.)
Deriv.: **bhās** E.+ **bhāsaka** C. **-bhāsana** E.+ **bhāsura** E.
bhāsá B.+ **bhāsin** E.+ **bhā́sas** RV. **bhāsvará** B.+
bhāsya C.
Doubtless a secondary root-form from √ **bhā**, perhaps through the noun **bhā́s.** Compare also √ **bhāṣ.**

√ bhikṣ, 'beg'.

Pres. [1.] bhíkṣate *etc.* V.+, -ti *etc.* E.
Perf. bibhikṣe B.U.
[*Aor.* abhikṣiṣṭa.]
Fut. 1. bhikṣiṣye E. [— 2. bhikṣitā.]
Verb. bhikṣita E.+; bhikṣitum E.; bhikṣitvā C.
Sec. Conj.: *Caus.* bhikṣayati C.
Deriv.: bhikṣā́ V.+ bhikṣaṇa S.+ bhikṣitavyà ÇB. bhikṣu C. bhikṣin E. bhikṣuka S.+

A desiderative formation from √ bhaj.

√ bhid, 'split'.

Pres. [7.] bhinátti bhindánti *etc.* V.+, bhintte C., bhindāná RV.
Perf. bibhéda bibhidús V.+, bibhide C.
Aor. 1. ábhedam -et *etc.* RV. (bhét bhédati bhidánt RV., bhidyús? MS.); abhedi B.E. — 2. [abhidat] bhideyam AV. [— 3. abībidhat.] — 4. [abhāitsīt,] bhitthās TS. [bhitsīṣṭa.]
Fut. 1. bhetsyati *etc.* S.+, -áte *etc.* B.+ (abhetsyat U.) [— 2. bhettā.]
Verb. bhinná V.+; bhettum B.+, bhéttavāí B.S.; bhittvā́ V.+; -bhídya V.+
Sec. Conj.: *Pass.* bhidyáte *etc.* B.+, -ti *etc.* E. [— *Int.* bebhid-.] — *Desid.* bíbhitsati *etc.* RV.E. — *Caus.* bhedayati *etc.* E.+, -te E. (bibhedayiṣa- *in d.*), bhidāpaya- (*in d.*).

Deriv.: bhíd V.+	bhedaka S.+	bhindú V.B.	bhettṛ́ V.+
-bhida E.+	bhedin B.+	bhidura C.	bibhitsā E.+
bhidā C.	bhedya E.+	bhitta? C.	bibhitsu E.+
bhídya V.+	bhedana S.+	bhittí B.+	bibhedayiṣu E.
bhedá V.+	bhedanīya E.	bhettavya E.+	bhidāpana C.

√ bhiṣaj, 'heal'.

Pres. [2.] bhiṣakti RV. — [7?] abhiṣṇak RV.
Deriv.: bhiṣáj V.+ bheṣajá V.+

The use of bhiṣaj as a verbal root in RV. is very abnormal. The denominative bhiṣajyáti *etc.* V.B., from the noun bhiṣáj, is quite common.

√ bhī, bhīṣ, 'fear'.

Pres. [3.] bibhéti bíbhyati *etc.* V.+ ([bibhitas *etc.*] bibhiyāt C.) — [1.] bibhyati -yanti *etc.* E.+ — bháyate *etc.* V.
Perf. bibhāya bibhyus *etc.* V.+ (bībhāya AB.AA.), bibhye E. — bibhayā́ṁ cakāra B.
Aor. 1. bhes B.S., bhema RV., bhiyāná RV. [abhāyi.] — 3. bībhayat ábībhayanta RV. — 4. ábhāiṣīt *etc.* V.+ (bhāis B.+)
Fut. 1. abheṣyat ÇB. [— 2. bhetā.]

Verb. bhītá v.+; bhetum E.; -bhīya C.; bhiyáse RV.

Sec. Conj.: [*Pass.* bhīyate. — *Int.* bebhī-. — *Desid.* bibhīṣa-. —] *Caus.* bhāyayati *etc.* C. (-bhāyya B.); bhīṣayate *etc.* B.+, -ti *etc.* E.+ (bībhiṣas TS., -ṣathās RV.; bhiṣayant C.)

Deriv.:

bhī́ v.+	bhiyásāna AV.	bheya E.	bhīṣā E.+
bhayá v.+	bhīti C.	bhīrú v.+	bhīṣaka E.+
bhayya B.	bhetavya E.+	-bhīla E.	bhī́ṣaṇa v.+
bhiyás v.	bhīmá v.+	bhī́s v.B.U.	bhīṣmá B.+

The 'causative' stem is, of course, a denominative from a derivative noun. Compare √ bhyas.

√ 1 bhuj, 'bend'.

Pres. [6.] bhujáti *etc.* v.+

Perf. [bubhoja] ábubhojīs RV.

[*Aor. etc.* abhāukṣīt; bhokṣyati, bhoktā.]

Verb. bhugna S.+; -bhujya S.+

Sec. Conj.: *Pass.* bhujyate C.

Deriv.:

-bhuj AV.	bhogá v.+	bhují RV.	bhujyú v.B.
bhuja E.+		bhujmán? RV.	

√ 2 bhuj, 'enjoy'.

Pres. [7.] bhuṅkté bhuñjáte *etc.* v.+ (-jaté RV.), bhunákti bhuñjanti *etc.* v.+ (bhuñjīyāt *etc.* S.+, bhuñjītam E.) — [1?] bhuñjati *etc.* U.+, -te *etc.* E.

Perf. bubhujé *etc.* v.+ (-jmáhe -jriré RV.), bubhujus E.+

Aor. 1. bhojam, bhójate RV. [bhujyāt; abhoji.] — 2. bhujema RV. — [3. abūbhujat, -jata. — 4. abhāukṣīt, abhukta. —] 6? bhukṣiṣīya B.S.

Fut. 1. bhokṣyate *etc.* S.+, -ti *etc.* E.+ — 2. bhoktā E.

Verb. bhukta E.+; bhoktum E.+; bhuktvā S.+, bhuṅktvā C.; bhójase RV.; bhújam bhujé RV.

Sec. Conj.: *Pass.* bhújyate *etc.* B.+, -ti M.? — *Int.* bobhujīti C., -jyate C. — *Desid.* bubhukṣate *etc.* E.+, -ti E. — *Caus.* bhojayati *etc.* AV.+, -te C.; bhuñjāpayati C.

Deriv.:

bhúj v.+	bhóga v.+	bhují RV.	bhujiṣyà AV.+
-bhoj- RV.	bhogin B.+	-bhogi RV.	-bhujiṣṭha? AV.
bhojá v.+	bhógya AV.+	-bhogaya RV.	bubhukṣā E.+
bhojaka E.+	bhójana v.+	bhukti S.+	bubhukṣu C.
bhojin S.+	bhojanīya B.+	bhoktavya S.+	bhojayitavya E.+
bhojyà v.+	bhójas v.	bhoktṛ U.+	bhojayitṛ C.

The word bhuṅkṣita R[1]. is perhaps an irregular formation from this root.

√ bhur, 'quiver'.

Pres. [6.] **bhurántu -ránta -rámāṇa** RV.
Sec. Conj.: Int. **járbhurīti -rat -rāṇa** RV.
Deriv.: **bhuraṇa** V. **bhurváṇi** RV. **bhū́rṇi** V. **bhuríj**? V.+

Doubtless a specialized root-form from √ **bhṛ**; all the forms and derivatives such as might come from √ **bhṛ**: *cf.* √ **tṛ**.

√ bhuraj.

The single form **bhurajanta** RV[1]. is regarded as coming from √ **bhṛjj** 'roast'.

√ bhū, 'be'.

Pres. [1.] **bhávati** *etc.* V.+, **-te** *etc.* B.+
Perf. **babhū́va** *etc.* V.+ (**babhū́tha -ū́vitha** V.B.; **babhūyās -yā́t babhūtu** RV.)
Aor. 1. **ábhūt -ūvan** *etc.* V.+ (**bhūyā́sam -sma** *etc.* V.+, **-yāma** V.B.U.; **bodhí** V.B., **bhū́tu** *etc.* V.); **abhāvi** C. — 2? **ábhuvat** *etc.* V. (**bhúvat** *etc.* V.B., **bhuvāni** RV.) — 3. **abūbhuvas** AV. [**abībhavat.**] — 5. **bhaviṣāt**? AB. [**abhaviṣṭa, bhaviṣīṣṭa.**]
Fut. 1. **bhaviṣyáti** *etc.* V.+, **-te** *etc.* E.+ (**abhaviṣyat** *etc.* U.+, **bhaviṣyadhvam** E.) — 2. **bhavitā́** B.U.E.
Verb. **bhūtá** V.+; **bhávitum** B.+, **-tos** B.; **bhūtvā́** V.+, **-tvī́** RV.; **-bhū́ya** V.+; **bhuvé -bhúve** V., **-bhvè** RV.; **bhūṣáṇi** RV.; **-bhū́yam** B., **-bhávam** ÇB.
Sec. Conj.: Pass. **bhūyate** *etc.* E.+, **-ti** U. — *Int.* **bóbhavīti** *etc.* V.+ — *Desid.* **búbhūṣati** *etc.* V.+, **-te** *etc.* E.+ — *Caus.* **bhāvayati** *etc.* AV.+, **-te** C. (**bhāvitum** E.; **bhāvyate** *etc.* E.+, **bibhāvayiṣati** B.)
Deriv.:

bhū́ V.+	**bhúvana** V.+	**bhū́yas** V.+	**bhāvyá** V.+
-bhu V.+	**-bhavas** B.	**bhávīyas** RV.	**bhāvana** E.+
-bhva V.	**bhúvas** B.+	**bhū́yiṣṭha** V.+	**bhāvanīya** E.+
bhúva B.+	**bhū́ti** V.+	**-bhaviṣṭha** RV.	**bhā́vuka** B.+
bhava V.+	**bhūtí** RV.	**bhū́ri** V.+	**bubhūṣā** B.+
bhavá AV.+	**bhávītva** RV.	**-bhū́varī** V.B.	**bubhūṣaka** E.
bhavaka C.	**bhavitavyà** B.+	**bhūṣṇu** B.+	**bubhūṣitavya** JB.
-bhavin C.	**bhavitṛ** E.+	**bhaviṣṇú** B.+	**bubhūṣu** S.+
bhávya V.+	**bhavítra** V.	**-bhū́ya** AV.+	**bhāvayitavya** B.+
-bhvan V.	**bhū́man** V.S.	**bhāva** U.S.+	**bhāvayitṛ** B.+
bhavana E.+	**bhūmán** V.+	**bhāvaka** E.+	**bhāvayú** RV.
bhavanīya C.	**bhū́mī** V.+	**bhāvin** E.+	

√ bhūṣ, 'attend upon, adorn'.

Pres. [1.] **bhū́ṣati** *etc.* V.B[1].
[*Perf. etc.* **bubhūṣa; abubhūṣat, abhūṣīt; bhūṣiṣyati, bhūṣitā.**]

Sec. Conj.: Caus. bhūṣayati *etc.* e.+, -te *etc.* e.+

Deriv.: bhūṣā e.+ bhūṣaṇa e.+ -bhūṣéṇya rv. bhūṣayitavya e.+ bhūṣya c. bhūṣitavya jb.

A secondary root-form, from √ bhū. The Vedic forms are divided by BR. between two roots: 1 bhūṣ, 'be, move' etc., 2 bhūṣ, 'attend upon' etc.

√ bhṛ, 'bear'.

Pres. [3.] bíbharti bíbhrati *etc.* v.b., bibhárti *etc.* rv[1].+, bibhṛṣva bibhrāṇa c. — [1.] bíbhramāṇa rv[1]. — bhárati -te *etc.* v.+ — [2.] bharti rv[2].

Perf. babhāra *etc.* b.+ (babhrima c.), babhre -rāṇá rv.; jabhā́ra *etc.* v.b., -bhre *etc.* v. (jabhartha -bhárat ajabhartana rv.) — bibharām babhūva c.

Aor. 1. bhartám bhṛtám b., abhṛta c.; bhriyāsam -yāt b.; abhāri v.b. — 3. bībharas e. — 4. abhārṣīt *etc.* v.b. (abhār v.b.; abhāriṣam av.; bharṣat rv.)

Fut. 1. bhariṣyáti *etc.* v.+ (ábhariṣyat rv.) — 2. bhartā́ çb.

Verb. bhṛtá v.+; bhártum v.+, -tave v., -tavāí v.; -bhṛ́tya v.+; bháradhyāi rv.

Sec. Conj.: Pass. bhriyate *etc.* v.+, -ti e. — *Int.* jarbhṛtás rv., bháribhrati *etc.* rv., barībharti c. — *Desid.* bubhūrṣati *etc.* b.+ [bibhariṣa-.] — *Caus.* bhārayati e.

Deriv.:

-bhrà? v.+	bhartṛ v.+	bhārá v.+	-bhṛtra rv.
bhára v.+	bhrā́tṛ? v.+	bhārin b.+	-bhṛ́tvan v.
-bhala? av.s.	bharítra rv.	bhāryà av.+	bhṛthá v.+
bháraṇa v.+	-bhárṇas rv.	-bhṛt v.+	-babhra b.
bharaṇīya e.+	bhárman rv.c.	bhṛtí v.+	babhrí v.
bharas v.b.	bhárīman rv.	bhṛ́ti çb[1].	jarbhári rv.
-bhári rv.c.	bhā́rman rv.	bhṛ́tya *gdve.* b.+	bámbhāri? b.
bharu c.	bhariṣá? rv.	bhṛ́tya *n.* av.	bubhūrṣā s.
bharatá v.+	bhrūṇá v.+	bhṛtyā́ v.	bubhūrṣu c.
bhartavyà v.+		bhṛtenya? av.	

√ bhṛjj, 'roast'.

Pres. [6.] bhṛjjáti *etc.* v.+ [-te.] — [4.] bhṛjyéyus? b.

[*Perf. etc.* babharjja -je, babhrajja -je; ababharjjat ababhrajjat, abhrākṣīt abhārkṣīt, abhraṣṭa abharṣṭa; bhrakṣyati -te, bharkṣyati -te, bhraṣṭā bharṣṭā.]

Verb. bhṛṣṭa s.+; bhṛṣṭvā c.

Sec. Conj.: Pass. bhṛjjyate c., -ti e. — [*Int.* barībhṛjjya-. — *Desid.* bibhrakṣa- bibharkṣa, bibhrajjiṣa- bibharjjiṣa-. —] *Caus.* [bhrajjayati;] bharjjayati *etc.* c.

Deriv.: bharjjana s.+ bhṛjjana b. bhráṣṭra b. bhrāṣṭra c.

√ bhyas, 'fear'.

Pres. [1.] ábhyasetām RV., bhyásāt SV.
[*Perf. etc.* babhyase; abibhyasat, abhyasiṣṭa; bhyasiṣyati, bhyasitā; bābhyas-, bibhyasiṣa-, bhyāsaya-.]
Deriv. -bhyasa AV.
A derivative root-form, from √ bhī (through bhiyas?).

√ bhrañç, bhraç, 'fall'.

Pres. [1.] bhráñçate *etc.* B.+, -ti AV[1].? — [4.] bhraçyate *etc.* S.+, -ti *etc.* E.+
[*Perf.* babhrañça -açus, babhrañçe.]
Aor. 2. bhraçat V.B. [— 3. ababhrañçat. — 5. abhrañçiṣṭa.]
[*Fut.* bhrañçiṣyati -te, bhrañçitā.]
Verb. bhraṣṭá AV.+, -bhṛṣṭa V.
Sec. Conj.: [*Int.* bābhraçya-, banībhraçya-, banībhrañc-. — *Desid.* bibhrañçiṣa-. —] *Caus.* bhrañçayati *etc.* E.+ (bhrañçyate *etc.* S.+); bhrāçáyan RV.
Deriv.: bhrañça B.+ bhráñçana AV.+ -bhráñçuka B. bhrā́çya RV. bhrañçin B.+ bhrañçathu C.

√ bhram, 'wander'.

Pres. [1.] bhramati *etc.* ÇB[1].? E.+, -te *etc.* E.+ — [4.] bhrāmyati *etc.* B.+
Perf. babhrāma babhramus *etc.* E.+, bhrematus -mus C.
Aor. 1. bhramyāt S.; abhrāmi E. — 3. abibhramat E. [— 5. abhramīt.]
Fut. 1. bhramiṣyati C. [— 2. bhramitā.]
Verb. bhrāṁta E.+; bhramitum C., bhrāṁtum C.; bhramitvā E., bhrāṁtvā C.; -bhramya C., -bhrāmya C.; -bhrāmam C.
Sec. Conj.: *Int.* bambhramīti *etc.* C., -myate *etc.* C. [— *Desid.* bibhramiṣa-.] — *Caus.* bhrāmayati *etc.* E.+, -te C. (bhrāmyate U.+); bhramayati *etc.* S.+ (bhramyate C.)
Deriv.: bhṛmá V. bhramá V.+ bhrami C. bhrāmaka C. bhṛmí RV. -bhramin C. bhrāṁti C. bhrāmin C. bhṛ́mi RV. bhramaṇa E.+ bhrāma C. bhrāmaṇa C. bhṛ́ñga? AV.+ bhramaṇīya C.

√ bhrāj, 'shine'.

Pres. [1.] bhrā́jate *etc.* V.+, -ti *etc.* V.+
Perf. babhrāja -ājatus E.+ [babhrāje, bhreje.]
Aor. 1. abhrāṭ RV.; bhrājyāsam AV.; abhrāji RV. — [3. ababhrājat, abibhrajat. — 5. abhrājiṣṭa.]
Fut. 1. bhrājiṣyate E. [— 2. bhrājitā.]
Sec. Conj.: [*Int.* bābhrāj-. — *Desid.* bibhrājiṣa-. —] *Caus.* bhrājayati *etc.* E.+

Deriv.:	**bhrā́j** V.+	**bhrājaka** C.	**bhrajas**? AV.B.	**-bhrāṣṭi** RV.
	-bhraj? V.	**bhrājin** C.	**bhárgas** V.+	**bhṛṣṭí**? V.B.S.
	bhárga B.+	**bhrājana** C.	**bhrājí** MS.	**bhrā́jiṣṭha** B.C.
	bhrājá V.+	**bhrā́jas** V.B.S.	**bhrājis-** B.E.	**bhrājiṣṇu** E.+
			bhṛ́gu? V.+	

√ **bhrī**, consume'.

Pres. [9.] **bhrīṇánti** RV[1].

[*Perf. etc.* **bibhrāya; abhrāiṣīt; bhreṣyati, bhretā; bebhrī-, bibhrīṣa-, bhrāyaya-.**]

√ **bhreṣ**, 'totter'.

Pres. [1.] **bhreṣati** B., **-te** RV.

[*Perf. etc.* **bibhreṣa -ṣe** *etc. etc.*]

Deriv. **bhréṣa** B.+

Doubtless related with √ **bhraṅç**.

√ **maṅh, mah**, 'be great, be liberal, bestow'.

Pres. [1.] **máṅhate** *etc.* V.B. — **mahe** RV.M., **-heta -hema** RV.

Perf. **māmahé -hāná** V.B. (**māmahanta** *etc.* **māmáhas** RV.) [**mamāha, mamaṅhe.**]

[*Aor. etc.* **amaṅhista, amahīt; maṅhiṣyate mahiṣyati, maṅhitā mahitā.**]

Verb. **mahitá** B.+; **mahitvā** E.; **mahé** V.B.; **maháye** RV.

Sec. Conj.: Caus. **maṅháyam** *etc.* RV.; **maháyati** *etc.* V.+, **-te** *etc.* V.B.

Deriv.:

maghá V.+	**makhá**? V.+	**mahana** C.	**mahmán** AV.
maṅhánā RV.	**majmán**? V.	**mahanīya** E.	**máhis-** RV.
maṅhanīya C.	**máh** V.+	**mahánt** V.+	**mahiṣá** V.+
máṅhīyas RV.	**maha** *n.* E.+	**mahás** V.+	**mahiṣṭha** C.
máṅhiṣṭha V.B.S.	**mahá** V.+	**máhas** V.+	**mahīyas** B.+
makṣú? RV.	**mahā́** V.+	**máhi** V.+	**mahayya** U.
mañkṣu? C.	**mahya**? E.	**mahín** RV.	**mahā́yya** RV.
maṅhayú RV.	**mahán** V.	**mahimán** V.+	**mahayā́yya** RV.

Generally divided into two (related) roots, but the forms and meanings are not separable with distinctness.

√ **majj**, 'sink'.

Pres. [1.] **májjati** *etc.* V.+, **-te** *etc.* E.+ (**majjāna** C.)

Perf. **mamajja** E.+

Aor. 1. **majjyāt** ÇB.; **amajji** C. [— 3. **amamajjat.** — 4. **amāñkṣīt.**] — 5. **majjīs** M.

Fut. 1. **mañkṣyati** *etc.* B.+, **-te** B.; **majjiṣyati** E. [— 2. **mañktā.**]

Verb. **magna** U.S.+; **majjitum** B.+ [**mañktum**; **mañktvā**, **maktvā**;] **-májjya** AV.+

Sec. Conj.: [*Int.* **māmañkti**, **māmajjyate**. —] *Desid.* **mimañkṣa-** (*in d.*). — *Caus.* **majjayati** *etc.* B.+, **-te** *etc.* E.+

Deriv.: **majján**? V.+ **majjana** S.+ **majjūka** C. **mañktavya** C. **madgú**? B.+ **-majra**? RV. **mimañkṣu** C. **majjayitṛ́** B.

√ mañc, 'purify' (?).

[*Pres. etc.* **mañcate**; **mamañce**; **amañciṣṭa**; **mañciṣyate**, **mañcitā**.]

Verb. **-mañcya** C[1].

Deriv.: **mañca**? E.+ **-mañcana** C.

Doubtless artificial.

√ maṇ, 'sound'.

Assumed for the *quasi*-pple **maṇita**, occurring once or twice in late Sanskrit.

√ maṇṭ, ?

Sec. Conj.: *Caus.* **maṇṭáyet** TB[1].

Probably a false reading.

√ maṇḍ, 'deck'.

[*Pres. etc.* **maṇḍati -te** *etc. etc.*]

Sec. Conj.: *Caus.* **maṇḍayati** *etc.* E.+, **-te** E.

Deriv.: **maṇḍa** U.+ **maṇḍana** E.+ **maṇḍitṛ** C.

√ math, manth, 'shake'.

Pres. [9.] **mathnā́ti** *etc.* V.+, **-nīte** *etc.* B. (**mathnadhvam** M.) — [1.] **mánthati** *etc.* V.+, **-te** V.B.; **máthati** *etc.* AV.E.+, **-te** *etc.* E.+

Perf. **mamā́tha** AV.+, **mamathus** C., **methus methire** B.; **mamantha -nthus** E.+

Aor. [3. **amīmathat**, **amamanthat**. —] 5. **mathīt** *etc.* V., **amathiṣata** JB.; **ámanthiṣṭām** RV.

Fut. 1. **mathiṣyati -te** *etc.* B.+; **manthiṣyati** B.S. — 2. **mathitā** E.

Verb. **mathitá** V.+; **mathitum** B.+, **-tos** B., **mánthitavāí** MS.; **mathitvā́** B.+ [**manthitvā**]; **-máthya** B.+, **-manthya** E.?; **-mātham** C.

Sec. Conj.: *Pass.* **mathyáte** *etc.* V.+, **-ti** *etc.* E.+ — [*Int.* **māmath-**, **mammath-**, **māmanth-**. — *Desid.* **mimathiṣa-**, **mimanthiṣa-**. —] *Caus.* **māthayati** *etc.* E.; **manthayati** *etc.* S.+; **mathayati** C.

Deriv.: **math** V.+ **-matha** E.+ **-mathyà** B. **máthya** B.+ **mathan** C. **mathana** U.+ **mathí** RV. **-máthi** V. **-mathitṛ** S. **mathná** RV. **mathrá** RV. **mātha** B.+ **-māthin** B.+ **manthá** V.+ **mánthā** V. **manthaka** C. **mánthya** B.S. **-mánthana** V.+ **-manthanī** B.S. **manthitavyà** MS.S. **mánthitṛ** AV.B. **manthu**? C. **manthāna** E.+ **manmatha** E.+

√ **mad, mand,** 'be exhilarated, exhilarate'.

Pres. [1.] **mádati** *etc.* V.B.S.C[1]., **-te** *etc.* AV.B.; **mándati -te** *etc.* V.B. — [3.] **mamatsi** *etc.* (**mamáttu** *etc.*, **mamádat** *etc.*, **ámamadus**) V. — [4.] **mā́dyati** *etc.* B.+, **-te** E. — 2. **mátsi -sva** V.

Perf. **mamā́da** V.B. (**māmadant**? S.); **mamanda** *etc.* RV. (**mamandat amamandus** RV.)

Aor. 1. **mandús -dānā́** RV. — 3. **ámīmadat** *etc.* **-danta** V.B.U. — 4. **amatsus** RV., **amatta** *etc.* V.B.S. (**mátsati** *etc.* **mátsat** RV.) — 5. **amādiṣus** *etc.* V.+ (**mādithās** M.); **ámandīt** *etc.* **mándiṣṭa** *etc.* (**mandiṣīmahi**) V.B.

[*Fut.* **madiṣyati, mandiṣyate; maditā, manditā.**]

Verb. **mattá** AV.+, **maditá** (*caus.*?) V.+; **maditos** B.; **mandádhyai** RV.

Sec. Conj.: Pass. **madyámāna** RV. — [*Int.* **māmad-** — *Desid.* **mimadiṣa-**. —] *Caus.* **madáyati** *etc.* AV.+, **-te** C.; **mādayati -te** *etc.* V.+; **mandáyati** *etc.* RV. (**mādayádhyāi mandayádhyāi** RV.)

Deriv.:

-mă̆d V.B.	**-madvara** E.+	**-mā́dya** V.	**-manda** S.
máda V.+	**mádiṣṭha** V.B.	**mā́dana** V.+	**mandín** RV.
madín V.B.	**madiṣṇu** B.+	**-mā́duka** B.	**mandána** V.B.
mádya V.+	**matsará** V.+	**medín**? V.+	**mandí** RV.
madana V.+	**mátsya**? V.+	**madāmada** U.	**mandāra** V.+
-maditavya U.	**maderú**? RV.	**madayitṛ** C.	**mandú** RV.
madirá RV.	**-mā́da** V.+	**mādayitṛ** C.	**mandrá** V.+
madrá? B.+	**mādaka** C.	**mādayitnú** RV.	**mándiṣṭha** RV.
mádvan RV.	**-mādin** E.+	**mādayiṣṇú** V.	**mandasānā́** V.
			mandayú RV.

Might well enough be divided into two different though related roots, of kindred meaning. BR. refer a few of the forms to a root 2 **mad** 'delay'.

√ **man,** 'think'.

Pres. [4.] **mányate** *etc.* V.+, **-ti** *etc.* U.+ (**manyā́sāi**? ÇB.) — [8.] **manuté** *etc.* V.+ (**manvaté** 3*p.* RV.) — [3.] **mamandhi -nyāt ámaman** RV.

Perf. **mene** *etc.* B.+ (**mamnā́the -ā́te** RV.)

Aor. 1. **amata** RV., **ámanmahi** V.B. (**mánāmahe** *etc.* **mananta manānā́** RV.) [— 3. **amīmanat.**] — 4. **amaṅsta** *etc.* V.+ (**máṅsate** *etc.* V.B.; **maṅsīṣṭá** *etc.* **-sīrata** V.; **masīya** RV.; **mā́ṅsta** AV.TA., **-stām** TA., **mandhvam** KB.) [— 5. **amaniṣṭa.**]

Fut. 1. **maṅsyate** *etc.* B.+ (**-syeran** M.), **-ti** E.; **maniṣye** V.B. [— 2. **mantā, manitā.**]

Verb. **matá** V.+ [**manita**]; **mantum** E.+, **mántave** RV., **-tavāí** V.B., **-tos** B.; **matvā́** U.+ [**manitvā**]; **-matya** B.+, **-manya** E.+

Sec. Conj.: Pass. **manyate** C. [— *Int.* **manman-**.] — *Desid.* **mīmāṅsate** *etc.* AV.+, **-ti** *etc.* B.U. (**amīmāṅsiṣṭhās** ÇB.; **mīmāṅsyáte** AV.+) [**mimaṅsa, mimaniṣa-**.] — *Caus.* **mānayati** *etc.* AV.+, **-te** *etc.* E.+ (**mānyate** E.+; **mīmānayiṣa-** *in d.*)

Deriv.:	-mana? TS.	matí V.+	-māti V.B.	-manya V.+
	manā́ RV.	mántu V.	māna V.+	-manyaka C.
	mánas V.+	mantavyà B.+	-mānaka C.	mīmāṅsā́ B.+
	manīṣā́ V.+	manotṛ RV.	mānin U.+	mīmāṅsaka C.
	mánu V.+	mantṛ́ B.+	mānya E.+	mīmāṅsya U.S.+
	manú V.	mántra V.+	mānana E.+	-mīmānayiṣu E.
	mánus V.B.	mánman V.B.S.	mānanīya E.+	mānayitṛ E.+
	manána RV.	manyú V.+	-mā́nuka B.	mānayitavya E.+
	mananā́ RV.		múni? V.+	

Compare √ mnā. BR. and Gr. refer, perhaps with reason, the reduplicated present forms to another root, meaning 'delay' (√ 2 mad, mand BR.; √ 2 man Gr.).

√ mah, *see* √ maṅh.

√ 1 mā, 'measure'.

Pres. [3.] mímīte mimate *etc.* V.+, mimīmas E., mimīyāt *etc.* mimātu mimīhí *etc.* V.(mimet KB.) — [2.] māti *etc.* V.+, māsva RV., mīmahe C. [— 4. māyate.]

Perf. mamé mamiré *etc.* V.+, mamāu *etc.* RV.C.

Aor. 1. [meyāt;] amāyi V.+ — 4. ámāsi AV. (mā́sātāi AV.) [māsīṣṭa. — 6. amāsīt.]

[*Fut.* māsyati -te; mātā.]

Verb. mitá V.+; mātum B.+, mitum C.; mitvā́ V.+, mītvā S.; -mā́ya V.+; -mé -māí RV.

Sec. Conj.: *Pass.* mīyate *etc.* E.+ — ⌊*Int.* māmā-, memīya-. —⌋ *Desid.* mitsati C. — *Caus.* māpayati -te *etc.* U.S.+ [amīmapat.]

Deriv.:	mā́ V.+	-mātavya C.	māyā́ V.+	-mitsā C.
	mā́na V.+	mā́tṛ V.+	māyú V.	māpaka C.
	mānā́? RV.	mā́tṛ́? V.+	mā́s, -mas V.+	-māpya C.
	miti U.+	mā́trā V.+	méya AV.+	-māpana E.

√ 2 mā, 'exchange'.

Pres. mayet M., mayante RV.

[*Perf. etc.* mame; amāsta; māsyate, mātā.]

Verb. -mítya AV.? [-māya.]

Sec. Conj.: *Pass.* mīyate C. [*Int. etc. as* √ 1 mā.]

Deriv.: -maya S.+ -mātavya C.

Doubtless a specialization of √ 1 mā in connection with certain prepositions.

√ 3 mā, 'bellow'.

Pres. [3.] mímāti V. (mimeti SV., mimanti RV.; mimīyāt K.)

Perf. mimāya V.B.

Aor. 3? ámīmet V. (mīmayat RV.)

Verb. **mā́tavāí** V.
Sec. Conj.: Int. **mémyat** RV.
Deriv.: **māyú** V.+ **mayú**? B. **mayū́ra**? V.+
Apparently an onomatopoetic root.

√ **mārg**, 'chase'.

Pres. [1.] **mārgati -te** *etc.* E.+
[*Perf. etc.* **mamārga**; **amārgīt.**]
Fut. 1. **mārgiṣyati** E. [— 2. **mārgitā.**]
Verb. **mārgita** E.+; **mārgitum** E.; **mārgitvā** E.
Sec. Conj.: Caus. **mārgayati** *etc.* E.+
Deriv.: **mārga** E.+ **mārgin** E. **mārgaṇa** E.+ **mārgitavya** E.+
Really a denominative formation from **mārga** 'track'.

√ **mi**, 'fix'.

Pres. [5.] **minóti** *etc.* V.+, **minute** S.
Perf. **mimāya mimyús** RV. [**mimye.**]
[*Aor.* **meyāt**; **amāyi**; **amāsīt, amāsta**; **māsīṣṭa.**]
Fut. 1. **meṣyant**? AB. [**māsyati -te.** — 2. **mātā.**]
Verb. **mitá** V.B.S.U.; **-mitya** AV.? AB. [**-māya.**]
Sec. Conj.: Pass. **mīyate** *etc.* V. [— **memi-**; **mitsati -te**; **māpayati.**]
Deriv.: **maya**? E.+ **mít** V. **-méka**? V.B. **métṛ** RV.
-mayana B. **mití** V.
Doubtless a form of √ 1 **mā**, with which it agrees also in meaning in later Sanskrit.

√ **mi**, 'damage', *see* √ **mī**.

√ **mikṣ** (**miç**), 'mix'.

Pres. [3.] **mimikṣvá** RV. — [1.] **mímikṣati** *etc.* V.B.S.
Perf. **mimikṣáthus** *etc.* **-ṣé -ṣire** RV.
Sec. Conj.: Caus. **mekṣayati** B.S.
Deriv.: **miçrá** V.+ **-miçla** V.B. **-míkṣā** V.B.S. **mékṣaṇa** B.S.
mimikṣú RV.
Seems a desiderative formation to a simpler √ **miç**; referred by the grammarians (and Gr.) to √ **mih.**

√ **migh**, *see* √ **mih.**

√ **mith**, 'alternate, altercate'.

Pres. [1.] **methati** *etc.* V.B.S., **methete** RV. — [6?] **mithatī** RV.
Perf. **mimetha** RV.
Verb. **mithita** RV.; **mithitvā** C.
Deriv.: **mithatí** RV. **míthu** V.B. **míthus** B. **-méthaka** ÇB.
mithás V.+ **mithuná** V.+ **mithyā́** B.+ **-méthana** S.

√ mid, mind, *see* √ med.

√ mil, 'combine'.

Pres. [6.] **milati** *etc.* C.
Perf. **mimilus** C.
[*Aor.* **amelīt, ameliṣṭa.**]
Fut. 1. **miliṣyati** B.+
Verb. **milita** C.; **militvā** C.; **-milya** C.
Sec. Conj.: *Caus.* **melayati** *etc.* C.; **melāpaya-** (*in d.*).
Deriv.: **milana** C. **mela** C. **melaka** C. **melana** C. **melāpaka** C. **melāpana**? C.

√ miṣ, 'wink'.

Pres. [6.] **miṣáti** *etc.* V.+, **-te** E.
Perf. **mimeṣa** C.
Aor. 3. **amīmiṣat** U. [— 5. **ameṣīt.**]
Fut. 1. [**meṣiṣyati**] (**miṣyanti**? R.) [— 2. **meṣitā.**]
Verb. **miṣita** C.; **-miṣya** C.; **-míṣas** RV.; **-meṣam** E.
Deriv.: **-miṣ** V.+ **miṣa** V.+ **-meṣa** V.+ **-meṣaṇa** C. **-memiṣa** B.

√ mih, '*mingere*'.

Pres. [1.] **méhati** *etc.* V.+, **-te** *etc.* B.+ — **méghamāna** RV[2].
[*Perf.* **mimeha.**]
Aor. [3. **amīmihat.** —] 7. **amikṣat** ÇB.
Fut. 1. **mekṣyáti** *etc.* AV.B.S. [— 2. **meḍhā.**]
Verb. **mīḍha** V.+; **mihé** RV.
Sec. Conj.: *Int.* **mémihat** ÇB. — [*Desid.* **mimikṣa-**, *see* √ **mikṣ.** —] *Caus.* **mehayati** *etc.* RV.C.
Deriv.: **míh** RV. **-míhya** ÇB. **meghá** V.+ **meha** B.+ **-mehin** C. **mehánā** RV. **méhana** V.+ **-mehanīya** S. **mehatnú** RV. **méḍhra** AV.+ **meṇḍhra**? C. **mīḍhá**? V.+ **mīḍhvā́ṅs**? V.+

Compare √ **mikṣ.**

√ mī, mi, 'damage'.

Pres. [9.] **minā́ti** *etc.* V.B., **aminanta minānā́** RV. (**minat -nan** RV., **minīt** AV.); **mīnāti** ÇB. [**mīnīte.**] — [5.] **minoti** *etc.* RV[1].C[1]. — [3.] **mimītas**? RV., **-īyāt**? V.B. — [4.] **mī́yate** *etc.* RV.B.+
Perf. **mimā́ya** *etc.* RV., **mimye** C. (**mīmaya** AV.) [**mamāu, mame.**]
Aor. 1. [**mīyāt;**] **ámāyi** B. — 4. [**amāsta, māsīṣṭa;**] **meṣṭa** *etc.* AV.B.S. [— 6. **amāsīt.**]
Fut. 1. **meṣyase** PB. [**māsyati, -te.** — 2. **mātā.**]
Verb. **mīta** V.+; **métos** B.; [**mītvā; -mīya, -māya;**] **-míyam -míye** RV.

Sec. Conj.: Pass. **mīyáte** *etc.* ÇB.MS. — *Int.* **mémyāna** RV. [— *Desid.* **mitsa-.**]
— *Caus.* **māpayati** *etc.* E. + [**amīmapat.**]

Deriv.: **-mi-?** RV.	**-mīya** B.	**-māyu** B.	**-mātavya** E.
-mī RV.	**-mayu** AV.	**máyuka** AV.B.	**-māpana** E. +
-maya B. +		**-mīti** C.	**-māpayitṛ** C.

√ mīl, 'wink'.

Pres. [1.] **mīlati** *etc.* B. +, **-te** S.
Perf. **mimīla** C.
Aor. 3. **amimīlat** C. [**amīmilat.** — 5. **amīlīt.**]
[*Fut.* **mīliṣyati, mīlitā.**]
Verb. **mīlita** B. +; **-mī́lya** V. +
Sec. Conj.: Pass. **mīlyate** C. — [*Int.* **memīl-.** — *Desid.* **mimīliṣa-.** —]
Caus. **mīlayati** B. +, **-te** E.

Deriv.: **-mīla** S. +	**mīlaka** C.	**-mīlin** AV.C.	**mīlana** E. +

√ mīv, mū, 'push'.

Pres. [1.] **mī́vati** *etc.* AV.B.
Verb. **mīvitá** B., **-mūta** V.S.; **-mī́vya** B.

Deriv.: **-mu?** C[1].	**mūrá** RV[1].	**-maviṣṇu?** RV[1].	**-móta?** AV[1].

√ muc, mokṣ, 'release'.

Pres. [6.] **muñcáti** *etc.* V. +, **-te** *etc.* V.+; **mucánti** *etc.* **mucasva** *etc.* (*aor.* 2?) RV.TA.
Perf. **mumóca mumucé** *etc.* V. + (**mumoktu** *etc.* V.B., **mumócat** *etc.* **mú-mocati mumucas amumuktam** RV.)
Aor. 1. **ámok** AV. (**mogdhí** TA.); **mucīṣṭa** RV.; **ámoci** V.+ — 2. **ámucat** *etc.* V. — 3. **amūmucat** C. — 4. **amāuk** *etc.* B. (**mokṣīs** C.), **ámukṣi** *etc.* V.; **mukṣīya** V.B.
Fut. 1. **mokṣyati -te** *etc.* B. + [— 2. **moktā.**]
Verb. **muktá** AV. +; **moktum** B. +; **muktvā́** B. +; **-múcya** V. +; **mókam** B.
Sec. Conj.: Pass. **mucyáte** *etc.* AV. +, **múcyase** *etc.* V., **-ti** *etc.* U.E. + — [*Int.* **momuc-.** —] *Desid.* **múmukṣati -te** *etc.* V. +; **mókṣate** *etc.* B. + — *Caus.* **mocayati -te** *etc.* E. + (**mocyate** C.; **mumocayiṣa-** C.)

Deriv.: **-muc** V. +	**mocya** E. +	**mucyu** GB.	**mumucu** E. +
-mucī AV.	**mócana** V. +	**-mukṣā** MS.	**mumukṣā** E. +
-muca E. +	**mocanīya** B. +	**mokṣa** B. +	**mumukṣú** V. +
moka, -kī V. +	**-muci** E.	**mokṣaka** E. +	**mocayitṛ** C.
-mokya AV.	**-mucu** E. +	**mokṣin** E. +	**mocayitavya** C.
moca E. +	**múkti** AV. +	**mokṣya** C.	**mumocayiṣu** E.
mocaka C.	**moktavya** E. +	**mokṣaṇa** E. +	**mokṣayitavya** C.
-mocin C.	**moktṛ** B. +	**mokṣaṇīya** E.	**mokṣayitṛ** E.
			mumokṣayiṣu E.

The desiderative formation **mokṣ** has nearly the same right to be treated as a separate root that √ **bhakṣ** has.

√ muṭ, 'break'.

Pres. [1.] moṭate c[1].
Sec. Conj.: *Caus.* moṭayati c[1].
Deriv.: moṭaka c. -moṭin c. moṭana c.

√ mud, 'be merry'.

Pres. [1.] módate *etc.* v.+, -ti *etc.* b.+
Perf. mumóda v.+, mumude *etc.* e.+
Aor. 1. mudīmahi rv. — [3. amūmudat. —] 5. modiṣīṣṭhās av.
Fut. 1. modiṣye e. [— 2. moditā.]
Verb. mudita e.+; -modam c.
Sec. Conj.: [*Int.* momud-. — *Desid.* mumudiṣa-, mumodiṣa-. —] *Caus.* modayati -te *etc.* b.+ (mumodayiṣati çb.)
Deriv.: múd v.+ -muda av.+ mudā e.+ móda v.+ modaka e.+ modin av.+ modana e.+ modanīya u.+ mudrá v. mudira? c. -mudvin? c.

√ muṣ, 'steal'.

Pres. [9.] muṣṇāti *etc.* v.+ (muṣāṇa c.) — [1.] móṣatha rv[1]. — [6.] muṣati *etc.* b.
Perf. mumoṣa c.
Aor. 1. amoṣi c. — [3. amūmuṣat. —] 5. moṣīs amoṣiṣus v.b.
[*Fut.* moṣiṣyati, moṣitā.]
Verb. muṣitá v.+, muṣṭa c.; muṣitvā c.; -múṣya v.+; muṣé rv.
Sec. Conj.: *Pass.* muṣyate *etc.* c., -yant e. [— *Int.* momuṣ-. — *Desid.* mumuṣiṣa-.] — *Caus.* [moṣaya-;] muṣayant? c.
Deriv.: -muṣ v.+ mū́s rv. mūṣa e.+ mū̆ṣaka c. -múṣi b. muṣīván rv. muṣṭí? v.+ moṣa b.+ -moṣaka e. -moṣin b.+ moṣya c. moṣaṇa s.c.

√ muh, 'be crazed'.

Pres. [4.] múhyati *etc.* v.+, -te *etc.* u.+
Perf. mumoha *etc.* b.+, mumuhe e.
Aor. 2. amuhat *etc.* b. — 3. amūmuhat *etc.* av.b.
Fut. 1. mohiṣyáti b. [mokṣyati. — 2. mohitā, mogdhā, moḍhā.]
Verb. mugdhá v.+, mūḍha av.s.u.+; muhé rv.; -móham b.
Sec. Conj.: *Int.* momuhat s., momuhyate e. — [*Desid.* mumohiṣa-, mumuhiṣa-, mumukṣa-. —] *Caus.* moháyati *etc.* v.+, -te *etc.* e.+ (mohyate c.)
Deriv.: -muh av.b. múhu v.b. múhus v.+ mudhā? e.+ mógha v.b. móha av.+ -mohaka e. mohin e.+ mohana e.+ móhuka b. momughá b. mohayitṛ e.

√ mū, *see* √ mīv.

√ mūrch, mūr, 'thicken'.

Pres. [1.] mūrchati *etc.* AV.+
Perf. mumūrcha E.+
[*Aor. etc.* amūrchīt; mūrchiṣyati, mūrchitā.]
Verb. mūrchita E.+, mūrtá B.+ [mūrtvā.]
Sec. Conj.: *Caus.* mūrchayati B.+, -te E.
Deriv.: mūrá? V.B. mūrkhá B.+ mūrchā E.+ mūrchana E.+
mū́rti B.+

√ 1 mṛ, 'die'.

Pres. [1.] maranti *etc.* márate *etc.* RV. (mara C[1].)
Perf. mamā́ra mamrus *etc.* V.+, mamre *etc.* C.
Aor. 1. amṛta *etc.* V.B.S.; murīya V. — 3. amīmarat *etc.* B.C. [— 4. mṛṣīṣṭa.]
Fut. 1. mariṣyati *etc.* AV.+, -te E. [— 2. martā.]
Verb. mṛtá V.+; martum E.+, -tave AVP.; mṛtvā́ B.+; -māram E.
Sec. Conj.: *Pass.* mriyáte *etc.* V.+, -ti *etc.* E.+ — *Int.* marīmarti C. [marmṛ-, memrīya-.] — *Desid.* mumūrṣati *etc.* S.+ — *Caus.* māráyati *etc.* AV.+, -te E. (māryate *etc.* E.+; mimārayiṣa- *in d.*)
Deriv.:

mara V.+	marā́yu V.B.	márman? V.+	mā́ruka B.S.
maraka C.	márta, -tya V.+	māra V.+	-mamri AV.
maraṇa B.+	mṛti C.	māraka C.	múrmura? B.+
maru? B.+	martavya E.+	mārin B.+	mumūrṣā E.+
-mura? AV.	mṛtyú V.+	mā́raṇa B.+	mumūrṣu B.+
			mimārayiṣu C.

The following root is doubtless the same with this.

√ 2 mṛ, mṛṇ, 'crush'.

Pres. [9.] mṛṇīhí *etc.* V. — [6.] mṛṇáti *etc.* V.B.
Perf. mumurat? RV.
Aor. 1. mṛṇyus K. — 3. ámīmṛṇan AV. [— 5. amārīt.]
Verb. mūrṇá AV.B.
Sec. Conj.: *Pass.* mūryáte ÇB.
Deriv.: múr RV. mura? E.+ -marītṛ RV. malímlu? B.
-múri RV. -mṛṇa V.B.

Hardly to be separated from the preceding.

√ mṛkṣ, 'stroke'.

Pres. [6.] mṛkṣā RV. — [1.] mrakṣanti C.
Perf. mimṛkṣus RV.
Sec. Conj.: *Caus.* mrakṣaya- C., mṛkṣayati E.
Deriv.: mṛkṣá RV. mṛkṣín RV. -mrakṣa RV. mrakṣaṇa C.

Doubtless a secondary root-form from √ mṛj.

√ mṛc, 'injure'.

Pres. [4.] mṛcyati? JB.
Aor. 4. mṛkṣīṣṭa RV.
Verb. mṛktá RV.
Sec. Conj.: *Caus.* marcáyati *etc.* V.B.S.
Deriv.: mṛ́c RV. marká RV. márka B.S. mṛcaya AB.

√ mṛch, 'perish'.

Pres. mṛchante U.
Very likely a false reading; if not, a secondary root-from √ 1 mṛ.

√ mṛj, 'wipe'.

Pres. [2.] mā́rṣṭi mṛjánti [mārjanti] *etc.* V.+, mṛṣṭé mṛjate *etc.* V.+ (mārjīta S.) — [7.] mṛñjata (*3p.*) RV., mṛṇajāni GB., mṛñjyāt ÇB. — [1.] mārjati -te *etc.* E.+ — [6.] mṛjati -te *etc.* AV[1].S.C.
Perf. mamā́rja mamṛjus *etc.* V.+ (mamārjus E., māmṛjus RV.), mamṛje AV. (māmṛjé -jīta RV.)
Aor. [1. amārji. —] 3. amīmṛjanta B. [amamārjat.] — 4. amārkṣīt *etc.* B. — 5. amārjīt *etc.* B. — 7. amṛkṣat *etc.* V.B.S., amṛkṣata *etc.* RV.E.
Fut. 1. mrakṣyate B., mārkṣyate B.S. [mārjiṣyati.] — 2. mraṣṭā JB. [mārṣṭā, mārjitā.]
Verb. mṛṣṭá V.+, mṛjita C., mārjita (*caus.*?) S.+; marṣṭum C., mārṣṭum C., mārjitum E.+; mṛṣṭvā́ AV., mārjitvā B.; -mṛ́jya AV.+, -mārjya C.; -mṛ́jas B.
Sec. Conj.: *Pass.* mṛjyáte *etc.* V. + — *Int.* marmṛjmá -janta *etc.* RV., -jyáte *etc.* V.B.S. (marmṛjāná RV.), marīmṛjyate B. [— *Desid.* mimārjiṣa-, mimṛkṣa-.] — *Caus.* marjayati -te *etc.* V.; mārjayati -te *etc.* B.+ (mārjyate C.).
Deriv.:

-mṛja C.	-mārjaka E.+	mārjāra E.+	mārṣṭavya C.
mṛjā E.+	mā́rjana V.+	mārjālyà RV.	-mṛgra RV.
márjya RV.	-mārjanīya E.	mṛ́ṣṭi B.+	-mṛ́gvan AV.
-mārga AV.+	-mā́rguka B.	mārṣṭi C.	marmṛjénya RV.

Compare √ mṛkṣ.

√ mṛḍ, 'be gracious'.

Pres. [6.] mṛḍáti *etc.* V.B.S., -ase B. [— 9. mṛḍnāti.]
Perf. [mamarḍa] (mamṛḍyus RV.)
[*Aor. etc.* amīmṛḍat amamarḍat, amarḍīt; marḍiṣyati, marḍitā.]
Sec. Conj.: [*Int.* marīmṛḍ-. — *Desid.* mimarḍiṣa-. —] *Caus.* mṛḍáyati *etc.* V.B.C., -te C.
Deriv.: mṛḍa B.+ mṛḍīká V.+ marḍitṛ́ RV. -mṛḍaya B.
mṛḍana C. mṛḍitṛ́ AV. mṛḍayā́ku RV.

√ **mṛṇ**, *see* √ 2 **mṛ**.

√ **mṛd, mrad**, 'rub, crush'.

Pres. [9.] **mṛdnāti** *etc.* s.+, **mṛdnīta** s. — [1.] **mardati -te** *etc.* E.+ — **mrada** RV., **-date** MS.
Perf. **mamarda mamṛdus** B.+ (**mamardus** M.), **mamṛde** E.
Aor. 1. **mṛdyāsam** B.S. — 3. **amīmṛdat** E. [**amamardat.** — 5. **amardīt.**]
Fut. 1. **mradiṣyati mardiṣyate** JB.
Verb. **mṛditá** AV.; **marditum** E.+, **-tos** B.; **mṛditvā** C.; **-mṛ́dya** B.+; **-mradé** B.; **-mardam** C.
Sec. Conj.: *Pass.* **mṛdyáte** *etc.* B.+ — *Int.* **marmarttu** RV. [**marīmṛd-.**] — *Desid.* **mimardiṣati** E. — *Caus.* **mardayati** *etc.* E.+, **-te** E. (**mardyate** C.; **mimardayiṣa-** *in d.*); **mradayati** TS.
Deriv.:
mṛ́d V.+ **mardin** E.+ **mṛ́ttikā** B.+ **mṛdú** AV.+
-mṛda S. **márdana** B.+ **marditavya** E. **mṛtsnā** B.+
marda E.+ **mardanīya** C. **-marditṛ** E. **mimardiṣu** E.
mardaka C. **-mradas** V.B.S. **mradīyas** B. **mimardayiṣu** E.

√ **mṛdh**, 'neglect'.

Pres. [1.] **márdhati** *etc.* RV. — [6.] **mṛdhāti** RV.S., **-asva** S.
Aor. 1. **mṛdhyās** RV. — 2. **mṛdhas** S. — 5. **mardhīs** *etc.* RV.B. (**márdhiṣat** RV.)
Verb. **mṛddhá** MS.
Deriv.: **mṛ́dh** V.B. **mṛdha** V.+ **mṛ́dhas** RV. **mṛdhrá** RV.
mardhuka JB.

√ **mṛç**, 'touch, feel'.

Pres. [6.] **mṛçáti** *etc.* V.+, **-te** *etc.* V.+
Perf. **mamarça mamṛçus** E.+ (**māmṛçús** RV.), **mamṛçe** B.+
Aor. 4. [**amārkṣīt amrākṣīt**] **mṛkṣīṣṭa**? RV. — 7. **ámṛkṣat** *etc.* V.B.
[*Fut.* **markṣyati mrakṣyati, marṣṭā mraṣṭā.**]
Verb. **mṛṣṭá** V.+, **mṛçita** C.; **marṣṭum** E.+; **-mṛ́çya** V.+; **-mṛ́çe** V.B.; **-márçam** B.S.
Sec. Conj.: *Pass.* **mṛçyate** *etc.* E.+ — *Int.* **mármṛçat** *etc.* V.B., **marīmṛçya-** B. — *Caus.* **marçayati** *etc.* B.+
Deriv.: **-mṛça** B.+ **marça** B.+ **-marçin** U.+ **marīmṛçá** AV.
-mṛçya B.+ **-marçaka** E. **márçana** V.+

√ **mṛṣ**, 'not heed'.

Pres. [4.] **mṛ́ṣyate** *etc.* V.+, **-ti** *etc.* E.+ [— 1. **marṣati -te.**]
Perf. **mamárṣa** RV.E., **mamṛṣe** E.

Aor. 1. mṛṣṭhās RV. — 2. amṛṣan M., mṛṣat S. (-ṣant? C.), -ṣanta RV. — 3. mīmṛṣas V. [amamarṣat.] — 5. [amarṣīt,] marṣiṣṭhās RV.
[*Fut.* marṣiṣyati -te, marṣitā.]
Verb. [mṛṣita; mṛṣitvā, marṣitvā;] -mṛṣya E.; -mṛ́ṣe RV.
Sec. Conj.: *Pass.* mṛṣyate E. — *Int.* māmṛṣat S. — *Caus.* marṣayati *etc.* E.+, -te *etc.* E.+
Deriv.: mṛ́ṣā V.+ -márṣa V.+ marṣaṇa E.+ -marṣi R.
-mṛṣya RV. marṣin E.+ marṣaṇīya E.+

√ med [mid], 'be fat'.

Pres. [4.] médyati *etc.* V.B. — [6.] medátām RV.
[*Perf. etc.* mimeda, mimide; amidat, amediṣṭa; mediṣyati-te, meditā; minna, miditvā meditvā.]
Sec. Conj.: [*Pass.* midyate. —] *Caus.* [mindayati;] medáyati *etc.* V.+
Deriv.: médana RV. medín V.+ médas V.+ medurá B.+
medya C.

√ mokṣ, *see* √ muc.

√ mnā, 'note'.

Pres. [1.] manati *etc.* S.+, -te S. — [2.] mnāyus C[1].
[*Perf.* mamnāu.]
Aor. [1. mnāyāt, mneyāt. —] 6. amnāsiṣus C.
[*Fut.* mnāsyati, mnātā.]
Verb. mnāta S.+
Sec. Conj.: *Pass.* mnāyate C. [— *Int.* māmnā-. — *Desid.* mimnāsa-. — *Caus.* mnāpaya-, amimnapat.]
Deriv.: -mnāna S.+ -mnātavya C. -mnāya S.+

Only with prefix ā: a secondary root-form from √ man — to which, indeed, the forms from stem mana- more properly belong.

√ myakṣ, 'be situated' (?).

Pres. [1.] myakṣa RV.
Perf. mimyákṣa mimikṣús -kṣire RV.
Aor. 1. amyak RV.; amyakṣi RV.

√ mrad, *see* √ mṛd.

√ mrit, mlit, 'dissolve'.

Pres. [4?] mrityét -yeyus ÇB.
Verb. -mletya S.
Deriv. -mretuka PB.

Perhaps related with √ mṛd.

√ mruc, mluc, mlup, 'set'.

Pres. [1.] **mrócati** *etc.* AV.B.; **mlócati** *etc.* B.+
Perf. **mumloca** ÇB.U.
Aor. 2. **amrucat** JB. [— 5. **amrocīt, amlocīt.**]
[*Fut.* **mrociṣyati, mrocitā; mlociṣyati, mlocitā.**]
Verb. **mrukta** B.+, **mlukta** RV., **mlupta** B.S.; **-mrúcas** RV.
Sec. Conj.: Int. **malimlucāmahe** S.
Deriv.: **-mruc** V.B. **mroká** AV. **-mloca** B.+ **-mrocana** C. **-mlocana** C. **-mloci** C. **-mrukti** B. **-mlukti** C. **malimlucá** AV.+ **malimluc** S.

√ mreḍ, 'gratify' (?).

Pres. [1.] **mreḍeran** U[1].
Sec. Conj.: Caus. **mreḍayati** *etc.* E.+ (**mrelayati** S.)
Deriv. **-mreḍa** C.

√ mlā, 'relax'.

Pres. [4.] **mlā́yati** *etc.* B.+, **-te** *etc.* E.+ — [2.] **mlānti** E.
Perf. **mamlāu** *etc.* E.+
Aor. [1. **mlāyāt, mleyāt.** —] 6? **mlāsīs** E.
Fut. 1. **amlāsyatām** B., **-yetām** U. [— 2. **mlātā.**]
Verb. **mlātá** RV., **mlāna** B.+
Sec. Conj.: Caus. **mlāpáyati** AV.+; **mlapayati** C.
Deriv.: **-mlāni** C. **-mlāyin** C. **-mlāpana** C. **mlāpin** C.

√ mluc, *see* **√ mruc.**

√ mlup, *see* **√ mruc.**

√ mlech, 'speak barbarously'.

Pres. [1.] **mlechati** *etc.* B.+
[*Perf. etc.* **mimlecha; amlechīt; mlechiṣyati, mlechitā; mlechita, mliṣṭa.**]
Deriv. **mlechá** B.+

√ yakṣ, 'press on' (?).

Pres. [1.] **yákṣati** *etc.* RV[1].B[1]., **-te** RV[1].
Verb. **-yákṣe** RV[2].
Deriv.: **yakṣá** V.+ **yakṣín** RV. **yákṣya** RV. **yákṣu** RV. **yákṣma** V.+ **yakṣman** B.+

The character of the root and the connection of its derivatives are very doubtful.

√ yach, *see* **√ yam.**

√ yaj, 'offer'.

Pres. [1.] **yájati -te** *etc.* V.+ — [2.] **yákṣi** V.B.S., **yákṣva** RV. — **yajase** (1s.) RV[1].

Perf. **iyāja** *etc.* E.+, **ījé** *etc.* V.+, **yejé** AV.?

Aor. [1. **ijyāt.** —] 3. **ayīyajat** *etc.* B. — 4. **ayākṣīt** *etc.* V.B.S. (**ayās** RV., **ayāṭ** V.B.S.; **yákṣat** V.B.S., **yakṣatas -ṣatām** RV.), **ayaṣṭa** *etc.* V.B.S. (**yakṣate** *etc.* V.B.; **yakṣīya** MS.) — 7. **ayakṣata** (3s.) AGS.

Fut. 1. **yakṣyati** *etc.* B.+, **-áte** *etc.* V.+ — 2. **yaṣṭā́** B.

Verb. **iṣṭá** V.+; **yáṣṭum** B.+, **-ṭave** V.B., **ījitum** M.; **iṣṭvā́** AV.+; [**-ijya;**] **yájadhyāi** V., **yajádhyāi** TS.; **-yā́jam** AV.

Sec. Conj.: Pass. **ijyate** *etc.* E.+, **-yant** E. — *Int.* **yāyaj-** (*in d.*). — *Desid.* **yiyakṣati -te** E.; **íyakṣati** *etc.* V., **-te** *etc.* V.B. — *Caus.* **yājayati** *etc.* B.+, **-te** E.

Deriv.:

-ij V.+	yajás RV.	yajñá V.+	-yājin B.+
yā́j V.+	-yaji RV.	yájyu V.	yājya B.+
yája B.	yájus V.+	yájīyas V.	yājyà B.+
yajā S.	yajatá V.	yájiṣṭha V.	yājana S.+
yajin B.+	íṣṭi V.+	yájvan V.+	yājanīya C.
-yájya RV.	yajati S.+	yajvin E.+	-yā́juka B.
-yajyā V.B.S.	yaṣṭavyà B.+	yajiṣṇu E.	yāyajū́ka B.+
ijya C.	yaṣṭṛ V.+	-yāga E.+	yiyakṣu E.+
ijyā S.+	yájatra V.B.	-yāja V.+	yājayitavyà B.
yájana AV.+	yajátha V.	yājaka E.+	yājayitṛ C.

Appears to be related with roots **yam** and **yach** and **yat**, and to mean originally 'reach out, extend'.

√ yat, 'stretch'.

Pres. [1.] **yátate** *etc.* V.+, **-ti** *etc.* V.+

Perf. **yete** *etc.* V.B.U.

Aor. 1. **yátāna, yatāná** RV. — [3. **ayīyatat.** —] 5. **ayatiṣṭa** B.

Fut. 1. **yatiṣyate** *etc.* B.+, **-ti** *etc.* E.+

Verb. **yatta** V.+, **yatita** E.; **yatitum** E.; **-yátya** B.

Sec. Conj.: Pass. **yatyate** C. — [*Int.* **yāyat-.** — *Desid.* **yiyatiṣa-.** —] *Caus.* **yātáyati -te** *etc.* V.+ (**yātyate** *etc.* B.+)

Deriv.:

-yā́t V.+	yátti MS.	-yātaka E.+	yatúna RV.
-yátana AV.+	-yattavya E.	-yātya S.+	yayā́ti? V.+
yatanīya C.	yatitavya E.+	yātanā́ E.+	
yáti V.+	yatna E.+		

√ yabh, '*futuere*'.

Pres. [1.] **yábhati** *etc.* AV.B.

[*Perf. etc.* **yayābha; ayāpsīt.**]

Fut. 1. **yapsyáti** *etc.* B.S.
Verb. **yabdhum** C., **yabhitum** C.
Sec. Conj.: *Desid.* **yiyapsate** *etc.* S.
Deriv.: **-yabhya** AV. **yābha** C.

√ yam, yach, 'reach'.

Pres. [1.] **yáchati -te** *etc.* V.+ — **yamati -te** *etc.* E.+ — [2.] **yáṁsi** RV.; **yamiti**? JB.
Perf. **yayāma yemús** *etc.* V.B. (**yayaṁtha** RV.; **yamátus -mus** RV.), **yeme** *etc.* V.+
Aor. 1. **áyamus** *etc.* RV. (**yámati yámat** *etc.* V., **yamate** *etc.* V.; **yamyās** 3*s.* **yamīmahi** RV.; **yaṁdhí** *etc.* RV.); **áyāmi** V.B. — [3. **ayīyamat.** —] 4. **áyāṁsam** *etc.* V.B. (**áyān** RV.; **yaṁsat** *etc.* V.B.S., **yaṁsatas** RV.), **áyaṁsta** *etc.* V.B. (**ayāṁsi** AB., **yaṁsate** RV.) — 5. **yámiṣṭa** (3*s.*) RV. [— 6. **ayaṁsiṣam.**]
Fut. 1. **yaṁsyáti** B., **yamiṣyati** C. [— 2. **yaṁtā.**]
Verb. **yatá** V.+; **yáṁtum** B.+, **-tave** RV., **yamitum** C., **yámitavāí** RV.; **yatvā** S., **yamitvā** C.; **-yátya** AV.B., **-yamya** S.+; **-yámam** V.B.
Sec. Conj.: *Pass.* **yamyáte** *etc.* V.+ — *Int.* **yaṅyamīti** RV. — *Desid.* **yiyaṁsati** B. — *Caus.* **yāmáyati** *etc.* V.E.+; **yamayati** *etc.* B.+, **-te** E.

Deriv.:	**yáma** V.+	**yáti** V.+	**yamúnā** V.+	**-yāmin** B.+
	yamá? V.+	**-yáṁtu** RV.	**-yamīyas** RV.	**-yāmana** C.
	-yamaka C.	**yaṁtavyà** B.+	**yámiṣṭha** RV.	**-yaṁsénya** RV.
	yamin B.+	**yaṁtúr** RV.	**yamasānā́** RV.	**-yachana** E.
	-yamya E.+	**yaṁtṛ** V.+	**yā́ma** V.+	**yaṣṭí**? B.+
	yámana B.+	**yaṁtrá** V.+	**yāmaka** B.+	

Compare √ **yaj** and √ **yat.**

√ yas, yeṣ, 'be heated'.

Pres. [4.] **yásyati** *etc.* AV.+ — [3.] **yayastu** RV. — [1.] **yéṣati** *etc.* V.B. [**yasati.**]
[*Perf.* **yayāsa.**]
Aor. 2. **ayasat** C. [— 3. **ayīyasat.** — 5. **ayāsīt.**]
[*Fut.* **yasiṣyati, yasitā.**]
Verb. **yastá** V.+, **yasita** B.C. [**yasitvā, yastvā.**]
Sec. Conj.: [*Int.* **yāyas-.** — *Desid.* **yiyasiṣa-.** —] *Caus.* **yāsayati** *etc.* E.+ [**-te.**] (**yāsyate** E.)

Deriv.:	**yās** V.B.S.	**-yāsaka** C.	**-yā́sya** V.+	**yaska**? B.+
	-yāsa B.+	**-yāsin** C.	**-yāsana** C.	

√ yah.

Such a root, of questionable meaning, is assumable for the derivatives:

yahú RV. **yahvá** V. **yahvánt** RV.

√ yā, 'go'.

Pres. [2.] yā́ti *etc.* V.+ (ayus B.+ [ayān]; yāmaki = yāmi KB.), yāmahe E[1].
Perf. yayāú *etc.* V.+ (yayā́tha V.), yaye C.
Aor. 4. ayāsam *etc.* V. (yā́sat V.B.; yeṣam RV.) — 6. ayāsiṣam *etc.* V.+ (yāsiṣat RV.; yāsisīṣṭhās V.B.)
Fut. yāsyati *etc.* AV.+, -te *etc.* E.+ — 2. yātā E.+
Verb. yātá V.+; yātum E.+, yā́tave V., -vāí B.; yātvā́ B.S.; -yā́ya B.+; -yāí V.B.; -yāyam S.
Sec. Conj.: Pass. yāyate E. — *Int.* īyāyate? U., yāyā- (*in d.*). — *Desid.* yiyāsati *etc.* E.+ — *Caus.* yāpáyati *etc.* B.+ [ayīyapat.]

Deriv.: -yā V.B., yā́na V.+, yú? V.B., -yāti U.+, yātú? V.+, yātavya E.+, yātṛ V.+, -yātra E.+, yātrā E.+, -yā́tha RV., yā́ma V.+, yā́man V.B.S., yāyin B.+, yā́van V.B., yéṣṭha RV., yayí, -í RV., -yayin RV., -yíyu RV., yayu V.E., yāyāvará B.+, yiyāsā C., yiyāsu E.+, -yāpa C., yāpaka C., yāpya B.+, yāpana S.+

[1] Doubtless a secondary form of √ i.

√ yāc, 'ask'.

Pres. [1.] yā́cati -te *etc.* V.+
Perf. [yayāca] yayāce B.+
Aor. [1. yācyāt. — 3. ayayācat. —] 5. ayācīt *etc.* V.E. (yāciṣat RV.), ayāciṣṭa B. (yāciṣāmahe RV.)
Fut. 1. yāciṣyati B.S., -te E. [— 2. yācitā.]
Verb. yācitá AV.+; yā́citum AV.+; yācitvā B.+; -yā́cya B.+
Sec. Conj.: Pass. yācyate *etc.* E.+ [— *Int.* yāyāc-. — *Desid.* yiyāciṣa-.] — *Caus.* yācáyati -te AV.+

Deriv.: yācaka E.+, yācin C., yācya E.+, yācana E.+, yācanā E.+, yācanīya E.+, yācitavya E.+, yācitṛ E.+, yāciṣṇu E.+, yācñā́ B.+, yācñyá AV.B.

√ yād, 'unite' (?).

Pres. [1.] yā́damāna RV.
Deriv.: yā́das B.+, yā́dura RV.

√ 1 yu, 'unite'.

Pres. [2.] yāúti yuvati *etc.* AV.B.S., yuté yuvate *etc.* V.B. — [6.] yuváti -te *etc.* V.B. [— 9. yunāti -nīte.]
Perf. [yuyāva] yuyuvé RV.
Aor. [1. yūyāt; ayāvi. — 3. ayīyavat. —] 5. yā́viṣṭam? RV. [ayaviṣṭa.]
Fut. [1. yaviṣyati -te. —] 2. yuvitā́ ÇB. [yavitā.]

Verb. yutá v.+; -yū́ya v.+, -yutya s.

Sec. Conj.: [*Pass.* yūyate. —] *Int.* yóyuvat av., yóyuve *etc.* rv. — *Desid.* yúyūṣati rv. [yiyaviṣa-. — *Caus.* yāvayati, yiyāvayiṣati.]

Deriv.:	yú b.+	yuti c.	yūna s.	yós? v.+
	-yava rv.	-yūti? v.+	yóni? v.+	yóṣaṇā *etc.*? v.+
	yávana av.+	yotra e.	yúvan? v.+	-yāva e.+
	-yuvana s.+	yūthá? v.+	yáviṣṭha v.+	-yāvana c.
	-yut v.b.		yavīyas s.+	yāvayitṛ c.

Compare √ yuj and √ 2 yu; from the latter, in combination with prefixes, the forms and derivatives of this root are not always separable with certainty.

√ 2 yu, yuch, 'separate'.

Pres. [3.] yuyóti *etc.* v.b., yuyudhvám *etc.* v.b. — [6.] áyuvanta *etc.* v.b.s. — [1.] yúchati *etc.* v.

Aor. 1. yuyāt b., yūyātām (3*d.*) b. (yūyās 3*s.* v.), yavanta rv.; áyāvi b. — 3. yūyot rv. — 4. ayāuṣīt *etc.* v.b. (yāus rv., yoṣati *etc.* v., yóṣat rv.; yoṣam *etc.* b.s., yūṣam av.), yoṣṭhās b.s. — 5. yā́vīs rv.

Verb. yutá rv.; yótave -tavāí -tos rv.; -yāvam av.b.

Sec. Conj.: *Int.* yóyuvat *etc.* v.b. (yoyāva ms.) — *Caus.* yāváyati *etc.* v.; yavayati *etc.* v.b.

Deriv.:	yáva av.c.	-yuti rv.c.	-yutvan rv.	-yā́vana av.
	-yávana ms.	-yotṛ rv.	-yā́van av.	yū́yuvi rv.
	-yut v.b.			

Compare √ 1 yu.

√ yuj, 'join'.

Pres. [7.] yunákti yuñkté *etc.* v.+ (yunañkṣi? c., yuñjīyāt r.) — [6?] yuñjati -te *etc.* u.e.+ — [2.] yujé v., yujmahe yujata (3*p.*) rv., yukṣvá v.

Perf. yuyója yuyujé *etc.* v.+ (yuyujma -jré v.; niniyoja ab.; yuyójate rv.)

Aor. 1. áyuji *etc.* v.b. (yojate yujāná rv.), (yojam yója yujyā́tām *etc.* rv.); áyoji v.c. — 2.? yujanta rv., ayujat -janta c. — 3. ayūyujat *etc.* e.+ — 4. ayokṣīt s., [ayāukṣīt] ayukṣi *etc.* v.+ (ayuñkṣmahi c.)

Fut. 1. yokṣyati *etc.* b.+, -te *etc.* av.+ — 2. yoktā́ b.

Verb. yuktá v.+; yoktum b.+; yuktvā́ v.+, -tvā́ya v.b.; -yujya e.+; yujé rv.

Sec. Conj.: *Pass.* yujyáte *etc.* v.+, -ti *etc.* e.+ — [*Int* yoyuj-. —] *Desid.* yuyukṣati *etc.* e.+ — *Caus.* yojayati *etc.* e.+, -te *etc.* e.+ (yojyate *etc.* c.)

Deriv.:	yúj v.+	yóga v.+	yójana v.+	yugma s.+
	-yuja v.s.	yógya av.+	yojanīya c.	yugmán b.
	yújya v.b.	yogyā́ rv.	yukti v.+	-yúgvan v.b.s.
	yugá v.+	yogin s.+	yoktavyà b.+	yuyukṣu c.
	yugya e.+	yojaka e.+	yoktṛ́ b.+	yojayitavya c.
	-yuṅga b.	yojya e.+	yóktra v.+	yojayitṛ s.c.
	yuñjaka e.+		yojitṛ c.	

√ yudh, 'fight'.

Pres. [4.] yúdhyate *etc.* v.+, -ti *etc.* v.+ — [1.] yodhati *etc.* av.pb. — [2.] yótsi rv.

Perf. yuyódha yuyudhé *etc.* v.+

Aor. 1. yódhi, yodhat, yodhānā́ rv., yudhāna ? c. — 3. yūyudhas m. — 4. yotsīs e., ayuddha c., yutsmahi av. — 5. ayodhīt *etc.* v. (yodhiṣat rv.)

Fut. 1. yotsyati -te *etc.* b.+ — 2. yoddhā e.

Verb. yuddhá v.+; yoddhum e.; -yuddhvī rv.; -yudhya e.; yudham jb., yudhé rv.; yudháye rv.

Sec. Conj.: Pass. yudhyate c. — *Int.* [yoyudh-] yavīyudh- (*in d.*) — *Desid.* yúyutsati -te *etc.* v.+ — *Caus.* yodhayati *etc.* v.+, -te *etc.* e. (yodhyate e.)

Deriv.:	yúdh v.+	yudhmá rv.	yodhana e.+	yúyudhi rv.
	-yudha v.+	yúdhvan rv.	yodhanīya c.	yū́yudhi rv.
	yudhi- av.	yodhá v.+	yodhuka jb.	yavīyúdh rv.
	-yudhya rv.	yodhaka e.	yódhīyas rv.	yuyutsā e.
	yudhénya v.	yodhin e.+	yoddhavya e.+	-yutsā ? c.
		yódhya v.+	yoddhṛ v.+	yuyutsu e.+

√ yup, 'obstruct'.

[*Pres.* 4. yupyati.]

Perf. yuyópa yuyopimá v.

Aor. [2. ayupat. —] 3. ayūyupan *etc.* b.

[*Fut.* yopiṣyati, yopitā.]

Verb. yupitá av.b.s.

Sec. Conj.: Int. yoyupyáte *etc.* b.s. — *Caus.* yopáyati *etc.* v.b.s.

Deriv.: yū́pa v.+ -yópana v. yoyupana c[1].

√ yeṣ, *see* √ yas.

√ raṅh, 'hasten'.

Pres. [1.] ráṅhate *etc.* rv., -ti rv.

Perf. rārahāṇá rv.b. [raraṅha.]

[*Aor. etc.* araraṅhat, araṅhīt; raṅhiṣyati, raṅhitā.]

Verb. raṅhita s.

Sec. Conj.: Caus. **raṅháyati -te** *etc.* RV.

Deriv.: **-raṅha** E. **ráṅhya** RV. **ráṅhas** V.+ **raṅghas** C. **rahas**? C. **ráṅhi** V.B. **ṛhánt**? RV. **raghú** V.+ **laghú** AV.+ **rághīyas** B. **lághīyas** AV.+ **laghiṣṭha** JB.

Compare √ **rah.**

√ rakṣ, 'protect'.

Pres. [1.] **rákṣati -te** *etc.* V.+

Perf. **rarákṣa** *etc.* V.+ (**rārakṣāṇá** RV.)

Aor. [1. **rakṣyāt.** — 3. **ararakṣat.** —] 4. **arakṣīt** *etc.* AV.+ (**rakṣiṣat** *etc.* RV.), **arākṣīt** *etc.* B.S. (**arāṭ**? MS.)

Fut. 1. **arakṣiṣyas** M., **rakṣye**? R[1]. — 2. **rakṣitā** E.C.

Verb. **rakṣitá** V.+; **rakṣitum** E.+; **-rakṣya** C.

Sec. Conj.: Pass. **rakṣyate** *etc.* U.+ — [*Int.* **rārakṣ-.** —] *Desid.* **rirakṣiṣati** *etc.* E. — *Caus.* **rakṣayati** *etc.* C., **-te** B.

Deriv.: **rakṣa** B.+ **rakṣā** E.+ **rakṣaka** C. **rakṣin** S.+ **rakṣya** E.+ **rákṣaṇa** V.+ **rakṣaṇā** C. **rakṣaṇīya** E.+ **rákṣas** V.+ **rakṣás** V.B. **-rákṣi** V.B. **rakṣitavya** E.+ **rakṣitṛ́** V.+ **rirákṣā** G. **rirakṣu** C. **rirakṣiṣā** C. **rirakṣiṣu** E.+

The relation of **rakṣas** 'demon' to this root is questionable. But **rakṣīs** AV[1]. is too weak evidence on which to accept a √ 2 **rakṣ** 'harm'.

√ raṅg, 'rock'.

Pres. [1.] **raṅgant** C[1].

Doubtless artificial.

√ rac, 'produce'.

Aor. 1. **araci** C. — 3. **arīracat** C.

Fut. 1. **raciṣyati** C.?

Sec. Conj.: Caus. **racayati** *etc.* E.+ (**racyate** C.)

Deriv.: **racana** E.+ **-racanā** C. **-rañca** C. **-rañcya** C. **-rañci** C. **racayitṛ** C.

√ 1 raj, 'direct', *see* √ ṛj.

√ 2 raj, rañj, 'color'.

Pres. [4.] **rajyati -te** *etc.* AV[1].E.+ — [1.] **rañjati** *etc.*? E.+ [**rajati -te.**]

[*Perf. etc.* **raranja raranje; rajyāt; arīrajat ararañjat, arāṅkṣīt araṅkta, raṅkṣīṣṭa; raṅkṣyati -te, raṅktā.**]

Verb. **raktá** B.+; [**raktvā, raṅktvā;**] **-rajya** C.

Sec. Conj.: Pass. **rajyate** C. — *Int.* **rārajīti** V. — [*Desid.* **riraṅkṣa-.** —] *Caus.* **rajayati** AV.; **rañjayati** *etc.* E.+, **-te** E.

Deriv.: **rañga** E.+ **rañjaka** E.+ **-rañjya** C. **rajaka** E.+ **rañjana** E.+ **rañjanīya** C. **rajana** AV.+ **rajanī̆** E. **rajanīya** E. **rájas**? V.+ **rají**? RV. **rajatá** V.+ **rakti** C. **rāga** U.+ **-rāgin** E.+ **rajayitṛ́** VS.

The forms with nasal belong to the later language.

√ rañch, 'mark'.

Only in (**ni-**) **-rañchana** C.: compare √ **lāñch.**

√ raṭ, 'howl'.

Pres. [1.] **rāṭati** *etc.* C.
[*Perf. etc.* **rarāṭa reṭus; arīraṭat, arāṭīt; raṭiṣyati, raṭitā.**]
Verb. **raṭita** C.
Sec. Conj.: *Int.* **rāraṭīti** *etc.* E.+
Deriv.: **raṭana** C. **-raṭi** C.

√ raṇv, 'delight'.

Pres. [1.] **raṇva** *etc.* TS.
Verb. **raṇvitá** RV.
A secondary formation from √ **ran,** apparently through **raṇvá.**

√ rad, 'dig'.

Pres. [1.] **rádati** *etc.* V.B., **-te** AV. — [2.] **ratsi** RV.
Perf. **rarā̆da** RV. [**redus.**]
[*Aor. etc.* **arā̆dīt; radiṣyati, raditā.**]
Verb. **raditá** AV.B.
Deriv.: **rada** RV.C. **radana** C.

√ radh, randh, 'be *or* make subject'.

Pres. [4.] **rádhyati** *etc.* AV.B. — [2.] **randdhi** RV[1].
Perf. [**rarandha rarandhima redhma**] **rāradhús** RV.
Aor. 2. **radham** *etc.* V. — 3. **rīradhas** *etc.* RV. (**rīradhā** 1*s.* RV.) [**ararandhat.**] — 5. **randhīs** RV.
[*Fut.* **radhiṣyati, ratsyati; radhitā, raddhā.**]
Verb. **raddhá** RV. [**radhitum.**]
Sec. Conj.: *Int.* **rāranddhi**? RV. [**rāradh-.**] — [*Desid.* **riradhiṣa-, riratsa-.** —] *Caus.* **randháyati** *etc.* V.+
Deriv.: **randhana** RV.C. **ránddhi** RV. **rándhra**? RV.+ **radhrá**? RV.

√ 1 ran, 'take pleasure'.

Pres. [1.] **ráṇati** *etc.* RV., **-anta** RV. — [4.] **ráṇyati** *etc.* RV. (**raṇyáthas** RV[1].)
Perf. **rāraṇa** RV. (**rāráṇas** *etc.* **rārán rārandhí** *etc.* **arāraṇus** RV.B.)
Aor. [3. **arīraṇat, ararāṇat.** —] 5. **arāṇiṣus** RV. (**ráṇiṣṭana** RV.)

[*Fut.* **raṇiṣyati, raṇitā.**]
Sec. Conj.: [*Int.* **raṅraṇ-.** — *Desid.* **riraṇiṣa-.** —] *Caus.* **raṇáyati** *etc.* V., **-anta** RV. [**rāṇayati.**]
Deriv.: **rán** RV. **rā́ṇya** V. **ránti**? V. **ráṇitṛ** RV.
ráṇa V.+ **raṇyà** AV. **rántya** V. **raṇvá** V.
ráṇvan RV.

Compare √ **ram.**

√ 2 ran, 'ring'.

Pres. [1.] **raṇati** *etc.* C.
Verb. **raṇita** C.
Sec. Conj.: *Caus.* **raṇayati** C.
Deriv. **-raṇana** C.
A late and probably artificial formation.

√ rap, 'chatter'.

Pres. [1.] **rápati** *etc.* V.B.
Sec. Conj.: *Int.* **rā́rapīti** *etc.* V.
Deriv.: **-rāp** RV. **-rāpin** AV.
A variant of √ **lap,** which compare.

√ rapç, 'be full'.

Pres. [1.] **rapçate** *etc.* V., **rapçant-** RV.
Perf. **rarapçe** RV.
Deriv.: **-rapça** RV. **-rapçin** V.B.

√ raph.

Perhaps to be seen in **raphitá** RV[1]. 'miserable'(?): compare √ **riph.**

√ rabh, rambh, 'take hold'.

Pres. [1.] **rábhate** *etc.* V.+, **-ti** *etc.* S.+; **rambhati -te** E.+
Perf. **rebhé** *etc.* V.+ (**rārabhe** RV.), **rarabhmá** RV.
Aor. 1. **arambhi** C. — [3. **ararambhat.** —] 4. **árabdha** RV.
Fut. 1. **rapsyate** *etc.* E.+, **-ti** E. [— 2. **rabdhā.**]
Verb. **rabdhá** V.+: **rabdhum** E.; **-rábhya** V.+; **-rábham** RV., **-rábhe** V.B.
Sec. Conj.: *Pass.* **rabhyate** *etc.* E.+ — [*Int.* **rārabh-, rārambh-.** —] *Desid.* **ripsate** *etc.* B.C. — *Caus.* **rambhayati** *etc.* B.+, **-te** B.
Deriv.:

rabha E.	**rábhi** V.+	**rábhiṣṭha** V.B.	**rambhín** V.+
-rábhya B.+	**-rabhin** V.S.	**rábhīyas** B.S.	**-rámbhana** V.+
rábhas V.+	**-rabdhi** C.	**rábhyas** RV.	**-rambhanīya** B.S.
rabhasānā́ RV.	**-rabdhavya** E.	**rambhá** V.+	**-ripsu** C.
	rabdhṛ C.	**rambhaka** C.	

Compare √ **labh,** which is the same in another phonetic form.

√ ram, 'be *or* make content'.

Pres. [1.] **rámate -ti** *etc.* V.+ — [9.] **ramṇāti** *etc.* V.B.
Perf. **rarāma remus** *etc.* E.+, **reme** *etc.* B.+
Aor. 1. **rántī**? SV. — 3. **árīramat** *etc.* RV. — 4. **araṁsīt** C., **áraṁsta** *etc.* V. [**raṁsīṣṭhās.**] — 6. **raṁsiṣam** SV.
Fut. 1. **raṁsyate** *etc.* B.+, **-ti** B. [— 2. **raṁtā.**]
Verb. **ratá** B.+; **raṁtum** E.+, **-tos** B., **ramitum** E.; **ratvā́** B., **raṁtvā** C.; **-ramya** S.+ [**-ratya**]; **-ramam** S.
Sec. Conj.: Pass. **ramyate** *etc.* E.+ — [*Int.* **raṅram-.** —] *Desid.* **riraṁsa-** (*in d.*) — *Caus.* **ramayati** *etc.* V.+, **-te** *etc.* E.+; **rāmayati** *etc.* V.+ (**riramayiṣa-** *in d.*)
Deriv.: **rama** E.+, **ramyà** B.+, **ramaṇa** B.+, **ramaṇīya** U.+, **ráti** B.+, **ráṁti** AV.+, **ramáti** AV.B., **rámati** AV.B., **raṁtavya** C., **ráṁtṛ** RV., **rā́trī**? V.+, **rā́ma** V.+, **-rāmin** RV., **rāmaṇa** E., **raṁsu-**? RV., **riraṁsā** E.+, **riraṁsu** C., **riramayiṣu** C.

Compare √ 1 **ran**, from which one or two of the derivatives here given may perhaps come, at least in part. Compare also √ **lam.**

√ ramb, 'hang down'.

Pres. [1.] **rámbate** *etc.* RV.
Deriv. **-rambaṇa** B.U.

Compare √ **lamb,** from which the verb-forms and derivatives mostly come.

√ rambh, 'roar'.

Pres. [1.] **rambhati -te** *etc.* C.

The isolated occurrences probably artificial.

√ raç.

Such a root inferable from the derivatives:
raçanā́ V.+ **raçman** RV. **raçmí** V.+ **rāçí** V.+

√ ras, 'roar'.

Pres. [1.] **rasati -te** *etc.* B.+
Perf. **rarāsa resus** *etc.* E.+
[*Aor. etc.* **arīrasat, arăsīt; rasiṣyati, rasitā.**]
Verb. **rasita** C.
[*Sec. Conj.* **rāras-; rirasiṣa-; rāsaya-.**]
Deriv.: **rasana** C. **rasitṛ** C.

Compare √ 1 **rās.**
The root 2 **ras** 'taste' is only a denominative of **rasa.**

√ **rah**, 'desert'.

[*Pres. etc.* **rahati; rarāha rehus; arīrahat, arahīt; rahiṣyati, rahitā.**]
Verb. **rahita** E.+; **rahitum** E.
Sec. Conj.: *Caus.* **rahayati** *etc.* S.+
Deriv.: **raha** RV.+ **rahaṇa** C. **rahas** E.+ **ráhū-**? RV. **-rahin** C. **rahasya, -yu** B.+

√ 1 **rā, rās**, 'give'.

Pres. [3.] **rirīhi** RV., **rarāsva** AV., **rarīdhvam** *etc.* (**rárate** ŚS., **rárāṇa**) V. — [2.] **rā́si** RV., **rāti** C., **rāté** B., **rā́sva** V.B.S. — [1.] **rā́sate** *etc.* V.B.S.
Perf. **rarimá -ivā́ṅs** RV., **raré** *etc.* RV.
Aor. 4. **árāsma** *etc.* V.B. (**rā́sat** *etc.* V.B.); **rāsāthām rāsīya** RV.
Fut. [1. **rāsyati.** —] 2. **rātā** C.
Verb. **rātá** V.+; **rātave** C.
Deriv.: **-rā** C. **rayí**? V.+ **rākā́**? V.+ **rárāvan** RV. **rāí** *or* **rā́**? V.+ **rayiṣṭha** B **rātí** V.+ **-ráru**? V.B. **-rāya** V. **rátna**? V.+ **rā́van** V.B.

The present-stem **rāsa** is plainly an extension of the aorist-stem **rās.**

√ 2 **rā**, 'bark'.

Pres. [4.] **rā́yati** *etc.* V.B.
[*Perf. etc.* **rarāu; arāsīt; rāsyati, rātā.**]
Deriv. **-rā́van**? VS.

√ **rāj**, 'be kingly'.

Pres. [1.] **rā́jati** *etc.* V.+, **-te** *etc.* E.+ — [2.] **rā́ṣṭi rā́ṭ** RV.
Perf. **rarāja rejus** *etc.* E.+, **rarājatus** M., **reje** *etc.* E.+ [**rarāje.**]
Aor. 1. **rājyāsam** S. [— 3. **ararājat.**] — 5. **arājiṣus** RV. [**arājiṣṭa.**]
[*Fut.* **rājiṣyati, rājitā.**]
Verb. **rājáse** RV.
Sec. Conj.: [*Int.* **rārāj-.** — *Desid.* **rirājiṣa-.** —] *Caus.* **rājayati** *etc.* B.+, **-te** *etc.* AV.E.
Deriv.: **rā́j** V.+ **rā́jan** V.+ **rājaná** B.+ **rā́ṣṭrī** V.B.S. **-rāja** V.+ **rāján** RV. **-rājin** RV.E. **rāṣṭrá** V.+

Is most probably an old denominative of **rā́j** 'ruler', from √ **ṛj, raj,** which see. The anomalous stem **irajyá-** (see ib.) is related with it.

√ **rādh**, 'succeed'.

Pres. [5.] **rādhnoti** *etc.* B.+ — [4.] **rā́dhyate** *etc.* AV.+, **-ti** *etc.* S.+
Perf. **rarā́dha** *etc.* V.B.
Aor. 1. **arādham** B. (**rādhati -dhat** *etc.* RV., **-dhās** ÇB.); **rādhyāsam -sma** AV.B.S.; **árādhi** V.B.U. — 3. **arīradhat** *etc.* B.C. — 4. **arātsīt** *etc.* AV.B.S. — 5. **rādhiṣi** *etc.* AV.B.U.

Fut. 1. **rātsyati** *etc.* AV.B.S. [— 2. **rāddhā.**]
Verb. **rāddhá** AV.+; **rāddhvā́** B.; **-rādhya** B.
Sec. Conj.: *Pass.* **rādhyate** C. — [*Int.* **rārādh-.** — *Desid.* **rirātsa-, ritsa-.** —] *Caus.* **rādhayati** *etc.* AV.+ (**rādhyate** E.; **rirādhayiṣati** B.)
Deriv.: **rā́dha** V.+ **rā́dhana** AV.+ **-rādhi** AV. **-rādhayitṛ** C. **-rādhin** E. **-rādhanīya** C. **rā́ddhi** AV.B.S. **-rādhayiṣṇu** E. **rā́dhya** V.+ **rā́dhas** V.+ **-rāddhṛ** C.

The form **iradhanta** RV¹., with the infin. **irádhyāi** (for **iradhádhyāi**) RV¹., appears to belong to this root.

√ 1 **rās**, 'roar'.

Pres. [1.] **rāsati -te** *etc.* E.+
Perf. **rarāse** C.
[*Aor. etc.* **arāsiṣṭa; rāsiṣyate, rāsitā.**]
Sec. Conj.: *Int.* **rārāsyate** E.
Deriv.: **rāsa**? C. **rā́sabha**? B.+

Compare √ **ras** and √ **2 rā.**

√ 2 **rās,** *see* √ **1 rā.**

√ **ri, rī,** 'flow'.

Pres. [9.] **riṇā́ti riṇīte** *etc.* V.B.S. — [5.] **ariṇvan** MS. — [4.] **rī́yate** V.B. [— 6. **riyati.**]
[*Perf. etc.* **rirāya; arīrayat, arāiṣīt; reṣyati, retā; reri-, rirīṣa-, rāyaya-, repaya- arīripat.**]
Deriv.: **-raya** E. **rít** RV. **rītí** V.+ **rétas** V.+ **reṇú** V.+

Compare √ **lī.**

√ **rikh,** 'scratch'.

Pres. [6.] **rikha** RV¹.
Deriv. **rekhā** E.

The usual form of this root is **likh,** which see.

√ **riṅkh, riṅg,** 'creep'.

Pres. [1.] **riṅkhati** *etc.* C.; **riṅgati -te** *etc.* C.
[*Perf. etc.* **ririṅkha, ririṅga** *etc. etc.*]
Sec. Conj.: *Caus.* **riṅgayati** C.
Deriv.: **riṅkhaṇa** C. **riṅgin** C. **riṅgi** C.

√ **ric,** 'leave'.

Pres. [7.] **riṇákti** *etc.* V.B. [**riṅkte.**] — [4?] **rícyate** *etc.* TS., **-ti** E.
Perf. **riréca ricicé** *etc.* V.B. (**riricyāt** *etc.* V., **ririkvā́ṅs** RV., **arirecīt** RV.)
Aor. 1. **riktam**? RV.; **areci** V.B.S. — 2. **aricat** C. — 3. **arīricat** *etc.* B.S. — 4. **ā́rāik** RV., **arikṣi** *etc.* V.B.
Fut. 1. **rekṣyate** B. [— 2. **rektā.**]

Verb. **riktá** v.+ [**ríkta.**]

Sec. Conj.: Pass. **ricyáte** *etc.* v.+ — [*Int.* **reric-.** — *Desid.* **ririkṣa-.** —]
Caus. **recayati** *etc.* B.+

Deriv.:	**-reka** V.+	**-recya** C.	**-riñca** E.+	**-rikti** JB.
	-rekin C.	**récana** V.+	**-riñcya** C.	**rikthá** V.+
	reca B.+	**-recanīya** C.	**-riñci** E.+	**réknas** RV.
	recaka E.+		**réku** RV.	**-ríkvan** RV.

The accent **rícyate** is quotable only from TS., and **ricyáte** only from ÇB.

√ rip, 'smear'.

Perf. **riripús** RV.
Verb. **riptá** RV.
Deriv.: **ríp** V. **répas** V. **ripú** V.+ **riprá** V.

Compare the other form of the root, **lip**, to which most of the formation belongs.

√ riph, 'snarl'.

Pres. [6.] **riphant -atī́** AV.B. — [1.] **rephant** B.
[*Perf. etc.* **rirepha** *etc. etc.*]
Verb. **riphitá** B.+
Sec. Conj.: Pass. **riphyate** S.
Deriv. **repha** S.+

√ ribh, 'sing'.

Pres. [1.] **rébhati** *etc.* V.B.C[1].?
Perf. **rirébha** RV.
[*Aor. etc.* **arebhīt; rebhiṣyati, rebhitā.**]
Sec. Conj.: Pass. **ribhyate** RV.
Deriv. **rebhá** V.+

√ riç, 'tear'.

Pres. [6.] **riçánt riçáte** *etc.* RV.
Verb. **riṣṭá** V.U.
Deriv. **riçā́** AV.

See the other form, **liç**, from which the forms mostly come.

√ riṣ, 'be hurt'.

Pres. [4.] **ríṣyati** *etc.* V.+, **-te** *etc.* E.+ — [1.] **reṣat réṣāt** V.
[*Perf.* **rireṣa.**]
Aor. 1. **rīḍhvam** TA. — 2. **ariṣan** *etc.* V.B.S. (**riṣātha** *etc.* RV., **ríṣant ríṣant?** RV.) — 3. **rīriṣat** *etc.* V.+ (**rīriṣīṣṭa** RV.C., **ririṣīṣṭa ririṣes** RV.) [— 5. **areṣīt.**]
[*Fut.* **reṣiṣyati; reṣitā, reṣṭā.**]
Verb. **riṣṭá** V.+; **riṣé riṣás** RV.

Sec. Conj.: [*Int.* **reriṣ-.** —] *Desid.* **rírikṣati** *etc.* RV. [**ririṣiṣa-, rireṣiṣa-.** —]
Caus. **reṣáyati** *etc.* V.+ (**riṣayádhyāi** RV.)

Deriv.: **ríṣ** V. **reṣa** C. **reṣaṇá** V. **reṣmán** AV.B.
réṣ? B. **-reṣin** S. **ríṣṭi** V.B.S. **ririkṣú** RV.
-riṣa AV. **riṣaṇa-** RV. **riṣīka**? C.

√ rih, 'lick'.

Pres. [2.] **reḍhi rihánti** *etc.* V.B., **rihaté** RV., **rihāṇá** V., **ríhāṇa** VS.
Perf. **ririhváṅs** RV.
Verb. **rīḍha** RV.
Sec. Conj.: *Int.* **rérihat -hāṇa** *etc.* V.B., **rerihyáte** *etc.* V.B.
Deriv.: **-réhaṇa** AV. **rerihá** AV.
The other verb-forms and derivatives made from √ **lih**, which see.

√ rī, *see* √ ri.

√ 1 ru, 'cry'.

Pres. [2.] **rāuti** [**ravīti**] **ruvanti** *etc.* B.+ (**rūyāt** S., **ravāṇa**? S.) — [6.]
ruváti *etc.* V.+ — [1.] **ravati -te** *etc.* JB.+
Perf. **rurāva** E., **ruruvire** B.
Aor. [1. **rūyāt.** —] 3. **arūruvat** C. [**arīravat.**] — 5. **árāvīt** *etc.* RV.
[*Fut.* **raviṣyati, ravitā rotā.**]
Verb **rutá** AV.+; **rotum** C.
Sec. Conj.: *Int.* **róravīti** *etc.* V.+, **róruvāṇa** B.; **rorūyate** *etc.* E.+, **-ti** E. —
[*Desid.* **rurūṣa-.** —] *Caus.* **rāvayati** *etc.* S.+

Deriv.: **ráva** V.+ **-rávas** V.+ **ruvátha** B. **rāva** E.+
ravaṇa C. **ravitṛ** B. **rúma**? RV. **rāvin** E.+
ruvaṇa- RV. **ravátha** V.B.S. **rāvaṇa** E.+

√ 2 ru, 'break'.

Pres. [2.] **rudhí** AV.? — [1.] **rávat** B.
Aor. 5. **rāviṣam** *etc.* V.B.
Verb. **rutá** V.B.
Sec. Conj.: *Int.* **róruvat** RV.
Deriv.: **ravitṛ** B. **-rāvin** B.
A very few sporadic occurrences, and not unquestionable.

√ ruc, 'shine'.

Pres. [1.] **rócate** *etc.* V.+, **-ti** *etc.* E.+
Perf. **ruroca rurucé** *etc.* V.+ (**rurukváṅs rurucyās rurucanta** RV.)
Aor. 1. **rucīya** TA., **rucāná** RV.; **aroci** RV. — 2. **arucat** C. — 3. **árūrucat**
RV., **-cata** (3*s.*) *etc.* B. — 4. **arukta** TA. — 5. **arociṣṭa** *etc.* B.+ (**rociṣīya**
B., **ruciṣīya** AV.)

Fut. 1. rociṣyate E. [— 2. rocitā.]
Verb. rucitá B.+; rocitum E.; rucé RV.
Sec. Conj.: *Int.* rórucāna RV. — *Desid.* rurucisate? AA. [rurociṣa-.] — *Caus.* rocáyati *etc.* V.+, -te *etc.* B.+ (rocyate E.); ruçayanta RV.

Deriv.:	rúc V.+	rocaka E.+	rúci AV.+	rucira E.+
	rucá B.	-rocin C.	roci C.	rukṣá RV.
	rucā E.	roká V.+	rocís V.+	ruciṣya C.
	rucaka E.+	róka RV.	rócuka MS.	rociṣṇú B.+
	rucya C.	-rokin V.B.	rukmá V.+	-ruça? RV.
	rocá AV.+	rocaná V.+	rúkmant V.B.	rúçant? V.
		-rocas B.		

√ ruj, 'break'.

Pres. [6.] rujáti *etc.* V.+, -te *etc.* E.+ — [2?] rukte B.
Perf. rurója rurujus *etc.* V.+ (rurójitha RV.)
Aor. 1. rok VS., ruk MS. — 3. arūrujat C. [— 4. arāukṣīt.]
[*Fut.* rokṣyati, roktā.]
Verb. rugṇá V.+; ruktvā́ B.; -rújya B.+; -rúje RV.
Sec. Conj.: *Pass.* rujyate E. — [*Int.* roruj-. —] *Desid.* rurukṣa- (*in d.*) — [*Caus.* rojayati.]

Deriv.:	ruj V.+	róga V.+	-rujana C.	-rujatnu RV.
	rujá V.+	logá? V.B.	-rogaṇa AV.	rurukṣáṇi RV.
	rujā E.+		rujā́nā RV.	

√ ruṭh, 'torment'.

Pres. [1.] roṭhamāna R[1].
Compare √ luṭh.

√ rud, 'weep'.

Pres. [2.] roditi rudanti *etc.* V.+ (rudimas rudihi C., arodīt B.+) — [6.] rudati -te *etc.* S.+ — [1.] rodati -te *etc.* S.+
Perf. ruroda rurudus *etc.* E., rurude E.
Aor. 2. árudat *etc.* AV.U. — [3. arūrudat. —] 5? arāudiṣīt C.
Fut. 1. rodiṣyati C. [— 2. roditā.]
Verb. rudita E.+; roditum C.; ruditvā E.+, roditvā E.; -rudya C.
Sec. Conj.: *Pass.* rudyate C. — *Int.* rorudat E., rorudyate *etc.* E.+ — *Desid.* rurudiṣa- (*in d.*) — *Caus.* rodáyati *etc.* V.+

Deriv.:	-rud AV.	rodana E.+	ródas *etc.*? V.+	-roruda AV.
	-ruda? C.	rudana C.	roditavya E.+	rurudiṣu C.
	róda AV.U.		rudrá? V.+	

√ 1 rudh, 'grow'.

Pres. [1.] ródhati ródhat RV. — [6.] rudhánt? RV[1].
Deriv.: -rudh V.+ -rodha AV.+ -ródhana V.B.
Appears to be another form of √ ruh.

√ 2 rudh, 'obstruct'.

Pres. [7.] ruṇáddhi rundhanti runddhé rundhate *etc.* V.+ — [2.] rudhmas AV. — [1.] rodhati E. — [6?] rundhati -te *etc.* B.+

Perf. rurodha rurudhe *etc.* V.+ (rurodhitha RV., rurundhatus E.)

Aor. 1. arodham RV., arudhma MS. (rudhánt? RV.); rudhyāt C. [arodhi.] — 2. arudhat *etc.* V.+ — [3. arūrudhat. —] 4. arāutsīt *etc.* B.+ (arāut AV., rotsīs U.), arutsi aruddha *etc.* B.U. (arāutsi AB.)

Fut. 1. rotsyati -te *etc.* B.+ [— 2. roddhā.]

Verb. ruddhá V.+; roddhum E.+, -dhos B., rodhitum E.; ruddhvā E.+; -rúdhya V.+, -rundhya E.; -rúdham AV.B., -rúndham B.; -ródham B.

Sec. Conj.: *Pass.* rudhyáte *etc.* V.+, -ti *etc.* E.+ — *Int.* rorudhas E. — *Desid.* rurutsate *etc.* B., -ti E. (-syamāna? B.S.) — *Caus.* rodhayati -te *etc.* E.+ (rodhyate E.); rundhayati E.

Deriv.: -rudh V.+   -rudha RV.   ródha V.+   rodhaka E.+   rodhin S.+   rodhya E.+   ródhana V.+   rodhanā́ RV.   ródhas V.+   -ródhuka B.   -ruddhi B.   roddhavya E.+   roddhṛ B.+

√ rup, 'break, pain'.

Pres. [4.] rúpyati *etc.* B.

[*Perf.* ruropa.]

Aor. [2. arupat. —] 3. arūrupat *etc.* AV.B.

[*Fut.* ropiṣyati, ropitā.]

Verb. rupita RV.

Sec. Conj.: *Caus.* ropayati B.

Deriv.: ropaṇá AV.   rópi AV.   rópuṣī RV.

Probably the same with √ lup, though differentiated from it in meaning.

√ ruṣ, 'be vexed'.

Pres. [1.] roṣati RV.B. — [4.] ruṣyati -te *etc.* E.+ — [6.] ruṣati *etc.* S.+

[*Perf. etc.* ruroṣa; aruṣat, arūruṣat, aroṣīt; roṣiṣyati, roṣitā roṣṭā.]

Verb. ruṣita E.+, ruṣṭa E.+; ruṣya E.

Sec. Conj.: [*Int.* roruṣ-. — *Desid.* ruruṣiṣa-, ruroṣiṣa-. —] *Caus.* roṣayati -te *etc.* E.+ (roṣyate E.+)

Deriv.: ruṣ E.+   roṣa E.+   roṣaṇa E.+

Occasionally written ruç; and part of the AV. forms of rúçant are referred here by BR.

√ ruh, 'ascend'.

Pres. [1.] róhati -te *etc.* V.+ — [6.] ruhati -te *etc.* E.+

Perf. ruroha ruruhús *etc.* V.+ (ruróhitha AV.), ruruhe *etc.* C.

Aor. 2. aruhat *etc.* V.+ (ruheyam *etc.* ruha rúhāṇa V.B.S.) — 7. árukṣat *etc.* V.B.S.

Fut. 1. rokṣyáti B.+, -te E., rohiṣye E. [— 2. roḍhā.]
Verb. rūḍhá V.+; róḍhum B.+, rohitum E.; rūḍhvā́ AV.; -rúhya AV.+, -rūhya AB.; -rúham RV.; róhiṣyāi TS.; -róham B.
Sec. Conj.: Pass. ruhyate E. — [*Int.* roruh-. —] *Desid.* rúrukṣati *etc.* V.+ — *Caus.* roháyati *etc.* V.+, -te *etc.* B.+; ropayati *etc.* B.+, -te E. (ropyate E.+, aropi C.)

Deriv.:	rúh V.+	róhaṇa V.+	-roḍhavya E.+	ropin E.+
	-ruha E.+	rohaṇīya S.+	-roḍhṛ C.	ropya E.+
	róha AV.+	róhas RV.S.	-rurukṣu E.+	ropaṇa E.+
	rohaka E.+	-róhuka B.	ropa E.+	ropaṇīya C.
	rohin B.+	rūḍhi B.+	ropaka E.+	ropayitṛ E.+
	-rohyà B.			

√ rūṣ, 'strew'.

[*Pres. etc.* rūṣati *etc. etc.*]
Verb. rūṣita E.+
Sec. Conj.: Caus. [rūṣayati;] roṣayati *etc.* C.
Deriv.: rūṣaṇa C. rūkṣá? V.+

√ rej, 'tremble'.

Pres. [1.] réjati -te *etc.* V.B.
Sec. Conj.: Caus. rejáyati *etc.* RV.

√ reḍ, 'deceive' (?).

Pres. [1.] -reḍant B.S.

Only in the phrase áreḍatā mánasā. Of wholly doubtful character.

√ rebh, *see* √ ribh.

√ lakṣ, 'mark'.

Pres. [1.] lakṣate C., -ti E.
Sec. Conj.: Caus. lakṣayati -te *etc.* E.+ (-lakṣita B.+, -lakṣya S.+; lakṣyate E.+)

Deriv.:	lakṣá V.+	lakṣya U.+	lakṣaṇīya C.	lakṣmī́ V.+
	lakṣaka C.	lakṣaṇa B.+	lákṣman V.+	-lakṣayitavya E.

Really a denominative formation from lakṣá, but having attained the position and value of a secondary root.

√ lag, 'attach'.

Pres. [1.] lagati *etc.* E.+
[*Perf. etc.* lalāga; alagīt.]
Fut. 1. lagiṣyati *etc.* C. [— 2. lagitā.]
Verb. lagna B[1].? E.+; lagitvā C.; -lagya C.

Sec. Conj.: Caus. lāgayati C.
Deriv.: -lagana C. laganīya C. liṅga? U.+

The lateness of this root is strongly opposed to the derivation from it of **lakṣá** etc.

√ laṅgh, 'leap'.

Pres. [1.] **laṅghati -te** C.
[*Perf. etc.* **lalaṅgha -ghe; alaṅghīt, alaṅghiṣṭa; laṅghiṣyati -te, laṅghitā.**]
Sec. Conj.: Caus. **laṅghayati** *etc.* E.+ (**laṅghita** S.+; **laṅghyate** C.)
Deriv.: **laṅghaka** C. **-laṅghin** C. **laṅghya** E.+ **laṅghana** S.+ **laṅghanīya** C.

Doubtless related with √ **raṅh.**

√ lajj, 'be ashamed'.

Pres. [6.] **lajjàte** *etc.* B[1].E.+, **-ti** *etc.* E.+
Perf. **lalajjire** C.
[*Aor. etc.* **alajjiṣṭa; lajjiṣyate, lajjitā.**]
Verb. **lajjita** C.; **lajjitum** E.
Sec. Conj.: [*Int.* **lālajj-.** — *Desid.* **lilajjiṣa-.** —] *Caus.* **lajjayati** *etc.* C.
Deriv. **lajjā** E.+

√ lap, 'prate'.

Pres. [1.] **lapati** *etc.* AV.E.+, **-te** *etc.* E. — [4.] **lapyant** M.
Perf. **lalāpa lepus** E.+
[*Aor.* **alīlapat, alalāpat; alāpīt.**]
Fut. 1. **lapiṣyati** *etc.* B.+ [— 2. **lapitā.**]
Verb. **lapitá** AV.+, **lapta** E.; **lapitum** C., **laptum** E.; **-lapya** E.+
Sec. Conj.: Pass. **lapyate** C. — *Int.* **lā́lapīti** *etc.* AV.B.; **lālapyate** *etc.* E.+, **-ti** E. — [*Desid.* **lilapiṣa-.** —] *Caus.* **lāpayati** *etc.* AV.+, **-te** *etc.* B.U.
Deriv.: **-lap** AV. **-lapya** C. **lapana** C. **lapanīya** C. **-lapti** C. **-lapitavya** C. **-lāpa** AV.+ **-lāpaka** E.+ **-lāpin** E.+ **-lāpya** C. **-lāpana** E.+

Compare the other root-form, **rap.**

√ labh, 'take'.

Pres. [1.] **labhate** *etc.* AV.+, **-ti** *etc.* AV.? E.+; **lambhate** *etc.* E.
Perf. **lalābha** C., **lebhé** *etc.* V.+
Aor. [1. **alambhi.** — 3. **alalambhat.** —] 4. **alabdha alapsata** B.; **lapsīya** S.
Fut. 1. **lapsyate** *etc.* B.+, **-ti** *etc.* B.+; **labhiṣyati** C. — 2. **labdhā** E.
Verb. **labdha** V.+; **labdhvā́** AV.+; **-lábhya** B.+; **-lámbham** B.S.
Sec. Conj.: Pass. **labhyáte** *etc.* B.+, **-ti** C. [— *Int.* **lālabh-, lālambh-.**] — *Desid.* **lípsate** *etc.* AV.+, **-ti** *etc.* E.+; **līpsate** *etc.* B.S. (**lipsyáte** ÇB.) — *Caus.* **lambhayati** *etc.* B.+, **-te** B.

Deriv.:	**-labha** s.+	**labhana** c.	**lambha** b.+	**lambhuka** b.u.
	labhya b.+	**-labhanīya** c.	**lambhaka** b.+	**lipsā** avp.e.+
	lābha b.+	**labdhi** e.+	**-lambhin** e.+	**lipsu** e.+
	-lābhaka rv.	**labdhavya** u.+	**-lambhyà** b.s.	**lipsitavya** e.
	lābhin c.	**labdhṛ** b.+	**lambhana** s.+	**līpsitavya** b.
			lambhanīya u.+	

Compare the other root-form, **rabh.**

√ lam, 'take pleasure'.

Pres. **lalāma** c[1].
Deriv. **lamaka**? s.
Sporadic variation of √ **ram.**

√ lamb, 'hang down'.

Pres. [1.] **lambate** *etc.* b.+, **-ti** *etc.* e.+
Perf. **lalambe** *etc.* e.+
[*Aor.* **alalambat, alambiṣṭa.**]
Fut. 1. **lambiṣyati** e., **alambiṣyata** c. — [2. **lambitā.**]
Verb. **lambita** e.+; **lambitum** e.+; **-lambya** e.+
Sec. Conj.: Pass. **lambyate** *etc.* e.+ — *Caus.* **lambayati** *etc.* e.+, **-te** c. (**lambyate** *etc.* e.+)

Deriv.:	**lamba** b.+	**lambin** b.+	**lambana** e.+	**-lambitavya** c.
	lambaka c.	**-lambya** c.	**-lambuka** b.	

Compare the other root-form, **ramb.**

√ lal, 'sport'.

Pres. [1.] **lalati -te** *etc.* e.+
Verb. **lalita** e.+
Sec. Conj.: Caus. **lālayati** *etc.* e.+, **-te** c. (**lālyate** c.); **lalayati** *etc.* c.

Deriv.:	**lalana** e.+	**lālaka** c.	**lālana** c.	**lālayitavya** e.+
	-lāla c.	**-lālya** c.	**lālanīya** e.+	

√ laṣ, 'desire'.

Pres. [1.] **laṣati -te** *etc.* e.+ [— 4. **laṣyati -te.**]
Perf. **lalāṣa leṣus** c. [**leṣe.**]
[*Aor.* **alīlaṣat; alăṣīt, alaṣiṣṭa.**]
Fut. 1. **laṣiṣyati** c. [**-te.** — 2. **laṣitā.**]
Verb. **laṣitá** e.+
[*Sec. Conj.:* **lālaṣ-; lilaṣiṣa-; lāṣaya-.**]

Deriv.:	**-laṣya** c.	**-laṣaṇīya** c.	**-lāṣa** c.	**-lāṣin** c.
			-lāṣaka e.+	**-lāṣuka** c.

Hardly occurs, in verb-forms or derivatives, except with **abhi.**

√ **las**, 'be lively'.

Pres. [1.] **lasati** *etc.* E.+, **-te** *etc.* C.
Perf. **lalāsa** C.
[*Aor. etc.* **alīlasat, alasīt; lasiṣyati, lasitā.**]
Verb. **lasita** E.+
Sec. Conj.: Caus. **lāsayati** *etc.* E.+ (**lāsyate** C.)
Deriv.: **-las** C. **-lasana** C. **lāsa** E.+ **-lāsin** E.+
-lasa B.+ **lāsana** E.+ **lāsaka** E.+ **lāsya** E.+
lālasa E.+

In meaning, **lālasa** belongs distinctly to √ **laṣ**, and the two roots are very possibly one in origin; **alasa** is the only pre-epic form.

√ **lā**, 'grasp'.

Pres. [2.] **lāti** C.
[*Perf. etc.* **lalāu; alāsīt; lāsyati, lātā.**]
Verb. **lātvā** C.

A few sporadic occurrences, probably artificial.

√ **lāñch**, 'mark'.

Only in **lāñchita** C. and **lāñchana** C.; perhaps connected with √ **lakṣ**.

√ **likh**, 'scratch'.

Pres. [6.] **likháti** *etc.* AV.+, **-te** B.S.
Perf. **lilékha** *etc.* B.+
Aor. [1. **alekhi.** —] 3. **alīlikhat** JB. — 5. **lekhīs** B.S.
Fut. 1. **likhiṣyati** C. [**lekhiṣyati.** — 2. **lekhitā.**]
Verb. **likhitá** AV.+ [**lekhitum, likhitum; lekhitvā,**] **likhitvā** C.; **-líkhya** B.+
Sec. Conj.: Pass. **likhyate** *etc.* S.+ — [*Desid.* **lilikhiṣa-, lilekhiṣa-.** —]
Caus. **lekhayati** *etc.* S.+; **likhāpayati** C.
Deriv.: **likhya** C. **lekha** S.+ **lekhaka** E.+ **lekhana** S.+
likhana C. **lékhā** B.+ **lekhin** E.+ **lekhanīya** C.
lekhya E.+

Compare the other root-form, **rikh.**

√ **lip, limp**, 'smear'.

Pres. [6.] **limpáti** *etc.* AV.+, **-te** *etc.* S.+
Perf. **lilepa lilipus** B.+
Aor. 1. **alepi** C. — 2. **alipat** C. [**alipata.** — 3. **alīlipat.**] — 4. **alipta** C., **alipsata** RV.
[*Fut.* **lepsyati -te; leptā.**]
Verb. **lipta** AV.+; **-lípya** B.+
Sec. Conj.: Pass. **lipyate** *etc.* B.+, **-ti** E. — [*Int.* **lelip-.** — *Desid.* **lilipsa-.** —]
Caus. **lepayati** *etc.* E.+; **limpayati** S.

Deriv.: **lepa** U.S.+ **lepin** E.+ **lepana** S.+ **-limpa** AV.B.
-lepaka C. **lepya** C. **lipi** E.+ **limpi** C[1].

Compare the other root-form, **rip**.

√ liç, 'tear'

Pres. [6.] **liçáte** *etc.* B. (**liçāna** JB.) [— 4. **liçyate.**]
Perf. **liliçire** B.
Aor. [3. **alīliçat.** —] 5. **aleçiṣi** B. [— 7. **alikṣata.**]
[*Fut.* **lekṣyate, leṣṭā.**]
Verb. **liṣṭá** B.S.
[*Sec. Conj.:* **leliç-; lilikṣa-; leçaya-.**]
Deriv.: **(ku-)liça**? V.+ **leça** B.+ **leṣṭu** E.+

Compare the other root-form, **riç.**

√ lih, 'lick'.

Pres. [2.] **leḍhi** *etc.* B.+, **līḍhe** *etc.* E.+ — [6.] **lihati** *etc.* B.+
[*Perf. etc.* **lileha, lilihe.**]
Aor. [1. **aḷehi.** — 3. **alīlihat.** — 4. **alīḍha.** —] 7. **alikṣat** S. [**-kṣata.**]
[*Fut.* **lekṣyati -te, leḍhā.**]
Verb. **līḍha** E.+; **-lihya** S.
Sec. Conj.: Pass. **lihyate** E. — *Int.* **lelihat** *etc.* E.+, **lelihāna** E.+, **-hita** JB., **lelihyate** *etc.* E.+, **-hyant** C. — [*Desid.* **lilikṣa-.** —] *Caus.* **leháyati** *etc.* B.+
Deriv.: **-lih** C. **leha** C. **-lehin** E.+ **lehana** S.+
-liha C. **-lehaka** E. **lehya** E.+ **leliha** E.+

Compare the other root-form, **rih.**

√ 1 lī, 'cling'.

Pres. [4.] **líyate** AV.? B.+, **-ti** *etc.* U.C. — [1.] **láyate** *etc.* V.B. — **(ni-)lāyata** B. [— 9. **lināti.**]
Perf. **lilye** *etc.* B.+, **lilyus** B.+ — **(ni-)layāṁ cakre** ÇB. [**lalāu.**]
Aor. 4. **aleṣṭa** ÇB. [**alāiṣīt.** — 6. **alāsīt.**]
[*Fut.* **leṣyati, lāsyati; letā, lātā.**]
Verb. **līna** AV.+; **-līya** E.+, **-lāya** S.; **-lā́yam** AV.B.
Sec. Conj.: [*Int.* **lelī-.** — *Desid.* **lilīṣa-.** —] *Caus.* **lāpayati** *etc.* B.+ (**lāpyate** C.); **lāyayati** *etc.* C.
Deriv.: **láya** B.+ **-līyana** C. **-lāyya**? RV. **-lāpya** C.
láyana AV.+ **lā́ya**? RV. **-lāyana** C. **-lā́pana** B.+
layú? MS. **-lā́yaka** VS. **-leya**? C. **-lāpayitavya** C.

Compare √ **ri, rī.**

√ 2 lī, 'be unsteady'.

Sec. Conj.: Int. **lelā́yati** B.U.S., **alelāyat** B., **alelet** B., **lelāyántī leláyatas** B.; **lelāyate** *etc.* U., **alelīyata** B.; **leláya**? ÇB., **lelā́ya** MS., **lelāyat** JB.
Deriv. **lelā́** ÇB.? JB.

Perhaps intensive of the preceding. The variety of form and accent is quite anomalous.

√ luñc, 'tear'.

[*Pres.* **luñcati.**]
Perf. **luluñcus** E., **-ñce** C.
[*Aor. etc.* **aluñcīt; luñciṣyati, luñcitā.**]
Verb. **luñcita** C.; **luñcitvā** C. [**lucitvā**]; **-luñcya** E.
Deriv.: **luk**? C. **-luñca** VS. **-luñcaka** C. **-luñcana** E.+

√ 1 luṭh, 'roll'

Pres. [6.] **luṭhati -te** *etc.* C.
Perf. **luloṭha** C.
[*Aor. etc.* **alūluṭhat aluloṭhat, aloṭhīt aloṭhiṣṭa; loṭhiṣyati, loṭhitā.**]
Verb. **luṭhita** C.
Sec. Conj.: Int. **loluṭhīti** C. — *Caus.* **loṭhayati** C.
Deriv. **loṭhana**? C.

√ 2 luṭh, luṇṭh, 'rob'.

Pres. [1.] **luṇṭhati** E[1].
Fut. **luṇṭhiṣyati** C.
Verb. **luṇṭhitum** C.
Sec. Conj.: Caus. **loṭhayati** *etc.* C.; **luṇṭhayati** *etc.* C. (**luṇṭhyate** C.)
Deriv.: **-luṇṭhā** C. **luṇṭhaka** C. **luṇṭhana** E[1].C. **luṇṭhi** C.

√ luḍ, 'stir up'.

[*Pres. etc.* **loḍati** *etc. etc.*]
Sec. Conj. Caus. **loḍayati** *etc.* E.+; **loḍita -loḍya** S.+ (**loḍyate** *etc.* E.+)
Deriv.: **-loḍana** E.+ **-loḍayitṛ** C.

Compare √ **lul.** A form or two from √ **luṇṭh** appear to have the meaning of √ **luḍ.**

√ lup, 'break'.

Pres. [6.] **lumpáti** *etc.* AV.+, **-te** *etc.* S.+
Perf. **lulopa** *etc.* B.+, **lulupe** E.
Aor. 1. **lopi** S. — [2. **alupat.** —] 3. **alūlupat** E. [**alulopat.**] — 4. [**alupta;**] **lopsīya** U.
[*Fut.* **lopsyati -te, loptā.**]
Verb. **lupta** AV.+; **loptum** C.; **luptvā** S.+; **-lúpya** AV.+; **-lúmpam** MS., **-lopam** S.

Sec. Conj.: Pass. **lupyáte** *etc.* AV.+ (**lúpyate** TS.), **-ti** S. — *Int.* **lolupat -pyate** *etc.* U.+ — [*Desid.* **lulupsa-, lulopiṣa-.** —] *Caus.* **lopayati -te** *etc.* JB.E.+ (**lopyate** C.)

Deriv.: **lup** C. **lopaka** E.+ **lopana** E.+ **-lumpaka** E.+ **-lupya** C. **lopin** E.+ **-lupti** B. **-lumpana** E. **lopa** B.+ **lopya** C. **loptṛ** E. **lolupa** E.+ **loptra** E.+

Compare the other root-form, **rup. Lolupa** belongs in meaning to √**lubh.**

√ **lubh**, 'be lustful'.

Pres. [4.] **lúbhyati** *etc.* AV.+ [— 6. **lubhati.**] — [1.] **lobhase** C[1].
Perf. **lulubhe** S.+ [**lulobha.**]
Aor. [2. **alubhat.** —] 3. **alūlubhat** JB. [— 5. **alobhīt.**]
[*Fut.* **lobhiṣyati; lobdhā, lobhitā.**]
Verb. **lubdha** B.+; **lobdhum** E.
Sec. Conj.: Int. **lolubhyate** C. — [*Desid.* **lulubhiṣa-, lulobhiṣa-.** —] *Caus.* **lobháyati** *etc.* V.+, **-te** *etc.* E.+ (**lobhyate** E.+; **lulobhayiṣati** AB.)

Deriv.: **lobha** E.+ **lobhin** E.+ **lobhana** S.+ **lobhanīya** E.+ **-lobhaka** C. **-lobhya** C.

√ **lul**, 'be lively'.

Pres. [1.] **lolati** *etc.* C.
Verb. **lulita** E.+
Sec. Conj.: Caus. **lolayati** *etc.* B.+
Deriv.: **lola** E.+ **lolana** C.
The same with √ **luḍ.**

√ **lū**, 'cut'.

Pres. [9.] **lunā́ti** *etc.* B.+ — [5.] **lunoti** *etc.* B.S.
Perf. **lulāva** C.
[*Aor. etc.* **alāvi, alīlavat -vata, alāvīt alaviṣṭa; laviṣyati -te, lavitā.**]
Verb. **lūna** B.+; **-lāvam** C.
[*Sec. Conj.:* **lolū-; lulūṣa-; lāvaya-.**]
Deriv.: **láva** B.+ **-lavya** C. **lavana** S.+ **lāva** C. **lāvaka** C.

√ **lok**, 'look'.

Pres. [1.] **lokate** *etc.* B[1].C.
Perf. **luloke** C.
Aor. 1. **aloki** C. [— 3. **alulokat.** — 5. **alokiṣṭa.**]
[*Fut.* **lokiṣyate, lokitā.**]
Verb. **lokitum** C.
Sec. Conj.: Caus. **lokayati** *etc.* E.+, **-te** *etc.* E.+ (**lokyate** *etc.* C.)

Deriv.: **-loka** E.+ **-lokin** S.+ **-lokana** C. **-lokayitṛ** C. **-lokaka** E.+ **-lokya** E.+ **-lokanīya** E.+ **-lokayitavya** C.

Doubtless from √ **ruc,** through a noun **loka:** compare also √ **loc.**

√ loc, 'see, consider'.

[*Pres.* locate.]
Perf. luloce c[1].
[*Aor. etc.* alulocat, aloċiṣṭa; lociṣyate, locitā.]
Sec. Conj.: [*Int.* loloc-. — *Desid.* lulociṣa-. —] *Caus.* locayati -te *etc.* B.+
Deriv.: -loca C. -locya C. locana E.+ -locanīya C.
-locaka C.

The same root with the preceding.

√ vak, *see* √ vañc.

√ vakṣ, ukṣ, 'increase'.

Pres. [1, 6.] úkṣant ukṣámāṇa āúkṣat RV.
Perf. vavákṣa vavakṣé *etc.* (vavákṣitha) V.
Aor. 3? vavákṣat SV. — 5. āúkṣīs RV.
[*Fut.* vakṣiṣyati, vakṣitā.]
Verb. ukṣitá RV.
Sec. Conj.: *Caus.* ukṣayanta RV.; vakṣayam RV.
Deriv.: vákṣaṇa RV. vakṣáṇā? V. vakṣáṇi RV. vakṣátha RV. vákṣas? V.+

√ vac, 'speak'.

Pres. [3.] vívakti *etc.* V. — [2.] vacmi vakṣi vakti E.+
Perf. uvā́ca ūcús *etc.* V.+ (uváktha AV.), ūcé *etc.* V.+ (vavā́ca vivakvā́ṅs RV., vavakṣé RV.)
Aor. 1. ucyāsam B.; avāci V.B. — 2. avocat -cata *etc.* V.+ (vócati -te *etc.* V.+; vocāti *etc.* V.B.S., vocét -ceta *etc.* V.B., vocatu *etc.* V.; vocant C.; avoci C.) [— 3. avīvacat.]
Fut. 1. vakṣyáti *etc.* V.+, -te *etc.* E.+ (avakṣyat *etc.* B.U.) — 2. vaktā́ B.+
Verb. uktá V.+; váktum B.+, -tave RV., -toṣ B.; uktvā́ B.+; -úcya B.+
Sec. Conj.: *Pass.* ucyáte *etc.* V.+ — *Int.* ávāvacīt RV. — *Desid.* vivakṣati -te *etc.* B.+ (vivakṣyate C.) — *Caus* vācayati *etc.* B.+, -te *etc.* S. (vācyate C.)

Deriv.:	vā́c V.+	vácana V.+	ukti V.+	vagnú V.B.
	-vaca E.+	vacaná RV.	vakti U[1].	vákman? RV.
	-úcya B.S.	vacanīya S.+	váktva RV.	vákmya? RV.
	vāká V.+	vācana V.+	vaktavyà B.+	vagvaná RV.
	-vākin U[1].	-vācanīya C.	vaktṛ V.+	vagvanú RV.
	vākyà V.+	vácas V.+	vaktra E.+	vivakṣā E.+
	vācaka E.+	-vā́cas V.	ukthá V.+	vivakṣu AV.+
	vācin C.	-vā́ku AV.+	ucátha RV.	vācayitṛ C.
	vā́cya V.+			vācayitavya S.

The aorist-stem voca is treated quite as a secondary root-form.

√ **vaj**, 'be strong'.

[*Pres. etc.* **vajati** *etc. etc.*]

Sec. Conj.: Caus. **vājáyati** *etc.* V.B.S. (**vājayánt** RV.; **vājayádhyāi** RV.)

Deriv.: **vā́ja** V.+ **ójas** V.+ **ójīyas** V.B. **ugrá** V.+
-vājana S. **oja-** RV. **ojmán** V. **vájra** V.+
óji̇ṣṭha V.B.

The verbal forms are really denominative, from **vāja**.

√ **vañc**, 'move crookedly'.

Pres. [1.] **váñcati** V.B.S., **-te** C[1].

Perf. [**vavañca**] **vāvakre** RV.

[*Aor. etc.* **vacyāt**, **avavañcat**, **avañcīt**; **vañciṣyati**, **vañcitā**; **vañcitvā** **vacitvā** **vaktvā**.]

Sec. Conj.: Pass. **vacyáte** *etc.* V.+ — *Int.* [**vanīvañc-**] **avāvacīt**? RV. — [*Desid.* **vivañciṣa-**. —] *Caus.* **vañcayati** *etc.* U.+, **-te** *etc.* E.+ (**vañcyate** E.+)

Deriv.: **vañcaka** E.+ **vañkú** RV. **vakrá** AV.+ **vañcayitṛ** C.
vañcana V.+ **váñkri** V.+ **vákva** RV. **vañcayitavya** E.+
vañcanīya E.+ **vákvan** RV.

It is hardly necessary to assume a different root-form **vak** for a part of these forms, since they are all such as sometimes show a guttural in place of a palatal of the root.

√ **vaṇṭ**, 'divide'.

[*Pres. etc.* **vaṇṭati** *etc. etc.*]

Sec. Conj.: Pass. **vaṇṭyate** C.

The single occurrence is doubtless artificial.

√ **vat**, 'apprehend'.

Pres. [1.] **vatema vátantas** RV.

Aor. 3. **avīvatan** V.

Sec. Conj.: Caus. **vātáyati** *etc.* RV.

Deriv. **-vāta**? RV.

Only with **api**.

√ **vad**, 'speak'.

Pres. [1.] **vádati -te** *etc.* V.+ (**vādata -deyus** E.; **udeyam** AV.)

Perf. **ūdimá ūdus** V.B., **ūde** *etc.* B.U.

Aor. 1. **udyāsam** *etc.* B.S.; **avādi** C. — [3. **avīvadat**. —] 5. **avādīt** *etc.* V.+ (**vā́diṣas** AV., **vadiṣma** AB.), **vadiṣṭhās** B. (**avādiran** AV.)

Fut. 1. **vadiṣyáti** *etc.* AV.+, **-te** B.

Verb. **uditá** V.+, **vadita** E.+; **vaditum** B.+, **váditos** B.S.; **uditvā** S.; **-udya** B.+; **-úde**? AV.

Sec. Conj.: *Pass.* udyáte *etc.* V.+ — *Int.* vā́vadīti *etc.* V.B., -dyáte *etc.* B. — *Desid.* vivadiṣati *etc.* B.S. — *Caus.* vādayati -te *etc.* B.+ (vādyate B.+, -ti E.)

Deriv.: -vada V.+ · -vadya V.+ · -udya AV.+ · vāda V.+ · vādaka E.+ · vādin V.+ · vā́dya AV.+ · vádana B.+ · vādana S.+ · -vādanīya S.+ · vaditavyà B.+ · vāditavya E. · vaditṛ B.+ · vāditra U.S.+ · -vadiṣu S. · -vadiṣṇu S. · vadiṣṭha B. · vāduka B. · vadmán RV. · -vadāvada B. · vadāvadin S. · -vādayitṛ B.+

Compare √ vand.

√ vadh, badh, 'slay'.

Pres. [1?] vadha? vadheyam AV., vadhet VS.

Aor. 1. badhyāsam -sus AV.B.S., vadhyāt B.; avadhi C. — 5. ávadhīt *etc.* V.+ (avadhīm vádhīm V.B.; vádhiṣas RV., badhīs TA.) [vadhiṣṭhās; vadhiṣiṣṭa.]

Fut. 1. vadhiṣyati -te *etc.* E.+

Sec. Conj.: *Pass.* vadhyate *etc.* E.+, -ti *etc.* E.+ — *Caus.* vadhayati *etc.* E.

Deriv.:

vadhá, ba- V.+ · vádhaka AV.+ · vádhya, bá- AV.+ · vadhánā RV. · vádhatra RV. · vádhar RV. · -vadhyā E.+ · -vadhra RV. · vádhri? V.+ · vadhasná RV. · vadhasnú V.

√ van, vā, 'win'.

Pres. [8.] vanóti vanuté *etc.* V.B.S. — [1.] vánati -te *etc.* V. — [6.] vanā́ti vanéma V.B.

Perf. vāvā́na vavanmá *etc.* vavné (vāvántha vāvánas vavandhí) RV.

Aor. 1. vanta? RV., váṅsva RV. — 4. váṅsat *etc.* RV., váṅsi (1*s*.) vaṅsate V.B., vaṅsīmahi vasīmahi RV. — 5. vaniṣat AV., vaniṣanta TS. (vanuṣanta RV.), vaniṣīṣṭa RV. — 6. vaṅsiṣīya? AV.

Fut. 1. vaniṣyate S. [— 2. vanitā.]

Verb. -vāta V.B., vanita E.+; -vantáve RV.

Sec. Conj.: *Int.* vanīvan- (*in d.*). — *Desid.* vívāsati -te *etc.* V. — *Caus.* vānayantu AV.

Deriv.: -van? B.S. · vana V.U. · vanín RV. · -ványa B. · vanád? RV. · -vánana V. · vanánā RV. · vananīya C. · vánas RV. · vaní V.B. · vanú RV. · vanús RV. · vantṛ́ RV. · vánitṛ RV. · vániṣṭha RV. · vánīyas RV. · -vānyà B.S. · vāmá? V.+ · vánīvan RV. · vāvā́ta V.+ · vāvā́tṛ RV. · vanayitṛ C.

√ vand, 'greet'.

Pres. [1.] vándate *etc.* V.+, -ti B.

Perf. vavanda *etc.* V.B., -dé *etc.* V.+

Aor. 1. **vandi** RV. — 5. **vandiṣīmáhi** RV.
[*Fut.* **vandiṣyate, vanditā.**]
Verb. **vanditá** AV.+; **vanditum** E.+; **vanditvā** E.+; **-vandya** E.+; **vandádhyāi** RV.
Sec. Conj.: *Pass.* **vandyate** *etc.* E.+ — *Desid.* **vivandiṣa-** (*in d.*). — *Caus.* **vandayati** *etc.* E.

Deriv.:			
-vanda V.	**vandin** C.	**vandanīya** E.+	**vanditavya** E.+
vándya V.+	**vándana** V.+	**vandā́ru** V.+	**vanditṛ** V.B.
			vivandiṣu C.

Doubtless the same with √ **vad.**

√ 1 **vap,** 'strew'.

Pres. [1.] **vápati -te** *etc.* V.+ (**upet** S.)
Perf. **uvāpa ūpús** *etc.* V.+ (**vavāpa** E.), **ūpe** *etc.* RV.
Aor. 1. [**upyāt**;] **vāpi** B. — [3. **avīvapat.** —] 4. **avāpsīt** *etc.* B.+ [**avapta.**]
Fut. 1. **vapsyáti** *etc.* B.S.; **vapiṣyati** *etc.* E.+ [— 2. **vaptā.**]
Verb. **uptá** V.+, **upita** E[1]., **vapta** E[1].; **uptvā** E.+; **-úpya** V.+
Sec. Conj.: *Pass.* **upyáte** *etc.* V.+ — [*Int.* **vāvap-.** — *Desid.* **vivapsa-.** —] *Caus.* **vāpayati** *etc.* B.+

Deriv.:			
vapá B.	**-vāpaka** E.	**vapanīya** C.	**vaptavya** C.
vapā́ V.B.S.	**-vāpin** C.	**vāpana** C.	**vaptṛ** E.+
-úpya B.	**vāpya** B.+	**vāpī** E.+	**vapra** S.+
vāpa B.+	**vápana** AV.+	**upti** C.	**-vapiṣṭha** B.
			-vāpayitṛ B.

Compare the following root.

√ 2 **vap,** 'shear'.

Pres. [1.] **vapati -te** *etc.* V.B.S.
Verb. **upta** S.; **uptvā** S.; **-upya** S.
Sec. Conj.: *Caus.* **vāpayati** *etc.* S., **-yīta** S.

Deriv.:			
vápana B.+	**vāpa** C.	**vāpana** S.+	**váptṛ** V.B.S.

Doubtless the same with the preceding root: 'scatter off from one'.

√ **vam,** 'vomit'.

Pres. [2.] **vámiti vamanti** *etc.* V.+ (**avamīt** V.B., **avamat** E.+) — [1.] **vamati** *etc.* E.+
Perf. **vavāma** E.+, **vemus** C. [**vavamus**] (**uvāma** ÇB.)
Aor. [1. **avāmi.** — 3. **avīvamat.** —] 4. **avān** KB. [— 5. **avamīt.**]
[*Fut.* **vamiṣyati, vamitā.**]
Verb. **vāṁtá** B.+; **vamitvā** C.
Sec. Conj.; [*Int.* **vaṅvam-.** — *Desid.* **vivamiṣa-.** —] *Caus.* **vāmayati** *etc.* C.; **vamayati** *etc.* C.

Deriv.:			
vami C.	**vamana** C.	**vamitavya** C.	**vamrá**? V.B.
vāmin B.+	**vāmanīya** C.	**vamathu** C.	

√ val, 'turn'.

Pres. [1.] **valati -te** *etc.* C.
Perf. **vavale** C.
[*Aor. etc.* **avīvalat, avaliṣṭa; valiṣyati, valitā.**]
Verb. **valitá** C.; **valitvā** C.
Sec. Conj.: Caus. **valayati** C.
Deriv.: **valana** C. **vali**? E.+ **valaya** E.+

Evidently a secondary root-form, probably from √ 1 **vṛ**, through some derivative.

√ valg, 'spring'.

Pres. [1.] **válgati** *etc.* AV.+, **-te** *etc.* E.+
Perf. **vavalga** *etc.* E.
[*Aor. etc.* **avalgīt; valgiṣyati, valgitā.**]
Verb. **valgita** E.+
Sec. Conj.: Caus. **valgayati** S.
Deriv.: **valgā** E.+ **-valgin** C. **valgana** C. **valgú** V.+

√ valh, 'challenge'.

Pres. [1.] **valhati -te** *etc.* B.S.
Verb. **valhita** C.; **-valhya** B.
Deriv.: **-valha** B.S. **-valhaka** B.S.

√ vaç, 'be eager'.

Pres. [2.] **váṣṭi uçánti** *etc.* V.+ (**çmasi** RV., **vaṣṭa** SV.) — [1.] **váçanti ávaçat** RV., **vaça -çet** AV.? — [3.] **vavákṣi vivaṣṭi** RV., **vivaṣṭu** SV. — [6.] **uçámāna** RV[1].
Perf. **vāvaçús -çe -çāná** RV. [**uvāça ūçus.**]
Aor. [1. **uçyāt.** — 3. **avīvaçat.** —] 5. **vaçīs** E. [**avāçīt.**]
[*Fut. etc.* **vaçiṣyati, vaçitā; uçita.**]
Sec. Conj.: [*Pass.* **uçyate.** — *Int.* **vāvaç-.** — *Desid.* **vivaçiṣa-.** —] *Caus.* **vaçayati** C.; **vāçitā**? AV.+
Deriv.: **váça** V.+ **uçá-**? RV. **uçánā, -nas** V.+ **uçénya** RV. **vaçí** B. **uçī-**? V.+ **uçíj** V.B.S. **váṣṭi** RV. **vaçitṛ** C. **váçīyas**? AV.

√ 1 vas, uṣ, uch, 'shine'.

Pres. [6.] **ucháti** *etc.* V.B.S. — [2.] **vaste**? ÇB[1].
Perf. **uvā́sa ūṣús** *etc.* V.B.
Aor. 1. **avasran** RV. — 4. **avāt**? AV.
Fut. 1. **avatsyat** ÇB.
Verb. **uṣṭá** V.+, **uṣita** S.E.; **vástave** RV.; **-úṣi** V.B.
Sec. Conj.: Caus. **vāsáyati** *etc.* V.B.

Deriv.: **úṣ** V.B. **uṣā́** RV. **-ūṣa** E.+ **uṣar-, usṛ́** RV. **uṣás** V.+ **-uṣṭi** V.+ **vástu** V.B. **vastṛ́** RV. **vásu** V.+ **vásiṣṭha** V.+ **vásīyas** B.S. **vásyas** V.B.U. **usrá** V.+ **úsri** RV. **-vāsa** AV.S. **-vāsana** C. **vāsará** RV. **vivásvan** RV. **vivasvant** V.+

√ 2 vas, 'clothe'.

Pres. [2.] **váste vásate vásāna** *etc.* V.+ (**vásiṣva** RV., **uṣāṇá** RV[1]., **vaddhvam** S.) — [6.] **uṣámāṇa** RV[1].

Perf. **vavase** C., **vāvase -sāná** RV.

Aor. [3. **avīvasat.** —] 5. **avasiṣṭa** *etc.* RV.

Fut. 1. [**vasiṣyate**;] **vatsyati** C[1]. [— 2. **vasitā.**]

Verb. **vasita** E.; **vasitum** E.+; **vasitvā** C.; **-vasya** E.

Sec. Conj.: [*Int.* **vāvas-.** — *Desid.* **vivasiṣa-.** —] *Caus.* **vāsáyati** *etc.* V.+, **-te** RV. (**vāsyate** E.)

Deriv.: **-vas** C. **vasa-** RV. **vásya** B.S. **-vāsa** V.+ **vāsin** B.+ **vásana** V.+ **vā́sana** AV.+ **vā́sas** V.+ **vasantá**? V.+ **vasitavya** E. **vasitṛ** C. **vastṛ** S. **vástra** V.+ **vásman** RV.

√ 3 vas, 'dwell'.

Pres. [1.] **vásati** *etc.* V.+, **-te** *etc.* B.+

Perf. **uvāsa ūṣus** *etc.* V.+; **-vāsāṁ cakre** U.

Aor. 1. **vásāna**? V.B.S. [**uṣyāt; avāsi.**] — 3. **avīvasat** MS. — 4. **avātsīt** *etc.* AV.+ (**avākṣam** AB **avāstam** U.)

Fut. 1. **vatsyati** *etc.* B.+, **-te** *etc.* E.+; **vasiṣyati** *etc.* E. [— 2. **vastā.**]

Verb. **uṣita** S.+, **uṣṭa** E., **vasita** C.; **vastum** E.+, **-tavāi** S., **vasitum** C.; **uṣitvā́** B.+, **uṣṭvā** E.+; **-úṣya** B.+; **-vāsam** C.

Sec. Conj.: *Pass.* **uṣyate** C. — [*Int.* **vāvas-.** —] *Desid.* **vivatsati** ÇB. — *Caus.* **vāsáyati** *etc.* V.+, **-te** *etc.* AV.+ (**vāsyáte** *etc.* B.+, **-yant** E.; **-vā́sas** TA.)

Deriv.: **vás** RV. **-vasa** E.+ **-uṣaka** C. **-uṣya** V.+ **vāsá** V.+ **-vāsaka** E.+ **vāsin** AV.+ **vāsya** E.+ **vásana** V.+ **-uṣaṇa** C. **vāsana** S.+ **-vāsanīya** E.+ **vāsas** U. **-vasu**? V. **vasatí** V.+ **vastu** E.+ **vastavyà** B.+ **uṣitavya** C. **vā́stu** V.+ **vástṛ** B. **-vasatha** V.B.S. **vásman** RV. **vāsayitavya** E. **vāsayitṛ** E.+

A few **vas**-forms, occurring in RV. in questionable connection, are referred in BR. to a root 4 **vas** 'aim'. The causative forms ascribed by BR. to a root 5 **vas** 'cut off' are also doubtless peculiar technical specializations from 3 **vas**.

√ vah, 'carry'.

Pres. [1.] **váhati -te** *etc.* V.+ — [2.] **vákṣi voḍham -ḍhā́m uhīta vákṣva voḍhvam ūḍhvam úhāna** V.B.
Perf. **uvāha ūhús** *etc.* V.+, **ūhé** *etc.* V. (**vavāha vavāhatus** E.+)
Aor. 1. **avāhi** C.; **uhyāt** S. — [3. **avīvahat.** —] 4. **ávākṣīt** *etc.* V.B.S. (**ávāṭ vāṭ** V.B.S., **vákṣat** *etc.* V.B.S., **vákṣati** *etc.* V.) [**avakṣi.**]
Fut. 1. **vakṣyáti** *etc.* AV.+, **-te** E.; **vahiṣyati** *etc.* E.+ — 2. **voḍhā́** B.
Verb. **ūḍhá** V.+, **voḍha**? E[1].; **vóḍhum** V.+, **-ḍhave** V.B.S., **-ḍhavāí** B.; **ūḍhvā́** B.; **-úhya** AV.+; **vā́he** RV.; **váhadhyāi** RV.
Sec. Conj.: *Pass.* **uhyáte** *etc.* V.+, **-yant** E.+ — *Int.* **vāvahīti** C., **vanīvāhyáte** *etc.* B.S. — [*Desid.* **vivakṣa-.** —] *Caus.* **vāhayati** *etc.* B.+, **-te** *etc.* E.+ (**vāhyate** *etc.* E.+)

Deriv.:

-vā̆h V.+	**vāhya** S.+	**voḍhavya** E.+	**váhīyas** V.B.
váha AV.+	**vahana** S.+	**-vāhitavya** E.	**váhni** V.+
vahín B.S.	**vā́hana** V.+	**voḍhṛ** V.+	**-vahman** RV.
vahyá V.S.	**vāhanīya** C.	**vāhitṛ** E.	**vákṣas**? V.
ogha U.+	**vahát** RV.	**-vahitṛ** U.	**vakṣáṇa**? V.
āughá B.	**vāghát**? RV.	**vahitra** C.	**vakṣī́**? RV.
vāhá V.+	**vā́has** V.B.S.	**váhiṣṭha** V.	**vā́vahi** RV.
vāhaka E.+	**ūḍhi** B.+	**vā́hiṣṭha** V.B.	**vīvadhá**? B.+
vāhín AV.+	**vahatú** V.B.		**-vāhayitṛ** C.

Compare roots 1, 2 **ūh.**

√ 1 vā, 'blow'

Pres. [2.] **vā́ti** *etc.* V.+ — [4.] **vā́yati** *etc.* V.+, **-te** *etc.* E.
Perf. **vavāu** *etc.* B.+
Aor. 6? **avāsīt** B.
Fut. 1. **vāsyati** *etc.* C.
Verb. **vāta** S., **vāna** C.; **vātum** C.
Sec. Conj.: *Caus.* **vāpáyati** *etc.* V.+

Deriv.:

-vā AV.B.	**vā́ta** V.+	**-vāpaka** C.	**-vāpayitṛ** C.
-vāna E.+	**vāyú** V.+	**-vāpana** C.	**-vāpayitavya** C.
	-vāyyà AV.		

The forms from pres.-stem **vāya** have mostly the sense 'be blown or exhausted', and are generally referred to a different root, 2 **vā.** The two, however, seem evidently only two sides of the same original root, nor are the forms capable of being clearly divided between them.

√ 2 vā, vi, u, 'weave'.

Pres. [4.] **váyati** *etc.* V.+, **-te** *etc.* B.+
Perf. **ūvus** RV. [**vavāu** *etc.*, **uvāya ūyus** *etc.*]
[*Aor.* 1. **ūyāt.** — 4. **avāsta, vāsīṣṭa.** — 6. **avāsīt.**]
Fut. 1. **vayiṣyáti** RV. [**-te; vāsyati.** — 2. **vātā.**]
Verb. **utá** V.+, **ūta** S.; **ótum** RV., **ótave** RV., **ótavāí** V., **vā́tave** AV.

Sec. Conj.: *Pass.* ūyate *etc.* B.S. [— *Int.* vāvā-. — *Desid.* vivāsa-. — *Caus.* vāyaya-.]

Deriv.: -vāya RV.C.	vāna S.+	ótu V.B.	veṇī? S.+
vāyaka C.	vayúna? V.+	-vātavya C.	vema E.
-vayana B.S.	ūti? C.	vayitṛ B.	véman B.+

√ 3 vā (*in* vivāsa-), *see* √ van.

√ vāñch, 'desire'.

Pres. [1.] vāñchati *etc.* V.+
[*Perf. etc.* vavāñcha; avāñchīt; vāñchiṣyati, vāñchitā.]
Verb. vāñchita E.+
Sec. Conj.: *Pass.* vāñchyate *etc.* C. — *Caus.* vāñchayati E.
Deriv. vāñchā C.

√ vāç, 'bellow'.

Pres. [4.] vā́çyate *etc.* AV.+, -ti E. — [1.] vā́çati *etc.* RV.E.+, -te *etc.* E.+
Perf. vavāçe *etc.* V.+ (vāvaçre -çāná avāvaçītam ávāvaçanta *etc.* RV.)
Aor. 3. avīvaçat *etc.* ávīvaçanta RV. [avavāçat.] — 5. avāçiṣṭhās B.
[*Fut.* vāçiṣyate, vāçitā.]
Verb. vāçita E.+; vāçitvā C.; -vāçya C.
Sec. Conj.: *Pass.* vāçyate C. — *Int.* vā́vaçat RV.; vāvāçyate E. — [*Desid.* vivāçiṣa-. —] *Caus.* vāçayati *etc.* V.S.

Deriv.: vaçā́? V.+	vāçaka C.	-vāçya S.	vāçrá V.+
vāçá V.S.	vāçin E.+	vāçana C.	

√ vāh, 'press'.

Pres. [1.] vāhate *etc.* C.
[*Perf. etc.* vavāhe; avāhiṣṭa; vāhiṣyate, vāhitā.]
Sec. Conj.: *Caus.* vāhayati C.

√ 1 vic, 'sift'.

Pres. [7.] vinákti *etc.* V.+ — [3.] vivekṣi RV[1].
Perf. viveca? AV. (vivikvā́ṅs RV.)
[*Aor.* avīvicat, avāikṣīt.]
Fut. 1. vekṣyati C. [— 2. vektā.]
Verb. vikta B.+; vektum E.; -vicya S.+; -vecam S.
Sec. Conj.: *Pass.* vicyáte *etc.* AV.+ — *Int.* vevekti S. — *Caus.* vecayati *etc.* C.

Deriv.: -veka U.+	-vecaka C.	-vikti B.+	-vektṛ C.
-vekin C.	-vecana E.+	-vektavya C.	vívici V.B.S.
-vekya C.			

√ 2 vic, *see* √ vyac.

√ vij, 'tremble'.

Pres. [6.] vijáte *etc.* V.+, -ti *etc.* E.+ — [1.] vejate B.
Perf. vivije *etc.* V.+
Aor. 1 (4?). vikthās V.B., vikta RV. — 3. vīvijas RV. [— 5. avijiṣṭa.]
Fut. 1. vijiṣyati E., vejiṣyati C. [— 2. vijitā.]
Verb. vikta RV., vigna E.+ [vijitum.]
Sec. Conj.: Int. vevijyáte RV., vévijāna RV. — [*Desid.* vivijiṣa-. —] *Caus.* vejayati *etc.* B.+, -te E.

Deriv.: víj RV. | -vejaka C. | -vejana C. | vevijá RV.
véga V.+ | -vejin C. | vigrá? RV.

√ 1 vid, 'know'.

Pres. [2.] vetti vidánti *etc.* V.+, vidmahe B.+ (avidus B., -dan C.; vidāṁ karotu *etc.* C.) — [1.] veda E., vedate U. — [6.] vidáti -te *etc.* AV.U.E.+; vindati -te *etc.* E.+
Perf. véda vidús *etc.* V.+, vidre RV.; viveda *etc.* C. — vidā́ṁ cakāra *etc.* B.U.S.
Aor. [1. avedi. — 3. avīvidat. —] 4. avāit? C. — 5. avedīt *etc.* B.+ — vidām akran B.
Fut. 1. vediṣyati -te *etc.* B.U. (avediṣyat U.); vetsyati -te *etc.* E.+ — 2. veditā́ ÇB., vettā E.
Verb. viditá AV.+; véditum B.+, -tos B., vettum E.; viditvā́ B.+
Sec. Conj.: Pass. vidyate C. — [*Int.* vevid-. —] *Desid.* vividiṣati *etc.* B.+, vivitsati *etc.* C. — *Caus.* vedáyate -ti *etc.* V.+ (vedyate *etc.* E.+; vivedayiṣa- *in d.*)

Deriv.: víd V.+ | vedana B.+ | veditavyà B.+ | vivitsā E.+
-vida B.+ | vedanīya E.+ | vidátha V.B. | vivitsu E.+
véda V.+ | -vedi B. | vidyā́ V.+ | vividiṣā C.
vedaka E.+ | vidú(s?) RV. | vidmán V. | vividiṣu C.
vedin B.+ | vitti C. | vidura E.+ | vedayitṛ C.
védya V.+ | vettṛ U.+ | vidván AV. | vivedayiṣu E.
vedyā́ RV.C. | véditṛ V.+ | vidvalá V.

See √ 2 vid.

√ 2 vid, 'find'.

Pres. [6.] vindáti -te *etc.* V.+ — [2.] vitté *etc.* V.B. (vidé 3*s.* V.B., vidré V.B., vidām 3*s.* AV.B., vidāná V.B., vídāna V.); vindate (3*p.*) B., vindyāt? C.
Perf. vivéda vividus *etc.* V.+ (vivéditha RV., vividat RV.), vividé *etc.* V.B.S.
Aor. 1. avedi védi RV. — 2. ávidat -data *etc.* V.B.S. (vidā́si *etc.* vidā́t *etc.* vidét -deta *etc.* V.B.S., videṣṭa AV.) — [3. avīvidat. —] 4. avitsi V.B.

Fut. 1. **vetsyati -te** *etc.* B.+ [**vediṣyati.** — 2. **vettā.**]
Verb. **vittá** V.+, **vinna** AV.+; **vettum** E., **véttave** AV., **-tavāi**? TB., **-tos** JB.; **vittvā́** AV.B.; **-vídya** B.+; **vidé** RV.
Sec. Conj.: Pass. **vidyáte** *etc.* V.+, **-ti** *etc.* E. — *Int.* **vévidat -dāna** *etc.* RV. — *Desid.* **vivitsati** *etc.* B.+ — *Caus.* **vedayati** *etc.* E.

Deriv.:			
-vid V.+	**vedya** B.+	**vitti** AV.+	**vidā́yya** RV.
-vídya V.	**védana** V.+	**-vettavya** C.	**-vinda** B.+
-véda V.+	**-vedanīya** C.	**-vettṛ** E.+	**-vindu** V.B.
-vedaka C.	**védas** V.+	**védiṣṭha** RV.	**-vindaka** C.
-vedin C.	**véduka** B.	**védīyas** RV.	**-vivitsu**? E.

Doubtless originally the same with the preceding root. In some of their meanings, the two are so close together as hardly to be separable; and there are instances, from the Veda down, of exchanges of form between them.

√ 1 vidh, 'worship'.

Pres. [6.] **vidháti** *etc.* V.B.U.C., **-te** *etc.* RV.
Deriv. **vedhás** V.+

√ 2 vidh, *see* √ vyadh.

√ vindh, 'lack'.

Pres. [6.] **vindháte** *etc.* RV.
Deriv.: **vidhú** V.+ **vidháva** V.+ **vidhura** E.+
A body of forms of not unquestionable connection.

√ vip, vep, 'tremble'.

Pres. [1.] **vépate** *etc.* V.+, **-ti** *etc.* E.+
Perf. **vivipre** RV., **vepus**? C. [**vivepe.**]
Aor. 1. **vipāná** RV. — 3. **avīvipat** *etc.* RV. — 5. **avepiṣṭa** *etc.* B.S.
[*Fut.* **vepiṣyate, vepitā.**]
Sec. Conj.: Caus. **vepáyati** *etc.* V.+; **vipáyanti** RV.

Deriv.:			
víp V.	**vépa** V.+	**vepaná** V.+	**vepáthu** AV.+
vipana-? RV.	**-vepin** C.	**vépas** RV.	**vépiṣṭha** RV.
vipas- V.+			**vípra** V.+

√ viç, 'enter'.

Pres. [6.] **viçáti -te** *etc.* V.+
Perf. **vivéça viviçe** *etc.* V.+ (**vivéçitha** RV., **viveçus** RV., **viveçatus** C., **-viçivā́ṅs** AV., **viviçyās** V., **áviveçīs** RV.)
Aor. 1. **áviçran** RV.; [**viçyāt;**] **aveçi** C. — 3. **avīviçat** C. — 4. **ávikṣmahi** *etc.* RV. — 5. **veçīt** RV. — 7. **avikṣat -ṣan** B.C. [**avikṣata.**]
Fut. 1. **vekṣyati** *etc.* B.+, **-te** *etc.* E. — 2. **veṣṭā** M.
Verb. **viṣṭá** V.+; **veṣṭum** E.+, **-ṭavāi** B.; **-víçya** AV.+; **víçam** RV.

Sec. Conj.: *Pass.* **viçyate** *etc.* C. — [*Int.* **veviç-.** —] *Desid.* **vivikṣati** *etc.* B.+ — *Caus.* **veçáyati** *etc.* V.+, **-te** *etc.* AV.+ (**veçyate** *etc.* S.+)

Deriv.: **víç** V.+ **-viça** B.+ **veçá** V.+ **veçī́** RV. **-veçaka** C. **veçin** S.+ **veçyà** V.+ **viçana** B.+ **véçana** V.+ **-veçanīya** C. **veçanta** V.B. **veçás** AV. **-viṣṭi** S. **veṣṭavya** B.+ **-veṣṭṛ** C. **véçman** V.+ **vivikṣu** B.+ **-veçayitavya** C.

√ viṣ, 'be active'.

Pres. [3.] **viveṣṭi** *etc.* RV. (**vivés víveṣas** *etc.* RV.) — [1.] **véṣati** *etc.* RV.B.

Perf. **viveṣa viviṣus** RV. (**aviveṣīs** RV.)

Aor. 1? **viḍḍhí** AV.B.S. — [2. **aviṣat.** —] 5. **veṣiṣas** RV. [— 7. **avikṣat.**]

Fut. 1. **vekṣyati -te** *etc.* B.+ [— 2. **veṣṭā.**]

Verb. **viṣṭá** V.+; **viṣṭvī́** RV.; **-víṣya** AV.B.; **-víṣe** RV.

Sec. Conj.: *Pass.* **viṣyate** B.+ — *Int.* **véveṣṭi** *etc.* V.B., **véviṣāṇa** RV., **veviṣyate** JUB. — *Desid.* **vivikṣa-** (*in d.*). — *Caus.* **veṣayati** *etc.* B.+

Deriv.: **-viṣ?** RV. **víṣa** V.+ **viṣá?** V.+ **veṣá** AV.+ **-veṣaka** B.+ **-veṣin** C. **-veṣya** AV.B.S. **véṣaṇa** V.+ **veṣáṇa** RV. **viṣaya?** B.+ **viṣṭí** V.+ **-veṣṭavya** C. **-veṣṭṛ** AV.+ **víṣṇu?** V.+ **-vivikṣu** B.

Divided by Grassmann into two roots.

√ viṣṭ, veṣṭ, 'wrap'.

Pres. [1.] **veṣṭate** *etc.* AV.+

[*Perf. etc.* **viveṣṭe; aviveṣṭat avaveṣṭat, aveṣṭiṣṭa; veṣṭiṣyate, veṣṭitā.**]

Verb. **viṣṭita** V.B.

Sec. Conj.: [*Int.* **veveṣṭ-.** — *Desid.* **viveṣṭiṣa-.** —] *Caus.* **veṣṭáyati** *etc.* AV.+, **-te** *etc.* B.+ (**veṣṭyate** *etc.* B.+)

Deriv.: **veṣṭa** S.+ **veṣṭaka** S.+ **veṣṭana** S.+ **-veṣṭanīya** C. **-veṣṭitṛ** U.

√ vī, 'enjoy' etc.

Pres. [2.] **véti vyánti** *etc.* V.B. (**vihí** RV., **viyantu** TS., **vema** VS.), **vyāná** RV.

Perf. **vivāya vivye** RV.

[*Aor. etc.* **avīvayat, avāiṣīt; veṣyati, vetā.**]

Verb. **vītá** V.B.

Sec. Conj.: *Pass.* **vīyáte** *etc.* AV.B. — *Int.* **veveti** RV., **vevīran** TS., **vevīyate** RV. [— *Desid.* **vivīṣa-.** — *Caus.* **vāyayati, vāpayati.**]

Deriv.: **vī** V.+ **-vīya** RV. **-vāya** AV. **vayā́** RV. **vayyà?** RV. **váyas** V.+ **vāyú?** V.B. **vayúna** V.+ **vītí** V.B. **vetra?** B.+ **vīrá?** V.+

A very perplexing root in its varieties of meaning; divided into two or three roots (on different lines) by BR. and Grassmann. It is treated by the grammarians as filling up the conjugation of √ **aj**.

√ **vīj, vyaj**, 'fan'.

Pres. [1.] **vījati** *etc.* E.+, **-te** E. — **vyajate**? C.
Perf. **vivyajus** E.
Sec. Conj.: *Caus.* **vījayati** *etc.* E.+ (**vījyate** E.+)
Deriv.: **vījana** C. **vyajana** E.+
Perhaps from √ **aj** + **vi**.

√ **vīḍ**, 'make strong'.

Sec. Conj.: *Caus.* **vīḍáyati -te** *etc.* V.B.S.
Deriv. **vīḍú** V.B.

√ 1 **vṛ**, 'cover'.

Pres. [5.] **vṛṇóti vṛṇuté** *etc.* V.+ (**vṛṇvaté** RV.); **ūrṇóti** (**ūrṇvánti ūrṇuvanti**) **ūrṇutė** (**ūrṇvīta ūrṇuvīta**) *etc.* V.+ (**ūrṇāuti** ÇB.S.) — [9.] **avṛṇīdhvam** AV. — [1.] **várati -te** *etc.* (*aor.* 1?) RV.C[1].
Perf. **vavāra vavrus vavré** *etc.* V.+ (**vavártha** RV. [**vavaritha, vavṛma** *etc.*], **vavrivā́ṅs vavavrúṣas** RV.) [**ūrṇunāva.**]
Aor. 1. **ávar avran** *etc.* (**vam**? **vartam** RV., **vṛdhi** RV.) [**vriyāt**], **avṛta** V. (**vrāṇá** RV.); **ávāri** RV. — 3. **avīvarat** AV., **avāvarīt**? RV. — 4. **varṣathas** RV. — 5. **avārīt** *etc.* B. [**avarīṣṭa; āurṇāvīt.**]
[*Fut.* **varīṣyati, varītā.**]
Verb. **vṛtá** V.+; **vartum** E., **vártave** RV., **varitum** C., **varītum** C.; **vṛtvā́** V.B., **-tvī́** RV., **-tvā́ya** B.; **-vṛ́tya** AV.+, **ūrṇutya** C.
Sec. Conj.: *Pass.* **vriyate** E. — *Int.* **avarīvar** RV., **várīvṛta** TA. [**varvṛ-, vovur-, vevri-.** — *Desid.* **vivarīṣa-.**] — *Caus.* **vāráyati -te** *etc.* V.+ (**vāryate** *etc.* E.+; **vivārayiṣate** B.)

Deriv.:	**vā́r**? RV.	**urú** V.+	**várṇa** V.+	**vāra** V.+
	vára V.+	**vṛ́t** V.B.	**váruṇa** V.+	**vāraka** E.+
	-varaka E.+	**vṛ́ti** V.+	**ū́rṇā** V.+	**-vārin** C.
	valá? V.+	**-vártu** RV.	**várman** V.+	**vārya** V.+
	úrā? RV.	**vartṛ́** RV.	**varī́man** V.B.S.	**vāraṇá** V.+
	vrá? V.	**-varītṛ** C.	**ūrmí**? V.+	**-vāraṇīya** E.+
	várana V.+	**varūtṛ́** V.B.	**várīyas** V.B.	**-ūrṇavana** C[1].
	varaṇá AV.+	**vártra** V.B.S.	**várivas** V.+	**vavrá** V.
	varaṇīya C.	**vṛtrá** V.+	**váriṣṭha** V.+	**vavrí** V.
	úraṇa V.+	**varatrā́** V.+	**úlba**? V.+	**-vārayiṣṇu** E.
	váras RV.	**várūtha** V.+	**ūrvá** V.B.	**vivārayiṣu** E.
	úras V.+			**vārayitavya** E.

See the following root. The present-stem **ūrṇu** is by the grammarians artificially provided with a complete set of forms, as if a root or conjugation-stem. As to **varṣman** etc., see under √ **vṛṣ**.

√ 2 vṛ, 'choose'.

Pres. [9.] vṛṇīté *etc.* v.+, vṛṇāti *etc.* E.+ — [5.] vṛṇoti vṛṇute *etc.* U.B.+
Perf. vavre *etc.* v.+ (vavṛṣé vavṛmáhe RV.)
Aor. 1. avri avṛta *etc.* v.+ (vurīta V.B., urāṇá RV.), váras *etc.* varanta RV. — 4. avṛṣi -ṣata *etc.* AV.B.U. (avṛḍhvam B.) [— 5. avarĭṣṭa.]
Fut. 1. variṣyate B. [varīṣyate. — 2. varĭtā.]
Verb. vṛtá v.+; varītum C. [varitum; varītvā,] varitvā S., vṛtvā S.
Sec. Conj.: Pass. vriyate S.C. — [*Int.* vevṛ-, varvṛ-, vovur-. — *Desid.* vivarĭṣa-, vovūrṣa-. —] *Caus.* varayati -te *etc.* E.+ (varyáte B.); vārayati E.

Deriv.:	vára v.+	-váryà *n.* B.	váreṇya v.+	vā́rya v.+
	vará v.+	-vū́rya V.S.	varas- RV.	-vāraṇa E.+
	varaka S.	varaṇa S.+	vṛ́thā, -thak V.	váriṣṭha V.+
	varya E.+	varaṇīya U.C.	vā́ra V.+	varīyas U.+
				varayitavya B.

Doubtless ultimately the same with the preceding; and the forms a little mixed up.

√ vṛṅh, bṛṅh, 'roar'.

Pres. [1.] vṛṅhati *etc.* E.+
Perf. vavṛṅhire C.
Verb. vṛṅhita E.+

√ vṛj, 'twist'.

Pres. [7.] vṛṇákti vṛṅkté *etc.* (vṛktām? M[1].)
Perf. vavṛjus *etc.* RV. (vavṛjyús vavṛktam RV., -varjúṣī AV.), vāvṛje RV.
Aor. 1. várk *etc.* RV. (varktam avṛjan varjati vṛjyām *etc.* RV., avṛk AV.), ávṛkta RV. (várjate RV.) — [3. avavarjat. —] 4. avārkṣīs B., avṛkṣmahi *etc.* V.B. — 7. avṛkṣat *etc.* V.B.
Fut. 1. varkṣyati -te B. [varjiṣyati. — 2. varjitā.]
Verb. vṛktá v.+; vṛktví RV.; -vṛ́jya B.S.; -vṛ́je vṛñjáse vṛjádhyāi RV.; -várgam V.S.
Sec. Conj.: Pass. vṛjyáte *etc.* V.B.S. — *Int.* várīvṛjat RV. [varvṛj-.] — *Desid.* vívṛkṣate B. — *Caus.* varjayati *etc.* AV.+, -te *etc.* E.+ (varjyate *etc.* E.+; varīvarjáyant AV.)

Deriv.:	-vṛj V.	varjaka E.	vṛjána V.	vṛñjana S.+
	ū́rj *etc.*? V.+	varjin E.+	vṛ́jana RV.	vṛjiná V.+
	varga V.+	varjya E.+	vṛjaní V.	-vṛkti V.B.
	-vargyà AV.+	vrajá V.+	varjana B.+	varjayitavya C.
	-varja S.+	vrājá V.	varjanīya B.+	varjayitṛ E.+
		-vṛ́jya V.B.S.		

√ vṛt, 'turn'.

Pres. [1.] **vártate** *etc.* V.+, **-ti** *etc.* U.+ — [3.] **vavartti vavṛtyām** *etc.* **-tīya** *etc.* **-tsva** *etc.* **ávavṛtran -ranta vavártat -tati vavṛtat** V.B. — [2.] **vartti** RV[1].

Perf. **vavarta vavṛtus** *etc.* V.+ (**vāvárta -vṛtús** V.), **vavṛte** *etc.* U.+ (**vāvṛté** V.)

Aor. 1. **avart** *etc.* (**vártat vartta**) RV., **avṛtran** V.B. — 2. **avṛtat** *etc.* AV.B.C. — 3. **avīvṛtat** *etc.* V. [**avavartat.**] — 4. **avṛtsan** C[1]., **avṛtsata** V.B.S. — 5. **vartithās** M.

Fut. 1. **vartsyáti** *etc.* AV.+ (**avartsyat** B.), **-te** *etc.* E.+; **vartiṣyati -te** *etc.* E.+ — 2. **vartitā** B.

Verb. **vṛttá** V.+; **vartitum** E.+; **-vṛ́tya** V.+; **-vṛ́te** RV., **-vṛ́tas** B.; **-vártam** B.+

Sec. Conj.: *Int.* **várvartti** *etc.* **várvṛtāna** V.; **varīvartti** *etc.* V.B. (**avarīvur** RV.), **varīvṛtyate** B. — *Desid.* **vívṛtsati** *etc.* V., **-te** B. [**vivartiṣa-.**] — *Caus.* **vartayati -te** *etc.* V.+ (**vartayádhyāi** RV.; **vartyate** *etc.* B.+)

Deriv.:

vṛ́t V.+	**vratá** V.+	**varti** E.+	**vratáti** V.+
vṛtā́ RV.	**vráta** AV.	**vartís** RV.	**vártman** V.+
-varta V.+	**vártana** V.+	**vṛtti** B.+	**varīvṛtá** AV.
vartaka V.+	**vartanīya** E.+	**várttu** V.+	**-vivṛtsu** C.
vartin V.+	**vartaní** V.B.U.	**-varttavya** E.	**-vartayitavya** E.+
-vartya E.+	**vártas** VS.	**vartitavya** E.+	**-vartayitṛ** C.
		-vartitṛ V.+	

Contracted in one or two forms with **anu** to **anvart**: see √ **ṛt**.

√ vṛdh, 'grow'.

Pres. [1.] **várdhati -te** *etc.* V.+

Perf. **vavárdha vavṛdhe** *etc.* V.+ (**vāvṛdhús** *etc.* **vāvṛdhé** *etc.* V.; **vāvṛdhāti -dhīthā́s -dhásva** *etc.* RV., **-dhéte** AV., **vā̆vṛdhánt** V.)

Aor. 2. **avṛdhat** *etc.* V.B.S. (**vṛdhātas vṛdhātu** B., **vṛdhánt** V., **vṛdhāná** RV.) — 3. **avīvṛdhat** *etc.* V.+, **-dhata** *etc.* V.B.S. — 5. **avardhiṣṭa** *etc.* E.+ (**vardhiṣīmáhi** B.S.)

Fut. 1. **vartsyati** C. [**vardhiṣyate.** — 2. **vardhitā.**]

Verb. **vṛddhá** V.+; **vardhitum** C.; [**vardhitvā, vṛddhvā;**] **vṛdhé** V., **vṛdhāse** RV., **vāvṛdhádhyāi** RV.

Sec. Conj.: [*Int.* **varīvṛdh-.** — *Desid.* **vivṛtsa-, vivardhiṣa-.** —] *Caus.* **vardháyati -te** *etc.* V.+ (**vivardhayiṣa** *in d.*); **vardhāpayati** C.

Deriv.:

vṛ́dh V.+	**várdhana** V.+	**vardhitṛ́** RV.	**vardhiṣṇu** C.
vṛdhá V.+	**vardhanīya** E.+	**vardhman** C.	**vāvṛdhénya** RV.
várdha V.+	**vṛdhás** RV.	**várddhra**? AV.B.	**vardhayitṛ** C.
-vardhaka C.	**vṛdhīká** RV.	**ūrdhvá** V.+	**vivardhayiṣu** E.+
vardhin E.+	**vṛ́ddhi** V.+	**vṛdhasāná** RV.	**vardhāpana** C.

Compare √ **ṛdh.** The asserted √ 2 **vṛdh** 'cut' (used only of the navel-string) rests on a too narrow foundation to be admitted: it is probably a specialized application of this root.

√ vṛṣ, 'rain'.

Pres. [1.] **várṣati** *etc.* V.+, **-te** *etc.* E.+ — [6.] **vṛṣate** *etc.* RV.S., **vṛṣant-** RV.
Perf. **vavarṣa vavṛṣus** *etc.* E.+ (**vavarṣus** E., **vavarṣvāṅs** MS.), **vavṛṣe** *etc.* E. (**vāvṛṣāṇá -ṣasva** RV.)
Aor. 2. **avṛṣāt**? TS. — 3. **avīvṛṣat** *etc.* E. [**avavarṣat.**] — 5. **ávarṣīt** *etc.* V.B.
Fut. 1. **varṣiṣyati** *etc.* B.U., **-te** E. — 2. **vraṣṭā́** MS.
Verb. **vṛṣṭá** V.+; **varṣitum** C., **-varṣṭos** B.; [**varṣitvā,**] **vṛṣṭvā** B., **-ṭvī́** RV.; **-vṛṣya** C.
Sec. Conj.: [*Int.* **varīvṛṣ-.** —] *Desid.* **vivarṣiṣa-** (*in d.*). — *Caus.* **varṣáyati** *etc.* V.+

Deriv.: **-vṛṣ** V.+	**varṣya** V.B.S.	**várṣṭṛ** B.	**vṛ́ṣan** V.+
vṛṣa- V.B.S.	**varṣaṇa** S.+	**varṣitṛ** C.	**vṛṣṇi** V.+
varṣá V.+	**várṣuka** B.	**vivarṣiṣu** E.	**vṛṣabhá** V.+
varṣin S.+	**vṛṣṭí** V.+		

The connection of **vṛ́ṣan** etc. with this root is questionable; and yet more that of **varṣman** V.+, **varṣimán** VS., **várṣīyas** V.+, **várṣiṣṭha** V.+, all of which may come from an aoristically extended form of √ 1 **vṛ** (like **párṣiṣṭha** etc. from √ 2 **pṛ**).

√ vṛh, bṛh, 'tear'.

Pres. [6.] **vṛháti bṛháti** *etc.* V.B.U.S.
Perf. **vavárha babarha vavṛhus** V.+
Aor. 1. **varhi** RV. — [3. **avīvṛhat, avavarhat.** —] 5. **barhīs -īt** RV. — 7. **avṛkṣat** *etc.* B.
[*Fut.* **varkṣyati, varhiṣyati; varḍhā, varhitā.**]
Verb. **vṛḍhá bṛḍha** B.S.; [**vṛḍhvā, varhitvā;**] **-vṛ́hya** B.U.S.; **-vṛhas** K.; **-várham -barham** B.
Sec. Conj.: *Pass.* **vṛhyate** *etc.* B. — [*Int.* **varīvṛh-.** — *Desid.* **vivṛkṣa-, vivarhiṣa-.** —] *Caus.* **barháyati** *etc.* RV. (**varhita** C.)

Deriv.: **-vṛha** S.+	**barhin, va-** E.	**bárhaṇa, vá-** AV.+	**barhís**? V.+
barha, va- AV.+			

Compare √ **bṛh.** The confusion of **b** and **v** goes back to the oldest time.

√ ven, 'long'.

Pres. [1.] **vénati** *etc.* V.B.
[*Perf. etc.* **vivena -ne; avivenat, avenīt -niṣṭa; veniṣyati -te, venitā; veven-, viveniṣa-, venaya-.**]
Deriv.: **vená** V.B. **venyá** RV.

√ vell, 'stagger'.

Pres. [1.] vellati *etc.* C.
Verb. vellita B.+
Deriv. vellana C.

√ veṣṭ, *see* √ viṣṭ.

√ vyac, vic, 'extend'.

Pres. [3.] viviktás vivyácat avivyak aviviktām avivyacus *etc.* vivyacanta RV. [— 6. vicati.]
Perf. vivyāca V.B., vivyáktha RV.; viveca? AV. [vivicus.]
[*Aor. etc.* vicyāt avyāci, avivyacat, avyăcīt; vyaciṣyati, vyacitā vicitā; vicita, vicitvā; vevic- vāvyac-, vivyaciṣa-, vyācaya-.]
Deriv.: vyácas V.B.S. vyáciṣṭha V.B. vícì? V.

Has a very suspicious likeness to √ añc, ac + vi.

√ vyaj, *see* √ vīj.

√ vyath, 'waver'.

Pres. [1.] vyáthate *etc.* V.+, -ti *etc.* E.+
Perf. vivyathe E.+, -thus E.
Aor. [1. avyăthi. —] 3. vivyathas B. — 5. vyathiṣi *etc.* AV.+, vyathiṣat B.
[*Fut.* vyathiṣyate, vyathitā.]
Verb. vyathitá AV.+; vyathiṣyāí B.S.
Sec. Conj.: [*Int.* vāvyath-. — *Desid.* vivyathiṣa-. —] *Caus.* vyatháyati *etc.* V.+ (vyathayīs AV.; vyathyate C.)
Deriv.: vyathā B.+ vyathana E.+ vyáthis RV. vyathayitṛ C. vyathaka C. vyáthi V. -vyātha B. -vyathya V.B. vyathí? AV. vithurá V.B.S.

√ vyadh, vidh, 'pierce'.

Pres. [4.] vídhyati *etc.* V.+, -te E.
Perf. vivyādha B.+, vivyadhus E., vividhus U., vividhváṅs RV.; vivyadhe E.
Aor. [1. vidhyāt. —] 3. avīvidhat E. [avivyadhat.] — 4. vyātsīs B.
Fut. 1. vetsyati -te E. [vyatsyati.] — 2. veddhā E. [vyaddhā.]
Verb. viddhá V.+; veddhum E.; viddhvā E.; -vidhya E.+; -vídhe RV.
Sec. Conj.: *Pass.* vidhyate E. — [*Int.* vāvyadh-, vevidh-. —] *Desid.* vivyatsati B. — *Caus.* vyādhayati B.; vyadhayati C.; vedhayati *etc.* E.

Deriv.:	-vidh V. +	vedhin E. +	vyādha AV. +	veddhavya U. +
	-vidhya E.	vedhya C.	vyādhin AV.B.	veddhṛ E. +
	vedha E. +	vyadha C.	-vyādhyà AV.	-vedhima C.
	vedhaka E. +	vyadhya C.	vedhana E. +	vyadhvará? AV.
			vyadhana AV.C.	

√ vyay, 'expend'.

Pres. [1.] vyayati -te *etc.* C.
[*Perf. etc.* vavyāya vavyaye *etc. etc.*]
Verb. vyayita C.
Is only a conjugation of √ i + vi, or denominative of vyaya.

√ vyā, vī, 'envelop'.

Pres. [4?] vyáyati -te *etc.* V. +
Perf. vivyathus RV., vivyé *etc.* RV. [vivyāya vivyayitha *etc.*]; -vyayāṁ cakāra ÇB.
Aor. [1. vīyāt. —] 2. ávyat *etc.* RV., avyata *etc.* V. [— 4. avyāsta, vyāsīṣṭa. — 6. avyāsīt.]
Fut. 1. [vyāsyati -te;] vyayiṣye S. [— 2. vyātā.]
Verb. vītá V. +; -vīya B.S.C. [-vyāya.]
Sec. Conj.: *Pass.* vīyáte B. [— *Int.* vāvyā-, vevī-. — *Desid.* vivyāsa-. — *Caus.* vyāyaya-.]
Deriv.: -vī V. + -vyāya B.S. -vyāna C. -vyayana B.S.

√ vraj, 'proceed'.

Pres. [1.] vrájati *etc.* V. +, -te C.
Perf. vavrāja *etc.* V. +
Aor. 5. avrājīt *etc.* B.U.
Fut. 1. vrajiṣyati *etc.* B. + [— 2. vrajitā.]
Verb. vrajita B. +; vrajitum E.; vrajitvā S. +; -vrájya B. +; -vrājam S.
Sec. Conj.: *Pass.* vrajyate C. — [*Int.* vāvraj-. —] *Desid.* vivrajiṣa- (*in d.*). — *Caus.* vrājayati *etc.* B. + (vrājyate E.)

Deriv.:	-vrāj E. +	vrajyā B. +	-vrājaka E. +	vrájana V. +
	-vrajya E. +	-vrāja V. +	-vrājin B. +	-vrājana E.
				-vivrajiṣu C.

√ vrad, vrand, 'weaken'.

Pres. [1.] avradanta RV[1].
Deriv. vrandín RV.

√ vran, 'sound' (?).

Pres. [1.] vraṇati C.
Deriv. vraṇa E. +
No real root; the single occurrence artificial.

√ vraçc, 'cut up'.

Pres. [6.] **vṛçcáti** *etc.* V.B.S.C. — [1.] **vraçcati**? C.
Perf. [**vavraçca vavraçcus**] **vavṛktam**? RV.
Aor. [3. **avivraçcat.** —] 4. [**avrākṣīt**] **vṛkṣi** B.S. [— 5. **avraçcīt.**]
Fut. 1. **vrakṣyánt** ÇB.? [**vraçciṣyati.** — 2. **vraçcitā, vraṣṭā.**]
Verb. **vṛkṇá** V.+; [**vraçcitvā,**] **vṛṣṭvā́** AV., **vṛktvī** RV.; **-vṛçcya** S.C.; **-vráçcam** B.S.
Sec. Conj.: *Pass.* **vṛçcyáte** *etc.* V.B. (**vṛçcáte** AV.) [— *Int.* **varīvṛçc-.** — *Desid.* **vivraçciṣa-, vivrakṣa-.** — *Caus.* **vraçcaya-.**]
Deriv.: **vṛ́ka**? V.+ **-vráçca** B. **-vraskya** S. **vráçcana** V.+ **vṛ́çcika** V.+ **-vraska** V.B.S. **vṛkṣá**? V.+

√ vrādh, 'stir up'.

Pres. [1.] **vrādhanta vrā́dhant** RV.

√ vrīḍ, 'be abashed'.

Pres. [1.] **vrīḍate** *etc.* E.+ — [4. **vrīḍyati.**]
[*Perf.* *etc.* **vivrīḍa; avrīḍīt; vrīḍiṣyati, vrīḍitā.**]
Verb. **vrīḍita** E.+
Sec. Conj.: *Caus.* **vrīḍayati** C.
Deriv.: **vrīḍā́** E.+ **vrīḍana** C.

√ vruḍ, 'sink'.

[*Pres.* *etc.* **vruḍati** *etc. etc.*]
Verb. **vruḍita** C.

The occurrence or two are doubtless artificial.

√ vlag, vlañg, 'pursue' (?).

Verb. **-vlágya** RV[2].
Deriv. **-vlañga** RV.

Only with **abhi.** Perhaps related with √ **valg.**

√ vlī, blī, 'crush'.

Pres. [9.] **vlīnāti** *etc.* B.; **vlināti** *etc.* ÇB.
[*Perf.* **vivlāya.**]
Aor. 4. **vleṣīs** S.
Fut. 1. **vleṣyati** B. [— 2. **vletā.**]
Verb. **vlīna** B., **blīna** AV.; **-vlī́ya** B.
Sec. Conj.: *Pass.* **vlīyate** *etc.* B.U. (**blīya-** K., **vliyeran** AB.) — *Int.* **avevlīyanta** B. [— *Desid.* **vivlīṣa-.** — *Caus.* **vlepayati, avivlipat.**]
Deriv.: **-vlaya** B.S. **vlayana** B. **vráyas**? RV.

√ çaṅs, 'praise'.

Pres. [1.] **çáṅsati -te** *etc.* V.+ (**çaṅsīyāt** C¹.)
Perf. **çaçaṅsa -se** *etc.* B.+ (**çaṅsus -sire** E.)
Aor. 1. **çasta** (2*p.*) RV., **çastāt** AB.; [**çasyāt**;] **çaṅsi** RV. — [3. **açaçaṅsat.** —] 5. **açaṅsīt** *etc.* V.+ (**çaṅsiṣat** *etc.* V.B.)
Fut. 1. **çaṅsiṣyati** B.S. [— 2. **çaṅsitā.**]
Verb. **çastá** V.+, **çaṅsita** E.+; **çaṅsitum** E.; **çastvā́** B.; **-çasya** S.+, **-çaṅsya** E.; **-çáse** RV.; **-çaṅsam** B.S.
Sec. Conj.: *Pass.* **çasyáte** *etc.* V.+ — [*Int.* **çāças-, çāçaṅs-.** — *Desid.* **çiçaṅsiṣa-.** —] *Caus.* **çaṅsáyati** *etc.* V.+, **-te** C.

Deriv.: **-ças** V.B.	**çáṅsa** V.+	**çaṅsanīya** C.	**-çastavya** E.
-çās V.	**çaṅsā** B.+	**-çaṅsu** S.	**çaṅsitṛ** E.+
-çasa B.	**-çaṅsaka** E.	**-çaṅsuka** B.	**çáṅstṛ** V.B.
çásā RV.	**çaṅsin** V.+	**çastí** V.+	**çastrá** B.+
çásya V.+	**çáṅsya** V.+	**-çastenya** B.	**çaṅsatha** S.
	çaṅsana E.+	**çaṅstavya** B.E.	**çásman** RV.

Compare the related √ 1 **çās.**

√ çak, 'be able'.

Pres. [5.] **çaknoti -nuvánti** *etc.* V.+
Perf. **çaçā́ka çekús** *etc.* V.+
Aor. 1. **çagdhí çaktam çákat** *etc.* **çakyām** V. — 2. **áçakat** *etc.* V.+ (**çakéyam** *etc.* V.B.S., **çakemahi** U.) [— 3. **açīçakat.**]
Fut. 1. **çakṣyati -te** *etc.* B.+ [— 2. **çaktā.**]
Verb. **çakta** E.+, **çakita** E.+; **-çaktave** RV.
Sec. Conj.: *Pass.* **çakyate** *etc.* E.+, **-ti** *etc.* E. — [*Int.* **çāçak-.** —] *Desid.* **çíkṣati -te** *etc.* V.+ (**çikṣāṇa** E.; **çiçikṣa** C.; **çikṣyate** *etc.* C.; **çikṣayati -te** *etc.* E.+) [— *Caus.* **çākayati.**]

Deriv.: **-çáka** RV.	**çákti** V.+	**çikvá** AV.	**çikṣaka** E.
çakya U.S.+	**çaktí** RV.	**çákvan** V.B.S.	**-çikṣin** C.
çā́ka V.	**çákman** RV.	**çíkvan** V.B.	**çikṣaṇa** C.
çākā́ RV.	**çā́kmaṅ** RV.	**çíkvas** RV.	**çikṣaṇīya** C.
çā́kī? RV.	**-çíkman** MS.	**çáciṣṭha** V.B.S.	**çikṣenya** S.
çácī V.+	**çagmá** V.B.S.	**çikṣā** V.+	**çikṣú** RV.
çāci? RV.	**çakrá** V.+	**çīkṣā** B.+	**çikṣuka** GB.

The desiderative **çikṣ** has won a so independent use and value that it might well enough have been treated (like **bhakṣ** *etc.*) as a separate root. BR. divide **çak** (and **çikṣ**) into two roots, the second meaning 'help', but favor their ultimate identity.

There are other groups of words, not connectable with this or any other verbal root: thus, **çakuná, çakúni, çakúnta, çakúnti** V.+; **çáka, çakán, çákṛt** V.+; **çañkú** V.+, **çakti** ('spear') E.+

√ çañk, 'doubt'.

Pres. [1.] çáñkate *etc.* B.+, -ti *etc.* E.
[*Perf.* çaçañke.]
Aor. 5. çañkīs çañkiṣṭhās E.+ (çañkithās E.)
[*Fut.* çañkiṣyate, çañkitā.]
Verb. çañkita E.+; çañkitum E.+; -çañkya C.
Sec. Conj.: Pass. çañkyate *etc.* C. — *Caus.* çañkayati C.
Deriv.: çañkā́ B.+ -çañkya S.+ çañkana E.? çañkitavya E.+
çañkin E.+ çañkanīya E.+

√ çat, 'cut in pieces'.

Sec. Conj.: Caus. çātáyati *etc.* AV.+, -te B.
Deriv.: çāta C. çātin C. çātana E.+ çātayitṛ C.

Called by the grammarians the causative of √ 2 çad.

√ 1 çad, 'prevail'

Perf. çāçadús RV.; çāçadmahe *etc.* (çā́çadāna) V.
Deriv. çátru? V.+

√ 2 çad, 'fall'.

Perf. çaçāda çedus B.
[*Aor.* 2. açadat.]
Fut. 1. çatsyati AV. [— 2. çattā.]
Verb. çanna S.
[*Sec. Conj.: Int.* çāçad-. — *Desid.* çiçatsa-. — *Caus.* çādaya-.]
Deriv.: çada AV.B.S. çā́da V.B. çādana C.

Compare √ çat, assigned by the grammarians to this root as another causative, and √ 1 çī, regarded by them as its present-system.

√ çap, 'curse'.

Pres. [1.] çápati *etc.* V.+, -te *etc.* B.+ [— 4. çapyati -te.]
Perf. çaçā́pa çepus AV.+, çepé *etc.* V.+
Aor. [3. açīçapat. —] 4. çāpta (2*p.*) B.S. [açapta.]
Fut. 1. çapiṣye E. [çapsyati -te. — 2. çaptā.]
Verb. çapta B.+, çapita E.; çapitum E., çaptum E.; [çaptvā,] çapitvā B.
Sec. Conj.: Pass. çapyate C. — [*Int.* çāçap-, çañçap-. — *Desid.* çiçapsa-. —]
Caus. çāpayati *etc.* AV.+
Deriv.: çāpa E.+ çápana AV. çaptṝ́ AV. çapátha V.+
çapaná ÇB.

√ 1 çam, çim, 'labor'.

Pres. [1.] çámant SV. — [2.] çamīṣva çamiṣva çamīdhvam B.S. — [9.] çamnīṣe -īṣva -īthās B.; çcámnan RV.? — [4.] çamyati *etc.* B., çimyati *etc.* B.
Perf. çaçamé -māná V.B. (çaçámate RV.)
Aor. 5. áçamiṣṭhās RV.
Verb. çamitá B.
Deriv.: çáma RV. çíma B. çamitṛ́ V.B. çamiṣṭha S.
çámī̆ V.B. çímī B.

Compare the two following roots.

√ 2 çam, 'be quiet'.

Pres. [4.] çā́myati *etc.* B.+, -te *etc.* B.+ — [1.] çamet E.
Perf. çaçāma çemus B.+
Aor. [1. çamyāt; açā̆mi. —] 2. açamat B. — 3. açīçamat *etc.* AV.+ [— 5. açamīt.]
[*Fut.* çamiṣyati; çamitā.]
Verb. çāṁtá AV.+ [çamitvā, çāṁtvā.]
Sec. Conj.: [*Int.* çaṅçam-. — *Desid.* çiçamiṣa-. —] *Caus.* çamáyati AV.+, -te *etc.* B.+; çāmayati *etc.* E.+ (çāmyate E.+)
Deriv.: çám? V.+ -çāmaka C. çaṁti- AV. çamatha C.
çama B.+ çāmya E.+ çā́ṁti AV.+ çamayitavya S.
çamin C. çámana AV.+ çamitṛ E.+ çamayitṛ S.+
çamanīya S.+

Probably ultimately the same with the preceding.

√ 3 çam, 'note'.

Perf. çemuṣī? C.
Verb. -çāṁta S.; -çamya E.+
Sec. Conj.: *Pass.* -çamyate *etc.* E.+ — *Caus.* -çāmayati *etc.* E.+ (-çāmyate E.)
Deriv.: -çāmana S. -çamaya C. -çāmayitavya C.

Only with prefix **ni-**, except in the strange **çemuṣī**; hence obviously a specialization from the preceding root, meaning 'settle in one's mind', or the like.

√ çal, 'leap'.

Pres. [1.] -çalant C.
[*Perf. etc.* çele, açaliṣṭa, çaliṣyate çalitā.]
Verb. -çalita C.

Only with prefix **ud**, and probably from √ **çri, çṛ**.

√ çaç, 'leap'.

Pres. [1.] çaçati *etc.* C.
[*Perf. etc.* çaçāça çaçaçus, açaçīt, çaçiṣyati çaçitā.]

Verb. çaçita c.
Deriv. çaçá v.+

Doubtless a denominative formation from **çaçá**. Only two or three occurrences.

√ ças, çās, 'cut'.

Pres. [2.] çasta (2p.) RV.; çāsti B.S., çā́sati -atu (3p.) B., açāt (3s.) B. — [1.] çasatha S., çásanti B., açasat C.
Perf. çaçāsa [çaçasus] E.
Fut. 1. çasiṣyati B. [— 2. çasitā.]
Verb. çasta E.; -çasya E.; -çásas B.
Sec. Conj.: Pass. çasyáte *etc.* B.+ — *Desid.* çiçāsiṣant S.
Deriv.: -ças B. çásana v.+ çástṛ v.+ -çāstṛ B.S. çāsá AV.B.S. çasitṛ B.+ çastrá B.+ -çiçāsiṣu B.

√ çā, çi, 'sharpen'.

Pres. [3.] çiçāti çiçīmasi çíçīte *etc.* v.+ (çiçanti -ntu S.) — [6?] çyáti *etc.* V.B.S., çyāna B.S.
Perf. [çaçāu] -çaçāná AV.
Aor. 1. áçīta? RV. [açāt; çāyāt. — 6. açāsīt.]
[*Fut.* çāsyati, çātā.]
Verb. çitá v.+, çāta E.+; -çā́ya v.
[*Sec. Conj.: Pass.* çāya-. — *Int.* çāçā-. — *Desid.* çiçāsa-, çīçāṅsa-. — *Caus.* çāyaya-.]
Deriv.: -çāna B.S. çāṇa? C. -çiti V.B. çiçayá RV.

Divided by BR. into two separate roots, with identical forms.

√ 1 çās, çiṣ, 'order'.

Pres. [2.] çā́sti çā́sati *etc.* ([çiṣṭas *etc.*] çāstána RV., çiṣyāt *etc.* U.S.+; açāt B.+) v.+, çā́ste çāsīta çā́sāna *etc.* v.+ — [1.] çāsati *etc.* E.+, -te E.
Perf. çaçāsa çaçāsus *etc.* v.+ (çaçādhi çaçās RV.)
Aor. 2. açiṣat *etc.* V.B.U. (çiṣánt RV.), çiṣāmahi RV. (-he SV.AV.) [— 3. açaçāsat.]
Fut. 1. çāsiṣyati -te *etc.* B.+ [— 2. çāsitā.]
Verb. çiṣṭá v.+, çāsta S.+, çāsita E.+; çāstum S.+, çāsitum E.+; [çiṣṭvā,] çāsitvā C.; -çiṣya B.U., -çāsya E.+
Sec. Conj.: Pass. çāsyate *etc.* E.+; çiṣyate *etc.* C. — [*Int.* çāçās-, çeçiṣ-. — *Desid.* çiçāsiṣa-. — *Caus.* çāsaya-.]
Deriv.: çā́s RV. çā́sa RV. çā́sana v.+ -çiṣṭi V.B.S. -çis v.+ -çāsaka C. çāsanīya C. çāsitṛ E.+ çāsá v. çāsin C. çā́sus RV. çāstṛ́ v.+ çāsā́ RV. çā́sya v.+ çāsti C. çāstrá v.+ çiṣya B.+

Compare the apparently related root **çaṅs**.

√ 2 çās, 'cut', *see* √ças.

√ çikṣ, *see* √ çak.

√ çiñgh, 'snuff'.

The occurrences of ucchiñghana and upaçiṅhana in Suçr. are doubtless artificial.

√ çiñj, 'twang'.

Pres. [2.] çiṅkte çiñjate *etc.* V.+, çiñjant C.
[*Perf. etc.* çiçiñje; açiñjiṣṭa; çiñjiṣyate, çiñjitā.]
Verb. çiñjita E.+
Sec. Conj.: Caus. çiñjayati *etc.* B.S.
Deriv.: çiñjin C. çiñjā́ra? RV. (*n. pr.*)

Probably an imitative root.

√ çip, 'be smooth'(?).

Such a root may possibly be inferred from çípi V.+, çíprā RV., çipitá ÇB.

√ çim, *see* √ 1 çam.

√ çiṣ, 'leave'.

Pres. [7.] çinásti *etc.* B.+ — [6?] çiṅṣati *etc.* B.S. — [1.] çeṣant C[1].
Perf. çiçiṣe *etc.* B. [çiçeṣa.]
Aor. 1. çeṣi AV.B.S. [çiṣyāt.] — 2. açiṣat *etc.* V.B. (-çíṣat RV.), çíṣātāi AV. [— 3. açīçiṣat.]
Fut. 1. çekṣyati -te B. [— 2. çeṣṭā.]
Verb. çiṣṭá V.+; -çiṣṭvā S.; -çiṣya B.+; -çeṣam S.+
Sec. Conj.: Pass. çiṣyate *etc.* AV.+ — [*Int.* çeçiṣ-. — *Desid.* çiçikṣa-. —] *Caus.* çeṣayati *etc.* E.+, -te B. (çeṣyate C.)
Deriv.: -çiṣa C. çeṣa B.+ -çeṣin C. çéṣaṇa AV.+ -çeṣaka E.+ çeṣya C. çéṣas V.

√ 1 çī, 'fall'.

Pres. [4?] çī́yate *etc.* AV.B.U.S. (çīyánte? ÇB[1].)
Deriv. -çāyana C.

Reckoned by the grammarians as present-system to √ 2 çad; and this is curiously supported by JB., which has (ii. 81) upaçīyate tasmād upaçadam, and (ii. 82) avaçīyante tasmāc chadaḥ. So far as the meaning is concerned, it might well be a specialization of √ 2 çī.

√ 2 çī, 'lie'.

Pres. [2.] çéte çérate *etc.* V.+ (çáye 3s. V.B., çére 3p. AV.B., çayire C.; çayām 3s. AV., áçeran V.B.) —¶[1.] çáyate *etc.* V.+, -ti *etc.* E.+ (áçayat V.B.) — açāyatam -yata (3s.) RV.
Perf. çiçye -yire B.+; çaçayāná V.
Aor. [1. açāyi. —] 3. açīçayat E. — 4. çéṣan RV[1]. — 5. açayiṣṭa *etc.* V.+
Fut. 1. çayiṣyate -ti B.+; çeṣyate -ti E. — 2. çayitā U.C. (-tāse ÇB.)
Verb. çayita E.+; çayitum E.; çayitvā U.+; -çayya C.; çayádhyāi RV.
Sec. Conj.: *Pass.* [çayyate;] çīyant M[1]. —. [*Int.* çeçī-, çāçay-. —] *Desid.* çiçayiṣate C. — *Caus.* çāyayati *etc.* S.+, -te E.

Deriv.:	-çī V.B.	çayyā B.+	-çāyana C.	-çīma V.B.S.
	-ça? B.+	-çāyaka C.	çayú V.	-çéyya V.
	-çaya V.+	-çāyin S.+	çayitavya C.	çayālu C.
	çayā́ RV.	çáyana AV.+	çayátha RV.	-çīvan V.B.
	çayin C.	-çayanīya C.	-çītha B.+	çiçayiṣu C.

√ çuc, 'gleam'.

Pres. [1.] çócati *etc.* V.+, -te *etc.* V.+ — [4.] çúcyati B[1]. — [2.] çocimi E[1].
Perf. çuçóca *etc.* V.+ (çuçukvā́ṅs RV., çuçugdhí V.), çuçucāná RV. (-cīta RV.)
Aor. 1. [çucyāsam;] áçoci RV. — 2. açucat *etc.* V.+ (çucánt V., çucámāna RV.) — 3. çūçucat *etc.* AV.B. — 5. çocīs B.
Fut. 1. çociṣyati *etc.* E.+, -te E. [— 2. çocitā.]
Verb. çuktá? (*adj.*) B.+; çocitum E.+, çoktum M.; çocitvā E. [çucitvā]; çucádhyāi RV.
Sec. Conj.: *Int.* çóçucan *etc.* çóçucāna *etc.* V.B. — *Desid.* [çuçuciṣa-, çuçociṣa-;] çuçukṣa- (*in d.*) — *Caus.* çocáyati *etc.* V.+ (çocyate C.); çucáyant RV.

Deriv.:	çúc V.+	çóka V.+	çocí V.	-çúkvan RV.
	çucá RV.C.	çoká AV.	çucis- RV.C.	çóciṣṭha RV.
	çúka? V.+	-çócana AV.+	çocís V.+	çuçukvaná RV.
	-çoca AV.	çocanīya C.	çukti S.+	çuçukváni RV.
	-çocin C.	-çokas RV.	çocitavya E.+	-çuçukṣáṇi RV.
	çocya E.+	çúci V.+	çukrá V.+	-çocayiṣṇu AV.
			çuklá AV.+	

√ çuj, 'swell' (?).

Sec. Conj.: *Int.* çū́çujāna RV.

√ çudh, çundh, 'purify'.

Pres. [1.] çundhati -te *etc.* V.B.S. — [4.] çudhyati *etc.* B.+, -te *etc.* E.+ — [2.] çunddhi AGS.

[*Perf. etc.* çuçodha, çuçundha; açudhat, açūçudhat, açundhīt; çotsyati çundhiṣyati, çoddhā çundhitā.]

Verb. çuddhá V.+

Sec. Conj.: [*Int.* çoçudh-. —] *Desid.* çuçutsat S. — *Caus.* çodhayati *etc.* B.+ (çodhyate E.+); çundhayati V.B.

Deriv.: -çodha C.	çodhya C.	çodhana S.+	çundhyú V.B.
çodhaka E.+	çúndhana B.	çodhanīya C.	çodhayitavya C.
çodhin C.		çúddhi B.+	

√ çubh, çumbh, 'beautify'.

Pres. [1.] çóbhate *etc.* V.+ (çóbhe 3*s.* RV.), -ti *etc.* E.+; çúmbhase *etc.* V., çúmbhati *etc.* AV. — [6.] çumbháti *etc.* V.C., -ámāna RV.C.

Perf. çuçobha çuçubhe E.+ [çuçumbha.]

Aor. 1. açobhi C.; çúmbhāna çubhāná RV. — [2. açubhat. —] 3. áçūçubhan RV., -bhanta B. [— 5. açobhiṣṭa, açumbhīt.]

Fut. 1. çobhiṣyati E. [çumbhiṣyati. — 2. çobhitā, çumbhitā.]

Verb. çubhitá B., çumbhita AV.; çubhé RV., çobháse RV.

Sec. Conj.: *Int.* çoçubhyate E. — *Desid.* çuçobhiṣate C. [çuçubhiṣa-.] — *Caus.* çobhayati *etc.* AV.+; çubháyati -te *etc.* V.B.

Deriv.: çúbh V.B.	çumbha E.+	çumbhú B.	çúbhvan RV.
çubha E.+	-çumbhaka E.	çobhátha SV.	çóbhiṣṭha RV.
çobha C.	çóbhana V.+	çubhrá V.+	çobhayitṛ C.
çobhā B.+	çobhaná B.+	çubhrí RV.	
-çobhin E.+	çúmbhana AV.+		

This root is, with considerable plausibility, divided by BR. into two: √ 1 çubh 'glide along', and √ 2 çubh 'beautify'; the former only in V.B.

√ 1 çuṣ, 'dry'.

Pres. [4.] çúṣyati *etc.* V.+, -te *etc.* E.+

[*Perf. etc.* çuçoṣa; açuṣat, açūçuṣat; çokṣyati, çoṣṭā.]

Verb. -çúṣya B.

Sec. Conj.: [*Int.* çoçuṣ-. — *Desid.* çuçukṣa-. —] *Caus.* çoṣáyati *etc.* AV.+, -te E. (çoṣyate C.)

Deriv.: çuṣa? V.	çoṣin E.+	çoṣaṇa E.+	çúṣka V.+
çoṣa E.+	-çoṣya E.+	çoṣaṇīya C.	çúṣṇa? V.B.S.
çoṣaka C.		çóṣuka B.	çoṣayitṛ C.

√ 2 çuṣ, 'blow', *see* √ çvas.

√ çū, çvā, çvi, 'swell'.

Pres. [1?] çváyati *etc.* V.B.

Perf. [çuçāva, çiçvāya] çūçuvus *etc.* (çūçuvat çūçávāma çūçuyáma) çūçuve çúçuvāna RV.

Aor. [1. çūyāt. —] 2. áçvat B. [— 3. açiçviyat, açūçuvat, açiçvayat. — 5. açvayīt.]

[*Fut.* çvayiṣyati, çvayitā.]
Verb. çūná C.; çváyitum B.; çūṣáṇi RV.
[*Sec. Conj.:* çūyate; çoçu-, çeçvi-; çiçvayiṣa-; çvāyaya-.]

Deriv.:	-çū? RV.	çáviṣṭha V.B.	çivá V.+	çvayathu C.
	çáva B.+	çotha C.	çéva V.+	çvātrá V.B.
	çāva E.+	çuná V.B.S.	-çévas AV.	çvāntá RV.
	-çvan V.+	çū̆na, -nyá V.+	-çvāyin B.	çíçu V.+
	çávas V.+	çū̆ra V.+	çvayana C.	-çíçvan RV.
	çavasāná RV.	çávīra RV.	çvayátha B.	-çiçvi RV.

The perfect forms in RV. are ascribed by BR. (perhaps with better reason) to a separate root çū 'prevail'. The connection of a part of the derivatives given here with one another and with any assignable root is open to much question.

√ 1 çṝ, 'crush'.

Pres. [9.] çṛṇā́ti *etc.* V.B.C[1]., çṛṇāná RV[1]. — [6.] çṛṇa AV. — [4.] çīryate ÇB.
Perf. [çaçāra çaçaritha çaçarus çaçrus] çaçré AV.
Aor. 1. açāri V.B. [çīryāt. — 3. açīçarat.] — 5. açarīt *etc.* AV.B. (-rāit AV.)
Fut. 1. çariṣyate B. [çarĭ̄ṣyati. — 2. çarĭ̄tā.]
Verb. çīrṇá AV.+, -çīrta MS., çūrtá? RV[1].; çárītos RV., çaritos AA.; -çī̆rya B.
Sec. Conj.: *Pass.* çīryate *etc.* V.+, -ti *etc.* U.E.+ [— *Int.* çāçṛ-, çeçīrya-. —]
Desid. çiçariṣa- (*in d.*), [çiçarīṣa-, çiçīrṣa-. — *Caus.* çāraya-.]

Deriv.:	-çir C.	çīrya B.S.	çárīra V.+	çīrti B.
	-çar AB.	çū̆la V.+	çarā̆ru RV.	çalúna AV.
	-çara V.+	çaraṇa C.	çā̆ri RV.	çarabhá V.+
	çará V.+	çaráṇi V.	çáru V.+	çalala, -lī́ B.+
	çalá AV.B.	çū̆raṇa RV.	çarvá AV.+	çalā̆ka B.+
	çalyá V.+	-çarīka AV.	-çāruka B.C.	-çiçariṣu C.

Part of the derivatives are of very questionable belongings.

√ 2 çṝ, *see* √ çrā.

√ 3 çṝ, *see* √ çri.

√ çṛdh, 'be defiant'.

Pres. [1.] çárdhati *etc.* V., -te *etc.* B.C.
[*Perf. etc.* çaçṛdhe; açṛdhat, açīçṛdhat, açardhiṣṭa; çartsyati çardhiṣyate, çardhitā.]
Sec. Conj.: [*Int.* çarīçṛdh-. — *Desid.* çiçardhiṣa-, çiçṛtsa-. —] *Caus.* çardháyati *etc.* RV.C.

Deriv.:	çárdha RV.	çárdhya RV.	çardhana C.	-çardhayitṛ C.
	-çardhin V.	çṛdhyā̆ RV.	çárdhas V.B.	

Not worth dividing into two roots.

√ çcand, cand, 'shine'.

[*Pres. etc.* candati, cacanda *etc. etc.*]
Sec. Conj.: Int. cániçcadat RV[1].
Deriv.: candana? E.+ çcandrá V.+ candrá V.+
The fuller form çcandra survives after V. only in the n. pr. háriçcandra.

√ çcam.

The single doubtful form çcámnan RV. was entered above under √ 1 çam.

√ çcut, 'drip'.

Pres. [1.] çcótati *etc.* V.+
Perf. cuçcota B.S.
Aor. [2. açcutat. —] 3. acuçcutat S. [— 5. açcotīt.]
[*Fut.* çcotiṣyati; çcotitā.]
Verb. çcutita B.+
Sec. Conj.: [*Int.* coçcut-. — *Desid.* cuçcotiṣa-, cuçcutiṣa-. —] *Caus.* çcotayati *etc.* B.S. (-çcotayitavāí ÇB.)
Deriv.: -çcut V.+ -çcotana C.
The forms are often, especially later, written with çcyu, and sometimes with cyu.

√ çnath, 'pierce'.

Pres. [2.] çnathihi çnáthat RV. [— 1. çnathati.]
[*Perf.* çaçnātha.]
Aor. 3. açiçnat çiçnáthat *etc.* RV. — 5. çnathiṣṭam -ṭana RV.
[*Fut.* çnathiṣyati; çnathitā.]
Verb. çnathitá RV.; -çnáthas RV.
Sec. Conj.: çnatháyati -te *etc.* RV.
Deriv.: çnáthana RV. çnáthitṛ RV. çiçnátha RV.

√ çyā, çī, 'coagulate'.

Pres. [4?] çyā́yati B., -te C.
[*Perf. etc.* çaçye; açyāsta; çyāsyate, çyātā.]
Verb. çītá V.+, çīná VS., çyāna C. [çyāta.]
Sec. Conj.: Pass. çīyáte *etc.* B. — [*Int.* çāçyā-. — *Desid.* çiçyāsa-. —] *Caus.* [çyāpaya-;] çyāyayati GB.
Deriv.: çyā́ TS.C. -çyāya E.+ çíçira? AV.+

√ çrath, çlath, 'slacken'.

Pres. [9.] áçrathnan çrathnās RV., çrathnīté *etc.* V. — [6?] çṛnthati TS[1]. — [1.] [çrathati çranthate;] çlathati -te *etc.* C.
Perf. çaçrathe RV. [çaçrantha çaçranthus çrethus.]

Aor. 3. çiçráthat *etc.* V.B. (çiçrathantu RV.) [— 5. açranthīt -thiṣṭa.]
[*Fut.* çranthiṣyati, çranthitā.]
Verb. çṛthitá RV., çlathita C.; [çrathitvā, çranthitvā;] -çrathya C.
Sec. Conj.: *Caus.* çratháyati *etc.* V.B., -te RV.; çlathayati C. (çlathyate C.) [çrāthayati, çranthayati.]
Deriv.: çratha- V. çrathar- RV. çlatha E.+

√ çran, 'give'.

[*Pres. etc.* çraṇati *etc. etc.*]
Sec. Conj.: *Caus.* çrāṇayati *etc.* S.+ [açiçraṇat, açaçrāṇat; çraṇayati.]
Deriv.: -çrāṇana C. -çrāṇika C.
Only with prefix vi.

√ çram, 'be weary'.

Pres. [4.] çrā́myati *etc.* V.+ — [1.] çramati -te *etc.* E.+
Perf. çaçrāma çaçramus V.+ (çremus KB.), çaçramāṇá RV.
Aor. [1. açrā̆mi. —] 2. áçramat *etc.* V. — 5. çramiṣma RV.B.
Fut. [1. çramiṣyati. —] 2. çramitā M.
Verb. çrāṁtá V.+; -çrámya B.+
Sec. Conj.: *Pass.* çramyate E.+ — *Desid.* çiçramiṣa- (*in d.*). — *Caus.* çramayati *etc.* S.+; çrāmayati *etc.* E.+ (çrāmyate E.+)
Deriv.: çráma V.+ çramaṇá B.+ çrāṁti E.+ -çiçramiṣu C.
-çrāma E.+ -çramaṇa V.+ -çramiṣṭha RV.

√ çrambh, 'trust'.

Pres. [1.] çrambhate *etc.* E.+
[*Perf. etc.* çaçrambhe; açrabhat, açrambhiṣṭa; çrambhiṣyate, çrambhitā.]
Verb. çrabdha E.+; -çrabhya C.
Sec. Conj.: *Caus.* çrambhayati *etc.* S.+
Deriv.: -çṛmbhá RV. -çrambha E.+ -çrambhana C. -çrabdhi C.
-çrambhin C. -çrambhanīya C.

√ çrā, 2 çrī, 2 çṛ, 'boil'.

Pres. [4?] çrā́yati *etc.* V.B. — [9.] çrīṇā́ti *etc.* V.B. [— 2. çrāti.]
[*Perf. etc.* çaçrāu; çrāyāt çreyāt, açrāsīt; çrāsyati, çrātā.]
Verb. çrātá V.B.S.; çṛtá V.+ [çrāṇa.]
Sec. Conj.: [*Int.* çāçrā-. — *Desid.* çiçrāsa-. —] *Caus.* çrapáyati *etc.* AV.+, -te *etc.* E. (açiçrapat *etc.* B.; çrapyáte *etc.* B.+)
Deriv.: çīrá? RV. çáras? B. -çrápa B. çrápaṇa B.+
çrāpin S. çrapayitṛ́ B.

√ çri, 3 çṛ, 'resort'.

Pres. [1.] çráyati *etc.* AV.+, -te *etc.* V.+
Perf. çiçrā́ya çiçriyé *etc.* V.+
Aor. 1. áçret -riyan *etc.* RV.; [çrīyāt;] áçrāyi RV. — 3. áçiçriyat *etc.* AV.+ (açiçret V.B., -çrema S., -çrayus RV.; -çriyus E., -çriyan C.; çiçrītá? RV.) — 4. açrāit AV. [— 5. açrā̆yiṣṭa.]
Fut. 1. çrayiṣyati -te *etc.* B.+ [— 2. çrayitā.]
Verb. çritá V.+; çrayitum E., -tavāí B.S.; çrayitvā E.+ [çritvā]; -çrítya B.+
Sec. Conj.: Pass. çrīyate *etc.* B.+ (çriyate *etc.* B.S.) — [*Int.* çeçri-. — *Desid.* çiçrayiṣa-, çiçrīṣa-. —] *Caus.* çrāpayati VS[1]. [çrāyayati, açiçrayat.]

Deriv.:	-çrī B.U.	-çāra AV.	çaraṇá V.+	çretṛ E.
	-çraya AV.+	çā́lā AV.+	-çrit V.+	çréṇi V.+
	-çrayin C.	çrayaṇa B.+	çrití RV.C.	çárman V.+
	çrāyá V.+	çrayaṇīya C.	-çrayitavya C.	çárīra? V.+

The derivatives from the root-form çṛ are probably best referred to a separate root çṛ or çar, çal, meaning 'cover' or the like.

√ çriṣ, *see* √ çliṣ.

√ 1 çrī, çṛ, 'mix'

Pres. [9.] çrīṇā́ti çrīṇīté *etc.* V.B.
Perf. çiçriye V.
Aor. 3. açiçrayus RV.
Verb. çrītá RV., çīrta RV.

Deriv.:	-çir V.B.S.	-çira S.+	-çrī V.	çrayaṇa S.

Is probably only a form of √ çri, from which it is at some points hardly separable. The interrelations of the roots çṛ, çrā, çri, çrī are intricate, and not yet fully worked out. Especially doubtful is it what is the connection with them of the noun çrī́ V.+ 'fortune', and the related çriyás RV., çréyas V.+, çréṣṭha V.+, çremán B.

√ 2 çrī, *see* √ çrā.

√ çru, 'hear'

Pres. [5.] çṛṇóti *etc.* V.+, çṛṇuté *etc.* V.+ (çṛṇviṣé -viré RV.) — [2.] çróṣi RV.
Perf. çuçrā́va çuçruve *etc.* V.+ (çuçrumas U.+; çuçravat çuçrūyā́s -yā́tam áçuçravi RV.)
Aor. 1. áçravam -rot -ravan V.B. (çrávat -vathas *etc.* V.B.S.; çrūyā́sam *etc.* V.C.; çrudhí çrótu *etc.* V.B.); açrāvi çrā́vi V.C. — 2? çruvam TA. — 3. açuçruvat B., -ravus RV. [açiçravat.] — 4. açrāuṣīt *etc.* B.+

Fut. 1. çroṣyáti *etc.* B.+, -te E. — 2. çrotā M.
Verb. çrutá V.+; çrotum E.+; çrutvā́ V.+; -çrútya AV.+; -çrāvam S.C.
Sec. Conj.: *Pass.* çrūyáte *etc.* V.+, -ti *etc.* E. — [*Int.* çoçru-. —] *Desid.* çúçrūṣate *etc.* V.+, -ti *etc.* E.+ (çuçrūṣyate *etc.* E.+) — *Caus.* çrāváyati *etc.* V.+, -te *etc.* E.+ (çrāvyate *etc.* E.+); çraváyati *etc.* RV.
Deriv.:

-çrū B.	-çrā́vaṇa B.S.	çrótra V.+	çuçrūṣaka E.+
çráva B.+	çrāvaṇīya E.+	çrāvitṛ E.	çuçrūṣin E.
çravya E.+	çrávas V.+	çrudhi- RV.	çuçrūṣya E.+
çravā́yya RV.	çlóka V.+	-çrúṇa RV.	çuçrūṣaṇa E.+
çrāva V.+	-çrut V.+	çrómata RV.	çuçrūṣéṇya B.S.
çrāvaka C.	çrúti V.+	çráviṣṭha AV.+	çuçrūṣú B.+
çrāvin C.	çrútya V.+	çrāúṣaṭ V.B.	çuçrūṣitṛ E.
çrāvya E.+	-çrótu RV.	-çuçruka? E.	çuçrūṣitavya E.
çrávaṇa V.+	çrotavyà B.+	çuçrūs E.	-çrāvayitṛ U.
çravaṇīya B.+	çrotṛ V.+	çuçrūṣā S.+	çrāvayitavya C.

Compare √ çruṣ; for √ 2 çru, see √ sru.

√ çruṣ, 'hear'.

Pres. [1.] çroṣan RV., çroṣantu V., çróṣamāṇa RV.
Deriv.: çruṣṭí RV. çrúṣṭi AV. çrāúṣṭi V.B.
A secondary root, growing out of the s-aorist-stem of √ çru.

√ çlath, *see* √ çrath.

√ çlā, 'dissolve' (?).

Pres. [4.] çlāyati JB.
Only in the passage tasmāt . . . vī 'va çlāyanti taruṇam iva hi tarhi reto bhavati JB. ii. 23. Probably a variant to √ çrā.

√ çlāgh, 'extol'.

Pres. [1.] çlā́ghate *etc.* ÇB[1].E.+, -ti E.
Perf. çaçlāghire C.
[*Aor. etc.* açaçlāghat, açlāghiṣṭa; çlāghiṣyate, çlāghitā.]
Verb. çlāghita C.
Sec. Conj.: *Pass.* çlāghyate *etc.* E.+ — *Caus.* çlāghayati *etc.* E.+
Deriv.: çlāghā B.+ çlāghin E.+ çlāghana E.+ çlāghiṣṭha B.
çlāghya E.+ çlāghanīya E.+

√ çliṣ, çriṣ, 'clasp'.

Pres. [4.] çlíṣyati *etc.* B.+, -te U. — [1.] çreṣāma RV. (√ çri?)
Perf. çiçléṣa B.+
Aor. 2. açliṣat E.+, çriṣat RV. [— 3. açiçliṣat. — 7. açlikṣat.]

[*Fut.* **çlekṣyati, çleṣṭā.**]
Verb. **çliṣṭa** B.+; **çleṣṭum** C.; **çliṣṭvā** C.; **-çliṣya** E.+; **-çríṣas** V.
Sec. Conj.: Pass. **çliṣyate** *etc.* C. — [*Int.* **çeçleṣ-.** —] *Desid.* **çiçlikṣa-** (*in d.*)? — *Caus.* **çleṣayati** *etc.* B.+, **-te** C.
Deriv.: **-çriṣ** AV. **-çreṣiṇa** AV. **çleṣin** B.C. **-çreṣman** AV. **-çliṣ** B.C. **çleṣa** AV.+ **-çleṣaṇa** B.+ **çleṣmán** B.+ **-çréṣa** AV.B. **çleṣaka** C. **-çiçlikṣu**? AV.

√ çvañc, 'spread'.

Pres. [1.] **çváñcate** *etc.* V. (**çmañc-** TA.)
Aor. 3? **çaçvacāí** RV.
Sec. Conj.: Caus. **çvañcáyas** RV.
Deriv. **-çvañka** B.

√ çvas, çuṣ, 'blow'.

Pres. [2.] **çvasiti** *etc.* V.+ (**çvasihí** AV.+; **açvasīt** B.+, **açvasat** E.+); **çuṣántam çuṣe çuṣāṇá** RV. — [1.] **çvásati -te** *etc.* AV.+
Perf. **çaçvāsa** *etc.* E.+
Aor. [3. **açiçvasat.** —] 5 (*or pres.*). **çvasīs** C.
Fut. 1. **çvasiṣyati** E. [— 2. **çvasitā.**]
Verb. **çvasita** B.+, **çvasta** E.+; **çvasitum** E.; **-çvasya** S.+; **-çvásas** RV.
Sec. Conj.: Int. **çā́çvasat** RV. — [*Desid.* **çiçvasiṣa-.** —] *Caus.* **çvāsayati** *etc.* V.+ (**çvasayati** C[1].?)
Deriv.: **-çvasa** AV. **çūṣá** V.B.S. **-çvāsana** E.+ **çvasátha** V.B. **çvāsa** V.+ **çóṣa**? VS. **-çvāsanīya** C. **çúṣma** V.B. **çvāsin** B.+ **çvasaná** V.+ **çvási-** RV. **çuṣman** C. **-çvāsya** E.+ **-çvasanīya** C. **-çvasitavya** B.+

√ çvā, çvi, *see* √ çū.

√ çvit, 'be bright'.

[*Pres. etc.* **çvetate; çiçvite.**]
Aor. 1. **açvitan çvitāná** RV. — 3. **áçiçvitat** RV. — 4. **açvāit** RV. [— 5. **açvetiṣṭa.**]
[*Fut. etc.* **çvetiṣyate, çvetitā; çvitta.**]
Deriv.: **-çvit** V.C. **çvetá** V.+ **çviti-** RV. **çvítna** RV. **çvetanā́** RV. **çvitrá** V.+

√ ṣṭhīv, 'spew'.

Pres. [1.] **ṣṭhīvati** *etc.* AV.+ [— 4. **ṣṭhīvyati.**]
Perf. **tiṣṭheva** B. [**ṭiṣṭheva.**]
Aor. 5. **aṣṭhaviṣam**? GB.S. [**aṣṭhevīt.**]
[*Fut.* **ṣṭheviṣyati, ṣṭhevitā.**]

Verb. **ṣṭhyūta** B.+, **ṣṭhīvita** C.; **ṣṭhutv** S.; **-ṣṭhīvya** C.
[*Sec. Conj.: Int.* **teṣṭhīv-, ṭeṣṭhīv-.** — *Desid.* **tiṣṭhīviṣa- ṭiṣ-, tuṣṭhyūṣa ṭuṣ-.** — *Caus.* **ṣṭhevayati.**]

√ sakṣ.

For the participle **sákṣant**, see √ **sah**.

√ sagh, 'be equal to'.

Pres. [5.] **ásaghnos** RV.
[*Perf.* **sasāgha.**]
Aor. 1. **sághat** RV.; **saghyāsam** B.S. [— 3. **asīṣaghat.** — 5. **asăghīt.**]
[*Fut. etc.* **saghiṣyati, saghitā; sāsagh-, sisaghiṣa-, sāghaya-.**]
Deriv. **sághan** B.
Doubtless another form of √ **sah.**

√ sac, 'accompany'.

Pres. [1.] **sácate** *etc.* V.B., **-ti** RV[1]. — [3.] **síṣakti** *etc.* RV.; **sáçcati** (3*p.*) RV., **saçcata** (3*p.*) RV. — [1.] **sáçcasi** *etc.* **saçce** RV.
Perf. **secire** AV.; **saçcima** V.B., **saçcus** *etc.* RV., **saçciré** RV.
Aor. 1. **sacāná** RV. — 4. **asakṣata** *etc.* (**sakṣat -ṣīmáhi**) RV. [— 5. **asaciṣṭa.**]
[*Fut.* **saciṣyate, sacitā.**]
Verb. **sacádhyāi** RV.; **sakṣáṇi**? RV.

Deriv.:	**-săc** V.S.	**săcya** RV.	**sācí**? V.B.	**-sakra** RV.
	-saca V.B.	**sacaná** RV.	**sákhi**? V.+	**sakṣáṇi** RV.
	sácā RV.B.	**sacas-** RV.	**sacátha** RV.	**saçcát** V.
	-sācin B.+	**sáci** V.+	**sákman, -mya** RV.	**sācayá** ÇB.

√ saj, sañj, 'hang'.

Pres. [1.] **sájati** *etc.* V.+, **-te** S.
Perf. **sasañja** B.+ ([**sasajus**] **sasañjus** C., **sasajjatus**? M., **sejus** ÇB.)
Aor. 1. **asañji** B. [**sajyāt.** — 3. **asasañjat.**] — 4. **sāṅkṣīt** *etc.* U.+, **ásakthās -ta** V.B.
[*Fut.* **saṅkṣyati, saṅktā.**]
Verb. **saktá** V.+; **saktum** E., **saṅktos** B.; **-sajya** B.+; **-sáṅgam** B.S.
Sec. Conj.: Pass. **sajyáte** *etc.* B.+, **-ti** B.; **sajjate** *etc.* E.+, **-ti** *etc.* E.+ — [*Int.* **sāsaj-, sāsañj-.** —] *Desid.* **sisaṅkṣati** ÇB. [**siṣaṅkṣa-.**] — *Caus.* **sañjayati** *etc.* E.+; **sajjayati** *etc.* E.+, **-te** E.

Deriv.:	**-saj** V.	**saṅga** V.+	**-sañjana** B.+	**sakti** V.+
	-saja RV.	**saṅgin** AV.+	**-sañjanīya** C.	**sáktu**? V.+
	-sajya C.	**-saṅgya** B.S.	**sajjana** C.	**-saktavya** C.
	-sañja C.			**-saṅktavya** C.

√ sad, 'sit'.

Pres. [1.] sīdati *etc.* V.+, -te *etc.* RV[1].E.+ — [2.] ṣátsi V

Perf. sasā́da sedús *etc.* V.+ (sasáttha RV.; sasadyāt AV.; sīdatus E.), sediré RV.

Aor. 1. ásādi sā́di RV. — 2. ásadat *etc.* V.+ (sádathas RV., sadas *etc.* V.+, sadeyam *etc.* V.B.S., sadatu *etc.* sádatam V.B.S., sádant RV., sadantām AV., sādat- RV.) — 3. asīṣadat *etc.* B. — 4. sátsat RV. — 5. asādīt TA.

Fut. 1. satsyati *etc.* B.S.; sīdiṣyati C. [— 2. sattā.]

Verb. sanná AV.+, sattá V.; sattum B., sīditum E.; -sádya V.+; -sádam RV., -sáde V.B.; -sādam B.

Sec. Conj.: Pass. sadyate B. — [*Int.* sāsad-. — *Desid.* siṣatsa-. —] *Caus.* sādáyati *etc.* V.+, -te *etc.* V.+ (sādyate *etc.* B.+; sisādayiṣa- *in d.*)

Deriv.:	sád V.+	sādín AV.+	sādi E.	sanni C.
	sada B.+	-sadya B.+	sedí AV.B.S.	sádman V.+
	-sádya V.B.S.	sádana V.+	-sandī? AV.B.S.	sadmán RV.
	-sádya *n.* V.B.	sā́dana V.+	seduka B.	-sádvan V.S.
	-sadyā ÇB.	-sādanīya E.+	sattí V.+	-sadvará B.S.
	sādá V.+	sádas V.+	sáttṛ V.B.U.	-satsnu RV.
	-sādaka E.+	-sádi AV.	sattrá V.+	sādayitavya E.+
				-sisādayiṣu E.

The stem sada, so far as accented sáda, is perhaps rather a present-stem.

√ san, 2 sā, 'gain'.

Pres. [8.] sanóti *etc.* V.B.S. — [1?] sánat *etc.* sánema sána sánant RV.

Perf. sasā́na RV. (sasavā́ṅs V., sasanúṣī B.S.) [sene.]

Aor. [1. asāta; sanyāt, sāyāt. —] 2. asanam *etc.* V.B. (sanéyam *etc.* B.S.; sanem B.S.) — [3. asīṣaṇat. —] 4? seṣam set B. — 5. asāniṣam RV. (saniṣat *etc.* V., sániṣantu SV.), [asaniṣṭa] (saniṣāmahe sániṣanta RV.)

Fut. 1. saniṣyáti V.B. [— 2. sanitā.]

Verb. sātá V.B.

Sec. Conj.: [*Pass.* sanyate, sāyate. —] *Int.* [sansan-, sāsā-,] saniṣṇata RV. — *Desid.* síṣāsati *etc.* V.B. [sisaniṣa-. — *Caus.* sānayati.]

Deriv.:	-san RV.	sani V.B.	sanítṛ V.B.	sanéru? RV.
	-sána RV.	-sani V.+	sanítra RV.	sánīyas B.
	sína? RV.	sānuká RV.	sanutṛ RV.	sániṣṭha RV
	-sānin C.	saniti RV.	sanítvan RV	sānasí RV.
	-sanana RV.	sānitva RV	sátvan? V.+	sásni V.B.
				siṣṇu RV.
	-sā V.B.	-seya V.	sā́tu? RV.	siṣāsátu RV.
	-sa RV.	sātí V.	sā́man? V.+	siṣāsáni RV.
				siṣāsú V.B.

Different from this is the root seen in sána 'old' V.+ and the related words.

√ sap, 'serve'.

Pres. [1.] **sápati -te** *etc.* v.b.
Perf. **sepus** rv.
Aor. 3. **sīṣapanta** rv.
[*Fut.* **sapiṣyati, sapitā.**]
Sec. Conj.: Caus. **sāpáyant**? b.
Deriv.: **-sāp** rv. **sápa** b.s. **sapar-** v.+ **sápti** v.+ **-sapin** rv.

The relations of part of these forms are very doubtful.

√ sarj, 'creak'.

Pres. [1.] **sárjati** *etc.* v.b.

Does not appear to admit of connection with √ **sṛj.**

√ saçc, *see* √ sac.

√ sas, 'sleep'.

Pres. [2.] **sásti** *etc.* (**sastás sasánt** *etc.*) v. — [3.] **sasásti** ts., **sásasti** vs., **sasat** c[1].
[*Perf. etc.* **sasāsa; asīṣasat, asāsīt; sasiṣyati, sasitā; sāsas-, sisasiṣa-, sāsaya-.**]
Deriv. **sasá**? rv.

The single later occurrence is doubtless artificial.

√ sah, 'prevail'.

Pres. [1.] **sáhate** *etc.* v.+, **-ti** *etc.* e.+ (**sáhant** rv.); **sā́hati** *etc.* rv[1].b[1]. — [4.] **sahyāmi** m[1]. — [2.] **sakṣi sákṣva sā́kṣva** rv.
Perf. [**sehe**] (**sehāná** rv.; **sasahe** av.; **sasāhé** *etc.* v.; **sāsahāná** v., **sāsahīṣṭhā́s** rv.), **sehima -hus** b. (**sāsā́ha** v.; **sāsáhat** *etc.* v., **sāsahyā́ma** *etc.* rv., **sāsahvā́ṅs** rv., **sasahvā́ṅs** ta., **sāhvā́ṅs** rv.)
Aor. 1. **sahāná** rv.; **sāhyā́ma** v., **sahyās** *etc.* rv. — [3. **asīṣahat.** —] 4. **asākṣi sākṣi** rv., **asakṣmahi** b. (**sākṣate** rv.; **sākṣīya** *etc.* av.b.), **sākṣīt** gb. (**sakṣati** av., **sakṣat** rv., **sákṣāma** rv., **sákṣat** *pple.* rv.) — 5. **ásahiṣṭa** rv., **sāhiṣīmáhi** *etc.* v.
Fut. 1. **sakṣyati** *etc.* e., **-te** b., **sākṣye**? av.; **sahiṣyati -te** *etc.* e.+ (**asahiṣyat** e.) — 2. **soḍhā** b.+ [**sahitā.**]
Verb. **sāḍhá** v.+, **soḍha** c.; **soḍhum** e.+, **sahitum** b.; [**sāḍhvā, sahitvā;**] **-sáhya** v.+; **-sáham** b.; **sáhadhyāi** rv.k.
Sec. Conj.: Pass. **sahyate** *etc.* c. — [*Int.* **sāsah-.** —] *Desid.* **síkṣati -te** *etc.* rv.ts. [**sisahiṣa-.**] — *Caus.* **sāhayati** *etc.* e.+

Deriv.: -săh V.+ sáha V.B. sahá V.+ sahaka C. -sahya SV.+ -sáhya *n.* RV. sāhá V.+ -sāha RV. -sāhin C. -sāhya V.+ -sabha? E.+ siṅhá? V.+ sáhan? RV. sahana C. sahanīya E.+ -sāhana E.+ sáhantya V.B. sáhas V.+ sahasānā RV. -sāhi C. séhu? AV.K. sā́ḍhi MS. soḍhavya C. sahitavya E. sā́ḍhṛ RV. soḍhṛ E. sáhuri V. sáhīyas V.+ sáhyas RV. sáhiṣṭha V.B. sáhyu RV. sahiṣṇu E.+ sáhvan B.S. sakṣa B. -sakṣin RV. sakṣáṇa RV. sakṣáṇi V. sāsahí V.

√ 1 sā, si, 'bind'.

Pres. [6?] syáti *etc.* V.+, -te *etc.* V.+ — [9.] sinā́ti *etc.* V.B.U. — [5.] asinot JB., -sinvant RV.? — [1?] sāmi santi seyam set M.

Perf. sasāu C.; siṣāya RV. (siṣet? RV.) [siṣye.]

Aor. 1. asāt *etc.* V.B. (sāhi sitam RV., sīmáhi RV.TS.?) [seyāt. — 3. asīṣayat. — 4. asāiṣīt, aseṣṭa. — 6. asāsīt.]

Fut. 1. [sāsyati] siṣyati M. [seṣyati -te. — 2. sātā, setā.]

Verb. sitá V.+; sātum JB., sétave AV., -situm C.; sitvā S.; -sā́ya V.+, -sya B.+; -sā́í RV.

Sec. Conj.: *Pass.* sīyate *etc.* E.+ — [*Int.* sāsā-, seṣi-. — *Desid.* siṣāsa-, sisīṣa-. —] *Caus.* sāyáyati *etc.* B.+

Deriv.: -sā? RV.+ -sāya E.+ -sāyin B.+ -seya C. -sā́na V.+ -sātṛ RV.C. -sya B. -siti V.? C. sétu V.+ setavya C. setṛ́ RV. -sinva? RV.

It is not practicable to separate the two forms of this root. Its prevailing use with ava has led to its reduction to mere s in some of the forms made from it.

√ 2 sā, *see* √ san.

√ sādh, sadh, 'succeed'.

Pres. [1.] sā́dhati -te *etc.* RV. — [5.] sadhnoti *etc.* JB.; [sādhnoti. — 4. sādhyati.]

[*Perf.* sasādha.]

Aor. 3. sīṣadhāti -dhas *etc.*, -dhema -dhātu V.B. [— 4, asātsīt.]

[*Fut.* sātsyati, sāddhā.]

Verb. sādhitum (*caus.*?) C.

Sec. Conj.: [*Int.* sāsādh-. — *Desid.* siṣātsa-. —] *Caus.* sādháyati *etc.* V.+, -te *etc.* E.+ (sādhyate *etc.* E.+; siṣādhayiṣati *etc.* sisādh- C.)

Deriv.: -sādh RV. sā́dha RV. sādhaka E.+ sādhin C. sādhyá V.+ sā́dhana V.+ sādhanīya E.+ sā́dhas V. sādhú V.+ sā́dhu RV. saddhi JB. sā́dhīyas B.+ sā́dhiṣṭha RV.U. sādhayitavya C. sādhayitṛ C. siṣādhayiṣā C. siṣādhayiṣu S.+

√ si, 'bind', see √ 1 sā.

From a root or roots si or sī appear to come sundry doubtful derivatives, as sā́yaka B.+, sénā V.+, sī́tā V.+, sīmán -mant -mā AV.+, sīrá V.+

√ sic, 'pour out'.

Pres. [6.] siñcáti *etc.* V.+, -te *etc.* V.+ — [1.] sécate RV[1].
Perf. siṣeca siṣice *etc.* V.+ (sisicus RV., sisice RV.C.)
Aor. 1. sicyāt B. (siñcyāt? AÇS.); aseci B.S. — 2. asicat *etc.* V.+, -cata *etc.* V.B. (sicāmahe V.B.) — [3. asīṣicat, asīsicat. — 4. asikta.]
Fut. 1. sekṣyati -te *etc.* B.B.
Verb. siktá V.+; sektum E., -tavāi B.; siktvā B.+, siñcitvā C.; -sícya AV.+; -secam S., -sekam S.
Sec. Conj.: Pass. sicyáte *etc.* V.+, -ti B. — [*Int.* sesic-. — *Desid.* sisikṣa-, siṣikṣa-. —] *Caus.* secayati *etc.* S.+, -te S,+; siñcayati E[1].

Deriv.:

síc V B.S.	-sekin C.	sécana V.+	séktṛ V.+
-sícya B	-sekyà B.+	-secanī́ya B.	-secitṛ E.
-sicya *n.* B.	-secaka E.	siktí V.B.	siktha C.
séka V.+	-secya E.	sektavya C	

√ 1 sidh, 'repel'.

Pres. [1.] sédhati *etc.* V.+, -te *etc.* S.+
Perf. siṣedha *etc.* V.+, śiṣidhe E.
Aor. 1. asedhi C. — [3. asīṣídhat. — 4. asāitsīt. —] 5. asedhīs *etc.* RV.E
Fut. 1. setsyati E., sedhiṣyati C. [— 2. seddhā, sedhitā.]
Verb. siddha B.+; seddhum B.+; -sídhya AV.+
Sec. Conj.: Pass. sidhyate *etc.* E.+ — *Int.* séṣidhat RV. — [*Desid.* sisedhiṣa-, sisidhiṣa-, siṣitsa. —] *Caus.* sedhayati *etc.* S.+

Deriv.:

sedha AV.+	-sedhya C.	-siddhi C.	-seddhra B.
-sedhaka E.+	-sedhana E.+	-seddhavya E.+	sidhmá, -man? B.+
-sedhin C.	-sedhanīya C.	-seddhṛ B.+	-sedhayitṛ C.

See the following root.

√ 2 sidh, 'succeed'.

Pres. [4.] sídhyati *etc.* RV[1].U.S.+, -te *etc.* E.+
Perf. siṣedha RV[1]?
Aor. [1. sidhyāsam; asedhi. — 2. asidhat. — 3. asīṣidhat. —] 4. sāitsīt C[1].
Fut. 1. setsyati -te *etc.* E.+ [— 2. seddhā.]
Verb. siddha B[1].E.+ [sedhitvā, sidhitvā, siddhvā.]
[*Sec. Conj.:* seṣidh-; siṣitsa-; sedhaya-.]

Deriv.: -sidh RV. siddhi U.+ sidhmá RV. -sídhvan RV.
sidhrá RV.

Appears to be a weakened form of √ sādh. Grassmann, however, considers 1 sidh and 2 sidh as one root, and there are in fact some difficulties in their separation.

√ sī, *see* √ si.

√ sīv, syū, 'sew'.

Pres. [4.] sívyati *etc.* V.+, -te V.
[*Perf. etc.* siṣeva; asīṣivat, asevīt; seviṣyati, sevitā.]
Verb. syūtá V.+; syūtvā S.; -sīvya AV.
Sec. Conj.: [*Int.* seṣīv-. — *Desid.* siseviṣa-, susyūṣa-. —] *Caus.* ⌊sevayati;⌋ sīvayati C.
Deriv.: syū́ B. seva B. sevitavya C syuman V.B.
sīvaka C. sevana B.+ sū́tra AV.+ syoná? V.B.S.
sīvya C. sīvana B.+ sūná V.B.S.

The noun sūcí (of which sūcay 'point out' is a denominative) can hardly be connected with this root.

√ su, 'press out'.

Pres. [5.] sunóti *etc.* V.+, sunute *etc.* V.+ (sunviré RV.) — [3.] suṣvati (3*p.*) RV.
Perf. suṣā́va suṣumá *etc.* V.B., suṣvāṇá RV.
Aor. 1. sótu sutám *etc.* RV., suvāná svāná V.; ásāvi RV. — 3. asuṣavus AB. ⌊asūṣavat. — 4. asāuṣīt, asoṣṭa. — 5. asāvīt, asaviṣṭa.⌋
Fut. 1. soṣyati KÇS., saviṣyati ÇB. — 2. sotā AB.
Verb. sutá V.+; sótave RV., -tos V.B.; -sútya B.+; -sūya E.
Sec. Conj.: *Pass.* sūyáte *etc.* V.+ — [*Int.* soṣu-. — *Desid.* susūṣa-. —] *Caus.* sāvayati S.
Deriv.: -suva B. sávana V.+ sótu RV. somán RV.
savá V.B.S. -sut V.+ sótva RV. sūya B.
sāvá RV. -suti V. sotṛ́ RV. súrā? V.+
-sāvin RV. sutya S.+ sútvan V -sunva RV.
-sāvya S.+ sutyā B.S. sóma V.+ súṣvi RV.

Doubtless the same with √ sū, and the forms and uses of the two not always clearly distinguishable.

√ sul (?).

Only in the single form prá sulāmi TS.TB., for which VS. has prá tilāmi: see √ til.

√ subh, sumbh, 'smother' (?).

Pres. [9.] **asubhnan** TS. — [6?] **sumbhan** K.
Verb. **subdha** TS.
Deriv. sóbharī? V.

√ sū, su, 'generate, enliven, impel'.

Pres. [2.] **sū́te súvate** *etc.* V.+ (**suvānā́ svānā́**? RV.), **sāuti** B.+, **sū́hi** S. — [6.] **suváti** *etc.* V.B.U. (**sva** AV.TA.), **suvate** *etc.* B. — [4.] **sūyate** *etc.* B[1].+, **-ti** *etc.* E.+ — [1.] **savati** *etc.* E.+
Perf. **suṣāva** *etc.* E.+, **suṣuvé** *etc.* AV.+ (**sasū́va** V.)
Aor. [1. **asāvi.**] — 3. [**asūṣavat,**] **asuṣot** MS., **-ṣavus** TB. — 4. [**asāuṣīt,**] **asoṣṭa** U.+ — 5. **asāvīt** *etc.* V.B. (**sāviṣat** V.B.) [**asaviṣṭa.**]
Fut. 1. **soṣyáti -te** *etc.* B.+ (**sū́ṣyant** RV[1].C[1].), **saviṣyati -te** *etc.* E.+ [— 2. **sotā, savitā.**]
Verb. **sūtá** V.+, **suta** B.+ [**sūna**]; [**sotum,**] **sū́tave** V., **-tavāí** AV., **sávitave** AV.; **sūtvā́** B.+; **-sūya** E.+; **-sútya** ÇB.
Sec. Conj.: *Pass.* **sūyáte** *etc.* V.+ — *Int.* **soṣavīti** RV. — [*Desid.* **susūṣa-.** — *Caus.* **sāvaya-.**]

Deriv.:			
sū́ V.+	**-savas** B.S.	**sūtrī́** AV.	**-sū́ya** AV.+
savá V.+	**sū́ti** V.+	**strī́**? V.+	**sū́ra**? V.
sávya? *n.pr.* RV.	**-suti** RV.	**savatha**? C.	**ṣūrí**? V.+
-savin C.	**sū́tu** AV.	**-sūna** S.+	**sávīman** V.B.S.
sávana V.+	**savitṛ́** V.+	**sūnú** V.+	**-sū́van** V.
-súvana AV.	**-savītṛ** RV.	**-sū́ma** V.	**sūṣā́** AV.
			sūṣaṇā? AV.

Usually divided into two roots, 1 **sū̆** 'impel', and 2 **sū̆** 'give birth' (the verb-forms of the former, with three or four sporadic exceptions, limited to the older language); but their forms and meanings are mixed beyond the possibility of successful separation.

√ sūd, 'put in order'.

[*Pres.* **sūdate.**]
Perf. [**suṣūde,**] **suṣūdima** RV. (**súṣūdati** *etc.* **súṣūdat** *etc.* RV., **suṣūdáta** AV.)
Aor. 3. **asūṣudanta** TS.
[*Fut.* **sūdiṣyati, sūditā.**]
Sec. Conj.: [*Int.* **soṣūd-.** — *Desid.* **suṣūdiṣa-.** —] *Caus.* **sūdáyati** *etc.* V.+, **-te** *etc.* B.+

Deriv.:			
-sūd RV.	**-sūdaka** E.+	**sū́daṇa** V.+	**sūdayitnú** RV.
sū́da V.+	**sūdin** B.		

√ sūrkṣ, 'heed'.

Pres. [1.] **sūrkṣati** *etc.* B.S.
[*Perf. etc.* **suṣūrkṣa; asūrkṣīt; sūrkṣiṣyáti, sūrkṣitā.**]
Deriv. **sū́rkṣya** B.

√ sṛ, 'flow'.

Pres. [3.] **sísarti sísrat** *etc.* RV., **sísrate** (3*p*.) *etc.* V. (**sísratus** RV[1].) — [1.] **sarati** *etc.* S[1].E.+, **-te** *etc.* E.+
Perf. **sasā́ra sasré** *etc.* V.+ (**sasṛva** ÇB., **sasṛvā́ṅs** V.+, **sasrāṇá** RV.; **sasṛmāṇá** RV.)
Aor. 1. **asāri** B. [**sriyāt.**] — 2. **asarat** *etc.* V.B. (**sárat** *etc.* **sára** RV.) — 4. [**asārṣīt,**] **sarṣat** AV.
Fut. 1. **sariṣyáti** *etc.* V.+ [— 2. **sartā.**]
Verb. **sṛtá** B.+; **sartum** C., **sártave** RV., **-tavā́í** RV.; **sṛtvā́** B.+; **-sṛ́tya** B.+; **-sā́ram** B.
Sec. Conj.: Int. **sarsré** *etc.* RV. (**sársrāṇa** V.) — *Desid.* **sisīrṣati** *etc.* B. — *Caus.* **sārayati -te** *etc.* V.+ (**sāryate** *etc.* B.+; **sisārayiṣa-** *in d.*); **saráyante** RV.

Deriv.:	**sará** V.+	**saraṇa** V.+	**-sṛ́tya** AV.	**sarámā?** V.+
	saraka E.+	**saraṇi** C.	**-sṛtyā** JB.	**sṛmará** B.+
	sárin? RV.	**sā́raṇa** B.+	**-sártu** RV.	**saráyu** V.+
	sā́ra V.+	**-sāraṇīya** C.	**-sartavyà** B.C.	**sarirá** B.
	sāraka B.+	**sáras** V.+	**sártṛ** B.	**salilá** V.+
	sārin B.+	**sarít** V.+	**sṛ́tvan** V.B.	**sarala?** E.+
	-sārya C.	**sáru?** AV.	**-sṛtvara** C.	**sasrá** RV.
	sirā́ V.+	**-sṛt** V.+	**sárma** RV.	**sásri** RV.
	sīrā́ RV.	**sṛtí** AV.+	**-sarman** RV.	**-sisārayiṣu** C.
			sárīman RV.	

√ sṛk, 'be pointed' (?).

A root **sṛk** or **sṛc** inferable with plausibility from the derivatives:

sṛká V.B.	**sraktí** V.B.S.	**sṛkva** C.	**sṛ́kvan** V.+
		srákva RV.	**sṛkvi** E.+

√ sṛj, 'send forth'.

Pres. [6.] **sṛjáti -te** *etc.* V.+ — [1.] **sárjatas** AV., **-anti** C. (**sarájant** RV[1]?)
Perf. **sasarja sasṛjé** *etc.* V.+ (**sasarktha** C. [**sasarjitha sasraṣṭha**]. **sasṛjmáhe -jrire** RV., **sasṛgmáhe** SV.; **sasṛjyāt asasṛgram** RV.)
Aor. 1. **ásṛgran -ram** RV.; **ásarji** V.B.; **sṛjāná** RV. — [3. **asīsṛjat, asasarjat.** —] 4. **asrākṣīt** *etc.* V.+ (**asrāk** V.B.C[1]., **asrāṭ** B., **srās** AV.; **srakṣat** B.), **ásṛkṣi ásṛṣṭa** *etc.* V.B.
Fut. 1. **srakṣyati -te** *etc.* B.+ — 2. **sraṣṭā?** PB.

Verb. sṛṣṭá v.+; sraṣṭum e.+; sṛṣṭvā b.u.; -sṛ́jya b.+; -sárgam b., -sárjam b.

Sec. Conj.: Pass. sṛjyáte *etc.* v.+ — [*Int.* sarīsṛj-. —] *Desid.* sisṛkṣati *etc.* b.+ (sisṛkṣmas c[1].), -te gb. — *Caus.* sarjayati -te *etc.* b.+

Deriv.: -sṛj v.+ sráj v.+ sṛjya b.+ sárga v.+ -sargin s.+ sarjá b.+ -sarjya e. sárjana v.+ sṛ́ṣṭi v.+ sṛṣṭí çb[1]. sraṣṭavya c. sraṣṭṛ v.+ sṛjayá -yā́ b. sisṛkṣā c. sisṛkṣu e.+ sarjayitavya u.+

√ sṛp, 'creep'.

Pres. [1.] sárpati *etc.* v.+, -te *etc.* e.+

Perf. sasarpa *etc.* b.+

Aor. 2. asṛpat *etc.* av.b. — 3. asīsṛpat b. [asasarpat.] — 4. [asārpsit, asrāpsīt;] asṛpta b.s.

Fut. 1. srapsyati *etc.* b.+, sarpsyati b. [— 2. sarptā, sraptā.]

Verb. sṛpta b.+; sarpitum e.+; sṛptvā b.; -sṛ́pya av.b.s.; -sṛ́pas b.; -sárpam b.s.

Sec. Conj.: Pass. sṛpyate *etc.* b.+ — *Int.* sarīsṛpant c., -pyate b. — *Desid.* sísṛpsati *etc.* v.+ — *Caus.* sarpayati *etc.* s.+

Deriv.: -sṛp b.s. -sṛpya c. sarpá v.+ -sarpaka s. -sarpin b.+ sárpaṇa v.+ sarpi b. sarpís v.+ -sṛpti c. sṛprá rv. sasarparī́ rv. sarīsṛpá v.+

√ sev, 'attend upon'.

Pres. [1.] sévate *etc.* v.+, -ti *etc.* rv[1].e.+

Perf. siṣeve *etc.* e.+, -va c.

[*Aor.* asiṣevat, aseviṣṭa.]

Fut. 1. seviṣyati e. [-te. — 2. sevitā.]

Verb. sevita e.+; sevitum c.; sevitvā e.; -sevya c.

Sec. Conj.: Pass. sevyate *etc.* e.+ — [*Int.* seṣev-. — *Desid.* siseviṣa-. —] *Caus.* sevayati c. (siṣevayiṣa- *in d.*)

Deriv.: sevā e.+ sevaka e.+ sevin e.+ sevya e.+ sevana b.+ sevanīya c. sevitavya b.+ sevitṛ e.+ siṣevayiṣu c.

√ skand, 'leap'.

Pres. [1.] skándati *etc.* v.+, -te c.

Perf. caskánda v.+, -de e.+

Aor. 1. askan skán v.b. [skadyāt.] — [2. askadat. — 3. acaskandat. —] 4. askāntsīt b. (áskān skān b.s.)

Fut. 1. skantsyati b. [— 2. skanttā.]

Verb. skanná v.+; [skanditum; skanttvā;] -skándya b.+, -skádya b.; -skáde -skádas rv.; -skándam av.b.

Sec. Conj.: [*Pass.* skadyate. —] *Int.* kániṣkan caniṣkadat RV. — [*Desid.* ciskantsa-. —] *Caus.* skandayati *etc.* B.+

Deriv.: skanda V.+ -skandya B. -skádvarī B. skandhá AV.+ skandin E.+ skandana B.+ skándhas? V.B.

√ skambh, skabh, 'prop'.

Pres. [9.] skabhnā́ti *etc.* V.B. (skabhāná B.) — [5.] skabhnuvánt B. [— 1. skambhate.]

Perf. caskambha C[1]. (cāskámbha skambháthus -bhus RV.), [caskambhe] caskabhāná AV

[*Aor. etc.* acaskambhat, askambhīt; skambhiṣyati, skambhitā.]

Verb. skabhitá V.; [skambhitum;] skabhitvī́ RV.; -skábhe RV.

Sec. Conj.: Caus. [skambhayati] (skambhita C.)

Deriv.: skabha- V.B. -skambhaka C. skámbhana V.B. skábhīyas RV. skambhá V.+ -skambhin E.

√ sku, 'tear'.

Pres. [2.] skāuti ÇB. — [5.] skunoti AV. [skunute. — 9. skunāti, skunīte.]

[*Perf. etc.* cuskāva cuskuve; acuskavat, askāuṣīt askoṣṭa; skosyati -te, skotā.]

Verb. skuta RV.; -skā́vam

Sec. Conj.: Pass. skūyáte MS. — *Int.* coṣkūyáte *etc.* RV. [— *Desid.* cuskūṣa-. — *Caus.* skāvayati.]

Deriv.: -skava AV. -skavana S.

The doubtful form skuptvā in Ap. Dh. S. (i. 31. 24) perhaps belongs here; compare dantaskavana ib. ii. 5. 9.

√ skṛ, *see* √ 1 kṛ.

√ skhal, 'stumble'.

Pres. [1.] skhalati *etc.* E.+, -te AB.

Perf. caskhāla caskhalus E.+

[*Aor. etc.* askhālīt; skhaliṣyati, skhalitā.]

Verb. skhalita B.+

Sec. Conj.: Caus. skhalayati *etc.* C. [skhālayati.]

Deriv.: skhala B.+ skhalana E.+

√ stan, 'thunder'.

Pres. [2.] stanihi stan RV. — [1.] stanati *etc.* AV.B.+, -se C[1]

[*Perf.* tastāna tastanus.]

Aor. [2. atiṣṭanat. —] 5. astānīt AV

[*Fut.* staniṣyati, stanitā.]

Verb. **stanita** s.+; **stanitvā** c.

Sec. Conj.: *Int.* **taṅstanīhi** AV. [— *Desid.* **tistaniṣa-**. —] *Caus.* **stanáyati** *etc.* V.+

Deriv.: **-stana** V.B. **stanana** c. **stanátha** RV. **iṣṭáni**? RV. **-stānaka**? c. **stāmú**? RV. **stanáthu** AV. **stanayitnú** V.+

Compare √ **2 tan**.

√ stambh, stabh, 'prop'.

Pres. [9.] **stabhnā́ti** *etc.* V.+ (**stabhāná** V.B.) — [5.] **stabhnoti** *etc.* B. — [1.] **stambhant** c., **stambhate** *etc.* c.; **stabhamāna** AA.

Perf. **tastámbha tastabhús** *etc.* V. (**tastámbhat** RV.), **tastambhe** *etc.* B.+ (**tastabhāná** V.B.)

Aor. 1. [**stabhyāt**;] **astambhi** c. — [2. **astabhat**. — 3. **atastambhat**. —] 4. **astāmpsīt** TB. — 5. **ástambhīt stámbhīt** RV.

[*Fut.* **stambhiṣyati, stambhitā**.]

Verb. **stabhitá** V., **stabdha** B.+; **stabdhum** c.; **stabdhvā́** AV.B., **stambhitvā** B.; **-stábhya** B.+; **-stambham** B.

Sec. Conj.: *Pass.* **stabhyate** c. — [*Int.* **tāstabh-**. — *Desid.* **tistambhiṣa-**. —] *Caus.* **stambhayati -te** *etc.* B.+ (**stambhayiṣa**? *in d.*)

Deriv.:

stambha V.+ **stabha-** RV. **stámbhana** B.+ **-stambhayitṛ** c.
stambhaka E.+ **-stabhya** c. **stambhanīya** E.+ **-stambhayiṣu** B.
stambhin E.+ **stabhu-** RV. **-stabdhi** B.+

Compare the parallel and equivalent root **skambh**.

√ stā, 'be stealthy'.

Is inferable from the derivatives:

stāyát AV.GB. **stāyú** VS. **stéya** V.+ **stāmán**? AV.
stāyāt JB. **tāyú**? V. **stená** V.+

GB. reads **stāyan**; JB. has **na stāyād bhavati** ii. 24 (*ter*).

√ stigh, 'mount'.

Pres. [5.] **stighnoti -nuyā́t** MS. [**stighnute**.]

[*Perf. etc.* **tiṣṭighe**; **atiṣṭighat, asteghiṣṭa**; **steghiṣyate, steghitā**.]

Verb. **-stígham** MS.

Sec. Conj.: [*Int.* **teṣṭigh-**. —] *Desid.* **tiṣṭighiṣati** MS. [**tistighiṣa-, tisteghiṣa-**. — *Caus.* **steghayati**.]

These forms are somewhat amended from the MSS. (which have **stiñnoti** *etc.*): see Schröder in ZDMG. xxxiii. 195.

√ stim, stīm, 'be stiff'

[*Pres. etc.* **stī́myati**; **tiṣṭema, tiṣṭīma**; *etc. etc.*]

Verb. **stimita** E.+

Compare √ **styā**.

√ 1 stu, 'praise'.

Pres. [2.] **stāúti stuvánti** *etc.* v.+, **stute stuváte** *etc.* v.+ (**stavīmi** c[1]., **stoṣi** RV., **stuvāná** v., **stávāna** v., **stavāná** RV.) — [1.] **stávate** *etc.* (**stave** 3*s.*) RV. — [6?] **astuvat** E., **stuvate** *etc.* AV.E. — [5.] **stunvanti** *etc.* U.C., **stunvāna** U. — **stuṣé** (1,3*s.*) v.

Perf. **tuṣṭāva tuṣṭuvús** *etc.* v.+ [**tuṣṭuva -ma**], **tuṣṭuvé** *etc.* v.+

Aor. 1. [**stūyāt;**] **ástāvi** RV. — 3. **átuṣṭavam** RV., **-ṭuvam** JB. (**tuṣṭávat** RV.) — 4. **astāuṣīt** *etc.* B.+ (**stoṣat** *etc.* **stoṣāṇi** RV.), **ástoṣṭa** *etc.* V.B. — 5. **astāvīt** *etc.* B.S.

Fut. 1. **stoṣyati** *etc.* B.+ (**astoṣyat** *etc.* B.U.), **-te** *etc.* B.+; **staviṣyati -te** *etc.* v. [— 2. **stotā.**]

Verb. **stutá** v.+; **stotum** B.+, **stótave** RV.; **stutvā́** AV.+; **-stútya** B.+, **-stūya** E.+; **stavádhyāi** RV.

Sec. Conj.: Pass. **stūyáte** *etc.* v.+ — [*Int.* **toṣṭu-.** —] *Desid.* **tuṣṭūṣita** c. — *Caus.* **stāvayati** *etc.* B.+, **-te** c.; **stavayati** c[1].

Deriv.: **-stu** RV. **stáva** v.+ **stavya** E. **stāva** B.+ **stāvaka** c. **-stāvya** s. **stavana** s.+ **-stavanīya** s. **-stāvanā** E.+ **stút** v.s. **stutí** v.+ **stútya** v.+ **stotavya** B.+ **stotṛ́** v.+ **stotrá** v.+ **stavátha** RV. **stóma** v.+ **stavā́n**? RV. **stuṣéyya** RV.

√ 2 stu, 'drip'.

Such a root is with probability inferable from the derivatives:

-stu RV. **-stāva** AV. **stúkā** V.B.S. **stoká** v.+ **stupá** AV.B. **stū́pa** v.+

√ stubh, 'praise'.

Pres. [1.] **stóbhati** V.B.S. [**-te**]. — [2.] **stobdhi** (3*s.*) JB., **stubhāná** RV.

[*Perf. etc.* **tuṣṭubhe; atuṣṭubhat, astobhiṣṭa; stobhiṣyate, stobhitā.**]

Verb. **stubdha** B.S.

Sec. Conj.: Caus. **stobhayati** RV.c[1].

Deriv.: **stúbh** v.+ **stubha** E. **-stobha** B.+ **stobhana** c. **stobdhavya** JB. **stúbhvan** RV.

Seems related with √ 1 stu.

√ stṛ, 'strew'.

Pres. [9.] **stṛṇā́ti stṛṇīté** *etc.* v.+ — [5.] **stṛṇóti stṛṇute** *etc.* v.+ — [1.] **starati** *etc.* E.+

Perf. **tastāra tastarus** B.+, **tastare -rire** c. (**tastriré** AV., **tistiré** 3*s.* **-rāṇá** RV.)

Aor. 1. **ástar star** RV., **astṛta** AB. (**stárate starāmahe** RV.); [**staryāt;**] **ástāri** RV. — [3. **atastarat.** —] 4. [**astārṣīt**] **astṛṣi** B.; **stṛṣīya** AV. — 5. **astarīs** AV. [**astariṣṭa, stariṣīṣṭa.**]

Fut. 1. stariṣyati -te B.C. [— 2. startā.]

Verb. stṛta V.+, stīrṇá V.+; stártave B., -tavāi B., staritavāi B., stárītave AV.B., -starītavāí B.; stṛtvā́ B.S., stīrtvā́ B.S.; -stṛtya E., -stī́rya B.+; -stíre RV.; stṛṇīṣáṇi RV.

Sec. Conj.: Pass. stīryate *etc.* S.+, -ti M.?; striyáte ÇB. [staryate. — *Int.* testīrya-, tastarya-. —] *Desid.* tistīrṣate JB.; tustūrṣate B.U.S. — *Caus.* stārayati *etc.* E.+

Deriv.: stṛ́? RV.	stárya B.	-stārin AV.+	-stárītu RV.
-stir RV.	-staryà B.	stáraṇa V.+	-staritṛ C.
-stur RV.	-stāra V.+	stṛ́ti B.+	stárīman RV.
-stára V.+	-stāraka C.	stṛtya B.	-stṛṇa C.

√ stṛh, 'crush'.

Pres. [6.] stṛhant S[1].

[*Perf. etc.* tastarha *etc. etc.*]

Seems to be a variant of √ tṛh.

√ styā, stī, 'stiffen'.

Pres. [4.] styāyate *etc.* B.C.

[*Perf. etc.* tastyāu; styāyāt styeyāt, astyāsīt; styāsyati, styātā.]

Verb. styāna C. [stīta, stīma]; -styā́ya B.

Deriv.: stíyā RV.	-styāya C.	-styāyana C.	stīmá AV.
			-stīmin AV.B.

The last two derivatives perhaps rather from √ stĭm (or this from them).

√ sthag, 'cover'.

[*Pres. etc.* sthagati; tasthāga; asthagīt; sthagiṣyati, sthagitā.]

Sec. Conj.: Caus. sthagayati *etc.* C.

Deriv.: sthagaka C.	sthagana C.

√ sthā, 'stand'.

Pres. [1.] tíṣṭhati *etc.* V.+, -te *etc.* V.+ (tiṣṭhāsam? GGS.)

Perf. tasthāú tasthe *etc.* V.+

Aor. 1. ásthāt *etc.* V.+ (sthāti sthā́thas stheyāma sthā́nt RV.), ásthithās -ita V.+, ásthiran V.B.; [stheyāsam;] asthāyi C. — 2? āsthat AV.K. — 4. [sthāsīṣṭa;] stheṣam B., -ṣus? AV. — 5. asthiṣi -ṣata B.+

Fut. 1. sthāsyati -te *etc.* B.+ — 2. sthātā *etc.* E.+

Verb. sthitá V.+; sthā́tum B.+, -tos B.S., -sthitum E.; sthitvā́ E.+; -sthā́ya V.+; -sthā́yam V.B.

Sec. Conj.: Pass. sthīyate *etc.* B.+ (asthāyiṣi C[1].) — [*Int.* tāsthā-, teṣṭhīya-. —] *Desid.* tiṣṭhāsati *etc.* B.+ (tiṣṭhā́set? ÇB.) — *Caus.* sthāpayati *etc.* V.+, -te *etc.* V.+ (átiṣṭhipat *etc.* V.B.; -sthā́pam B.; sthāpyate *etc.* B.+; -sthāpayiṣati B.)

Deriv.:

sthā́ v.+	**-sthu** v.+	**sthā́man** v.c.	**tiṣṭhāsā** c.
-stha v.+	**-sthṛ** b.	**sthemán** b.+	**tiṣṭhāsu** c.
-sthin av.+	**sthāyuka** b.	**sthéyas** v.+	**sthāpaka** e.+
-sthāya e.	**sthíti** b.+	**sthirá** v.+	**sthāpin** c.
-sthāyaka c.	**sthití** çb[1].	**sthāla, -lī́?** v.+	**sthā́pya** b.+
sthāyin b.+	**sthātavya** e.+	**-sthā́van** v.b.	**sthāpana** e.+
sthā́na v.+	**sthātúr** rv.	**sthāvará** b.+	**sthāpanīya** b.+
-sthi rv.	**sthātṛ** v.+	**sthāsnu** s.+	**sthāpitṛ** c.
stheya b.+	**sthātrá** v.	**tasthu** c.	**sthāpayitavya** e.+
-sthéya *n.* b.	**sthāṇú** v.+		**sthāpayitṛ** e.+

A number of derivatives are also made from a root **sthū**, which appears to be only a form of **sthā**. They are

sthūrá v.b.	**sthávira** v.+	**sthū́ṇā** v.+	**sthávimau** b.
sthūlá av.+	**sthā́vira** rv.	**sthū́ri?** v.b.	**sthávīyas** b.+
	-sthāva b.		**sthávi̤ṣṭha** b.+

√ snā, 'bathe'.

Pres. [2.] **snā́ti** *etc.* v.+, **snāyīta** e. — [4.] **snāyate** *etc.* e.
Perf. **sasnus** c.
Aor. 1. [**snāyāt, sneyāt**;] **asnāyi** c. [— 6. **asnāsīt.**]
Fut. 1. **snāsyati -te** *etc.* e.+ [— 2. **snātā.**]
Verb. **snātá** av.+; **snātum** b.+; **snātvā́** av.+; **-snā́ya** v.b.
Sec. Conj.: [*Int.* **sāsnā-**. —] *Desid.* **siṣṇāsa-** (*in d.*). — *Caus.* **snāpáyati** *etc.* rv.s.+, **-te** gb.; **snapáyati** *etc.* av.+

Deriv.:

-snā v.c.	**snéya** b.+	**snā́tva** v.b.	**snāpaka** e.+
-sna e.+	**snāna** av.+	**snātavya** e.+	**snāpana** e.+
snāyin e.+	**-snātṛ** v.c.	**siṣṇāsu** e.	**snápana** av.+

√ snih, 'be sticky'.

Pres. [4.] **snihyati** *etc.* e.+, **-te** *etc.* e.+
[*Perf. etc.* **siṣṇeha; asnihat, asiṣṇihat; snehiṣyati, snekṣyati, snehitā snegdhā sneḍhā.**]
Verb. **snigdha** e.+ [**snīḍha; snehitvā, snihitvā, snigdhvā, snīḍhvā.**]
Sec. Conj.: [*Int.* **seṣṇih-**. — *Desid.* **sisnehiṣa-, sisnihiṣa-, sisnikṣa-.** —] *Caus.* **sneháyati** *etc.* rv.c.

Deriv.:

sníh ta.	**snehin** c.	**snīhán** b.	**snīhiti** v.
sneha b.+	**snehya** c.	**snehana** e.+	**snéhiti** rv.
snehaka c.			**snehayitavya** c.

√ snu, 'distil'.

Pres. [2.] **snāuti** *etc.* b.+ [**snute.**]
[*Perf. etc.* **suṣṇāva suṣṇuve; asnāvi, asnoṣṭa, asnāvīt; snaviṣyati snoṣyate, snavitā snotā.**]

Verb. snuta s.? E. +
[*Sec. Conj.:* soṣṇu-; susnūṣa-; snāvaya-.]
Deriv.: -snu RV. -snava E. + -snāvin c.

√ spand, 'quiver'.

Pres. [1.] spandate *etc.* V. +, -ti *etc.* E. +
[*Perf. etc.* paspande; aspandiṣṭa; spandiṣyate, spanditā.]
Verb. spandita c.; spanditum c.
Sec. Conj.: Int. paniṣpad- (*in d.*). — [*Desid.* pispandiṣa-. —] *Caus.* spandayati -te *etc.* B. +
Deriv.: spanda E. + spandin c. spandaná AV. + paniṣpadá AV.

√ spaç, *see* √ paç.

√ spūrdh, *see* √ spṛdh.

√ spṛ, 'win'.

Pres. [5.] spṛṇoti spṛṇute *etc.* V.B.U.S. (spṛṇvaté RV.) — [9.] spṛṇāti JUB.
Perf. paspāra B.
Aor. 1. aspar *etc.* V. (spárat V., spṛdhi *etc.* RV.) — 4. áspārṣam RV.
[*Fut.* spariṣyati, spartā.]
Verb. spṛtá V.B.; spṛtvā́ B.; spárase RV.
Deriv.: spara B. spárana AV.B. spṛ́t V.B. -spartṛ RV. spṛ́ti B.S.

√ spṛdh, spūrdh, 'contend'.

Pres. [1.] spárdhate *etc.* V. +, -ti *etc.* E. + — [6.] spūrdhán RV[1].
Perf. paspṛdhé *etc.* V.B. (ápaspṛdhethām V.), paspardha E. +
Aor. 1. aspṛdhran spṛdhāná RV. [— 5. aspardhiṣṭa.]
[*Fut.* spardhiṣyate, spardhitā.]
Verb. spardhita E. +; spárdhitum AV.B.; -spṛ́dhya RV.; spūrdháse RV.
[*Sec. Conj.:* pāspṛdh-; pispardhiṣa-; spardhaya-.]
Deriv.: spṛ́dh RV. spardhin E. + spardhanīya c. -spardhas V. + spardhā B. + spardhya E.

√ spṛç, 'touch'.

Pres. [6.] spṛçati *etc.* V. +, -te *etc.* AV. + (spṛçāna E.) — [1.] asparçat c[1].
Perf. paspṛçus -çe *etc.* E. + (pasparçus? U.; paspárçat RV.)
Aor. 1. spṛçyāt B. — 3. pispṛças -çati RV. — 4. asprākṣam *etc.* B.E. [aspārkṣīt.] — 7. áspṛkṣat *etc.* AV.B.
Fut. 1. sprakṣyati *etc.* B. [sparkṣyati. — 2. spraṣṭā, sparṣṭā.]

Verb. **spr̥ṣṭá** AV.+; **spraṣṭum** E.+; **spr̥ṣṭvā** B.+; **-spŕ̥çya** B.+; **-spŕ̥çe** RV., **-spŕ̥ças** B.

Sec. Conj.: Pass. **spr̥çyate** *etc.* E.+ — [*Int.* **parīspr̥ç-**. —] *Desid.* **pispr̥kṣa-** (*in d.*). — *Caus.* **sparçayati** *etc.* B.+, **-te** RV.

Deriv.:

-spr̥ç V.+	**sparça** AV.+	**spr̥çi** C.	**sparçitr̥** E.
-spr̥ça E.+	**sparçin** S.+	**spŕ̥ṣṭi** B.+	**pispr̥kṣu** E.+
spr̥çya E.+	**sparçana** U.S.+	**spraṣṭavyà** B.+	**sparçayitavya** U.
	sparçanīya E.+	**spraṣṭŕ̥** B.+	

Compare √ **pr̥ç, pr̥ṣ**; a part of the words there given may with considerable plausibility be connected with this root.

√ spr̥h, 'be eager'.

Pres. [6.] **spr̥hantī** S.

Sec. Conj.: Caus. **spr̥hayati** *etc.* V.+, **-te** *etc.* E.+

Deriv.:

-spr̥h V.	**spārhá** V.+	**spr̥haṇa** E.	**spr̥hayālu** E.+
spr̥hā E.+		**spr̥haṇīya** E.+	**spr̥hayā́yya** RV.

The non-causative form only in Āp. Dh. S. i. 31. 9 (perhaps an error?).

√ sphaṭ, 'split'.

Sec. Conj.: Caus. **sphāṭita** C.

Deriv. **sphaṭiká** U.+

No proper root; the participle probably a denominative formation.

√ sphar, *see* √ sphr̥.

√ sphal, 'strike'.

Sec. Conj.: Caus. **sphālayati** *etc.* TA.C.

Deriv. **sphālana** E.+

√ sphā, 'fatten'.

[*Pres. etc.* **sphāyate; pasphāye; apisphavat, asphāyiṣṭa; sphāyiṣyate, sphāyitā.**]

Verb. **sphīta** E.+

Sec. Conj.: Pass. **sphīyate** B. — *Caus.* **sphāvaya-** (*in d.*).

Deriv.:

-sphāka AV.	**sphātí** V.B.S.	**sphirá** RV.	**sphāvayitr̥** AB.
-sphā́na V.C.	**sphīti** C.		

√ sphuṭ, 'burst'.

Pres. [6.] **sphuṭati** *etc.* B.+ — [1.] **sphóṭati** B.B.

Perf. **pusphoṭa** C.

[*Aor.* **apusphuṭat, asphoṭīt.**]

Fut. 1. **sphuṭiṣyati** *etc.* E. [— 2. **sphuṭitā.**]
Verb. **sphuṭita** E. +; **sphuṭitvā** C.
Sec. Conj.: *Caus.* **sphoṭayati** *etc.* E. +
Deriv.: **sphuṭa** E. + **sphoṭa** E. + **sphuṭana** C. **sphoṭana** E. +

√ sphur, sphul, *see* sphṛ.

√ sphūrj, 'rumble'.

Pres. [1.] **sphū́rjati** *etc.* AV. +
[*Perf. etc* **pusphūrja; apusphūrjat, asphūrjīt; sphūrjiṣyati, sphūrjitā.**]
Verb. **sphūrjita** E. +; **-sphūrjya** E.?
Sec. Conj.: [*Int.* **posphūrj-.** — *Desid.* **pusphūrjiṣa-.** —] *Caus.* **sphūrjáyati** *etc.* V. +
Deriv.: **sphūrja** C. **-sphūrjana** C. **-sphūrjathu** C. **-sphūrji** C. **sphū́rjaka** B.+

√ sphṛ, sphar, sphur, sphul, 'jerk' etc.

Pres. [6.] **sphuráti** *etc.* V. +, **-te** *etc.* B. +
[*Perf.* **pusphora pusphure.**]
Aor. [1. **sphūryāt.** — 3. **apusphurat.** —] 5. **spharīs** RV. [**asphorīt.**]
[*Fut.* **sphuriṣyati, sphuritā.**]
Verb. **sphurita** E. +. **sphulita** C[1].; **spharitvā** C.
Sec. Conj.: [*Int.* **posphur-.** — *Desid.* **pusphuriṣa-.** —] *Caus.* **sphārayati** *etc.* E. +; **sphurayati** C. [**sphorayati.**]
Deriv.: **-sphur** RV. **-sphāra** E. + **sphuraṇa** S. + **-sphuliṅga** V. + **-sphura** V. + **-sphūrti** C.

Does not seem worth the attempt to divide into different roots, as the whole considerable range of meanings appears in the forms of **sphur.**

√ smi, 'smile'.

Pres. [1.] **smáyate** *etc.* V. +, **-ti** *etc.* E. +
Perf. **siṣmiyé** *etc.* V.B.; **sismiye** *etc.* E.+, **sismāya** *etc.* E.+; **-smayām āsa** E.
Aor. [1. **asmāyi.** — 3. **asiṣmayam.** — 4. **asmeṣṭa.** —] 5. **asmayiṣṭhās** E.
[*Fut.* **smeṣyate, smetā.**]
Verb. **smita** E. +; **smitvā** C., **-smayitvā** E.; **-smitya** E.
Sec. Conj.: [*Int.* **seṣmi-.** — *Desid.* **sismayiṣa-.** —] *Caus.* **smāpayati** *etc.* E. + (**sismāpayiṣa-** *in d.*); **smāyayati** C.
Deriv.:

smaya E. +	**smayana** S. +	**smera** RV.C.	**-smāpanīya** C.
smayā́ka TA.	**-smayanīya** E. +	**-smāpaka** C.	**-smāpayanīya** E.
smāya C.	**smetavyà** TA.	**-smāpana** E. +	**-sismāpayiṣu** E.

√ smṛ, 'remember'.

Pres. [1.] smárati *etc.* v.+, -te *etc.* v.+
Perf. sasmāra sasmarus E.
Aor. [1. smaryāt, asmāri. — 3. asasmarat. —] 4. asmārṣus M.
Fut. 1. smariṣyati E. — 2. smartā E.
Verb. smṛta v.+; smartum E.; smṛtvā S.+, smaritvā E.; -smṛtya S.+; smāram C.
Sec. Conj.: *Pass.* smaryáte *etc.* B.+ — [*Int.* sāsmṛ-. — *Desid.* susmūrṣa-. —] *Caus.* smārayati *etc.* E.+, -te *etc.* E.+ (smāryate *etc.* E.+); smarayati *etc.* C.
Deriv.: smará AV.+ smāraka C. smaraṇa E.+ smṛti AV.+ smarya C. smārin C. smaraṇīya E.+ smartavya E.+ smāra B.+ smāraṇa E.+ -smṛt C. smartṛ C.

√ syand, syad, 'move on'.

Pres. [1.] syándate *etc.* v.+, -ti *etc.* E.+
Perf. siṣyanda siṣyadús -de AV.B.; sasyande C. [-dimahe -dmahe.]
Aor. 1. syándi ÇB. — [2. asyadat. —] 3. ásiṣyadat -danta V. — 4. asyān RV. [— 5. asyandiṣṭa.]
Fut. 1. syantsyáti B. [syandiṣyate. — 2. syanttā, syanditā.]
Verb. syanná v.+; syánttum B.; syanttvā́ B., syattvā́ B.; -syadya B.; -syáde RV.
Sec. Conj.: *Pass.* syandyate C. — *Int.* sániṣyadat V.B. — [*Desid.* sisyandiṣa-, sisyantsa-. —] *Caus.* syandayati *etc.* B.+ (syandayádhyāi RV.)
Deriv.: -syad V. syandaka E.+ syandaná V.+ syandrá RV. syáda B. syandin S.+ syédu AV. sasyád RV. syanda B.+ syandyā̀ B.S. syánttṛ RV. saniṣyadá AV.

√ sraṅs, sras, 'fall'.

Pres. [1.] sráṅsate *etc.* B.+, -ti *etc.* E.+
Perf. sasraṅsus B., sraṅsire? C.
Aor. 1. asrat B. — 2. asrasat *etc.* V.+ (srasema RV.) — 3. asisrasat *etc.* AV.B. — 5. asraṅsiṣata B.
[*Fut.* sraṅsiṣyate, sraṅsitā.]
Verb. srasta AV.+; [sraṅsitvā, srastvā;] -sráṅsya B.S., -srasya S.; -srásas V.B.U.
Sec. Conj.: [*Pass.* srasyate. —] *Int.* sanisras- (*in d.*). — [*Desid.* sisraṅsiṣa-. —] *Caus.* sraṅsayati *etc.* AV.+ (sraṅsyate B.)
Deriv.: -sras V.B. -srásya B. -sráṅsaka B. sraṅsana E.+ -srásā B.S. sraṅsa AV.+ sraṅsin C. sanisrasá AV.

√ sridh, 'blunder' (?).

Pres. [1.] srédhati *etc.* RV.
Aor. 2. sridhat sridhāna RV.
Deriv. sridh V.

√ srīv, 'fail'.

Pres. [4.] srīvyanti B[1].
[*Perf. etc.* sisreva; asrevīt; sreviṣyati, srevitā; srūta, srevitvā srūtvā.]
Sec. Conj.: [*Int.* sesrīv-. — *Desid.* sisreviṣa-, susrūṣa-. —] *Caus.* srevāyant RV., çrīvayati AV.
Deriv.: -srīví? B. -sreman? RV.
Sometimes found written with ç for s.

√ sru, 'flow'

Pres. [1.] srávati *etc.* V.+, -te *etc.* B.+; çrúvat RV.
Perf. susrāva susruvus AV.+ [susruma], susruve *etc.* E.+
Aor. 3. ásusrot *etc.* V.B. [asusruvat; asusravat asisravat.] — 5. asrāvīs JB.
Fut. 1. sraviṣyati *etc.* E. [sroṣyati. — 2. srotā.]
Verb. srutá AV.+, çruta AV.; srávitave RV., -tavāí RV.
Sec. Conj.: [*Int.* sosru-. — *Desid.* susrūṣa-. —] *Caus.* srāvayati *etc.* AV.+, -te *etc.* B.; sravayati C.

Deriv.:	srú RV.	srāvín B.+	sravát V.	srótas V.+
	sruvá V.+	srāvya E.+	srúc? V.+	srotyā́ V.B.
	srava V.+	srávaṇa V.+	-srut V.+	sravatha RV.
	-sravin C.	srāvaṇa AV.+	srútya B.	srāvayitavyà MS.
	-srāva AV.+	-sravas E.	srutí V.+	

Apparent forms and derivatives of this root are occasionally found with initial ç, even in V.; and BR. recognize a root 2 çru, equivalent in meaning with sru.

√ svaj, svañj, 'embrace'.

Pres. [1.] svájate *etc.* V.+, -ti *etc.* RV[1].B.+ (svajāna B.)
Perf. sasvajé *etc.* V.+, -jus C. [sasvañje.]
Aor. 3. ásasvajat (*plpf.*?) RV. [— 4. asvañkṣi.]
Fut. 1. svajiṣyate B. [svañkṣyate. — 2. svañktā.]
Verb. svakta B.+; svaktum B.; svajitvā B.; -svajya E.+; -sváje V.
[*Sec. Conj.:* svajya-; sāsvañj-, sāsvajya-; sisvañkṣa-; svañjaya-.]

Deriv.:	svajá AV.B.	-svañga B.+	-svajana C.	-svañjalya AV.
	-svajya B.	-svañgin C.	-svajīyas AV.	

√ **svad, svād,** 'sweeten'.

Pres. [1.] **svádati -te** *etc.* V.+; **svādate** RV[1].
Perf. **sasvade** C. [**sasvāde.**]
Aor. 3. **asiṣvadat** *etc.* V.B.
[*Fut.* **svădiṣyate, svăditā.**]
Verb. **svāttá** V.B.; **-súde** RV.; **-svādam** S.
Sec. Conj.: [*Int.* **sāsvăd-.** — *Desid.* **sisvădiṣa-.** —] *Caus.* **svadáyati -te** *etc.* V.B., **svādayati** *etc.* E.+ (**svādyate** C.)
Deriv.: **svada-?** RV. **svāda** C. **-svādaka** C. **svādin** C. **-svādya** E.+ **svā́dana** RV.C. **svādanīya** B. **-svādas** RV. **svādú** V.+ **svā́dīyas** V.+ **svā́diṣṭha** V.+ **svā́dman** RV. **svādmán** RV. **svādiman** C. **svadayitṛ́** B.
Compare √ **sūd,** which is perhaps related.

√ **svan,** 'sound'.

Pres. [1.] **svanati -te** *etc.* E. — [2.?] **asvanīt** RV.
Perf. **sasvāna sasvanus** E.+ [**svenus.**]
Aor. 1. **sváni?** RV. — [3. **asisvanat.** —] 5. **svānīt** RV.
[*Fut.* **svaniṣyati, svanitā.**]
Verb. **svanita** RV.
Sec. Conj.: *Int.* **saniṣvanat** RV. [**sañsvan-.** — *Desid.* **sisvaniṣa-.**] — *Caus.* **svanayati** *etc.* RV.C.
Deriv.: **-svan** RV. **svaná** V.+ **svāná** V.+ **svānín** RV. **-svanas** RV. **sváni** RV. **svanáya** RV.

√ **svap,** 'sleep'.

Pres. [2.] **svapiti -panti** *etc.* V.+ (**svapihi** C., **sváptu** AV.), **svapīta** B. — [1.] **svápati** *etc.* V.+, **-te** *etc.* E.+
Perf. **suṣvāpa suṣupus** *etc.* V.+, **suṣupāṇá** RV. (**suṣupthās** B.S.)
Aor. 1. **supyāt** S.; **asvāpi** C. — 3. **siṣvapas síṣvap** RV. [**asūṣupat.**] — 4. **asvāpsam** *etc.* S.+
Fut. 1. **svapsyati** *etc.* B.+, **-te** *etc.* E.+; **svapiṣyati** AV., **-te** E. — 2. **svaptā** M.
Verb. **suptá** AV.+; **svaptum** B.+; **suptvā́** AV.+; **-svā́pam** RV.
Sec. Conj.: *Pass.* **supyate** *etc.* E.+ [— *Int.* **sāsvap-, soṣup-.**] — *Desid.* **suṣupsa-** (*in d.*). — *Caus.* **svāpáyati** *etc.* V.+; **svapayati** C[1].
Deriv.: **-sup** RV. **svāpa** E.+ **-svāpin** C. **svapaná** B.C. **svāpana** S.+ **supti** C. **svaptavya** B.+ **svapitṛ** C. **svápna** V.+ **suṣupsā** E. **suṣupsu** B.+

√ **svar,** 'sound'.

Pres. [1.] **svárati** *etc.* V.B.U.S.
Perf. [**sasvāra sasvarus**] (**sasvár?** RV.)

Aor. [3. asisvarat. —] 4. ásvār asvārṣṭām RV. — 5. asvārīs JB.
[*Fut.* svariṣyati, svartā svaritā.]
Verb. svaritos JB.; -svāram S.
Sec. Conj.: [*Int.* sāsvar-. — *Desid.* sisvariṣa-, susvūrṣa-. —] *Caus.* svaráyati AV.+ (svaryate C.) [svārayati.]
Deriv.: -svar RV. svaryà RV. sváraṇa RV. sváritṛ RV.
svára AV.B. svārá V.+ -svaras RV. -svartṛ RV.
svará V.+ -svārya C. svarí? RV. svarīyas C.
sváru? V.B.S. svarayitavya C.

Hardly to be separated from this root are the derivatives showing the radical sense of 'brightness': namely,
svàr V.+ sū́ra V.B. sū́rya V.+ sū́rta? V.
-svara U.C. sūrí? V.+

√ svād, *see* √ svad.

√ svid, 'sweat'.

Pres. [1.] svedate B.U. — [4.] svidyati *etc.* E.+, -te *etc.* C.
Perf. siṣvide E. -dāná RV. [siṣveda.]
Aor. 1. svidyāt S. [— 2. asvidat. — 3. asisvidat.]
[*Fut.* svetsyati, svettā.]
Verb. svinná AV.+; -svedam B.
Sec. Conj.: [*Int.* seṣvid-. — *Desid.* siṣvitsa-. —] *Caus.* svedayati *etc.* B.+
Deriv.: svéda V.+ svedin E.+ svedya C. svedana C. svédu-? RV.

√ had, '*cacare*'.

Pres. [1.] hadati C. [-te.]
[*Perf. etc.* jahade; ahatta; hatsyate, hattā.]
Verb. hanna C.
[*Sec. Conj.*: jāhad-; jihatsa-; hādaya-.]
Deriv.: -hāda E.+ -hadana C.

√ han, 'smite'.

Pres. [2.] hánti hatás ghnánti *etc.* V.+, hate ghnate *etc.* V.+ (hanma E.; ghnīya -īta B.C., hánīta *etc.* B.; jahí V.+, handhí TA.; ahata 3*p.* AB.) — [1.] hanāmi TA., ahanat -nan B.+ — [6?] aghnam E., ghnata (2*p.*) B.+, aghnanta ghnamāna B. — [8.] hanomi PGS. — [1.] jíghnate *etc.* RV.B., -ti *etc.* B.; jaghnant B.
Perf. jaghā́na jaghnús *etc.* V.+ (jaghántha V.; jaghanvā́ṅs V.B., jaghnivā́ṅs B.+; jaghánat RV.), jaghne *etc.* B.+
Aor. [1. aghāni.] — 3. ajīghanat *etc.* E.+ — 4. ghān? S. [ahasta.] — 5. ahānīt JB.
Fut. 1. haniṣyáti *etc.* V.+, -te *etc.* B.+ (ahaniṣyat E.+); haṅsyati E. — 2. hantā B.

Verb. hatá V.+, ghāta B.; hántum V.+, -tave V.B., -tavāí V.B.S., -tos V.B., hanitum C[1].; hatvā́ V.+, -tvī́ RV., -tvā́ya V.; -hátya V.+, -hanya E.+; -ghā́tam B.+

Sec. Conj.: Pass. hanyáte *etc.* V.+, -ti E. — *Int.* jáñghanti *etc.* -ananta V.B., jañghanyate U.; ghánighnat RV.; jījahi? E. [jeghnīya-.] — *Desid.* jíghāṅsati *etc.* V.+ (ajighāṅsīs ÇB.), -te *etc.* E.+ — *Caus.* ghātayati *etc.* B.+, -te *etc.* E.+ (aghātayithās E.) [ajīghatat.]

Deriv.:

-han V.+	-hanas? V.B.	hantṛ V.+	jighatnú RV.
-ha V.+	hánu? V.+	hátha RV.	jighāṅsā E.+
-hána V.+	-hat RV.	hatnú V.	jighāṅsu B.+
-gha U.+	hati V.+	hánman V.B.	-hāta C.
ghaná V.+	-hátya *n.* V.+	hánīyas B.	ghāta B.+
-ghna V.+	hatyā V.+	hániṣṭha RV.	ghātaka E.+
-ghnya V.+	-hanti B.	jaghána? V.+	ghātin AV.+
-ghni AV.	-hántu V.+	ghanāghaná V.+	ghātya C.
-ghnī V.B.	hántva V.B.	jághni V.S.	ghātana E.+
hánana AV.+	hantavya E.+	jáñghā V.+	ghā́tuka AV.B.

√ har, 'be gratified'.

Pres. [4.] háryati -te *etc.* V.B.

[*Perf. etc.* jaharya; ajaharyat, aharyīt; haryiṣyati, haryitā; jāharya-, jiharyiṣa-, haryaya-.]

Deriv. haryatá V.B.

Perhaps a derivative from √ hṛ.

A conspicuous group of words show an inferable root har or hir 'be yellow': thus,

hári V.+	hárita V.+	harimán V.	híraṇya V.+
harít V.+	hariṇá V.+		híri- RV.

√ has, 'laugh'.

Pres. [1.] hásati *etc.* B.+, -te *etc.* E.+

Perf. jahāsa jahasus E.+, jahase C.

Aor. 1. ahāsi C. [— 3. ajīhasat. — 5. ahasīt.]

Fut. 1. hasiṣyati E.+ [— 2. hasitā.]

Verb. hasita E.+; hasitum E.; hasitvā E.+; -hasya E.+

Sec. Conj.: Pass. hasyate *etc.* C. — *Int.* jāhasyate E. — [*Desid.* jihasiṣa-. —] *Caus.* hāsayati *etc.* C.

Deriv.:

has- RV.	hāsa B.+	hasanā́ RV.	hāsana C.
hása V.+	hāsaka E.	hasana E.+	hasrá RV.
hasá AV.	hāsin AV.+	hasanīya C.	-hásvan RV.
-hásya AV.	hāsya E.+		

Compare the derivative root 2 jakṣ.

√ 1 hā, 'leave'.

Pres. [3.] jáhāti jahati *etc.* V.+ (jahītam -īta -ītāt AV., jahīhi C. [jahihi, jahāhi], jahimas *etc.* jahitam ajahitām AV.B., jahyāt *etc.* AV.+) — [1.] jahat AB., -hati *etc.* E.+

Perf. jahāu jahús *etc.* V.+ (jahā RV.?), jahe B.

Aor. 1. ahāt B.C.; ahāyi AV.B. [heyāt.] — 3. ajījahat C. — 4. ahās (3s.) RV., ahāsma hāsus *etc.* V.B., áhāsi -sthās *etc.* AV.B. — 6. hāsiṣam *etc.* V.+

Fut. 1. hāsyati *etc.* AV.+, -te *etc.* B.+; jahiṣyati *etc.* E.+ [— 2. hātā.]

Verb. hīná V.+, hāta C., hāna AB., jahitá V.+; hātum B.+; hitvā́ V.+, -tvī́ RV., -tvā́ya RV. [hītvā]; -hā́ya B.+; -hī́yam TS.

Sec. Conj.: Pass. hīyáte *etc.* V.+ (hī́yate *etc.* TS.ÇB.), hīyanti E. — [*Int.* jāhā-, jehīya-. —] *Desid.* jihāsati *etc.* C. — *Caus.* hāpayati *etc.* E.+, -te C. (jīhipas RV. [ajīhapat.])

Deriv.:			
-hā V.B.	-hāyya B.	-hi? C.	jihāsā C.
-ha E.+	hāna B.+	heya C.	jihāsu C.
hāyaka E.	-hāyas V.+	-hāvarī MS.	jáhāka B.
hāyin JB.	hātavya E.+	hāpana C.	jahana C.
	hāni U.S.+	-hāpanīya C.	

Compare the next root. Two or three of the forms given above show the establishment of a secondary root-form jah.

√ 2 hā, 'go forth'

Pres. [3.] jíhīte jíhate *etc.* V.+ (jihīthām ÇB.)

Perf. jahiré AV.

Aor. 4. ahāsta *etc.* V.+

Fut. 1. hāsyate *etc.* B.E. [— 2. hātā.]

Verb. hāna B.; hā́tum B.E.; [hātvā;] -hā́ya V.+

Sec. Conj.: [*Pass.* hāyate. — *Int.* jāhā-. —] *Desid.* jihīṣate AV.? — *Caus.* hāpayati *etc.* AV.B. [ajīhapat.]

This is only the middle conjugation of 1 hā, with the signification slightly weakened or generalized. The forms of the two cannot everywhere be distinctly separated, and one or two of the derivatives given under 1 hā have an equal or better claim to be placed here. Compare also √ hās, which is a secondary form of hā (doubtless through the aorist-stem)

√ hās, 'go emulously'.

Pres. [1.] hā́sate *etc.* V.

Sec. Conj.: Caus. hāsayanti RV.

A secondary form of √ 1, 2 hā (hā́sante AV. iv. 36. 5 is omitted in the Atharva-Veda Index).

√ hi, 'impel'.

Pres. [5.] **hinóti hinvánti** *etc.* V.+, **hinvé** *etc.* V. (**hinviré** RV.) — [1.] **hínvati** *etc.* V.+ — **jighyati -tu** AB. — **háyant** RV.TS. — **hiṣe** (1s.) RV.
Perf. **jighāya jighyus** B.+
Aor. 1. **áhema áhetana ahyan heta** RV., **hiyāná** RV.S. [**hīyāt.**] — 2. **ahyam**? AV. — [3. **ajīhayat.** —] 4. **ahāiṣīt** B. (**áhāit** AV.), **aheṣata** RV.
Fut. 1. **heṣyati** *etc.* E.+ [— 2. **hetā.**]
Verb. **hitá** V.+; **-hyè** RV.
Sec. Conj.: *Pass.* **hīyate** C. [— *Int.* **jeghīya-**, — *Desid.* **jighīṣa-**. — *Caus.* **hāyaya-**.]

Deriv.:			
háya V.+	**hetí** V.+	**hetṛ́** RV.	**hinvá** RV.
-héya AV.B.	**hetú** V.+	**-héman** V.B.	**héṣas**? RV.
-hit B.	**hétva** RV.	**hemán** RV.	**-hāyyà** AV.
-hiti RV.	**hetavya** C.	**hítvan** RV.	

Probably another form of √ **hā**, with causative value. Some of its uses are equivalent with those of √ **hā**; and the stem **jighya** perhaps belongs directly to the latter.

√ hiṅs, 'injure'.

Pres. [7.] **hinásti híṅsanti** *etc.* V.+ (**hiṅsyāt** *etc.* B.+; **ahinat** 3s. B.; **hiṅsi** 2s. E.), **híṅste** *etc.* V.B. — [1.] **hiṅsati -te** *etc.* B.+
Perf. **jihiṅsa -simá** AV.B.S. (**jíhiṅsīs** AV.)
Aor. [3. **ajihiṅsat.** —] 5. **ahiṅsīt** *etc.* V.+
Fut. 1. **hiṅsiṣyati -te** *etc.* B.+ [— 2. **hiṅsitā.**]
Verb. **hiṅsitá** AV.+; **hiṅsitum** B.+, **híṅsitos** B.; **hiṅsitvā** AV.B.; **-hiṅsya** E.
Sec. Conj.: *Pass.* **hiṅsyate** V.+ — [*Int.* **jehiṅs-**. —] *Desid.* **jíhiṅsiṣati** ÇB. — *Caus.* **hiṅsayati** E.

Deriv.:			
hiṅsā B.+	**hiṅsaka** E.+	**hiṅsana** E.+	**hiṅsitavyà** AV.
	hiṅsya S.+	**hiṅsanīya** E.+	**hiṅsrá** V.+

Probably an abbreviated desiderative of √ **han.**

√ hikk, 'sob'.

Pres. [1.] **hikkati -te** *etc.* C
[*Perf. etc.* **jihikka -ke**; **ajihikkat, ahikkīt ahikkiṣṭa**; **hikkiṣyati -te, hikkitā.**]
Sec. Conj.: [*Int.* **jehikk-**. — *Desid.* **jihikkiṣa-**. —] *Caus.* **hikkayati** C.
Deriv.: **hikkā** E.+ **hikkin** C.

√ hiṇḍ, 'be empty' (?).

Pres. [1.] **ahiṇḍanta** C[1].
[*Perf. etc.* **jihiṇḍe**; **ahiṇḍiṣṭa**; **hiṇḍiṣyate, hiṇḍitā.**]

Deriv.: -hiṇḍaka E.+ -hiṇḍuka E.+
The single occurrence is probably artificial.

√ hīḍ, hel, 'be hostile'.

Pres. [1.] heḍant RV., heḍamāna RV., helamāna E., hīḍamāna B.; ahiḍat? GB.
Perf. jihīḍa RV. (jīhīḍa AV.), jihīḍé *etc.* V.B.
Aor. 3. ajīhiḍat AV. [ajiheḍat.] — 5. hīḍiṣātām TA.
[*Fut.* heḍiṣyate, heḍitā.]
Verb. hīḍitá V.B.
Sec. Conj.: *Caus.* heḍayant RV. (helayām āsa C.), helayate E.
Deriv.: hīḍá? RV. helā E.+ helana E.+ heḍas V.B.
héḍa V. -héḍana V. helanīya C. helitavya E.

√ hu, 'sacrifice'.

Pres. [3.] juhóti júhvati *etc.* V.+, juhuté júhvate *etc.* V.+ (juhudhí B.S., juhvant E.+, ajuhavus V.B., -huvus ÇB.?) — [2.] hoṣi RV[1].
Perf. juhāva juhuvus E., juhuve E., juhvire B. (juhve juhuré RV.); juhavā́ṁ cakāra *etc.* B.U.
Aor. 1. áhāvi RV. [hūyāt. — 3. ajūhavat.] — 4. ahāuṣīt *etc.* B.+
Fut. 1. hoṣyáti *etc.* AV.+, -te E. (ahoṣyat B.) [— 2. hotā.]
Verb. hutá V.+: hótum B.S., -tavāí B.S., -tos B.S.: hutvā B.+
Sec. Conj.: *Pass.* hūyáte *etc.* V.+ — *Int.* johavīti C. — *Desid.* juhūṣati *etc.* S.+ (juhuṣet? GGS.) — *Caus.* hāvayati *etc.* S.+
Deriv.: -hava E.+ havís V.+ hótṛ? V.+ hóman RV.
havyá V.+ -hut V.B.S. hotrá V.+ -hoṣa RV.
-hāva RV. -huti V.B. hótrā V.+ juhū́ V.+
hávana V.B.S. hotavyà B.+ hóma AV.+ juhūṣu C.

√ hur, *see* √ hvṛ.

√ hū, hvā, 'call'.

Pres. [4?] hváyati -te *etc.* V.+ (hvayāna E.) — [1.] hávate *etc.* V.B. — [6?] huvé *etc.* V.B. (huvéya *etc.* áhuve *etc.* huvāná V.B.; hve AV., hvāmahe VS.), huvat -véma -vánt RV. — [2.] hóma RV., -hvatī KÇS., hūte K., hūmáhe RV. — [3.] juhūmási RV.
Perf. juhā́va juhuvus V.+, juhvé juhūré RV., juhuve -vire B.; hvayām āsa E., hvayāṁ cakre E.
Aor. 1. ahvi AV., áhūmahi RV. [hūyāt; ahvāyi.] — 2. áhvat *etc.* V.B., ahvata *etc.* V.B. — [3. ajūhavat. —] 4. ahūṣata RV. [ahvāsta.] — 6? ahvāsīt GB.
Fut. 1. hvayiṣyati -te B., hvāsyate S. [— 2. hvātā.]
Verb. hūtá V.+; hávītave RV., hváyitum B., -tavāí B.S., hvātum C.; hūtvā́ C.; -hū́ya B.+; huvádhyāi RV.; -hāvam B.S.

Sec. Conj.: Pass. **hūyáte** *etc.* V.+ — *Int.* **jóhavīti** *etc.* V.C., **johuvanta** **jóhuvāna** V.B. — *Desid.* **juhūṣati** B. — *Caus.* **hvāyaya-** (*in d.*).

Deriv.:			
-hū V.+	**huvana-** RV.	**hótrā** V.+	**-hváyana** B.
-hū́ya V.B.	**hávana** V.+	**hóman** RV.	**hvāna** B.+
háva V.+	**havás** RV.	**hávīman** RV.	**hvātavya** C.
havín AV.B.	**hūti** V.+	**haviṣṭha**? C.	**-hvayitavya** E.
hávya V.+	**-hávītu** RV.	**-hvā** C.	**hvātṛ** E.+
hávyā RV.	**-hūtavya** C[1].	**-hva** AV.C.	**jihvā́**? V.+
-hāva B.+	**hótṛ** V.+	**-hvaya** E.+	**johū́tra** RV.
		-hvāyaka C.	**-hvāyayitavya** C.

√ hūrch, 'fall away'.

Pres. [1.] **hūrchati** *etc.* B.U.

[*Perf. etc.* **juhūrcha**; **ahūrchīt**; **hūrchiṣyati**, **hūrchitā**; **hūrchita** **hūrṇa**.]

Sec. Conj.: Caus. **hūrchayati** B.

Probably related with √ **hvṛ**.

√ 1 hṛ, 'take'.

Pres. [1.] **hárati** *etc.* V.+, **-te** *etc.* V.+ — [2.] **harmi** RV[1]. — [3.] **jiharti** S[1].
Perf. **jahāra jahrus** *etc.* AV.+ (**jahártha** B.+: **jaharus**? AV.), **jahre** *etc.* B.+
Aor. 1. **ahṛthās** JB.; **ahāri** C. [**hriyāt**. — 3. **ajīharat**.] — 4. **ahārṣīt** *etc.* V.B.U.S.E. (**ahār** AV.B.; **hāriṣīt** S[1].), **ahṛṣata** RV. [**hṛṣīṣṭa**.]
Fut. 1. **hariṣyati -te** *etc.* B.+ (**ahariṣyat** *etc.* B.U.) — 2. **hartā** B.E.
Verb. **hṛtá** V.+; **hártum** B.+, **-tave** C[1]., **-tavāí** B.S., **-tos** B.S., **haritum** R[1].; **hṛtvā** B.S.; **-hṛ́tya** AV.+; **-hā́ram** B.+
Sec. Conj.: Pass. **hriyáte** *etc.* AV.+, **-ti** *etc.* E.+ — *Int.* **jarīharti** C. [**jarhṛ-**, **jehrīya-**.] — *Desid.* **jíhīrṣati** *etc.* AV.+ (**-ṣyate** C.) — *Caus.* **hārayati** *etc.* B.+, **-te** *etc.* B.S. (**hāryate** *etc.* E.+); **harayanta** RV[1].

Deriv.:			
-hara U.S.+	**háraṇa** AV.+	**-hṛt** V.+	**jihīrṣā** E.+
hāra V.+	**-haraṇīya** E.+	**hṛti** B.+	**jihīrṣu** E.+
-hāraka E.+	**-hāraṇa** C.	**-hṛ́tya** B.	**-hārayitavya** C.
hārin E.+	**háras** V.+	**hartavya** E.+	
hāryà AV.+	**hā́ruka** B.	**hartṛ** B.+	

Apparently a variant to √ **bhṛ**; making a very small figure in the oldest language, it gains rapidly in use, and becomes extremely common.

√ 2 hṛ, 'be angry'.

Pres. [9.] **hṛṇīté** *etc.* V. (**ahṛṇāt** KB.?)
Deriv.: **hṛṇāy- hṛṇīy-** V.

Compare the √ **bhur** beside √ **bhṛ**.

√ hṛṣ, 'be excited'

Pres. [4.] hṛṣyati *etc.* v[1].b.+, -te *etc.* e.+ — [1.] hárṣate *etc.* v.c[1]., hárṣant rv[1].
Perf. jaharṣa jahṛṣus e.+, jahṛṣe -ṣire e.+ (jāhṛṣāṇá rv.)
Aor. 2. ahṛṣat e. [— 3. ajīhṛṣat, ajaharṣat.]
[*Fut.* harṣiṣyati, harṣitā.]
Verb. hṛṣitá v.+, hṛṣṭa e.+; -hṛṣya e.+
Sec. Conj.: *Int.* jarhṛṣanta rv., járhṛṣāṇa v.b. [jarīhṛṣ-. — *Desid.* jiharṣiṣa-.] — *Caus.* harṣáyati *etc.* v.+, -te v.e.

Deriv.:	harṣa e.+	hárṣaṇa av.+	harṣú- rv.e.+	ghṛ́ṣu rv.
	harṣaka e.+	hṛ́ṣī- rv.e.+	hṛṣṭi c.	ghṛ́ṣvi rv.
	harṣin v.+	hárṣi rv.		

√ heṭh.

The apparent derivative vi-heṭhaka (or -ṭaka) m[1]. is probably only a misreading for -ḍaka; and vi-heṭhā c[1]. a like case or artificial.

√ heḍ, hel, *see* √ hīḍ.

√ heṣ, 'whinney'.

Pres. [1.] héṣati *etc.* v.+, -te *etc.* e.+
Perf. jiheṣire c.
[*Aor. etc.* aheṣiṣṭa; heṣiṣyate, heṣitā.]
Verb. heṣita e.+

Deriv.:	heṣá-? rv.	heṣā c.	héṣas? rv.

√ hnu, 'hide'.

Pres. [2.] hnuté *etc.* v.+, hnāuti (hnoti?) b., hnutas rv., hnuyāt c. — [1.] hnave b.s., hnavanti e[1].
[*Perf. etc.* juhnuve; ahnoṣṭa; hnoṣyate, hnotā.]
Verb. hnutá av.+; hnotum c.; -hnutya c.
[*Sec. Conj.:* johnu-; juhnūṣa-; hnāvaya-.]

Deriv.:	-hnava b.+	-hnavana s.+	-hnuti c.	-hnavāyya rv.
		-hnuvana s.	-hnotṛ c.	

√ hras, 'shorten'

Pres. [1.] hrasati -te *etc.* s.+
[*Perf. etc.* jahrāsa; ajihrasat, ahrāsīt; hrasiṣyati, hrasitā.]
Verb. hrasta s., hrasita c.
Sec. Conj.: [*Int.* jāhras-. — *Desid.* jihrasiṣa-. —] *Caus.* hrāsayati *etc.* s.+

Deriv.:	hrāsa s.+	hrāsana c.	hrásiṣṭha b.	hrasvá b.+
		hrāsanīya c.	hrásīyas b.+	

√ **hrād**, 'make a noise'.

Pres. [1.] **hrādate** *etc.* S.+
[*Perf. etc.* **jahrāde; ahrādiṣṭa; hrādiṣyate, hrāditā.**]
Verb. **hrādita** C.
Sec. Conj.: Caus. **hrādayati** *etc.* B.+
Deriv.: **hrāda** B.+ **hrādin** E.+ **-hrādana** E.+ **-hrādi** U.E.

√ **hrī**, 'be ashamed'.

Pres. [3.] **jihreti** *etc.* B.+ (**jíhriyat** MS.)
Perf. **jihrāya** C. [**jihrayām āsa.**]
Aor. 1. **-hrayāṇa**? RV. [**hrīyāt.** — 4. **ahrāiṣīt.**]
[*Fut.* **hreṣyati, hretā.**]
Verb. **hrīta** B.+, **hrīṇa** E.
Sec. Conj.: Int. **jehrīyate** C. — [*Desid.* **jihrīṣa-.** —] *Caus.* **hrepayati** *etc.* C. [**ajihripat.**]
Deriv.: **hrī́** B.+ **-hraya** RV. **hrīti** E. **hrepaṇa** C. **-hri** RV.

√ **hru**, *see* √ **hvṛ**.

√ **hreṣ**, 'neigh'.

Pres. [1.] **hreṣati -te** *etc.* E.+
[*Perf. etc.* **jihreṣe; ahreṣiṣṭa; hreṣiṣyate, hreṣitā.**]
Verb. **hreṣita** E.+
Sec. Conj.: Caus. **hreṣayati** *etc.* E.
Deriv.: **hreṣin** E. **hreṣuka** E.

√ **hlād**, 'refresh'.

Pres. [1.] **hlādate** *etc.* C.
[*Perf. etc.* **jahlāde; ajihladat, ahlādiṣṭa; hlādiṣyate, hlāditā; hlanna.**]
Sec. Conj.: Caus. **hlādayati -te** *etc.* TA[1].E.+ (**ahlādayiṣata** C.)
Deriv.: **hradá** V.+ **hlādaka** V.C. **hlāduka** TA. **-hlādayitṛ** C. **hlāda** U.+ **hlādin** E.+ **hlāduni** C. **hlādana** E.+ **hrādúni** V.B.U.

Only one or two late sporadic forms outside the causative conjugation; and the proper form of the root seems to be **hlad** (or **hrad**).

√ **hval**, 'go wrong'.

Pres. [1.] **hválati** *etc.* ÇB.E.+, **-te** E.
[*Perf. etc.* **jahvāla; ajihvalat, ahvālīt; hvaliṣyati, hvalitā.**]
Verb. **hvalita** E.+; **hválitos** ÇB.; **-hvā́lam** ÇB.S.
Sec. Conj.: Caus. **hvaláyati** ÇB. [**hvālayati.**]
Deriv.: **-hvala** E.+ **hvalā́** ÇB. **-hvalin** C. **hvāla** S.

Is only a specialized form of the following root.

√ **hvṛ, hru, hur,** 'be *or* make crooked'.

Pres. [1.] **-hvarant hvárate** RV. — [9.] **hruṇāti** RV. [**hvṛṇāti.**] — [3?] **juhuras** RV., **juhūrthās juhuranta -rāṇá** RV.

[*Perf.* **jahvāra jahvartha jahvarus.**]

Aor. [1. **hvaryāt; ahvāri.** —] 3. **jihvaras** V., **-ratam** VS. (**jīhv-** TS.TA.) — 4. **hvārṣīt** *etc.* B. (**hvār** B., **hvāriṣus** K.)

Fut. 1. **hvadiṣyati**? TA. [— 2. **hvartā.**]

Verb. **hvṛta** RV., [**hvarita,**] **hrutá** V.+

Sec. Conj.: [*Pass.* **hvaryate.** — *Int.* **jāhvṛ-, jarīhvṛ-.** — *Desid.* **juhvūrṣa-.** —] *Caus.* **hvārayati** *etc.* B.

Deriv.: **-hū́rya** RV. **-hvara** V.+ **hvaraka** C. **hvārá** V. **hurás** RV. **hváras** V.B. **-hvṛt** RV. **hrút** V.B. **-hvṛti** V.+ **-hruti** V.C.?

INDEXES

OF

TENSE- AND CONJUGATION-STEMS.

The following lists give the stems of the various tense- and conjugation-systems, each mode of formation by itself. Mode-stems are not added, except in the case of the aorist-optatives, among which the so-called precatives are included. For the sake of illustrating more clearly the history of the language, the stems of each formation are presented in three divisions.

A. Stems found only in the earlier language (of Veda, Brāhmaṇa, Upanishad, Sūtra);

B. Stems found in both the earlier and the later language;

C. Stems found in the later (epic and classical) language only.

In these divisions the stems follow one another not alphabetically, but in the order of the roots as presented above. The references to periods are in an abbreviated form: only the five principal periods are noted — namely, Veda, Brāhmaṇa, Sūtra, epos, classics (the Vedas are not separated, and Upanishad is included in Brāhmaṇa); and, in each division, all references are omitted if the stem is found through the whole division (that is, in **A.** is omitted the specification of V.B.S.; in **B.**, that of V.+; in **C.**, that of E.+). Also, all accents, question-marks, variety of stem-forms, and the like, are left out; for such details, when desired, the body of the work may be consulted.

Further particulars as to some of the lists are given under the different heads below.

I. PRESENT-STEMS. [1136.]

1. Root-class (ad-class, second class). [143.]

A. Earlier Language. [80.]

am V.B.
īḍ V.B.
īr V.B
u V.
ūh V.
ṛ B.
kṛ V.
1 kṣi V.B.
2 kṣi V.
kṣṇu
gam V.
ci V.
chand V.B.
2 jakṣ V.B
jan V.B.
ji V.
juṣ V.
tak V.
takṣ V.B.
taḍ V.
tu V.
tur V.
tvakṣ V.
tviṣ V.

dan V.
dah V.
1 dā V.
2 dā
di B.
dāç V.
dṛ V.
dṛbh B.
1 drā V.
dhā V.
dhū B.
dhṛṣ V.
niṅs V.
nī V.S.
2 nu S.
1 pā V
pī̆ V.
pṛ V.
prā V.
psā V.B.
bhaj V.
bhiṣaj V.
bhṛ V.
mad V.
yaj
yam V.B.
yu
yuj V.
yudh V.
rad V.
randh V.
rāj V.
rih V.B.
2 ru V.
ruj B.
rudh V.
1 vas B.
vah V.B.
vī̆ V.B.
vṛt V.
çam B.S.
1 çās
çundh S.
çnath V.
çru V.
çuṣ V.
sad V.
sas V.
sah V.
sku B.
stan V.
stubh V.B
svan V.
hu V.
hū
hṛ V.

B. Earlier and Later Language. [49.]

ad
an
as
ās
i
ī
īç
kṣu B.+
gā B.E.
ghrā B.E.
cakṣ
1 jakṣ B.+
trā
dih
duh
2 drā B.+
dviṣ
dhī B.+
dhyā B.+
nij V.C.
1 nu
2 pā
plu S.E.
brū
bhā
mā
mṛj
yā
rā
1 ru B.+
rud
lih B.+
vam
vaç
2 vas
vā
1 vid
2 vid
2 çās
çiñj
çī
çvas
sū
stu
snā
snu B.+
svap
han
hnu

C. Later Language. [14.]

kū C.
khyā
glā E.
cakās C.
dad
dyu C.
dhmā C.
pad E.
mnā C.
mlā E.
lā C.
vac
vind
çuc E.

2. Reduplicating-class (hu-class, third class). [49.]

A. Earlier Language. [33.]

iyar V.B
cakṛ V.
jigā V.B.
jighṛ V.B.
ciki V.B.
didiç V.
dīdī
dīdhī V.B.
ninij V.
ninī V.B.
pipā V.B.
pīpī̆ V.B.
pipṛc V.B.
mamad V.
maman V.
2 mimā V.B.
mimikṣ V.
mimī V.B.
yayas V.
yuyu V.B.
rarā V.
vivac V.
vavaç, vivaç V.
vivic V.

viviṣ v.	siṣac v.	sisṛ v.	jihṛ s.
vavṛt v.b.	susu v.	juhū v.	juhur v.
vivyac v.			

B. Earlier and Later Language. [16.]

jighrā	1 pipṛ v.c.	bibhṛ	jahā
titṛ v.c.	2 pipṛ	1 mimā	jihī
dadā	babhas v.b.c.	çiçā	juhu
dadhā	bibhī	sasas b.c.	jihrī b.+

3. Nasal-class (rudh-class, seventh class). [29.]

A. Earlier Language. [16.]

unad	kṛṇat	tuñj v.	pṛṇac v.b.
unabh v.b.	gṛṇath v.	tund v.	bhiṣṇaj v.
ṛñj v.	chṛṇad b.	tṛṇad v.b.	mṛṇaj v.b.
ṛṇadh v.	tanac b.s.	tṛṇah v.b.	riṇac v.b.

B. Earlier and Later Language. [13.]

anaj	bhanaj	yunaj	vṛṇaj
inadh	bhinad	ruṇadh	çinaṣ b.+
chinad	bhunaj	vinac	hinas
pinaṣ			

4. nu-class (su-class, fifth class). [50.]

A. Earlier Language. [24.]

akṣṇu v.b.	jinu v.b.	1 pṛṇu s.	sadhnu b.
inu v.	takṣṇu b.s.	pruṣṇu v.	skabhnu b.
unu v.	daghnu b.	riṇu b.	skunu v.
ṛṇu v.	dabhnu v.b.	lunu b.s.	stabhnu b.
kṛṇu	dāçnu v.	saghnu v.	stighnu b.
kṣubhnu b.	pinu v.b.	sinu v.b.	spṛṇu

B. Earlier and Later Language. [22.]

açnu	dunu	rādhnu b.+	çṛṇu
āpnu	dhinu b.+	1 vṛṇu	sunu
ṛdhnu	dhūnu	ūrṇu	stunu b.c.
kṣiṇu	dhṛṣṇu	2 vṛṇu b.+	stṛṇu
1 cinu	1 minu	çaknu	hinu
tṛpṇu, -nu v.b.c.	2 minu v.c.		

C. Later Language. [4.]

2 cinu	jaghnu c.	tinu c.	2 pṛṇu c.

5. u-class (tan-class, eighth class). [8.]

The stems of this class are too few to be worth dividing by periods.

kuru V.+
kṣaṇu B.+
tanu V.+
taru V.
manu V.+
vanu V.B.S.
sanu V.B.S.
hanu S.

6. nā-class (krī-class, ninth class). [53.]

A. Earlier Language. [31.]

inī V.
iṣṇā
ubhnā V.
uṣṇā V.
kṣiṇā V.B.
2 gṛṇā V.S.
gṛbhṇā V.B
junā V.
jinā
dṛṇī B.
drūṇā V.B.
pṛṇā
pruṣṇā B.
bhrīṇā V.
mĭ̄nā V.B.
mṛṇā V.
ramṇā V.B.
riṇā
1 vṛṇī V.
vlĭ̄nā B.
çamnī B.
çcamnī V.
çrathnā V.
1 çrīṇā V.B.
2 çrīṇā V.B.
sinā V.B.
subhnā B.
skabhnā V.B.
spṛṇā B.
hṛṇā V.B.
hruṇā V.

B. Earlier and Later Language. [17.]

2 açnā
krīṇā
1 gṛṇā
grathnā B.+
gṛhṇā
jānā
punā
prīṇā
badhnā
mathnā
muṣṇā
mṛdnā S.+
lunā B.+
2 vṛṇā
çṛṇā
stabhnā
stṛṇā

C. Later Language. [5.]

1 açnī E.
kuṣṇā C.
kliçnā
dhŭ̄nī C.
puṣṇā

7. a-(unaccented)-class (bhū-class, first class). [529.]

A. Earlier Language. [175.]

akṣa V.B.
aca
añja S.
ata V.
ana V.B.
ama V.B.
inva V.
īḍa V.S.
īra V.
īrṣya B.S.
īça V.B.
īṣa V.B.
2 eṣa V.
oha V.
arça B.
arṣa V.B.
īja V.
kara V.
kṛpa V.
krakṣa V.
klatha B.
kṣada V.B.
1 kṣaya V.
kṣoda V.
kṣobha U.
kṣveda B.
kharja S.
gama V.
garda B.
gūrda B.
cata V.
cāya V.B.
1 caya V.
2 caya V.B.
ceta V.
coda V.
jana V.B.
jasa V.
jinva
java V.B.
jūrva V.
2 jara V.
jeha V.
jraya V.
taṭa B.
tanda V.
tāva V.
teja V.B.
tuñja V.
tunda V.
tūrva V.B.
toça V.
tsara
thūrva B.
dakṣa V.B.
dabha V.B.

dāsa
dāça v.
dodha v.
darpa s.
dṛṅha v.b.
dhanva v.b.
dhava v.
dhūrva v.b.
dhrăja v.b.
dhvara b.
nakṣa v.b.
nabha v.
2 naça v.
nasa v.
nādha v.
ṇikṣa v.
1 nava v.
2 nava v.
ṇeda b.
patha s.
pana v.
pāya b.
paya v.
pinva
pibda v.b.
pīya v.b.
pūya b.s.
para b.
pṛñca v.
prava
protha v.b.
bṛṅha b.
bhana v.
bhanda v.
bharva v.
bhasa v.
bhaya v.
bhūṣa v.b.
bibhra v.
bhyasa v.
bhreṣa v.b.
maṅha v.b.
manda v.b.
metha
megha v.
mīva v.b.
moṣa v.
mara v.
mṛcha b.
mrada v.b.
mardha v.
myakṣa rv.
mroca v.b.
mreḍa b.
yabha v.b.
yeṣa v.b.
yāda v.
yucha v.
yodha v.b.
raṅha v.
raṇva b.
rada v.b.
1 raṇa v.
rapa v.b.
rapça v.
ramba v
1 rāsa
repha b.
reṣa v.
2 rava b.
1 rodha v.
roṣa v.b.
reja v.b.
reḍa b.s.
laya v.b.
ukṣa v.
vañca
vata v.
vadha v.b.
vana v.
2 vapa
valha b.s.
vaça v.
vena v.b.
vrada v.
vrādha v.
1 çama v.
çāya v.
çundha
çumbha v.
çvaya v.b.
çroṣa v.
çreṣa v.
çvañca v.
çmañca b.
saca v.b.
saçca v.
sána v.
sapa v.b.
1 sarja v.b.
sādha v.
seca v.
sūrkṣa b.s.
stabha b.
stava v.
stobha
sredha v.
svāda v.
svara
sveda b.
jighna v.b.
hāsa v.
jighya b.
haya v.b.
heḍa v.
hĭḍa b.
hava v.b.
hūrcha b.
hvara v.

B. Earlier and Later Language. [212.]

añca
aja
arca
arha
ava
asa
aya
īkṣa
īṅkha b.+
īha b.+
oṣa
1 ūha
arja b.
arda
eja
edha
kampa b.+
kaṣa
kasa v.c.
kāṅkṣa b.+
kāça b.+
kūja
karṣa
kalpa
kranda
krăma
krīḍa
kroça
kvatha b.+
kṣapa
kṣama
kṣara
khana
khāda
gada s.+
gacha
garha
gāha
gūha
gṛhṇa b.+
grasa
ghoṣa
jighra
cakṣa
căma b.+
cara
cala
ceṣṭa
cyava
cyota s.+
chanda b.e.
jaksa b.+

C. Later Language. [142.]

kuñca c.
kuñja c.
kūṇa c.
kūrda
karta e.
klanda c.
klinda c.
kvaṇa c.
2 kṣaya
kṣveḍa
kṣvela e.
khaca c.
khañja c.
khalla c.
khela
garja
gala c.
galbha c.
guñja c.
gopa c.
gumpha c.
glaha e.
ghaṭa
ghūrṇa
gharṣa
caka c.
cakāça
cañca c.
caṭa c.
cinva c.
copa e.
cumba
chaya c.
chinda c.
jhaṇa c.
jhara c.
ṭala c.
ṭīka c.
ḍama c.
ḍamba c.
ḍaya c.
ḍhāuka c.
tarja
tarpa e.
trapa
tvañga c.
dañça c.
dala
deva
dunva e.
dhukṣa e.
dhvana c.
naṭa c.
naha e.
paṭa c.
parda c.
poṣa c.
pūja e.
ploṣa c.
phakka c.
phaṇa c.
1 phala
2 phala
bandha
badhna e.
bhakṣa
bhaṣa
bibhya
mathna e.
mārga
moṭa c.
mrakṣa c.
mārja
marda
yama
rañga c.
rañja
raṭa c.
2 raṇa c.
1 rambha
2 rambha c.
2 rāsa
riñkha c.
riñga c.
roṭha e.
2 rodha e.
lakṣa
laga
lañgha c.
laḍa c.
lambha e.
lala
laṣa
lasa
luṇṭha e.
lobha c.
lola c.
vama
vala c.
vāha c.
veja e.
vīja
vyaja c.
vṛñha
vella c.
1 vyaya c.
vraṇa c.
vraçca c.
vrīḍa
2 çama e.
çala c.
çaça c.
çāsa
çeṣa c.
çlatha c.
çrama
çrambha
sa e.
sava
stambha c
stara
sparça c.
svana e.
hada c.
jaghna e.
hikka c.
hiṇḍa c.
hela e.
hreṣa
hlāda c.

8. á-(accented)-class (tud-class, sixth class). [142.]

A. Earlier Language. [72.]

ana v.
iṭa v.b.
2 iṣa v.
unda b.s.
ubja
umbha v.b.
ṛṇva v.
ra v.
ṛñja v.b.
ṛda v.
ṛṣa
kuva b.
kṣiya v.b.
khada b.
khuda v.
gṛṇa v.
cṛta
chya v.b.
jura v.
tila b.
tuja v.
tira
tura v.b.
tṛmpa
tviṣa v.
1 dya
2 dya v.b.
dṛbha b.
dṛñha v.
dhŭva v.b.
piñça v.b.
pīṣa v.
pṛṇa v.b.
pruṣa v.
bṛha v.b.
bhura v.
mima b.
mitha v.
mina v.
muca v.b.

B. Earlier and Later Language. [53.]

C. Later Language. [17.]

9. ya-class (div-class, fourth class). [133.]

A. Earlier Language. [41.]

B. Earlier and Later Language. [64.]

asya	dīpya	bhraçya s.+	vaya
īya	dī̆vya	mādya b.+	vāçya v.e.
2 iṣya	duṣya b.+	manya	vidhya
ṛdhya	dṛpya	mīya	2 vyaya
krudhya	druhya b.+	muhya	çāmya b.+
kṣudhya	dhaya	mṛṣya	çudhya b.+
gāya	dhyāya b.+	mlāya b.+	çuṣya
gṛdhya	naçya	yasya	çyāya b.c.
glāya	nahya	yudhya	çrāmya
jāya	nṛtya	rajya	çliṣya b.+
jīrya	padya	rādhya	sidhya
tapya b.+	paçya	ricya b.e.	sīvya
tāmya b.+	puṣya	riṣya	sūya b.+
tuṣya s.+	pyāya	līya	styāya b.c.
tṛpya	prī̆ya b.+	lubhya	hvaya
trāya	budhya	vāya	hṛṣya

C. Later Language. [28.]

āsya e.	kṣubhya	dahya e.	bhrāmya
1 iṣya	ghuṣya c.	1 dāya e.	ruṣya
kupya	ḍīya c.	2 dāya c.	lapya e.
klāmya c.	timya c.	diçya e.	sahya e.
klidya	trasya	duhya	snāya e.
kliçya	truṭya, -ḍya c.	drāya	snihya
kṣamya	tviṣya c.	dhāya b.	svidya

II. PERFECT-STEMS. [473.]

The variety of stem-forms is not given, except in the case of medial e from a. The rare intensive and desiderative simple perfects are included in the list.

A. Earlier Language. [169.]

ākṣ v.	3 īṣ v.	cikrī s.	cicyu v.
ac b.	ūc v.	cakṣad v.	cachand v.
aj v.	ūd v.	jugur v.	jajas v.
ānaj v.b.	uvoṣ b.	1 jagṛ b.	jijinv v.
ān v.	ūh v.	jagṛbh	jūju v.
ām, em v.b.	ānṛj v.	jagras v.	jajṛ v.
ānṛh v.e.	ānṛdh v.b.	jaghas v.b.	jujur v.
1 āç v.	ānṛṣ b.	jughuṣ b.	jijyā b.
īdh v.b.	cā̆kan rv.	1 ciki b.	tatas rv.
2 īṣ v.	cakā	cikit	tatam b.
īr v.	cakṛp v.	cacṛt v.	titij b.s.
īç v.	cakṛç v.	cucyu v.	tūtu v.

B. Earlier and Later Language. [191.]

tatṛ, ter	babādh	lalabh, lebh	çiçri
tatṛd v.c.	bubudh	lilikh b.+	çuçru
tătṛp v.e.	babhaj, bhej	lilip b.+	çiçliṣ b.+
dadaç v.e.	babhañj	lilī b.+	sasañj, sej b.+
dadah, deh b.+	babhāṣ b.+	lulup b.+	sasad, sed
1 dadā	bibhid	lulubh s.+	săsah, seh
didiç	bĭbhī	uvac	siṣic
didīkṣ b.c.	2 bubhuj	vavand	1 siṣidh
duduh	băbhū	uvap	suṣu
dadṛ	babhṛ	vavam, vem b.+	suṣū
dadṛç	mamath, meth	văvas v.c.	sasṛ
didyut	maman, men	2 uvas	sasṛj
1 dadrā v.c.	1 mamā	uvah	sasṛp b.+
dudru b.c.	2 mimī v.c.	vavā b.+	caskand
dudruh	mumuc	2 văvaç	caskambh v.c.
1 dadhā	mumud	vivij	tastambh
dudhū	mumuh b.+	vid	tuṣṭu
dădhṛ	mamṛ	2 vivid	tastṛ
dadhyā b.+	mămṛj	viviç	tasthā
dadhvas	mămṛç	1 vavṛ	paspṛdh
nănam, nem	mamṛṣ v.e.	2 vavṛ	paspṛç
nanaç, neç	īj, yej	văvṛt	siṣmi
ninind	yayam, yem	văvṛdh	sasraṅs b.c.
ninī	yayā	văvṛṣ	susru
nunud	yayāc b.+	vavṛh	sasvaj
papac, pec	yūyuj	vivyadh b.+	suṣvap
papat, pet	yuyudh	vavraj	siṣvid v.b.
papad, ped	rărakṣ	çaçaṅs b.+	jaghan
papā	rărabh, rebh	çaçak, çek	1 jahā
pipiṣ	raram, rem b.+	çaçap, çep	jighi b.+
pupuṣ	ruru b.e.	2 çaçam, çem b.+	juhu
paprach b.+	ruruc	çaçās	juhū
paprath	ruruj	çiçī b.+	jahṛ
puplu b.+	rurudh	çuçuc	jăhṛṣ
babandh, bedh	ruruh	çaçram, çrem.	

C. Later Language. [113.]

ānarch e.	cukūrd c.	jagarj	jughūrṇ
edh c.	2 cakṛ e.	jagarh	jaghṛṣ c.
cakamp e.	cukruç c.	jagalbh c.	jaghrā c.
cakas c.	caklam c.	jagāh c.	cacaṭ c.
cakāṅkṣ	cikliç c.	juguh	cacam, cem b.
cakāç	cakṣar c.	jajāgṛ	cacal, cel
cukuc c.	cukṣud b.	jaghaṭ c.	cucumb
cukūj c.	jagad	jaghaṭṭ b.	ciceṣṭ b.

cachṛd C.
jajap, jep E.
jajalp E.
jajṛmbh
ḍuḍhāuk C.
tataḍ C.
tutuṣ
tatyaj
tatras, tres
tutruṭ C.
tatvar
didih E.
didīp C.
2 dadrā C.
dadhmā E.
dadhāv C.
dadhvan C.
nanad, ned
nanand
nanard E.
nunu C.
nanṛt
papaṭh C.
pupūj E.
pupūr C.
paphal E.
phel C.
babhaṇ C.
babhā
babhās
babhram, bhrem
babhrāj
mamajj
mamanth
mimil C.
mimiṣ C.
mimīl C.
mumuṣ C.
mumūrch
mamṛd
mamlā
raras, res
rarāj, rej
rarās C.
rurud E.
lalajj C.
lalap, lep
lalam C.
lalamb
lalaṣ, leṣ C.
lalas C.
luluñc
luluṭh C.
lulū C.
lulok C.
luloc C.
vavap E.
vaval C.
vavalg E.
vavah
1 vivid C.
vivyaj E.
vavṛṅh C.
vivyath
çiçikṣ *desid.* C.
3 çem C.
çaças E.
çuçubh
çaçlāgh C.
çaçvas
sasā S.
siṣev
caskhal
sasnā C.
pusphuṭ C.
sasmṛ E.
sasyand C.
sasvad C.
sasvan
jahas
jiheṣ C.
jihrī C.

III. AORIST-STEMS. [737.]

From stems with *p.* added, only optative or «precative» forms occur.

1. Root-aorist. [140.]

Simply the root is given. The passive-aorist third persons will be found further on, under VII.

A. Earlier Language. [112.]

ad *p.* B.
av *p.*
aç
āp *p.* B.
idh V.
uh *p.* B.
ṛ V.B.
ṛdh
kṛp V.
kram V.
gam
gur V.
gṛ V.
grabh V.B.
ghas
ghrā *p.* S.
1 ci V.
2 ci V.
cit V.B.
cyu V.
chid V.
jan B.S.
jīv *p.*
jñā *p.* V.
tan V.B.
tap V.
tṛd V.S.
tṛp *p.* B.
dagh V.
dabh V.
dī̆ B.
2 dṛ B.
dyut V.B.
2 dhā V.
dhṛ V.
naç V.B.
nas *p.* V.
nid V.B.
nṛt V.
pad V.
spaç V.
piç V.
pṛ V.
pṛc V.S.
prath V.
prā V.B.
budh V.
bhid V.B.
bhī
bhuj V.
bhram *p.* S.
bhrāj V.
majj *p.* B.
mand V.
man V.B.
muc V.B.
mud *p.* V.
mṛ
mṛṇ *p.* B.
mṛd *p.* B.S.
mṛdh *p.* V.
mṛṣ V.
myakṣ V.
yat V.

yam v.	vadh p.	ças v.b.	sṛj v.
yu v.b.	van v.	çak v.	skand v.b.
yuj v.b.	1 vas v.	çā v.	stṛ v.b.
ram v.	2 vas	çubh v.	spṛ v.
rāj p. s.	vah p. s.	çri v.	spṛdh v.
rādh	vij v.b.	çvit v.	sras b.
ric v.	vip v.	sagh v.	svap p. s.
riṣ b.	viṣ v.	sac v.	svid p. s.
ruc v.b.	viç v.	sah v.	hi v.s.
ruj b.	1 vṛ v.	sā, sĭ v.b.	hū v.
vac p. b.	vṛj v.	sic p. b.s.	hṛ b.
vad p. b.s.	vṛt v.b.	su v.	hrī v.

B. Earlier and Later Language. [18.]

i p. b.+	dā	bhū	2 vṛ
kṛ	dṛç	bhṛ b.c.	çru
gā	1 dhā, dhĭ, hi	yudh v.c.	sthā
ji p. b.e.	pā	rudh v.b.c.	hā b.c.
juṣ	puṣ p. b.c.		

C. Later Language. [10.]

as p. e.	dah p. e.	piṣ c.	brū p. e.
kir p. c.	1 dṛ p. c.	prī p. c.	spṛç p. e.
jā p.	nud p.		

2. a-aorist. [86.]

A. Earlier Language. [61.]

aça v.	tṛpa v.b.	budha v.	vya v.
ara v.b.	tṛṣa v.b.	bhida v.	çama b.
ṛdha v.b.	tṛha v.	bhuja v.	1 çiṣa v.b.
kara	dagha b.	bhuva v.b.	2 çiṣa v.b.
kṛta v.	dasa	bhraça v.b.	çva b.
krada v.	da v.b.	muca v.	çrama v.
krama v.b.	duṣa b.	muha b.	çruva b.
kṣudha v.	dṛpa b.	mṛdha s.	çriṣa v.
khya	dṛça v.b.	mruca b.	sana
guha v.	dha v.	radha v.	sara v.b.
gṛdha v.b.	dhṛṣa v.b.	riṣa	sṛpa v.b.
gṛha v.b.	dhvasa v.	ruda v.b.	stha v.b.
ghasa b.	nija v.s.	vida	sridha v.
tasa v.b.	nṛta v.	vṛdha	hya v.
tana v.	puṣa	vṛṣa b.	hva v.b.
tama			

B. Earlier and Later Language. [18.]

astha
āpa
krudha
gama
chida
dyuta b.+
druha v.e.
mṛṣa
yuja v.c.
rudha
ruha
voca
vṛta
çaka
çuca
săda
sica
srasa

C. Later Language. [7.]

naça
yasa c.
rica c.
ruca c.
lipa c.
çliṣa
hṛṣa e.

3. Reduplicated Aorist. [154.]

A. Earlier Language. [101.]

amama v.b.
āpipa b.
cīkama b.
cīkṛta b.
cīkṛṣa v.
cikrada v.b.
cukrudha v.
cikṣipa v.
jīgama v.b.
jŭ̄gupa b.s.
1 jīgṛ v.
2 jĭ̄gṛ v.
jigrabha b.
jīghasa b.
cīcata b.
cucyava v.b.
cucyu v.
jījabha v.
jījasa b.
jajas v.
tataṅsa v.
tītara v.
tītṛṣa v.b.
titrasa v.
dadakṣa b.
didīkṣa b.
dūduṣa v.
didyuta v.b.
dudru v.
dadhāv v.
dīdhara
dĭ̄dhṛ v.
neç v.b.
nūnu v.
pīpata v.
papta
pīpada v.b.
pūpura v.b.
1 pīpara v.
2 pīpara v.b.
papratha v.
piplava b.
būbudha v.
babhakṣa b.
bībhaj b.
bībhaya v.
bibhīṣa v.b.
būbhuva v.
mīmada v.b.
mīmī v.
mīmiṣa b.
mūmuha v.b.
mīmṛṇa v.
mīmṛja b.
mīmṛṣa v.
yīyaja b.
yūyu v.
yūyupa b.
1 rīradha v.
rīrama v.
rīrica b.s.
rūruca v.b.
rūrupa v.b.
līlikha b.
lūlubha b.
vavakṣa v.
vīvata v.
vīvasa b.
vīvaça v.
vīvija v.
vīvipa v.
vīvara v.
vāvṛ v.
vīvṛta v.
vivyatha b.
çūçuca v.b.
çūçubha v.b.
cuçcuta s.
çiçnath v.
çiçratha v.b.
çiçrī v.
çuçruva v.b.
çaçvaca v.
çiçvita v.
sīṣada b.
sīṣapa v.
sīṣadha v.b.
suṣu b.
suṣū b.
sūṣuda b.
sīsṛpa b.
tuṣṭava v.b.
pispṛça v.
siṣyada v.
sisrasa v.b.
susru v.b.
sasvaja v.
siṣvada v.b.
siṣvap v.
jīhiḍa v.
jĭ̄hvara v.b.

B. Earlier and Later Language. [17.]

cīkḷpa
cīcara
jījana
tītapa v.e.
tītṛpa
didīpa v.c.
dīdipa b.e.
dīdṛça b.+
dudruva b.+
nīnama v.c.
nīnaça
mīmara b.c.
2 rīradha b.c.
rīriṣa
vīvṛdha
çīçama
çiçriya

C. Later Language. [30.]

cīkasa c.
cīkara c.
jigraha c.
cūcuda e.
cūcura c.
cachada c.
cichida e.
jījaya e.
titvara e.
dīdaha c.
dūduha c.
dīdara
pīpiṣa e.
bībhara e.
bibhrama e.
mimīla c.
mūmuca c.
mīmṛda e.
yūyuja
yūyudha e.
rīraca c.
rūruva c.
rūruja c.
lūlupa e.
vīviça c.
vīvṛṣa e.
vīvidha e.
çīçaya e.
jīghana
jījaha c.

Here appended are the reduplicated aorists from causative stems in **p.** [6.]

arpipa v.
jījapa, jījipa b.
jijñapa, jijñipa b.c.
çiçrapa b.
tiṣṭhipa v.b.
jīhipa v.

4. s-aorist. [145.]

A. Earlier Language. [99.]

akṣ v.b.
kīrṣ b.
2 **kārṣ** v.
krānts v.b.
kraṁs
kṣārṣ v.
1 **kṣeṣ** v.
2 **kṣeṣ**
khāṅs b.
gas v.b.
gās v.
cārṣ b.s.
cāiṣ b.
cāits v.
cyoṣ v.b.
chānts v.
jñās v.b.
tāṅs, tas v.b.
tāps
trās v.b.
tsārṣ v.
2 **diṣ** p. v.
3 **diṣ** v.
dikṣ v.
dhukṣ v.b.
darṣ v.
dṛṣ b.
dyāuts v.b.
1 **drās** v.
2 **drās** b.
dhās v.
dhūṣ v.s.
dhūrṣ v.
naṁs v.b.
nāikṣ v.
nūṣ v.b.
nuts v.b.
pakṣ v.
pats v.b.
1 **pās** v.
2 **pās** v.
parṣ v.b.
1 **prākṣ**
prās v.b.
prāiṣ v.b.
proṣ s.
ploṣ b.
bhits b.
bhārṣ v.b.
mats
mas p. v.
mās v.
meṣ
mṛkṣ p. v.
mārkṣ b.
yakṣ
yaṁs
yās v.
yāuṣ
raps v.
rās v.b.
rāts
rāikṣ v.b.
rukṣ b.
laps b.s.
leṣ b.
lops p. b.
vaṅs, vas p. v.b.
vāṁs b.
1 **vāts** v.
vakṣ
vits v.b.
vikṣ v.
varṣ v.
vṛṣ v.b.
vārkṣ v.b.
vyāts b.
vṛkṣ b.s.
vleṣ s.
çāps b.s.
çeṣ v.
çrāiṣ v.
çvāits v.
1 **sakṣ** v.
2 **sakṣ** v.b.
sats v.
sākṣ v.b.
sarṣ v.
sṛps b.s.
skānts b.s.
stāmps b.
stṛṣ v.b.
spārṣ v.
syānts v.
svārṣ v.
ghāṅs s.
hāiṣ v.b.
hūṣ v.
hvārṣ b.

B. Earlier and Later Language. [37.]

1 **kārṣ** b.+
gaṁs s.+
gīṣ b.+
chāits
jāiṣ
tārṣ s.+
dhākṣ
dās, diṣ

drākṣ
dhiṣ B.+
nāiṣ
2 prākṣ
bhuts
bhakṣ
bhāiṣ
mǎṅs
māukṣ
yokṣ
yots
raṁs V.C.
rāuts
lips V.C.
vāps B.+
2 vāts
vṛts
çrāuṣ B.+
sāñkṣ B.+
soṣ B.+
srākṣ
stāuṣ
sthiṣ B.+
sprākṣ B.E.
svāps S.+
1 hās V.B.E.
2 hās
hāuṣ B.+
hārṣ

C. Later Language. [9.]

āps E.
ceṣ C.
tyākṣ
drokṣ E.
dhyās E.
bhāñkṣ
vāits C.
sāits C.
smārṣ E.

5. iṣ-aorist. [174.]

A. Earlier Language. [123.]

akṣiṣ V.
ajiṣ S.
añjiṣ B.
aniṣ V.
aviṣ
āsiṣ B.S.
indhiṣ B.
idhiṣ S.
1 iṣiṣ B.
īkṣiṣ B.
ukṣiṣ B.
uṣiṣ B.S.
1 ūhiṣ B.
2 ūhiṣ V.
artiṣ B.
ardhiṣ B.
edhiṣ *p.* V.B.
kāniṣ V.
1 kāriṣ V.
2 kāriṣ V.
kartiṣ B.
krapiṣ V.
krǎmiṣ V.B.
kṣaṇiṣ V.
gamiṣ V.B.
gāriṣ V.
grabhīṣ V.B.
caniṣ V.
cāriṣ
cāyiṣ V.
cayiṣ V.
codiṣ V.
japiṣ B.
jambhiṣ V.
joṣiṣ V.
jūrviṣ V.
jāriṣ V.
takṣiṣ V.S.
tāniṣ B.
tāriṣ
trāsiṣ B.
tsāriṣ B.
dambhiṣ
dāsiṣ V.
dadiṣ V.
dīkṣiṣ B.
doṣiṣ B.
dṛṅhiṣ B.
dhanviṣ V.B.
dhāyiṣ V.
1 dhāviṣ B.
2 dhāviṣ V.
dhinviṣ B.
dhūrviṣ B.
dharṣiṣ B.
dhrājiṣ *p.* B.
dhvaniṣ V.
nindiṣ V.S.
naviṣ V.
nudiṣ V.
nartiṣ V.
paniṣ V.
paviṣ V.B.
pūriṣ B.
pāriṣ V.
pyāyiṣ *p.* S.
prathiṣ V.
bādhiṣ V.B.
bhaviṣ B.
mathiṣ V.B.
manthiṣ V.
mandiṣ V.B.
modiṣ *p.* V.
moṣiṣ V.B.
mārjiṣ B.
mardhiṣ V.B.
marṣiṣ V.
yatiṣ B.
yamiṣ V.
1 yāviṣ V.
2 yāviṣ V.
yodhiṣ V.
randhiṣ V.
rǎṇiṣ V.
rājiṣ V.
rādhiṣ V.B.
1 rāviṣ V.
2 rāviṣ V.B.
lekhiṣ B.S.
leçiṣ B.
āukṣiṣ V.
vaniṣ V.B.
vandiṣ *p.* V.
vasiṣ V.
vāçiṣ B.
vepiṣ B.S.
veçiṣ V.
veṣiṣ V.
vāriṣ B.
varṣiṣ V.B.
barhiṣ V.
vrājiṣ B.
çamiṣ V.
çociṣ B.
çariṣ V.B.
çnathiṣ V.
çramiṣ V.B.
ṣṭhaviṣ B.S.
sādiṣ B.
sǎniṣ V.
sǎhiṣ V.
sāviṣ V.B.
stāniṣ V.
stambhiṣ V.
stāviṣ B.S.
stariṣ V.
sphariṣ V.
sraṅsiṣ B.
srāviṣ B.
svāniṣ V.
svāriṣ B.
hāniṣ B.
hīḍiṣ B.

B. Earlier and Later Language. [21.]

açiṣ	**nā̆yiṣ** v.s.c.	**rociṣ** b.+	**vyathiṣ**
grahīṣ	**bodhiṣ** v.c.	**vā̆diṣ**	**çaṅsiṣ**
janiṣ	**mādiṣ**	**vadhiṣ**	**çayiṣ**
jayiṣ b.c.	**yāciṣ**	**vediṣ** b.+	**sedhiṣ** v.b.
jīviṣ	**rā̆kṣiṣ**	**vardhiṣ** b.+	**hiṅsiṣ**
jvā̆liṣ b.+			

C. Later Language. [16.]

2 iṣiṣ	**grasiṣ** c.	**majjiṣ** e.	**çaṅkiṣ**
ujhiṣ c.	**daliṣ** c.	**rāudiṣ** c.	**çvasiṣ** c.
kopiṣ e.	**deviṣ** e.	**vaçiṣ** e.	**sthāyiṣ** c.
krandiṣ c.	**bhāṣiṣ** c.	**vartiṣ** e.	**smayiṣ** e.

Here are added, without classification by periods, the **iṣ**-aorists from desiderative and causative conjugation-stems. [14.]

īpsiṣ b.	**cikīrṣiṣ** b.	**jijñāsiṣ** b.	**mīmāṅsiṣ** b.
īrtsiṣ v.	**cikitsiṣ** v.	**dhitsiṣ** b.	**jighāṅsiṣ** b.
ilayiṣ v.	**pyāyayiṣ** b.		
dhvanayiṣ v.	**vyathayiṣ** v.	**ghātayiṣ** v.	**hlādayiṣ** c.

6. siṣ-aorist. [19.]

In this aorist and the one following, the numbers being so small, the headings of the divisions are omitted. From those of the **siṣ**-stems that are followed by a question, no forms have been met with that might not belong to the **s**-aorist (2d and 3d singular).

gāsiṣ v.b.	**dhyāsiṣ** b.	**bhukṣiṣ** *p.* b.s.	**vaṅsiṣ** *p.* v.
jyāsiṣ b.	**pyāsiṣ** *p.* v.b.s.	**raṁsiṣ** v.	**vāsiṣ**? b.
drāsiṣ? b.			**hvāsiṣ**? b. [10.]
jñāsiṣ b.+	**yāsiṣ** v.+	**hāsiṣ** v.+	[3.]
glāsiṣ? e.	**dhmāsiṣ**? c.	**naṁsiṣ**? c.	**mnāsiṣ** c. [6.]
		pāsiṣ? c.	**mlāsiṣ**? e.

7. sa-aorist. [19.]

kṛkṣa b.	**dṛkṣa** b.	**pikṣa** b.	**likṣa** s.
krukṣa v.b.	**drukṣa** b.	**mikṣa** b.	**1 vṛkṣa** v.b.
ghukṣa v.b.	**dvikṣa** v.	**rukṣa** v.b.s.	**2 vṛkṣa** b.
dhikṣa b.			**spṛkṣa** v.b. [14.]
dikṣa b.c.	**dhukṣa, du-** v.+	**1 mṛkṣa** v.+	**vikṣa** b.c.
		2 mṛkṣa v.b.	[5.

IV. FUTURE STEMS. [347.]

1a. Sibilant Future without i. [131.]

If from any root there are made both a future-stem without and one with i, each of the stems has a + prefixed to it.

A. Earlier Language. [46.]

atsya B.S.	2 dāsya S.	mekṣya	varkṣya B.
+ arkṣya B.	+ drapsya B.	2 meṣya B.	vrakṣya B.
+ kartsya V.	drāsya B.	mrakṣya B.	vleṣya B.
+ krakṣya B.S.	droṣya B.	mārkṣya B.S.	çatsya V.
+ klapsya B.	dhrokṣya B.	mlāsya B.	çekṣya B.
kreṣya B.S.	+ naṁsya B.	yapsya B.S.	+ satsya B.S.
1 kṣeṣya V.	pekṣya B.	+ yaṁsya B.	+ 1 soṣya S.
+ 2 kṣeṣya B.	ploṣya B.	rātsya	sarpsya B.
cyoṣya B.	+ bhantsya B.S.	rekṣya B.	skantsya B.
jyāsya B.	+ bhakṣya B.	+ vapsya B.S.	syantsya B.
taṅsya B.	bheṣya B.	1 vatsya B.	+ hvāsya S.
trapsya B.	1 meṣya B.		

B. Earlier and Later Language. [59.]

āpsya B.+	drakṣya B.+	yakṣya	çakṣya B.+
+ eṣya	1 dhāsya B.+	yāsya	çroṣya B.+
+ kraṁsya	+ neṣya	yokṣya	+ săkṣya
khyāsya B.+	notsya B.E.	yotsya B.+	sekṣya B.E.
gāsya B.+	pakṣya B.+	raṁsya B.+	+ 2 soṣya B.+
gopsya	patsya B.+	rotsya B.+	sūṣya V.C.
1 ceṣya B.+	pāsya B.+	+ rokṣya B.+	srakṣya B.+
chetsya B.+	prakṣya E.+	+ lapsya B.+	srapsya B.+
+ jeṣya	bhotsya B.E.	1 vakṣya	+ stoṣya B.+
jñāsya B.+	bhāsya B.+	+ 3 vatsya B.+	sthāsya B.+
+ tapsya B.+	bhetsya B.+	+ 2 vakṣya	+ svapsya B.+
trāsya B.+	bhokṣya S.+	2 vetsya B.+	1 hāsya
+ dhakṣya	+ mañkṣya B.+	2 vekṣya B.+	2 hāsya B.E.
1 dāsya	+ maṅsya B.+	3 vekṣya B.+	hoṣya
dekṣya S.+	mokṣya B.+	+ 1 vartsya	

C. Later Language. [26.]

+ kṣaṁsya E.	dhyāsya E.	1 vekṣya C.	+ 1 setsya E.
kṣepsya	+ nañkṣya E.+	+ 1 vetsya	2 setsya
2 ceṣya E.	bhañkṣya E.	2 vartsya C.	snāsya
jāsya E.	+ rakṣya E.	3 vetsya E.	sprakṣya E.
+ tyakṣya E.	rapsya	+ çeṣya E.	+ haṅsya E.
dhokṣya C.	2 vatsya C.	siṣya E.	heṣya E.+
2 dhāsya E.	vāsya C.		

1b. Sibilant Future with i. [158.]

The prefixed sign + shows that from the same root is also made a future-stem without i.

A. Earlier Language. [44.]

aniṣya B.	kaṣiṣya B.	+ darpiṣya B.	+ vediṣya B.
aviṣya V.B.	+ karṣiṣya B.	dyotiṣya B.	variṣya B.
açnuviṣya B.	+ khyāyiṣya B.	dhaviṣya B.S.	vyayiṣya S.
indhiṣya S.	1 gariṣya S.	proṣiṣya B.	çaṅsiṣya B.S.
eṣiṣya B.	gardhiṣya B.	manthiṣya B.S.	çasiṣya B.
īçiṣya B.	granthiṣya B.	+ maniṣya V.B.	çariṣya B.
ukṣiṣya B.S.	japiṣya B.	mohiṣya B.	saniṣya V.B.
ariṣya B.	jinviṣya B.	mardiṣya B.	+ 1 saviṣya B.
artiṣya V.	dakṣiṣya B.	mradiṣya B.	+ staviṣya V.
ardhiṣya B.	daghiṣya B.	vaniṣya S.	+ hvayiṣya B.
kamiṣya B.	dadiṣya B.	vayiṣya V.	hvadiṣya B.

B. Earlier and Later Language. [43.]

açiṣya B.+	grahīṣya B.+	patiṣya	vrajiṣya B.+
asiṣya	cariṣya B.+	bhaviṣya	çāsiṣya B.+
āsiṣya B.+	janiṣya	bhariṣya	+ çayiṣya B.+
+ ayiṣya B.+	+ jayiṣya B.E.	mathiṣya B.+	çrayiṣya B.+
īkṣiṣya B.+	jīviṣya B.+	miliṣya B.+	sariṣya
1 kariṣya	jvaliṣya B.+	mariṣya	stariṣya B.C.
+ kramiṣya B.+	tariṣya S.+	yatiṣya B.+	+ svapiṣya V.E.
+ kṣamiṣya B.+	dīkṣiṣya B.+	yāciṣya B.+	+ haniṣya
khaniṣya B.+	dhariṣya	lapiṣya B.+	hiṅsiṣya B.+
gamiṣya	+ naçiṣya	vadiṣya	hariṣya B.+
2 gariṣya B.C.	+ nayiṣya B.+	varṣiṣya B.E.	

C. Later Language. [71.]

aṭiṣya E.	jvariṣya E.	+ bandhiṣya	rodiṣya C.
+ arciṣya C.	+ tapiṣya E.	bādhiṣya	+ rohiṣya E.
2 kariṣya E.	+ tyajiṣya	+ bhajiṣya E.+	lagiṣya C.
+ kartiṣya C.	trasiṣya E.	bhāṣiṣya C.	+ labhiṣya C.
+ kalpiṣya C.	daçiṣya E.	bhikṣiṣya E.	lambiṣya
krīḍiṣya C.	daliṣya C.	bhramiṣya C.	laṣiṣya C.
+ kṣayiṣya E.	+ dahiṣya	bhrājiṣya E.	likhiṣya C.
khādiṣya E.	deviṣya	+ majjiṣya E.	luṇṭhiṣya C.
gadiṣya E.	dhamiṣya	mārgiṣya E.	vadhiṣya
gāhiṣya	dhāviṣya C.	modiṣya E.	+ vapiṣya
grasiṣya	nandiṣya B.	+ yamiṣya C.	+ vasiṣya E.
glahīṣya E.	+ namiṣya C.	+ rakṣiṣya B.	+ vahiṣya
ghaṭiṣya C.	nartiṣya C.	raciṣya C.	vijiṣya, vej-
caliṣya	phaliṣya	rociṣya E.	+ vartiṣya

çapiṣya E.
çociṣya
çobhiṣya E.
çvasiṣya E.
+ sīdiṣya C.
+ sahiṣya
+ sedhiṣya C.
+ 2 saviṣya
seviṣya E.
sphuṭiṣya E.
smariṣya E.
sraviṣya E.
svajiṣya E.
hasiṣya
jahiṣya

2. Periphrastic Future. [58.]

A. Earlier Language. [18.]

āptā B.
ardhitā B.
kamitā B.
jñātā B.
dhātā B.
dhyātā B.
paktā B.
bhartā B.
mraṣṭā B.
yaṣṭā B.
yuvitā B.
yoktā B.
voḍhā B.
veditā B.
vartitā B.
vraṣṭā B.
sotā B.
sraṣṭā B.

B. Earlier and Later Language. [10.]

etā B. +
kartā S. +
gaṁtā B. +
janitā B. +
jetā B.E.
dātā B.E.
bhavitā B.E.
vaktā B. +
çayitā B.C.
hartā B.E.

C. Later Language. [30.]

avitā C.
grahītā E.
ghaṭṭitā E.
cetā E.
tāyitā C.
taptā E.
draṣṭā E.
dhartā C.
naçitā E.
ninditā E.
netā, nayitā E.
patitā E.
bhañktā E.
bhoktā E.
mathitā E.
yātā
yoddhā E.
rakṣitā
rātā C.
labdhā B.
vettā E.
veṣṭā E.
veddhā E.
çramitā E.
çrotā E.
soḍhā
sthātā
smartā E.
svaptā E.
hantā E.

V. SECONDARY CONJUGATION-STEMS. [1153.]

1. Passive Stems. [259.]

For causative passives etc., see under VI.

A. Earlier Language. [37.]

1 ajya V.
amya B.
ṛcya V.
udya V.
krūḍya B.
gupya B.
ghriya B.
cāyya B.
cṛtya B.
2 jīya V.B.
tāyya B.
tujya V.
tṛhya V.
dabhya V.
dadya V.
nidya V.
panya V.
piçya V.
psīya B.
madya V.
3 mīya V.
4 mīya B.
mūrya B.
riphya S.
ribhya V.
ūya B.S.
1 vīya V.B.
vṛjya
vṛhya B.
2 vīya B.
vṛçcya V.B.
vlīya B.
2 çīya B.
sadya B.
skūya B.
striya B.
sphīya B.

B. Earlier and Later Language. [105.]

acya
2 ajya
adya B.+
açya
asya
āpya B.+
idhya
īkṣya S.+
ukṣya B.+
ū̆hya B.+
ṛdhya
kriya
kīrya B.+
kṛtya
kṛṣya B.+
kramya S.+
krīya B.+
kṣīya
khāya B.+
khyāya B.+
gamya
gīya
guhya
gṛhya
carya B.+
1 cīya B.+
chidya
jīvya B.+
jñāya
tāya
tapya
dahya
1 dīya
2 dīya
dūya B.+
duhya
dīrya B.+
driya B.+
dṛçya
dhamya
dhmāya B.+
dhīya
dhūya
dhriya
dhvasya B.C.
namya B.+
nīya
pacya
pīya
piṣya B.+
pūya
pūrya B.+
pṛcya
pṛchya
badhya
1 bhajya
2 bhajya
bhidya B.+
2 bhujya B.+
bhūya B.+
bhriya
mathya
mucya
mriya
mṛjya
mṛdya B.+
yamya
yujya
rakṣya B.+
ricya
rudhya
labhya B.+
likhya S.+
lipya B.+
lupya
ucya
vacya
udya
upya
uhya
vicya
2 vidya
viṣya B.+
2 vriya S.C.
1 çasya
2 çasya B.+
2 çiṣya
çīrya
çrī̆ya B.+
çrūya
sajya B.+
sicya
1 sūya
2 sūya
sṛjya
stūya
stīrya S.+
sthīya B.+
smarya B.+
hanya
1 hīya
hiṅsya
1 hūya
2 hūya
hriya

C. Later Language. [117.]

āsya
īya C.
iṣya
īḍya C.
uṣya C.
kucya C.
kruçya E.
kṣamya
kṣipya
khanya
khādya C.
khidya
gadya
garhya C.
gāhya
gīrya E.
grathya C.
grasya E.
ghuṣya
ghṛṣya
ghrāya C.
cakṣya
carvya C.
2 cīya C.
cumbya C.
cūṣya C.
japya E.
jalpya C.
1 jīya
jīrya C.
jvarya C.
ḍīya C.
tanya C.
tudya
tīrya E.
tyajya
trāya C.
daçya E.
diçya
dihya C.
dhāvya C.
dhyāya C.
nadya E.
nandya C.
nahya C.
nāthya C.
nijya
nindya C.
nūya
nṛtya C.
paṭhya
paṇya E.
puṭya C.
puṣya C.
priya
pluṣya C.
bādhya
budhya C.
bhaṇya C.
bhāṣya

1 bhujya c.
bhṛjjya
manya c.
1 mīya
2 mīya c.
mīlya c.
muṣya
mṛçya
mṛṣya e.
mnāya c.
ijya
yatya c.
yāya e.
yācya
yudhya
rajya c.
rabhya
ramya
rādhya c.
rujya b.
rudya c.
ruhya e.
lapya c.
lambya
lihya e.
vaṇṭya c.
vadhya
vandya
uṣya
vāñchya c.
vāçya c.
1 vidya c.
viçya c.
1 vriya e.
vidhya e.
vrajya c.
çakya
çañkya c.
çapya c.
çamya
çāsya
1 çiṣya c.
1 çīya e.
çramya
çlāghya
çliṣya c.
sahya c.
sīya
sidhya
sṛpya
sevya
stabhya c.
spṛçya
syandya c.
supya
hasya c.
2 hīya c.

2. Intensive Stems. [167.]

A + prefixed shows that there is another stem from the same root in another division.

A. Earlier Language. [105.]

īyāy b.
alar v.
cākaç, -çya
karikṛ, carikṛ v.b.
carkṛ v.
carkṛṣ v.b.
kanikrand, -kradya v.b.
canīkhud s.
kanīkhun b.
+ ganīgam v.b.
+ jāgam v.
+ galgal b.
jañgah v.
jogu v.b.
1 jargur v.
2 jargur, jalgul v.
+ carcar v.b.
calcal, cācal v.b.
jañjapya b.
+ jañjabh v.s.
tantas v.
tetij v.b.
tavītu v.
totudya s.
tartṛ, tartur, tarītṛ v.
tātrasya b.
dandaç v.
dediç, -çya v.b.
dedī b.
dardṛ, dādṛ v.b.
davidyut v.b.
dandramya b.
dodru b.
dedhī b.
+ davidhu v.
dardhṛ, dādhṛ v.b.
nannam, -mya
navīnu, nonu v.
nonudya b.
pāpat v.
panīpan v.b.
pepiç v.b.
popruth v.
panīphaṇ, pamphaṇ v.s.
parphar v.
balbal b.
bābadh, badbadh v.b.
barbṛh v.
jarbhur v.
+ jarbhṛ, bharībhṛ v.
1 memī v.
memih b.
2 memī v.
+ momuh s.
marmṛj, -jya, marīmṛjya
marmṛd v.
marmṛç, marīmṛçya v.b.
māmṛṣ s.
malimluc s.
yañyam v.
1 yoyu v.
2 yoyu v.b.
yavīyudh v.
yoyupya b.s.
rāraj v.
rārandh v.
rārap v.
rerih, -hya v.b.
2 roru v.
roruc v.
+ lālap v.b.
lelī b.s.
vāvac v.
vāvad, -dya v.b
vanīvan v.
+ vanīvāhya b.s.
+ vāvaç v.
vevic s.
vevij, -jya v.
vevid v.
veviṣ, -ṣya v.b.
vevī, -īya v.b.
varīvṛ v.b.
varīvṛj v.
varvṛt, varīvṛt, -tya v.b.
vevlīya b.
çoçuc v.b.
çūçuj v.
caniçcad v.
çāçvas v.
sanīṣan v.
seṣidh v.
soṣū v.

sarsṛ v.
+ sarīsṛpya b.
kaniṣkand, caniṣkad v.
coṣkūya v.
taṅstan v.
paniṣpad v.
saniṣyad v.b.
sanisras v.
saniṣvan v.
jaṅghan, -nya v.b.
ghanīghan v.
jarhṛṣ v.b.

B. Earlier and Later Language. [21.]

caṅkram, -mya
+ jaṅgam b.+
jāgṛ
+ carcūrya
cekit v.c.
+ jañjabhya b.+
daridrā b.c.
+ dodhū v.e.
nānad, -dya
nenij
nenīya
pepīya b.c.
poplūya b.+
bobudh b.c.
bobhū
yāyaj b.+
yāyā b.+
+ 1 roru
+ lelih b.+
lolup, -pya b.+
johū

C. Later Language. [41.]

jāgadya c.
+ galgalya c.
jegīya
jāghaṭ c.
jājam e.
jarījṛmbh c.
jājval, -lya
tātapya
dandah, -hya c.
dedīpya
darīdṛçya c.
dādhmāya c.
+ dodhūya
dandhvan e.
nānardya c.
narīnṛt, -tya c.
pāpacya c.
pāpaṭh, -ṭhya c.
panīpadya c.
bobhuj, -jya c.
+ barībhṛ c.
bambhram, -mya c.
+ momuhya e.
marīmṛ c.
rāraṭ
rārāsya e.
+ rorūya
rorud, -dya
rorudh e.
+ lālapya
+ lelihya
loluṭh c.
lolubhya c.
+ vāvah c.
+ vāvāçya e.
çoçubhya e.
+ sarīsṛp c.
jāhasya e.
johu c.
jarīhṛ c.
jehrīya c.

3. Desiderative Stems. [162.]

A prefixed + in either class indicates that from the same root is made also a stem of the other class.

a. Stems without i. [122.]

A. Earlier Language. [48.]

īrtsa v.b.
cukṣūṣa b.
jigāsa b.
jugukṣa v.
+ cicarṣa b.
2 cikīṣa
cikṣīṣa b.
cichitsa b.
+jujyūṣa, jijy- b.
jijyāsa v.b.
tūtūrṣa v.
titṛtsa v.b.
titṛpsa v.
dip-, dhīpsa v.b.
dhīkṣa b.
didāsa
didhiṣa v.
dhīṣa v.
didhyāsa b.
dudhūrṣa v b.
inakṣa v.
ninitsa v.s.
pipīṣa v.
piprīṣa v.
mimikṣa
iyakṣa v.b.
yiyapsa s.
yiyaṅsa b.
yuyūṣa v.
ririkṣa v.
1 rurukṣa v.
vivāsa v.
vivatsa b.
vivṛkṣa b.
vivṛtsa v.b.
vivyatsa b.
çuçukṣa v.
çuçutsa s.
çiçlikṣa v.
sisaṅkṣa b
siṣāsa v.b.
sīkṣa v.b.
sisīrṣa b.
tistīrṣa b.
tustūrṣa b.s.
jihīṣa v.,
1 juhūṣa s.
2 juhūṣa b.

B. Earlier and Later Language. [44.]

īpsa
cikīrṣa
+ jigāṁsa
1 jigīṣa V.C.
+ jugupsa B.+
+ jighṛkṣa B.+
jighatsa
1 cikīṣa B.+
cikitsa
2 jigīṣa
jijñāsa
titikṣa
titīrṣa B.+
ditsa
dudukṣa, dudhu- V.C.
didṛkṣa
dudrukṣa, dudhru- B.C.
dhitsa
ninīṣa
2 pitsa B.C.
pipāsa
+ bībhatsa
bibhitsa V.B.
bubhūṣa
bubhūrṣa B.+
mīmāṅsa
mumukṣa
mokṣa B.+
mumūrṣa S.+
yuyutsa
ripsa B.C.
rurutsa B.+
2 rurukṣa
lĭpsa
vivakṣa B.+
2 vivitsa B.+
çikṣa
çuçrūṣa
sisṛkṣa B.+
sisṛpsa
tiṣṭhāsa B.+
suṣupsa B.+
jighāṅsa
jihīrṣa

C. Later Language. [30.]

cikrīṣa C.
cikṣipsa C.
cikhyāsa C.
cicīṣa C.
titāṅsa C.
tityakṣa C.
didhakṣa
didikṣa C.
didrāsa C.
didhīrṣa C.
ninaṁsa C.
nunutsa C.
+ 1 pitsa C.
pupūṣa C.
+ pipṛkṣa C.
bubhutsa C.
bubhukṣa
mimaṅkṣa C.
mitsa C.
yiyakṣa B.
yiyāsa
yuyukṣa
riraṁsa
+ 1 vivitsa C.
1 vivikṣa
2 vivikṣa B.
tuṣṭūṣa C.
siṣṇāsa B.
pispṛkṣa
jihāsa C.

b. Stems with i. [40.]

A. Earlier Language. [12.]

edidhiṣa B.
cikramiṣa B.
+ jigrahīṣa B.
+ cicariṣa B.
jijaniṣa B.
didīkṣiṣa B.
+ pipatiṣa V.B.
ruruciṣa B.
vivadiṣa B.S.
çiçāsiṣa S.
tiṣṭighiṣa B.
jihiṅsiṣa B.

B. Earlier and Later Language. [5.]

açiçiṣa B.+
+ jigamiṣa B.+
+ jijīviṣa B.+
+ bibādhiṣa B.C.
+ vividiṣa B.+

C. Later Language. [23.]

eṣiṣiṣa C.
īcikṣiṣa C.
cikartiṣa C.
cikrīḍiṣa C.
cikhādiṣa
jigadiṣa B.
+ jugupiṣa B.
cicaliṣa C.
cucumbiṣa C.
ninartiṣa C.
+ pipṛchiṣa C.
bibhakṣiṣa B.
bibhaṇiṣa C.
mimardiṣa B.
rirakṣiṣa B.
rurudiṣa C.
vivandiṣa C.
vivarṣiṣa B.
vivrajiṣa C.
çiçayiṣa C.
çuçobhiṣa C.
çiçariṣa C.
çiçramiṣa C.

For desideratives from causatives, see below, under VI.

4. Causative Stems. [565.]

A. Earlier Language. [100.]

āmaya V.B.
āvaya V.B.
2 āsaya B.
ilaya V.B.S.
iṣaya RV.
kṛntaya S.
kṛpaya V.B.
krāthaya B.
krūḍaya B.
1 kṣayaya V.
gādaya S.
gāyaya B.
gulphaya S.
gūrdhaya V.
gṛbhaya V.
grāsaya B.S.
cakṣaya V.B.
2 çātaya V.B.
citaya V.
chadaya V.B.
chāyaya B.
jambhaya V.B.
jyotaya V.
taṅsaya V.B.
tamaya B.S.
tujaya V.
toçaya V.
tuṣaya V.
turaya V.
tardaya S.
daṅsaya V.
dakṣaya B.
dambhaya V.B.
dā̆saya V.B.
dāçaya B.
dṛṅhaya
dyutaya V.
dhanaya V.
dhvasaya V.
dhvanaya V.B.
nabhaya B.
nambhaya B.S.
nardaya B.
nāvaya B.
pāthaya B.S.
panaya V.
spāçaya
pinvaya B.
prothaya S.
phāṇaya
baṅhaya B.
barhaya V.
bhrāçaya V.
maṅhaya V.
maṇṭaya B.
mandaya V.
mekṣaya B.S.
marcaya
mradaya B.
yā̆vaya V.B.
yopaya
raṅhaya V.
rajaya V.
1 raṇaya V.
riṣaya V.
rucaya V.
1 ropaya B.
rejaya V.
limpaya S.
ukṣaya V.
vakṣaya V.
vājaya
vātaya V.
vānaya V.
2 vāpaya S.
valgaya S.
1 vāsaya V.B.
vāçaya V.S.
vipaya V.
vīḍaya
barhaya V.
çiñjaya B.S.
çucaya V.
çundhaya V.B.
çubhaya V.B.
çcotaya B.S.
çnathaya V.
çyāyaya B.
çrathaya V.B.
çvañcaya V.
sāpaya B.
sāvaya S.
sphāvaya B.
srevaya V.
çrīvaya V.
2 hāsaya V.
heḍaya V.
hūrchaya B.
hvalaya B.
hvāraya B.

B. Earlier and Later Language. [231.]

añjaya S.+
ā̆ḍaya B.+
ānaya
arcaya
arhaya S.+
āçaya B.+
1 āpaya B.+
iṅgaya
īkṣaya
īṅkhaya
īraya
ukṣaya S.+
arjaya S.+
ardaya
ardhaya
ejaya B.C.
edhaya S.+
kāmaya
kampaya B.+
kālaya B.+
kāçaya
kopaya
kūḍaya
kūlaya S.+
kāraya B.+
1 kartaya S.+
karçaya
kalpaya
krandaya
krā̆maya B.+
krīḍaya S.+
krodhaya
kledaya S.+
kvāthaya S.+
kṣāraya B.+
kṣālaya B.+
kṣodaya V.C.
khā̆naya S.+
gā̆maya
garhaya B.+
gūhaya S.+
grāhaya B.+
ghoṣaya
ghāraya
cā̆maya B.+
cāraya B.+
cetaya
cintaya B.+
codaya
ceṣṭaya B.+
cyā̆vaya
chādaya
chandaya
chedaya S.+
chardaya B.+
janaya
jāsaya B.+
jīvaya
joṣaya
jā̆raya

Ç. Later Language. [1040.]

añcaya C.
1 āsaya E.+
āyaya C.
indhaya C.
1 eṣaya C.
ichaya E.
2 eṣaya E.+
īḍaya C.
1 ūhaya C.
2 ūhaya E.
katthaya E.
kalaya E.+
kāsaya C.
kāñkṣaya E.
kuñcaya E.+
kocaya E.+
kuṭṭaya C.
kothaya C.
kūṇaya C.
kīraya E.
2 kartaya C.
karṣaya E.+
kroçaya
klāmaya C.
kleçaya E.+
kvaṇaya C.
kṣā̆maya E.+
2 kṣayaya E.+
kṣepaya E.+
kṣobhaya E.+
kṣveḍaya E.
khādaya E.+
khedaya E.+
khelaya C.
gālaya C.
gāhaya C.
guṇṭhaya C.
gopaya E.+
gumphaya C.
gūraya C.
giraya C.
granthaya E.
grathaya C.
ghā̆ṭaya E.+
ghaṭṭaya E.+
ghūrṇaya C.
gharṣaya E.
cakāsaya C.
cāṭaya C.
carcaya E.+
carvaya C.
cā̆laya E.+
cāyaya C.
cumbaya C.
coraya E.+
cūṣaya C.
cyotaya C.
choḍaya C.
churaya E.+
choraya C.
jāvaya C.
jṛmbhaya C.
jvaraya C.
ṭañkaya C.
ḍambaya C.
ḍāyaya C.
ḍvālaya C.
ḍhāukaya C.
tāḍaya E.+
tarkaya E.+
tarjaya E.+
tejaya E.+
todaya E.+
tolaya E.+
tulaya E.+
tyājaya E.+
trapaya C.
troṭaya C.
dayaya C.
dā̆laya
dāhaya
deçaya
dehaya
1 devaya C.
2 devaya
dāvaya C.
dolaya C.
darpaya
darbhaya C.
dveṣaya C.
dhukṣaya
dhūnaya
nāṭaya C.
nādaya
nāyaya
pāṭhaya C.
paṇaya C.
pothaya
2 pāraya C.
phālaya E.
bolaya C.
bṛñhaya
bhartsaya
bhikṣaya C.
bhedaya
bhūṣaya
bhāraya E.
bharjjaya C.
bhrañçaya
bhrājaya
maṇḍaya
mā̆thaya
mārgaya
melaya C.
mocaya
moṭaya C.
muṣaya C.
mrakṣaya C.
mṛkṣaya E.
mardaya
marṣaya
mreḍaya
yāsaya
yojaya
racaya
rañjaya
2 raṇaya C.
riñgaya C.
rodhaya
rundhaya E.
1 roṣaya
2 roṣaya C.
lakṣaya
lā̆gaya C.
lañghaya
lajjaya C.
lambaya
lā̆laya
lāsaya
lepaya
lāyaya C.
1 loṭhaya C.
2 loṭhaya C.
luṇṭhaya C.
loḍaya
lolaya
lokaya
locaya
vadhaya E.
vandaya E.
vā̆maya C.
valaya C.
vaçaya C.
vāñchaya E.
2 vāhaya C.
vecaya C.
2 vedaya E.
veṣaya
vījaya
2 vā̆raya
vedhaya E.
vrīḍaya C.
çañkaya C.
2 çāmaya
çeṣaya
çlathaya C.
çlāghaya
sañjaya
sajjaya
sāhaya
siñcaya E.
sīvaya C.
sevaya C.
skambhaya C.
skhalaya C.
stambhaya

stāraya
sthagaya c.
sphāṭaya c.
sphoṭaya
sphāraya
sphuraya c.
smāyaya c.
smăraya
1 hāsaya c.
hiṅsaya b.
hikkaya c.
helaya
hvāyaya c.
hreṣaya b.

The causative stems showing a p added to a final vowel may be given by themselves, as follows (with headings of divisions omitted): [33.]

kṣāpaya
kṣepaya v.
gāpaya b.+
jāpaya b.s.
2 dāpaya s.
drāpaya b.
2 dhāpaya v.b.
çrāpaya b.
2 hāpaya v.b.

2 āpaya b.+
arpaya
khyāpaya b.+
glăpaya
ghrāpaya b.+
jñăpaya
1 dāpaya
1 dhāpaya
1 māpaya b.+
mlăpaya
yāpaya b.+
2 lāpaya b.+
vāpaya
çrapaya
sthāpaya
snăpaya

knopaya c.
kṣapaya
kṣmāpaya c.
dhmāpaya
2 māpaya
smāpaya
1 hāpaya
hrepaya c.

Finally, the bastard stems with āp added (as in Prākrit) to a final consonant: [11.]

açāpaya s.
kṣālāpaya s.

krīḍāpaya b.
kṣamāpaya c.
jīvāpaya
dīkṣāpaya b.
bhidāpaya c.
bhuñjāpaya c.
melāpaya c.
likhāpaya c.
vardhāpaya c.

VI. TERTIARY (derivative from secondary) CONJUGATION-STEMS. [202.]

1a. Passives from Desideratives. [11.]

cikitsya b.+
jijñāsya b.+
jñīpsya c.
dhitsya c.
mīmāṅsya v.+
rurutsya b.s.
lipsya b.
vivakṣya c.
çikṣya c.
çuçrūṣya b.+
jihīrṣya c.

1b. Passives from Causatives. [147.]

A. Earlier Language. [9.]

iṅgya b.
īkṣya s.
ghārya s.
jyotya b.
dāhya b.
dohya b.
pāyya s.
bhājya v.b.
varya b.

B. Earlier and Later Language. [28.]

arcya b.s.
īrya b.+
kālya s.+
kalpya b.+
cintya b.+
codya s.+
chādya s.+
jñăpya b.+
jvālya b.+
tāpya b.e.
dīpya b.b.
dhārya b.+
pādya b.+
pīḍya b.+
pyāyya b.+
bhakṣya b.+
bhrañçya s.+
bhrămya b.+
yātya b.+
vādya b.+
2 vāsya b.+
veçya s.+
veṣṭya b.+
vartya b.+
çrapya b.+
sādya b.+
sārya b.+
sthāpya b.+

C. Later Language. [110.]

eṣya E.
arpya C.
ardya
kampya C.
kāsya C.
kāçya E.
kārya
krāmya C.
krodhya E.
kvāthya
kṣobhya
khyāpya C.
gopya E.
grāhya C.
ghăṭya
ghaṭṭya C.
ghoṣya C.
ghūrṇya C.
cārya
cālya E.
corya C.
chandya
jāsya E.
ḍambya C.
tāḍya
tarkya
tarjya E.
todya
tolya C.
toṣya C.
tārya
tarpya E.
tyājya C.
trāsya E.
tvarya E.
dălya C.
dūṣya
dārya
dyotya C.
drāvya E.
dhmāpya E.
dhāpya C.
dhukṣya C.
nādya
nāmya
nodya
pācya E.
pāṭya C.
pāṭhya C.
pātya
pāvya C.
pūjya
pūrya
pārya C.
plāvya C.
bodhya E.
bhartsya
bhāsya C.
bhāvya
mānya
mocya C.
mohya C.
mārya
mārjya C.
mardya C.
yāsya E.
yojya C.
yodhya E.
racya C.
rādhya E.
rocya E.
rodhya E.
roṣya
ropya
lakṣya
laṅghya C.
lambya
lālya C.
lāsya C.
lāpya C.
luṇṭhya C.
loḍya
lopya C.
lobhya
lokya C.
vācya C.
vañcya
1 vāsya E.
vāhya
vedya
vījya
vārya
varjya
vyathya C.
vrājya E
1 çāmya
2 çāmya E.
çeṣya C.
çocya C.
çodhya
çoṣya C.
çlathya C.
çrāmya
çrāvya
sādhya
smārya
sraṅsya E.
svādya C.
svarya C.
hārya

2. Desideratives from Causatives. [38.]

A. Earlier Language. [12.]

āpipayiṣa B.
cikalpayiṣa B.
jijanayiṣa B.
titarpayiṣa B.S.
didrāpayiṣa B.
pipāyayiṣa B.
bibhāvayiṣa B.
mumodayiṣa B.
rirādhayiṣa B.
lulobhayiṣa B.
vivārayiṣa B.
sthāpayiṣa B.

B. Earlier and Later Language. [5.]

didarçayiṣa S.+
didhārayiṣa S.C.
pipādayiṣa B.+
bibhakṣayiṣa S.+
siṣādhayiṣa S.+

C. Later Language. [21.]

cukopayiṣa E.
cikārayiṣa
cukṣobhayiṣa E.
cikhyāpayiṣa C.
jijīvayiṣa E.
nināçayiṣa C.
bubodhayiṣa
bibhedayiṣa E.
mimānayiṣa E.
mumocayiṣa
mumokṣayiṣa E.
mimārayiṣa C.
mimardayiṣa E.
riramayiṣa C.
vivedayiṣa E.
vivardhayiṣa
sisādayiṣa E.
sisārayiṣa C.
siṣevayiṣa C.
stambhayiṣa E.
sismāpayiṣa E.

3a. Causatives from Intensives.

jāgaraya B. +	dandaçaya C.	dādhāraya B.	varīvarjaya V.

3b. Causatives from Desideratives.

cikīrṣaya C.	çikṣaya E.+

VII. SUNDRIES.

1. Passive Aorists (third persons singular). [92.]

The unaugmented form is given, if the augmented does not occur.

A. Earlier Language. [47.]

ārdhi B.	apāyi V.	avāci V.B.	asādi V.
kṣāyi B.S.	aprāyi V.	vandi V.	aseci B.S.
ghoṣi V.	abhāri V.B.	vāpi B.	asāvi V.
aceti V.	abhrāji V.	avedi V.	asāri B.
achedi	2 amāyi B.	avāri V.	asarji
ajā̆ni V.B.	amyakṣi V.	varhi V.	astāvi V.
atāyi B.	ayāmi V.B.	çaṅsi V.	astāri V.
atāpi V.B.	ayāvi B.	çeṣi	syandi B.
atāri V.B.	arādhi V.B.	açoci V.	svani V.
dāyi V.B.	areci	açāri V.B.	ahāyi V.B.
adarçi V.	aroci V.	açrāyi V.	ahāvi V.
apāti B.	lopi S.	asañji B.	

B. Earlier and Later Language. [12.]

āpi B.+	ajñāyi	abodhi	amoci
akāri	adhāyi	abhedi B.E.	ayoji V.C.
agā̆mi V.C.	apādi	1 amāyi	açrāvi V.C.

C. Later Language. [33.]

āsi C.	abhāji C.	aropi C.	açobhi C.
āikṣi C.	abhāṇi C.	alepi C.	asedhi C.
ohi C.	abhāvi C.	aloki C.	astambhi C.
akūji C.	abhrāmi E.	avoci C.	asthāyi C.
agādi C.	amajji C.	avādi C.	asnāyi C.
aṭaṅki C.	amoṣi C.	avadhi C.	asvāpi C.
adhāri C.	araci C.	avāhi C.	ahāsi C.
apūri C.	arambhi C.	aveçi C.	ahāri C
abhakṣi C.			

2. Aorist Optatives (including Precatives). [118.]

Those stems from which actual precative forms (with sibilant between mode-sign and ending) are made are to be recognized by their final sibilant. The optatives of the **a**-aorist (2d form) are not included (excepting **videṣṭa**). The aorist-stems here instanced have all been given above in the aorist-lists, whether other than optative-forms are made from them or not.

a. Active Stems. [63.]

A. Earlier Language. [48.]

adyās B.	**jñeyā** V.	**bhriyā, -yās** B.	**ucyās** B.
avyā, -yās	**tṛdyā** S.	**bhramyā** S.	**udyā, -yās** B.S.
açyā, -yās	**trpyās** B.	**bhrājyās** V.	**badhyā, -yās**
āpyās B.	**daghyās** V.	**majjyā** B.	**uhyā** S.
iyās S.	**dahyā** E.	**mṛṇyā** B.	**vṛjyā, -yās** V.
uhyā B.	**deyā** V.	**mṛdyās** B.S.	**çakyā** V.
aryā B.	**dīdyās** B.S.	**mṛdhyā** V.	**saghyās** B.S.
ṛdhyā, -yās	**dheyā** V.	**yamyās** V.	**sā̆hyā, -yās** V.
kriyā, -yās	**nindyā** B.	**yū̆yā, -yās** V.B.	**sicyā** B.S.
gamyā, -yās	**peyās** V.	**yujyā** V.	**stheyā** V.
ghrāyā S.	**priyās** V.	**rājyās** S.	**supyā** S.
jīvyās	**bhidyā** B.	**rādhyās**	**svidyā** S.

B. Earlier and Later Language. [5.]

īyā B.+	**puṣyā, -yās** B.C.	**bhūyā, -yās**	**çrūyā, -yās** V.C.
jayyā B.E.			

C. Later Language. [10.]

asyā E.	**juṣyā** C.	**prīyā** C.	**rudhyā** C.
kīryā C.	**dīryā** C.	**brūyās** E.	**spṛçyā** E.
jāyā	**nudyā**		

b. Middle Stems. [55.]

A. Earlier Language. [54.]

açī	**tāriṣī** V.	**pyāyiṣī** S.	**murī** V.
idhī V.	**trāsī** V.	**pyāsiṣī**	**mṛkṣīṣ** V.
indh-, idhiṣī B.S.	**diṣī** V.	**bhakṣī, -īṣ**	**yakṣī** B.
	dhukṣī B.	**bhukṣiṣī** B.S.	**yamī** V.
arī V.	**darṣīṣ** V.	**mandiṣī** V.B.	**yāsisīṣ** V.B.
ṛdhī V.	**dhiṣī, dheṣī** B.S.	**maṅsī, -īṣ** V.	**rāsī** V.
edhiṣī V.B.	**dhrājiṣī** B.	**masī** V.	**rucī** B.
gmī B.	**naçī** V.	**mucīṣ** V.	**roc-, ruciṣī** V.B.
gmiṣī B.	**nasī** V.	**mukṣī** V.B.	**lapsī** S.
cucyuvī V.	**padīṣ** V.	**mudī** V.	**lopsī** B.
janiṣī, -īṣ	**pṛcī** V.S.	**modiṣīṣ** V.	**vaṅsī, vasī** V.

vaniṣīṣ v.	**videṣ** v.	**sakṣī** v.	**sāsahīṣ** v.
vaṅsiṣī v.	**vurī** v.b.	**sākṣī** v.b.	**stṛṣī** v.
vandiṣī v.	**vardhiṣī** b.s.	**săhiṣī** v.	

B. Earlier and Later Language. [1.]

rĭriṣīṣ v.c.

Here may be added the problematical optatives in **eṣ** from roots in **ā**: namely, **khyeṣ** b.s., **geṣ** v.b.s., **jñeṣ** v.b., **deṣ** b.s., **yeṣ** v., **seṣ** b., **stheṣ** v.b.; and **jeṣ** v.b.s. (√ji).

3. Periphrastic Perfects (primary conjugation).

The periphrastic perfects of secondary conjugation (very numerous for the causative, quite rare for the desiderative, unknown for the intensive, except √ jāgṛ) are not given. With **vidām** are made also a periphrastic aorist (b.) and present (c.). The headings of the divisions are omitted.

cāyāṁ kṛ b.	**bibhayāṁ kṛ** b.	**vāsāṁ kṛ** b.	**vyayāṁ kṛ** b.
tāyāṁ kṛ b.	**layāṁ kṛ** b.	**vidāṁ kṛ** b.s.	**juhavāṁ kṛ** b.
āsāṁ kṛ b.+	**īkṣāṁ kṛ** b.+	**edhāṁ kṛ, bhū** b.c.	
ayāṁ kṛ	**jayām as** c.	**nayām as, kṛ** e.	**smayām as** e.
ujhāṁ kṛ c.	**dayām as** c.	**bibharām bhū** c.	**hvayām as, kṛ** e.
jāgarām as c.			

4. Vedic Sibilant Presents (first persons singular).

arcase	**kṛṣe**	**gṛṇīṣe**	**stuṣe**
ohiṣe	**gāyiṣe**	**punīṣe**	**hiṣe**
ṛñjase		**yajase**	

There are certain odd or questionable forms given here and there under the roots above, of which no account is made in the Indexes. Those most worthy of note are as follows:

Pres. **āitat, iṅkṣva, inttām, kurmi, kṣāmat, gṛhī-, glapet, jiharti, chāyati, achinam atṛṇam abhanas, jajhatī, jañjatī, jña, tandrat, taruṣa- vanuṣa-, dadīyam, dadāyant, dūṣya-, dughāna, dhuṅgdhvam, duhīya-, dart, dhunet,** participles like **namāna, nahyus, pīpṛhi pipīpṛhi, apiprata, pṛkṣase, bhuñjīyāt yuñjīyāt çaṅsīyāt, bhuraja saraja minīt, rīṣant, lāyata** (√i + nir?), **vāda, ude- upe- uṣa-, çmasi, avākṣam, avāstam, vema, tiṣṭhāsam, çruvat, jihīthām, hiṅsi.**

Perf. **erire, jigāhīre, jakṣīyāt, dīdidāya, dudūhus, vavavruṣas, māmada- vāvṛdha- vāvṛṣa- suṣūda-, sīdatus, siṣet.**

Aor. **āpīpipat, aprāiṣit, akat, ajīgṛbham, cacārīt, neṣa puṣa parṣa, abhāriṣam hāriṣīt hvāriṣus, ririṣes, vam, avarīvur.**

Fut. **gṛhīṣyati, grahiṣyati.**

Sec. Conj. **ajagrabhāiṣan, titikṣmahe sisṛkṣmas, prathayi, jījahi.**

Sunds. **cukrūḍāyati.**

INDEX OF ROOTS.

Arranged in reversed alphabetical order.

The designation of periods is according to the verb-forms only. Roots having no such forms are left undesignated. It seemed better not to classify by periods; but it may be added that of the more than 800 roots here recorded as making forms of conjugation, nearly 200 occur only in the earlier language, nearly 500 in both earlier and later, and less than 150 only in the later language.

sru V.+
hru (hvṛ)
plu V.+
kṣu B.+
su V.+
hu V.+
kū V.+
jū V.+
1 dū (du)
2 dū
dhū V.+
nū (1 nu)
knū B.C.
pū V.+
bhū V.+
mū (mīv)
syū (sīv)
drū V.B.
brū V.+
lū B.+
çū V.+
sū V.+
hū V.+
ṛ V.+
1 kṛ V.+
2 kṛ V.+
3 kṛ V.
skṛ (1, 2 kṛ)
1 gṛ V.+
2 gṛ V.+
3 gṛ V.+
jāgṛ (3 gṛ)
ghṛ V.+
1 jṛ V.+
2 jṛ V.
tṛ V.+
stṛ V.+
1 dṛ V.+
2 dṛ B.+
dhṛ V.+
nṛ
1 pṛ V.+
2 pṛ V.+
3 pṛ E.+
spṛ V.B.S.
sphṛ V.+
bhṛ V.+
1 mṛ V.+
2 mṛ V.B.
smṛ V.+
1 vṛ V.+
2 vṛ V.+
dhvṛ V.+
hvṛ V.+
1 çṛ V.+
2 çṛ (çrā)
3 çṛ (çri)
sṛ V.+
1 hṛ V.+
2 hṛ V.B.
cak C.
tak V.
vak (vañc)
çak V.+
ṭīk C.
sṛk
lok B.+
ḍhauk E.+
phakk C.
hikk C.
ṭaṅk C.
çaṅk B.+
tark B.+
rikh V.
likh V.+
riṅkh C
īṅkh V.+
sthag C.
lag B.+
vlag V.
aṅg C.
raṅg C.
vlaṅg (vlag)
tvaṅg C.
iṅg V.+
riṅg C.
mārg E.+
valg V.+
jagh C.
dagh V.B.
sagh V.B.S.
çlāgh B.+
stigh B.
migh (mih)
laṅgh S.+
çiṅgh
ac V.+
khac E.+
tac (tañc)
pac V.+
vyac V.B.
rac B.+
vac V.+
tvac
sac V.B.
yāc V.+
ric V.+
1 vic V.+
2 vic (vyac)
sic V.+
uc V.+
kuc S.+
tuc
muc V.+
ruc V.+
mruc V.+
mluc (mruc)
çuc V.+
ṛc (arc)
pṛc V.+
mṛc V.B.S.
loc E.+
añc (ac)
cañc C.
tañc B.S.
mañc C.
çmañc B.
vañc V.+
çvañc V.
kuñc (kuc)
luñc E.+
arc V.+
carc E.+
vraçc V.+
saçc (sac)
gach (gam)
yach (yam)
prach V.+
ich (1 iṣ)
uch (1 vas)
yuch (2 yu)
ṛch (ṛ)
mṛch B.
mlech B.+
rañch
āñch C.
lāñch C.
vāñch V.+
uñch S.+
mūrch V.+
hūrch B.
aj V.+
paj V.
bhaj V.+
yaj V.+
tyaj V.+
vyaj (vīj)
1 raj (ṛj)
2 raj V.+
bhuraj V.
dhraj V.B.
vraj V.+
vaj V.B.S.
svaj V.+
bhiṣaj V.
saj V.+
rāj V.+
dhrāj (dhraj)
bhrāj V.+
ṭij V.+
nij V.+
vij V.+
īj (ej)
vīj E.+
tuj V.
1 bhuj V.+
2 bhuj V.+
yuj V.+
ruj V.+
çuj V.
kūj V.+
pūj S.+
1 ṛj V.+
2 ṛj
mṛj V.+
vṛj V.+
sṛj V.+
ej V.+
rej V.B.
majj V.+
lajj B.+
bhṛjj V.+
añj V.+
khañj C.
jañj V.
bhañj V.+
rañj (raj)
svañj (svaj)
sañj (saj)
çiñj V.+
kuñj C.
guñj C.
ṛñj (ṛj)
ubj V.B.S.
arj (ṛj)
kharj S.
garj E.+
tarj E.+
sarj V.B.
sphūrj V.+
jajh V.
ujh E.+
aṭ E.+
ghaṭ E.+
caṭ C.
jhaṭ C.
taṭ B.
naṭ C.
paṭ B.+
sphaṭ C.
bhaṭ C.
raṭ E.+
iṭ V.B.
ghuṭ B.+
chuṭ C.

ADDITIONS AND CORRECTIONS.

Of the following *emendanda*, some are corrections of discovered oversights, some are the results of continued collection, and a large part are gleanings from the last-issued portion (to end of l) of Böhtlingk's minor dictionary. A few obvious misprints are passed unnoticed. The modifications and new material here given are included in the Indexes.

p. 1, √ **ac**, l. 1 — read **añcati** *etc.* AV.B.

- 2, l. 1 — read **acyate** *etc.* V.B.

- 2, √ **aj**, l. 1 — read *etc.* V.B.

- 2, √ **aṭ** — to *deriv.* add **aṭāṭyā** C.

- 2, bottom — add √ **aṇṭh**, 'visit': *pres.* **aṇṭhati** C.; *verb.* **aṇṭhita** C. (Bö.)

- 4, √ **arc**, l. 7 — read (**arcyate** U.E.).

- 5, l. 1 — read **açīta** *etc.* V.B.S.

- 6, √ **āp**, l. 3 — read 1. **āpyāsam** AA., **āpi**; l. 12, col. 3 — read **āpayitṛ** U.C.

- 7, √ 1 **i**, l. 6 — read **īyāt** *etc.* B.+; to *deriv.* add **-āpin** C.

- 9, √ 1 **iṣ** — to *deriv.* add **-eṣiṣiṣu** C.

- 9, √ 2 **iṣ** — to *deriv.* add **-eṣitṛ** C.

- 14, √ **ṛ**, l. 8 — read **ṛtvā́** AV.B.U.

- 16, √ **ṛç**, — perhaps **árçat** VS. (xl. 4) belongs here.

- 20, √ **kū**, l. 1 — add [2.] **kāuti** C.

- 26, √ **krudh**, l. 8 — read **krúdhmi** RV.

- 29, √ **kṣip**, l. 2 — read **cikṣepa** *etc.* U.E.+

- 34, √ **gam**, l. 4 — add **jagmyātam** RV.; — to *deriv.* add **-jigamiṣā** C.

- 38, √ 1 **gṛ**, l. 6 — read **-gī́rya** B.S., and add **gṛṇádhyāi** AA.

- 40, √ **grabh**, l. 10 — for **agrabhiṣṭa** *etc.* read **agrabhīṣata**; — to *deriv.* add **grāhayitavya** C.

- 45, l. 1 — read **-cámya** B.+

- 46, l. 5 — read **cālayati** S.+

- 47, l. 5, col. 4 — read **ceya** S.E.

- 47, √ **cit**, l. 7 — add **acíte** RV.

- 50, √ **chand**, l. 1 — dele MS. (Bö.)

- 50, √ **chuṭ** — to *deriv.* add **choṭana** C.

- 54, √ **juṣ**, l. 2 — add **jujuṣan** RV.

- 55, √ 1 **jṛ**, l. 2 — read **-te** *etc.* B.+; — to *deriv.* add **-jariṣṇu** C.

- 56, √ **jñā**, l. 11 — add **jñīpsyate** C.; l. 14, col. 3 — read **jñapana** AV.B.

p. 56, √ jyā, l. 1 — read jīyate.
- 60, √ tan, l. 16 — read tanitṛ C.; — add -titāṅsu C.
- 61, √ tap, last l. — read tāpaka C.
- 63, √ tuj, l. 7 — read túj V.C.
- 63, √ tud, l. 8 — read -tud S.E.C.
- 65, l. 19, col. 1 — read turá V.+
- 70, √ dabh, l. 3 — add dambhiṣak S.
- 72, l. 17, col. 3 — read dāda E.+
- 82, √ dhā, l. 7 — read dhīmahe V.B.; l. 16 — add adhitsiṣam AA.
- 84, √ dhū, l. 7 — read dhūtvā B.U.
- 87, l. 2 — read dhūrtí RV. MS.
- 88, nam, l. 10 — read namayati *etc.* V.+, -te C.
- 91, l. 8 — read -tavāí B., -tos B.S.
- 92, √ ned, l. 1 — read nédati.
- 94, 1 pat, l. 14, col. 4 — read patayālú AV.C.; l. 16, col. 3 — read pātuka B.+
- 94, √ pad, l. 3 — read *Aor.* 1. apadi ÇB. (3*s. pass.*?), apadmahi etc.
- 95, l. 6, col. 3 — read pā́duka B.C.
- 95, √ pard — pardate C[1]. is now quotable (Bö.).
- 96, l. 2 — read -tavāi B.S.
- 99, √ pū, l. 8 — pupūṣati C[1]. is now quotable (Bö.).
- 101, √ pṛc, l. 10, col. 4 — read prakṣá? V.AA.
- 101, √ pyā, l. 3 — dele 4. apyāsam AA. —
- 102, √ prach — to *deriv.* add prā́ç AV. (see J.A.O.S., vol. xiii., p. xlii.), pipṛkṣu C.
- 103, l. 6 — add prīṇayitṛ C.
- 103, √ plu, l. 5 — read -plutya U.S.+
- 106, √ bādh, l. 8 — read bibādhiṣate ÇB.C.; — to *deriv.* add bādhayitṛ C.
- 107, √ brū, l. 2 — add bravīthās -īta U.
- 107, √ bhakṣ, l. 5 — read bibhakṣayiṣati S.+
- 111, √ bhikṣ, l. 5 — read bhikṣitvā U.C.
- 112, √ 2 bhuj, l. 9 — read bhuktvā B.+
- 118, √ mad — to *deriv.* add mandayitṛ C.
- 119, l. 9 — add mananīya C.
- 125, √ mṛc, l. 3 — read mṛktá RV.AA.
- 125, √ mṛj, l. 11 — read mṛṣṭvā́ AV.S.
- 126, √ mṛd — to *deriv.* add -mṛdya C.
- 129, √ yaj, l. 6 — dele — 7. ayakṣata (3*s.*) AGS.
- 135, √ raṭ, l. 1 — read raṭati.
- 137, √ ram, l. 2 — read remus *etc.* B.+
- 140, √ riph, l. 1 — read -atí AV.B.S.
- 140, √ ribh — to *deriv.* add rebhin C.
- 141, l. 3, col. 2 — read reṣa B.C.
- 141, √ rih, l. 1 — add rehāṇa S.

p. 141, √ 1 **ru** — to *deriv.* add **rā́van** B.
- 142, l. 2 — read **rucé** V.; l. 5 — add **rucí** MS.
- 142, √ **rud** — to *deriv.* add **rurudiṣā** C.
- 143, √ 2 **rudh** — to *deriv.* add **rurutsu** C.
- 143, √ **ruṣ** — to *deriv.* add **roṣin** C.
- 144, √ **rūṣ**, l. 2 — add **ruṅṣita** C.
- 145, l. 2 — read **liñgá** ÇB.U.+
- 145, after √ **lajj** — add √ **laḍ** 'move about': *pres.* **laḍati** C[1]. (Bö.)
- 145, √ **lap**, l. 10, col. 4 — read **lāpana** E.+
- 146, √ **lal** — to *deriv.* add **lālin** C.
- 147, √ **likh** — to *deriv.* add **likhitṛ** C.
- 148, l. 2 — read **lepaka** C., and add **lipti** C.
- 148, √ **lih**, l. 5 — add **leham** S.
- 148, √ 1 **lī**, l. 6 — add **letum** C., and read **-lā́ya** B.S.
- 149, √ **lup**, l. 7 — read **lopam** S.C.
- 150, √ **lubh**, l. 5 — add **lubhita** S.
- 150, √ **lul**, l. 1 — read **lolati -te** *etc.*
- 150, √ **lū**, l. 4 — add **lutvā** S.; to *deriv.* add **lavitavya** C.
- 151, √ **loc**, l. 6, col. 1 — read **locaka** C.
- 151, √ **vac**, l. 8 — add **-vā́ce** RV.
- 153, l. 8 — add **-vivādiṣu** C.
- 156, √ 3 **vas**, l. 12, col. 2 — read **vā́sya** B.+
- 159, √ **vij**, — to *deriv.* add **vijitavya** C.
- 163, √ **vṛj**, l. 1 — add (at end) V.+
- 166, √ **vyath** — to *deriv.* add **-vyathin** C.
- 168, √ **vlī**, l. 1 — read ÇB.S.
- 169, √ **çaṅs**, l. 11, col. 4 — read **çaṅsitṛ** B.+
- 173, √ **çiṣ**, l. 1 — read **çináṣṭi.**
- 179, √ 1 **çrī**, l. 4 — add **çrītvā** S.
- 183, √ **sad**, l. 3 — read **sedire** RV.
- 185, l. 6, col. 3 — read **soḍhṛ** E.+
- 187, √ **su**, l. 1 — read **sunuté.**
- 189, √ **sṛj**, l. 4 — read **ásarji** V.B.S.
- 190, l. 7, col. 1 — read **sṛ́jya** B.+
- 193, √ **stu**, l. 4 — read **stuṣé** (1*s.*), and add in l. 12 **stuṣé** RV.
- 194, √ **sthā**, l. 5 — dele — 5.
- 200, √ **sru**, l. 12, col. 4 — read **srāvayitavyà** MS.S.
- 207, l. 9, col. 4 — read **johū́tra** RV.AA.